SHANGRI-LA

M.BABLET

MW00789127

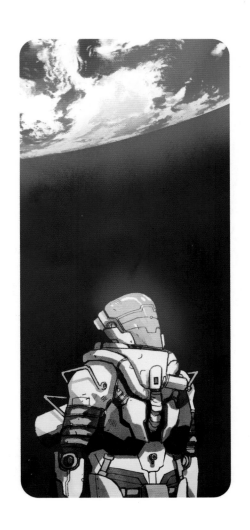

Written, designed, and illustrated
by
MATHIEU BABLET

Design Direction by Gaël Cecchin

Translation by Dan Christensen
Editing by Mike Kennedy

ISBN: 978-1-951719-98-2
Library of Congress Control Number: 2021913144

Shangri-La, Published 2021 by Magnetic Press, LLC.
Originally published as *Shangri-La* © LABEL 619 - ANKAMA EDITIONS 2016, by Bablet. www.ankama.com. All rights reserved.
MAGNETIC PRESS™, MAGNETIC™, and their associated distinctive designs are trademarks of Magnetic Press, LLC. No similarity
between any of the names, characters, persons, and/or institutions in this book with those of any living or dead person or institution is
intended and any such similarity which may exist is purely coincidental.

Printed in China.

10 9 8 7 6 5 4 3 2 1

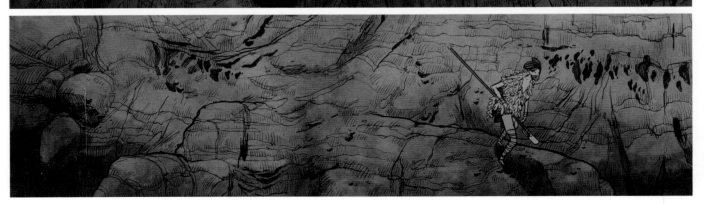

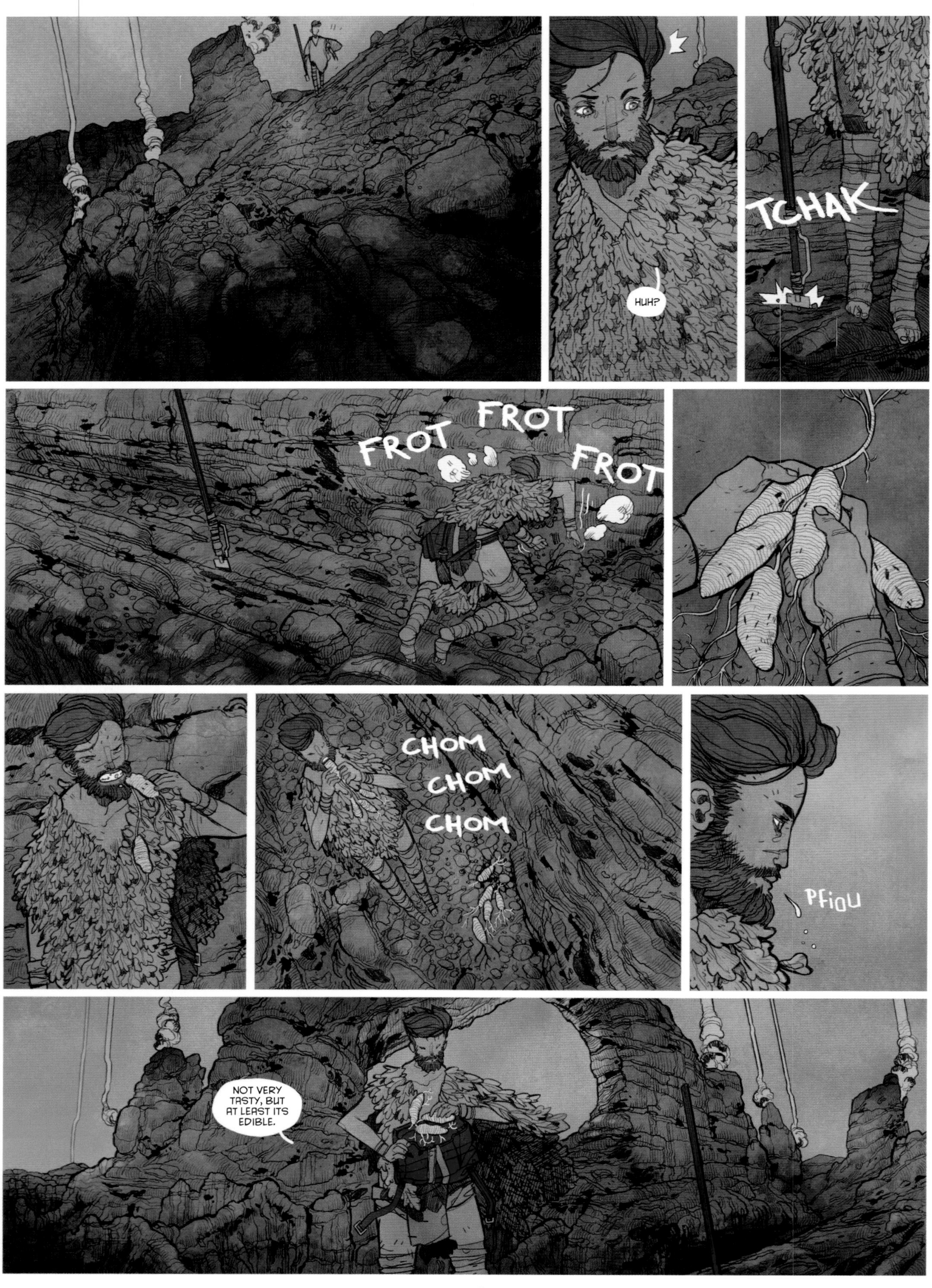
HUH?
TCHAK
FROT FROT FROT
CHOM CHOM CHOM
PFIOU
NOT VERY TASTY, BUT AT LEAST ITS EDIBLE.

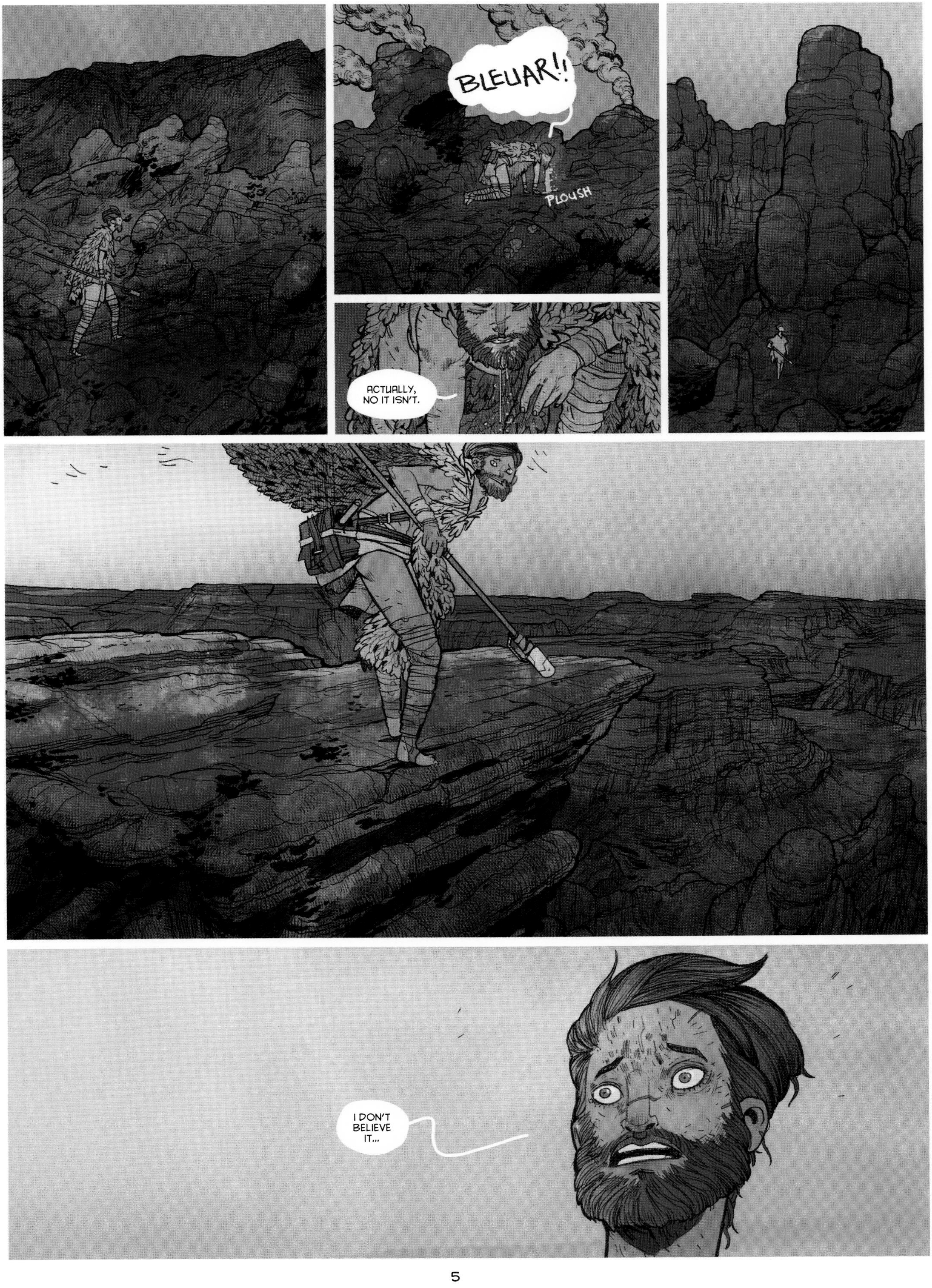
BLEUAR!!
PLOUSH
ACTUALLY, NO IT ISN'T.
I DON'T BELIEVE IT...

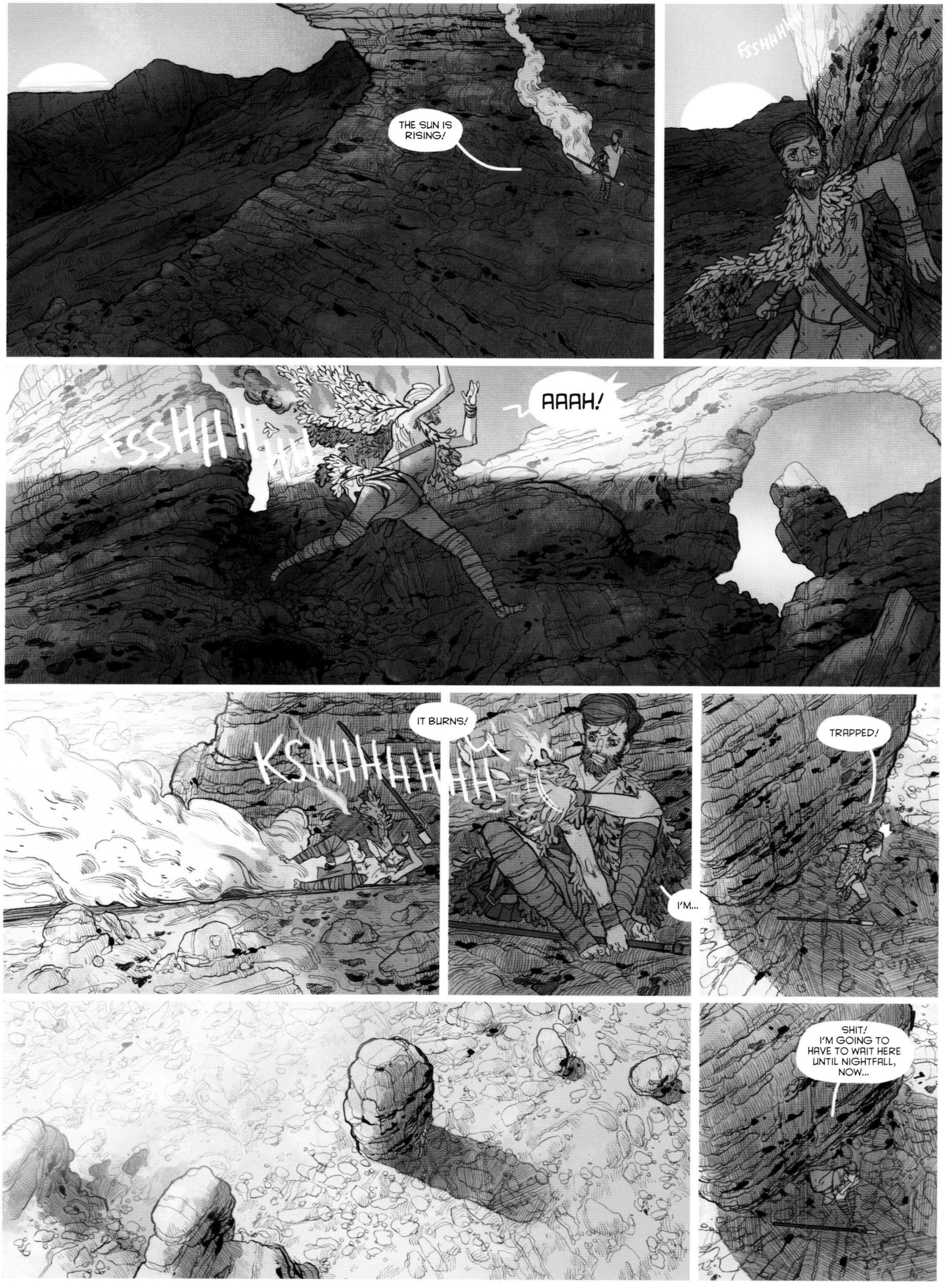
THE SUN IS RISING!
FSSHHHH
FSSHHHHH
AAAH!
IT BURNS!
KSHHHHHHHH
I'M...
TRAPPED!
SHIT! I'M GOING TO HAVE TO WAIT HERE UNTIL NIGHTFALL, NOW...

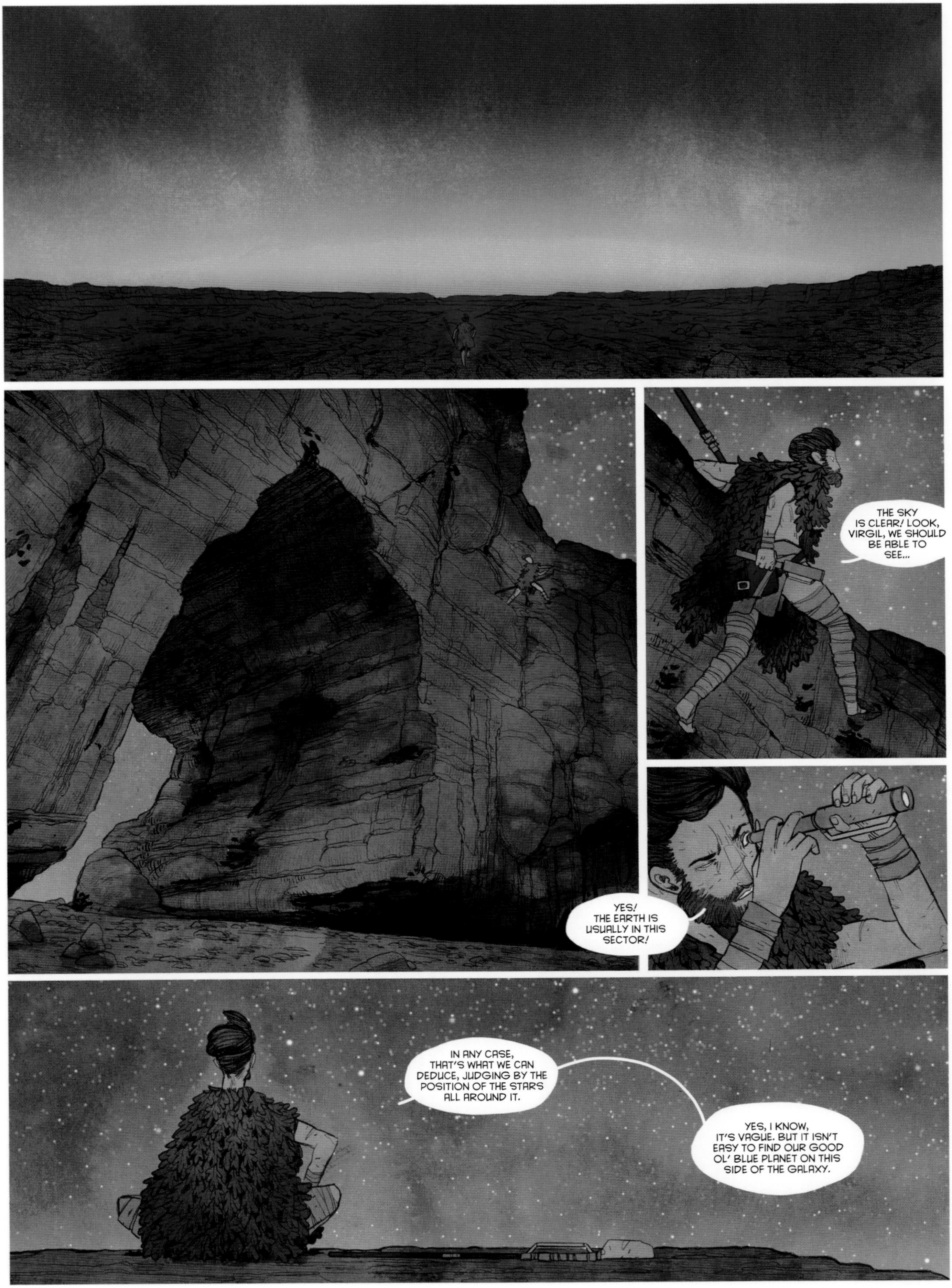
THE SKY IS CLEAR! LOOK, VIRGIL, WE SHOULD BE ABLE TO SEE...
YES! THE EARTH IS USUALLY IN THIS SECTOR!
IN ANY CASE, THAT'S WHAT WE CAN DEDUCE, JUDGING BY THE POSITION OF THE STARS ALL AROUND IT.
YES, I KNOW, IT'S VAGUE. BUT IT ISN'T EASY TO FIND OUR GOOD OL' BLUE PLANET ON THIS SIDE OF THE GALAXY.

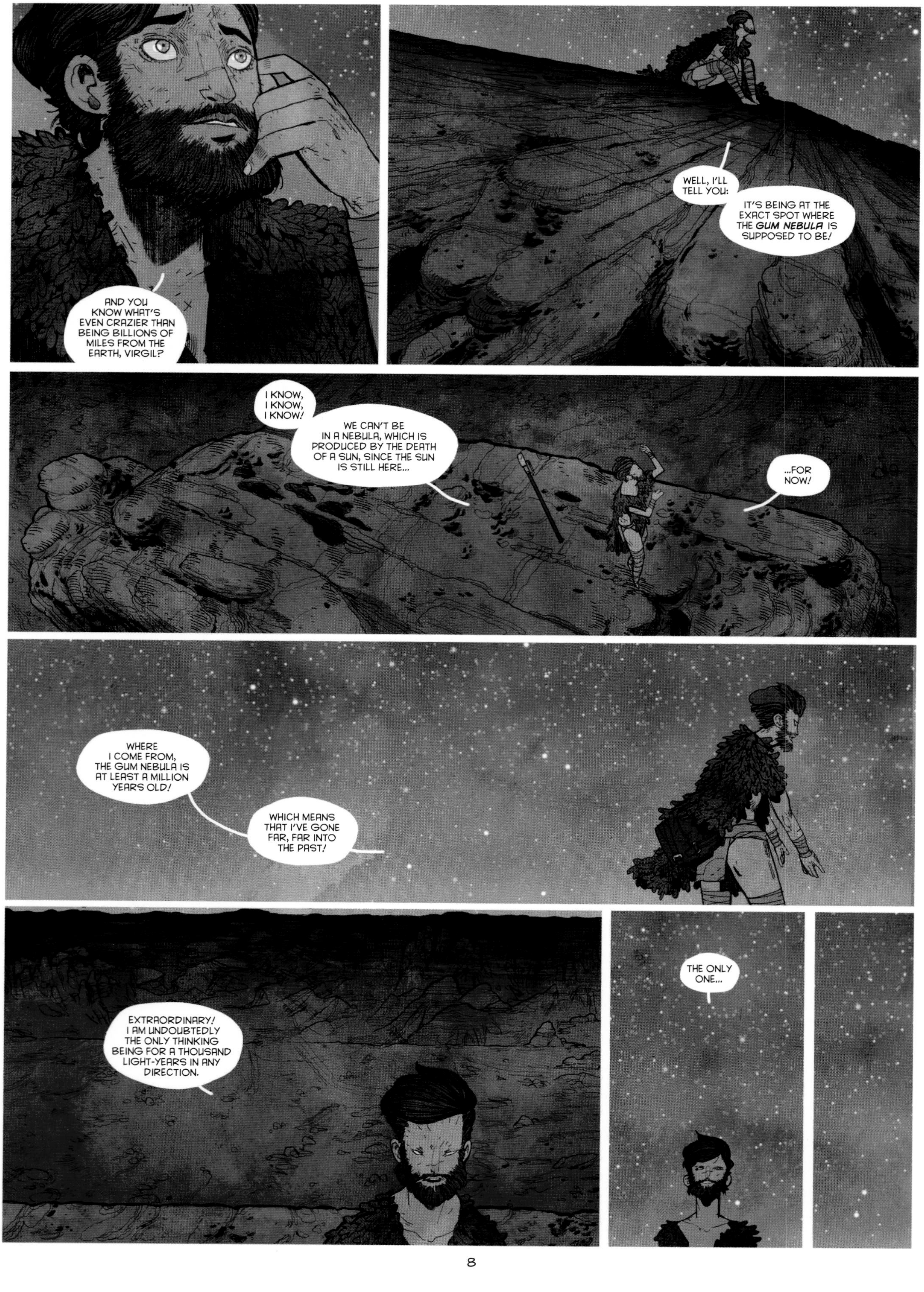
AND YOU KNOW WHAT'S EVEN CRAZIER THAN BEING BILLIONS OF MILES FROM THE EARTH, VIRGIL?
WELL, I'LL TELL YOU:
IT'S BEING AT THE EXACT SPOT WHERE THE **GUM NEBULA** IS SUPPOSED TO BE!
I KNOW, I KNOW, I KNOW!
WE CAN'T BE IN A NEBULA, WHICH IS PRODUCED BY THE DEATH OF A SUN, SINCE THE SUN IS STILL HERE...
...FOR NOW!
WHERE I COME FROM, THE GUM NEBULA IS AT LEAST A MILLION YEARS OLD!
WHICH MEANS THAT I'VE GONE FAR, FAR INTO THE PAST!
EXTRAORDINARY! I AM UNDOUBTEDLY THE ONLY THINKING BEING FOR A THOUSAND LIGHT-YEARS IN ANY DIRECTION.
THE ONLY ONE...

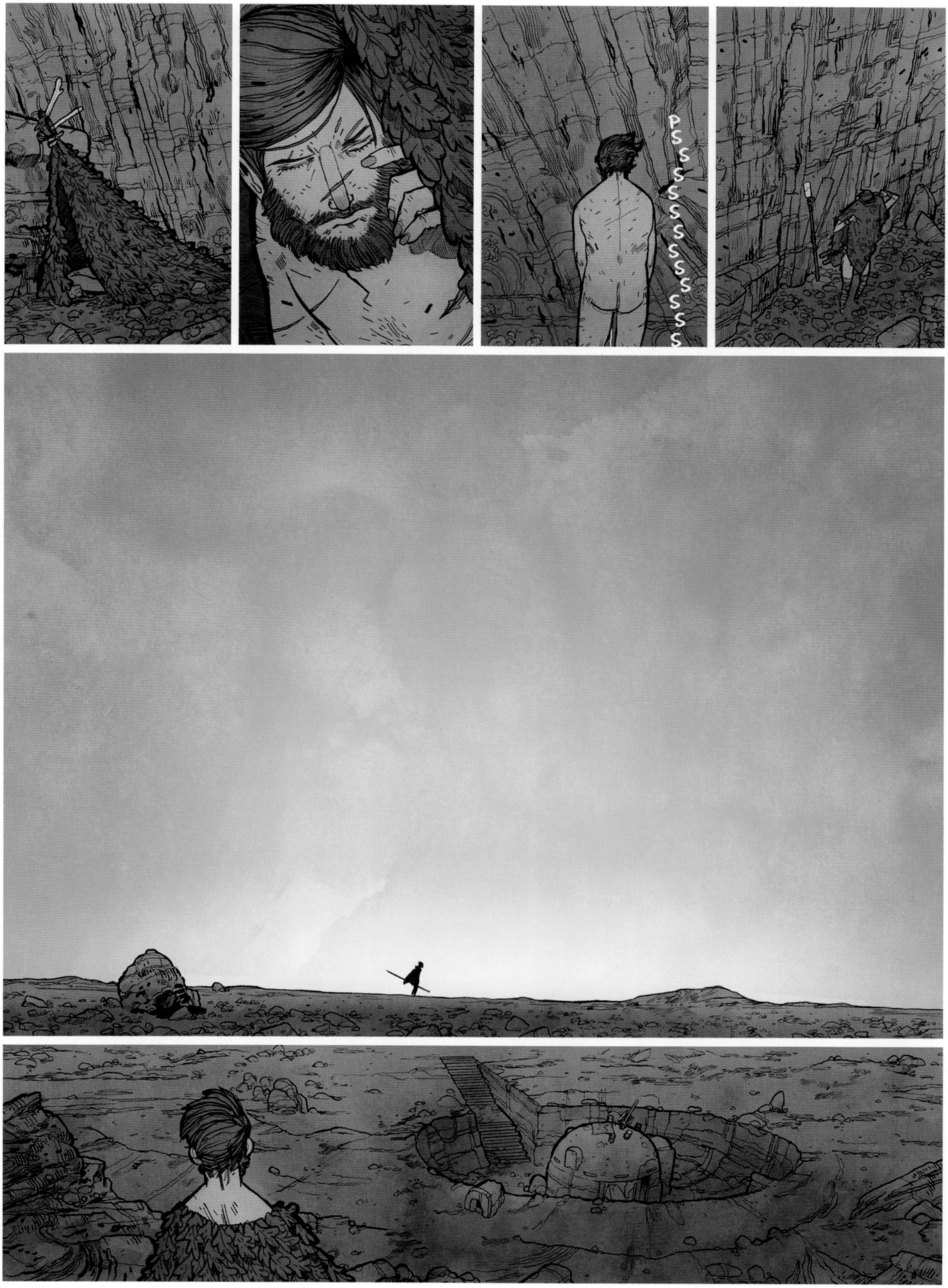
PSSSSSSSSSSSS

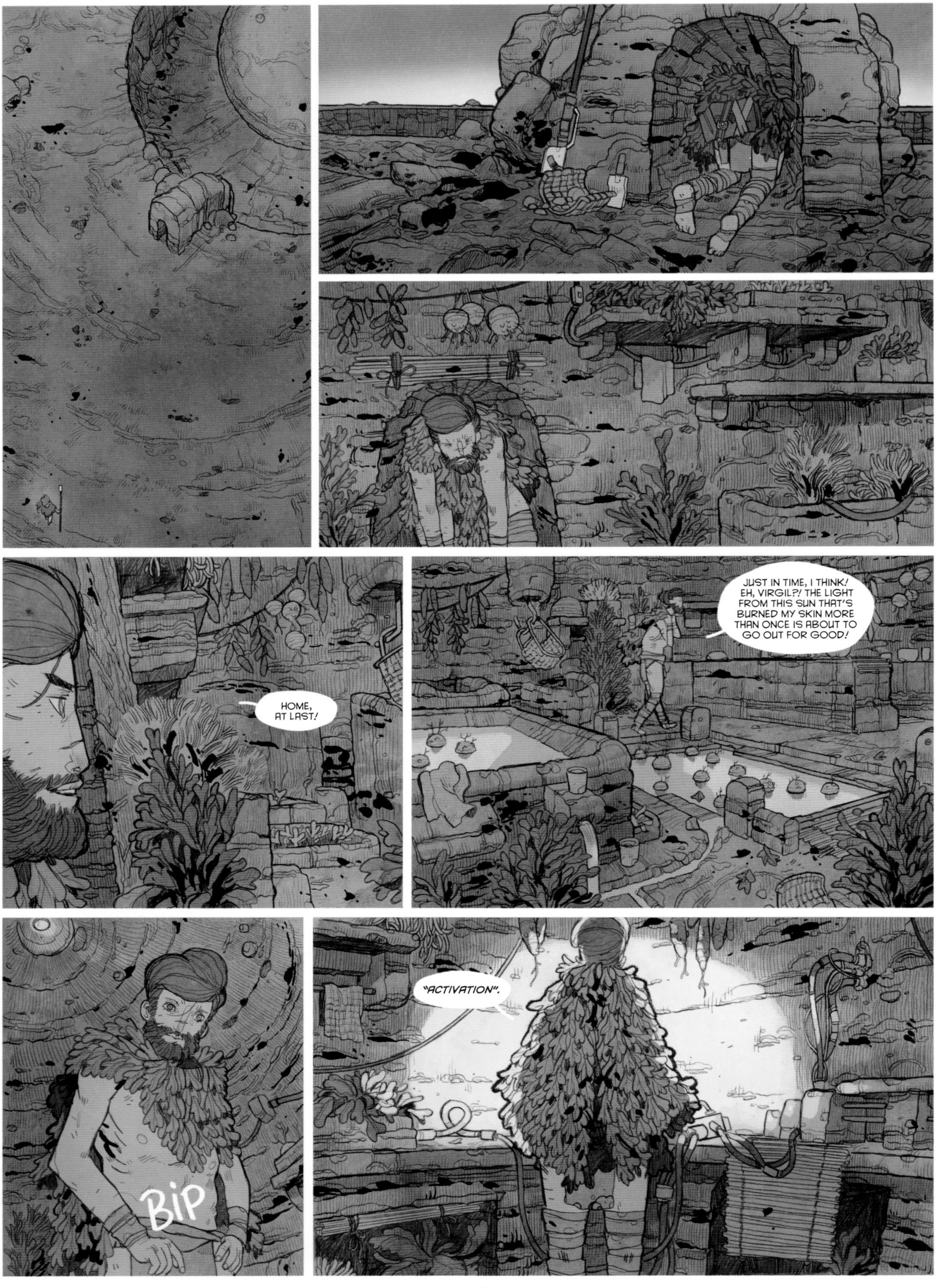
HOME, AT LAST!
JUST IN TIME, I THINK! EH, VIRGIL?! THE LIGHT FROM THIS SUN THAT'S BURNED MY SKIN MORE THAN ONCE IS ABOUT TO GO OUT FOR GOOD!
BIP
"ACTIVATION".

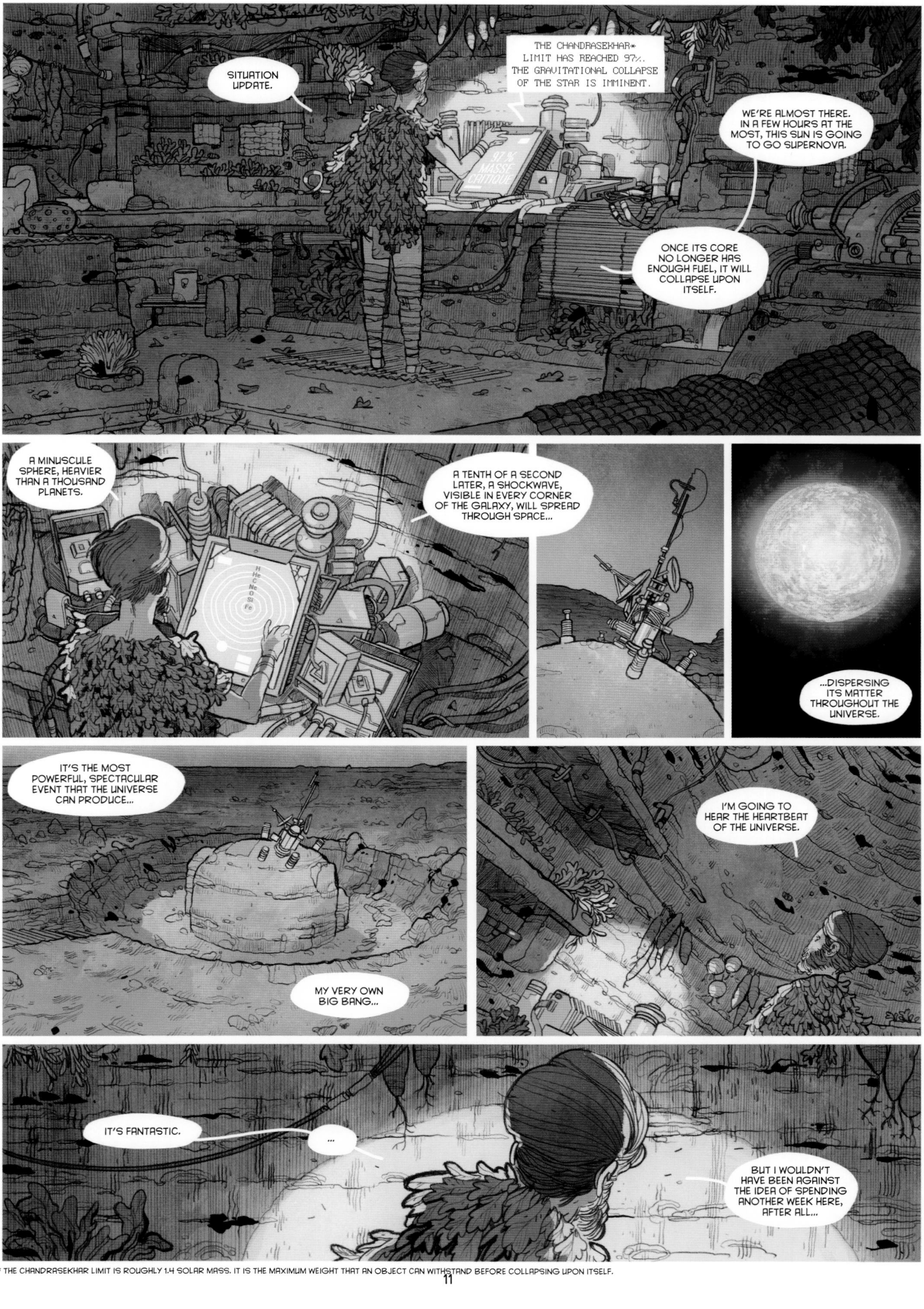
SITUATION UPDATE.
THE CHANDRASEKHAR* LIMIT HAS REACHED 97%. THE GRAVITATIONAL COLLAPSE OF THE STAR IS IMMINENT.
97% MASSE CRITIQUE
WE'RE ALMOST THERE. IN A FEW HOURS AT THE MOST, THIS SUN IS GOING TO GO SUPERNOVA.
ONCE ITS CORE NO LONGER HAS ENOUGH FUEL, IT WILL COLLAPSE UPON ITSELF.
A MINUSCULE SPHERE, HEAVIER THAN A THOUSAND PLANETS.
A TENTH OF A SECOND LATER, A SHOCKWAVE, VISIBLE IN EVERY CORNER OF THE GALAXY, WILL SPREAD THROUGH SPACE...
...DISPERSING ITS MATTER THROUGHOUT THE UNIVERSE.
IT'S THE MOST POWERFUL, SPECTACULAR EVENT THAT THE UNIVERSE CAN PRODUCE...
MY VERY OWN BIG BANG...
I'M GOING TO HEAR THE HEARTBEAT OF THE UNIVERSE.
IT'S FANTASTIC.
...
BUT I WOULDN'T HAVE BEEN AGAINST THE IDEA OF SPENDING ANOTHER WEEK HERE, AFTER ALL...

* THE CHANDRASEKHAR LIMIT IS ROUGHLY 1.4 SOLAR MASS. IT IS THE MAXIMUM WEIGHT THAT AN OBJECT CAN WITHSTAND BEFORE COLLAPSING UPON ITSELF.

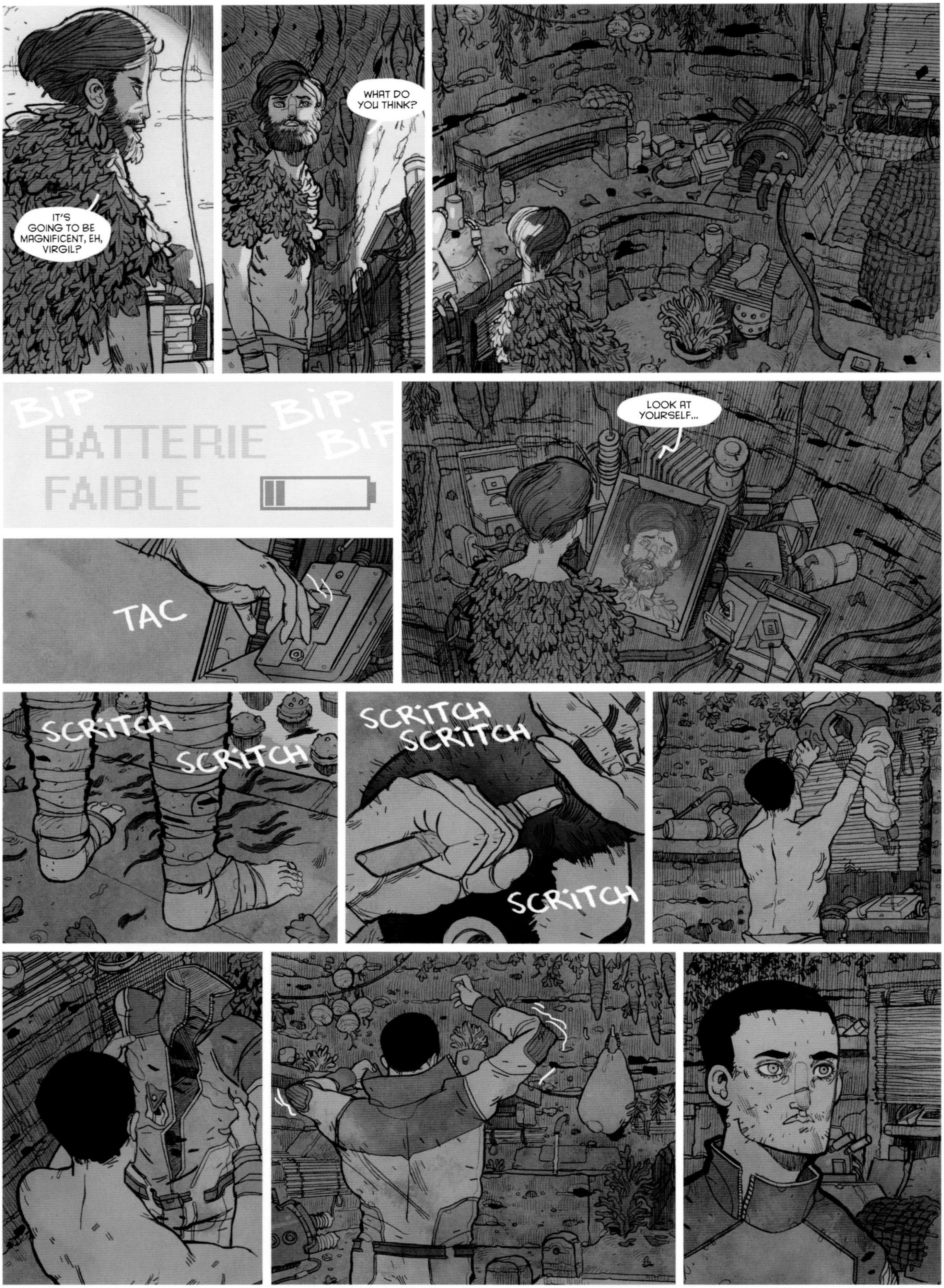
IT'S GOING TO BE MAGNIFICENT, EH, VIRGIL?
WHAT DO YOU THINK?
BIP
BATTERIE FAIBLE
BIP BIP
TAC
LOOK AT YOURSELF...
SCRITCH
SCRITCH
SCRITCH
SCRITCH
SCRITCH

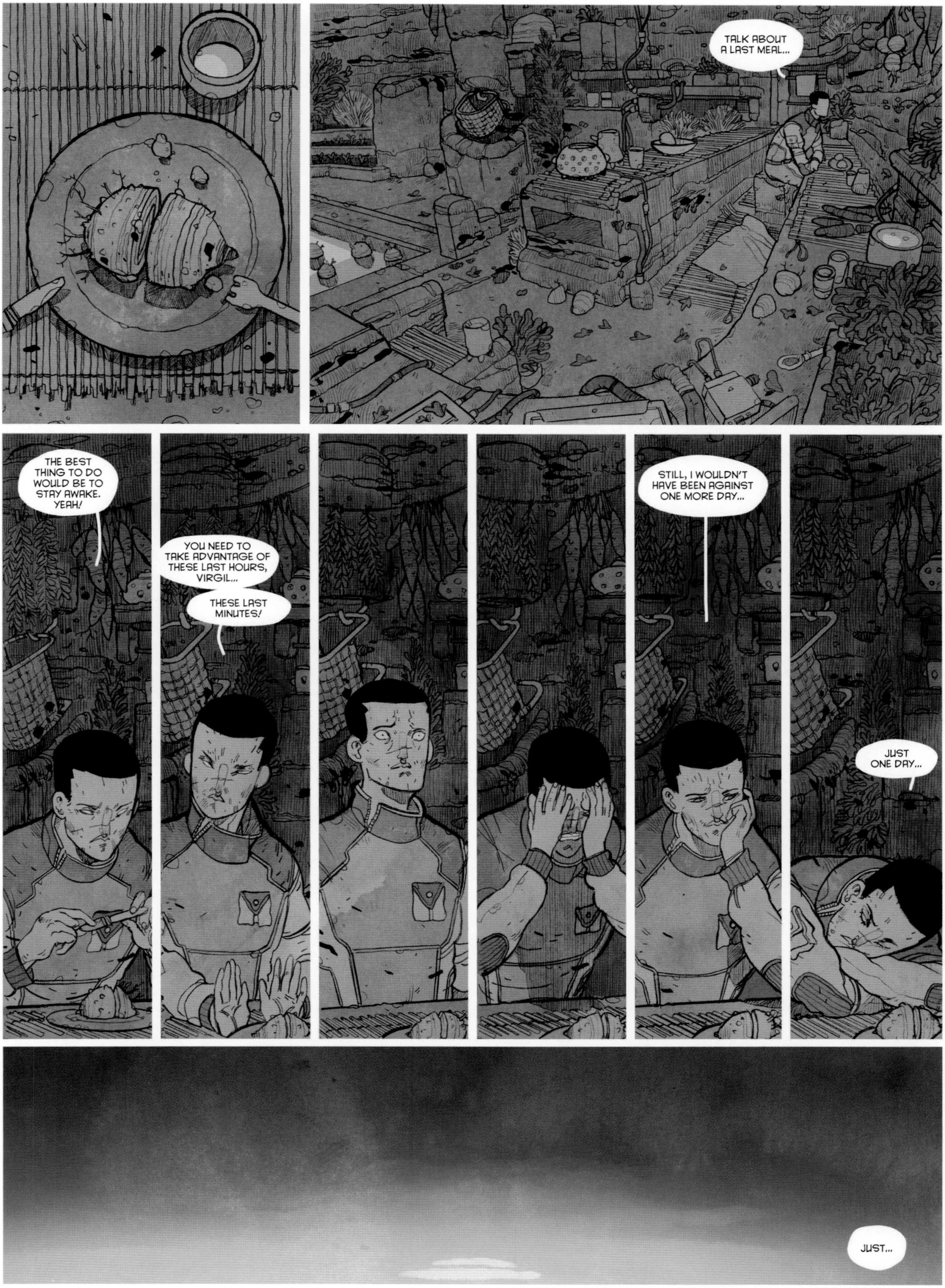
TALK ABOUT A LAST MEAL...
THE BEST THING TO DO WOULD BE TO STAY AWAKE. YEAH!
YOU NEED TO TAKE ADVANTAGE OF THESE LAST HOURS, VIRGIL...
THESE LAST MINUTES!
STILL, I WOULDN'T HAVE BEEN AGAINST ONE MORE DAY...
JUST ONE DAY...
JUST...

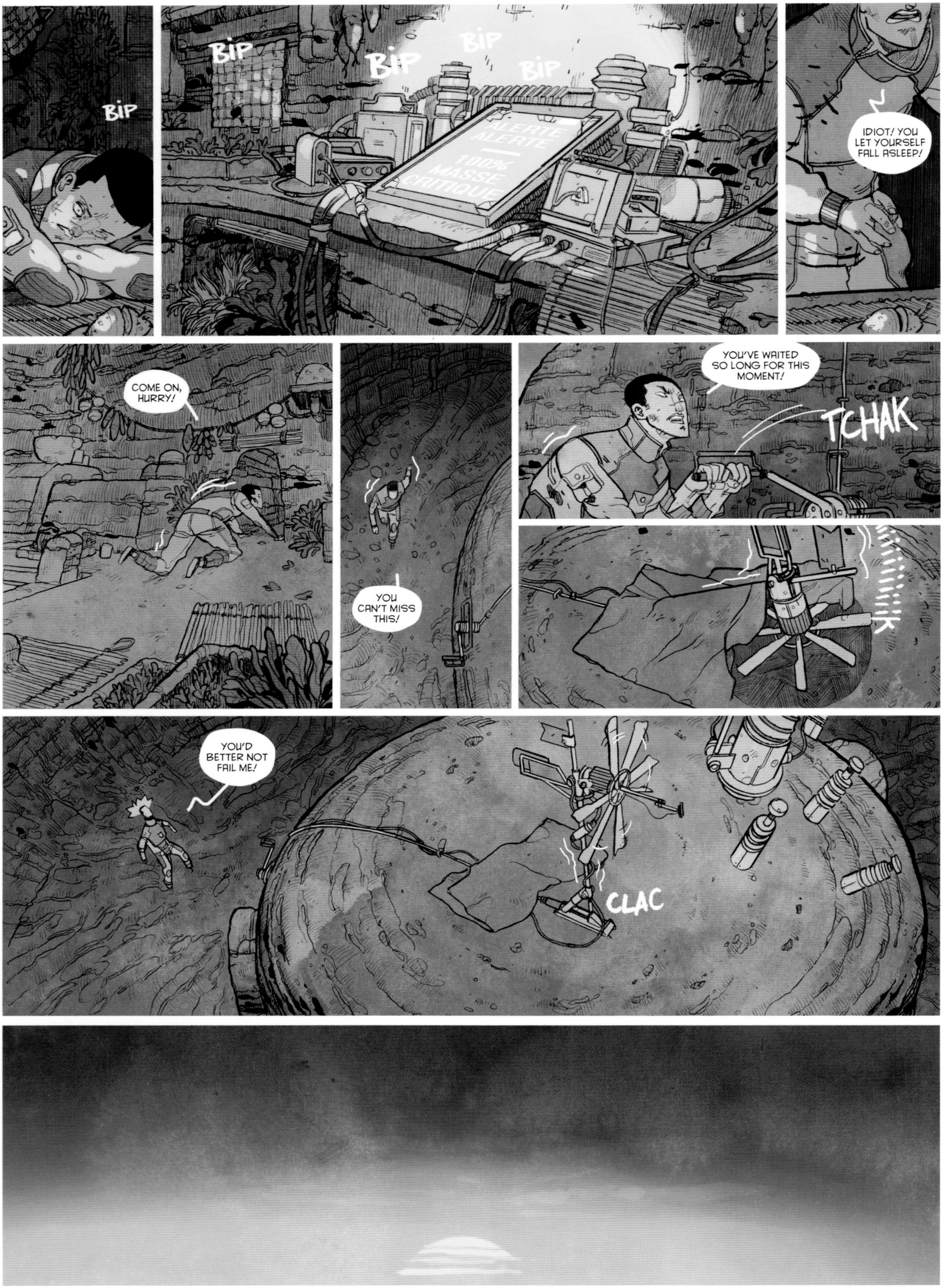
BIP
BIP
BIP
BIP
BIP
ALERTE ALERTE 100% MASSE CRITIQUE
IDIOT! YOU LET YOURSELF FALL ASLEEP!
COME ON, HURRY!
YOU CAN'T MISS THIS!
YOU'VE WAITED SO LONG FOR THIS MOMENT!
TCHAK
YOU'D BETTER NOT FAIL ME!
CLAC

I CAN HARDLY BELIEVE THAT IT'S HAPPENING RIGHT NOW!

EVERYTHING HAS TO BE PERFECT!

FWOOOSHH

HAH!

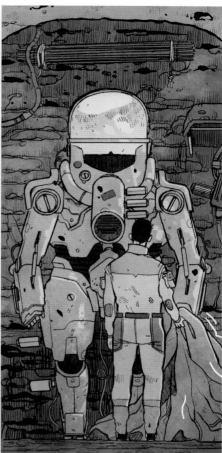

FZZZZZZZZZZZ

11 YEARS!

BZZZ

11 YEARS, 4 MONTHS, AND 26 DAYS SINCE I MATERIALIZED IN THIS SECTOR OF THE GALAXY...

...AND LANDED ON THIS GODFORSAKEN, ARID PLANET!

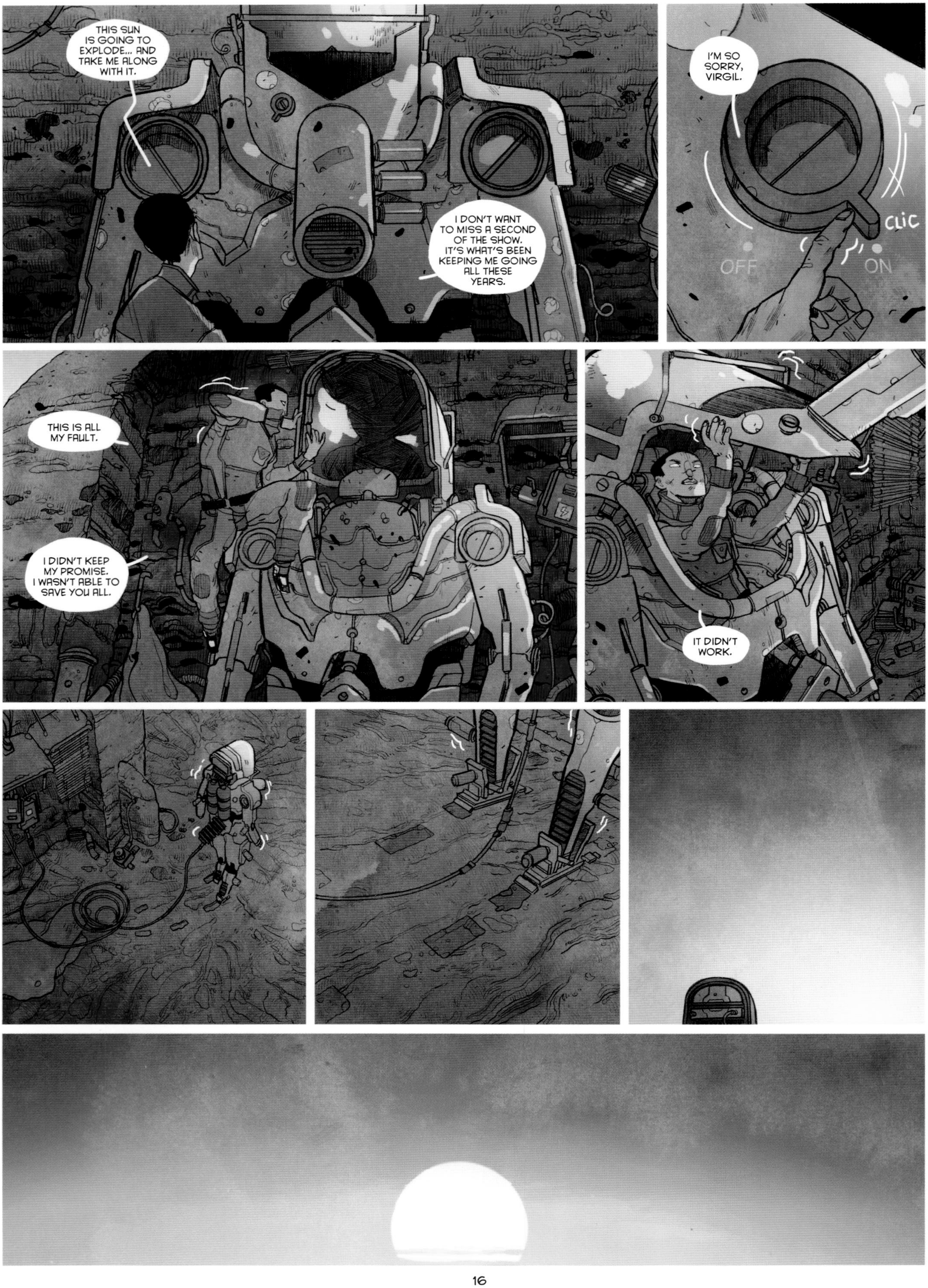

THIS SUN IS GOING TO EXPLODE... AND TAKE ME ALONG WITH IT.
I DON'T WANT TO MISS A SECOND OF THE SHOW. IT'S WHAT'S BEEN KEEPING ME GOING ALL THESE YEARS.
I'M SO SORRY, VIRGIL.
OFF
ON
CLIC
THIS IS ALL MY FAULT.
I DIDN'T KEEP MY PROMISE. I WASN'T ABLE TO SAVE YOU ALL.
IT DIDN'T WORK.

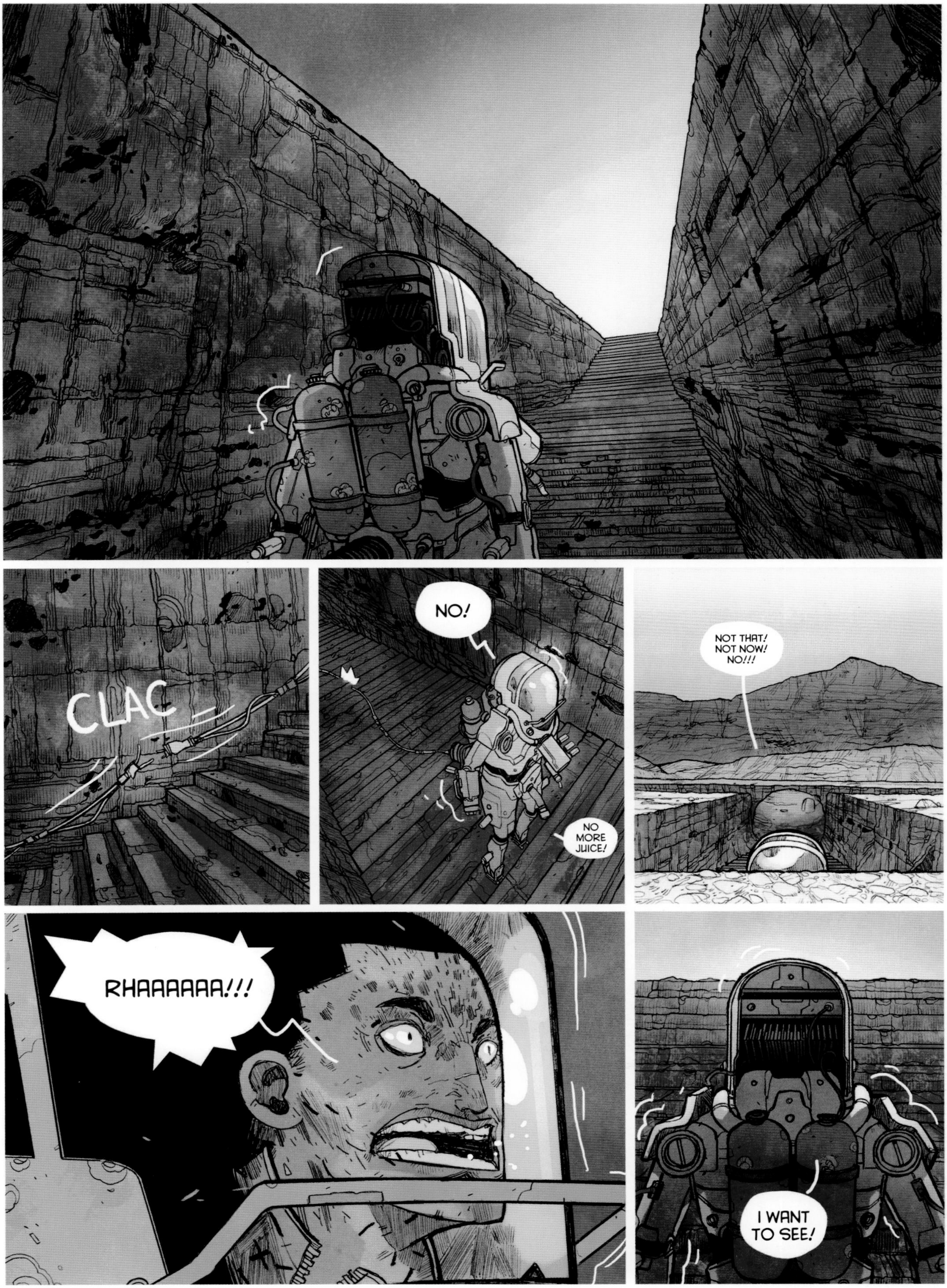
CLAC
NO!
NO MORE JUICE!
NOT THAT! NOT NOW! NO!!!
RHAAAAAA!!!
I WANT TO SEE!

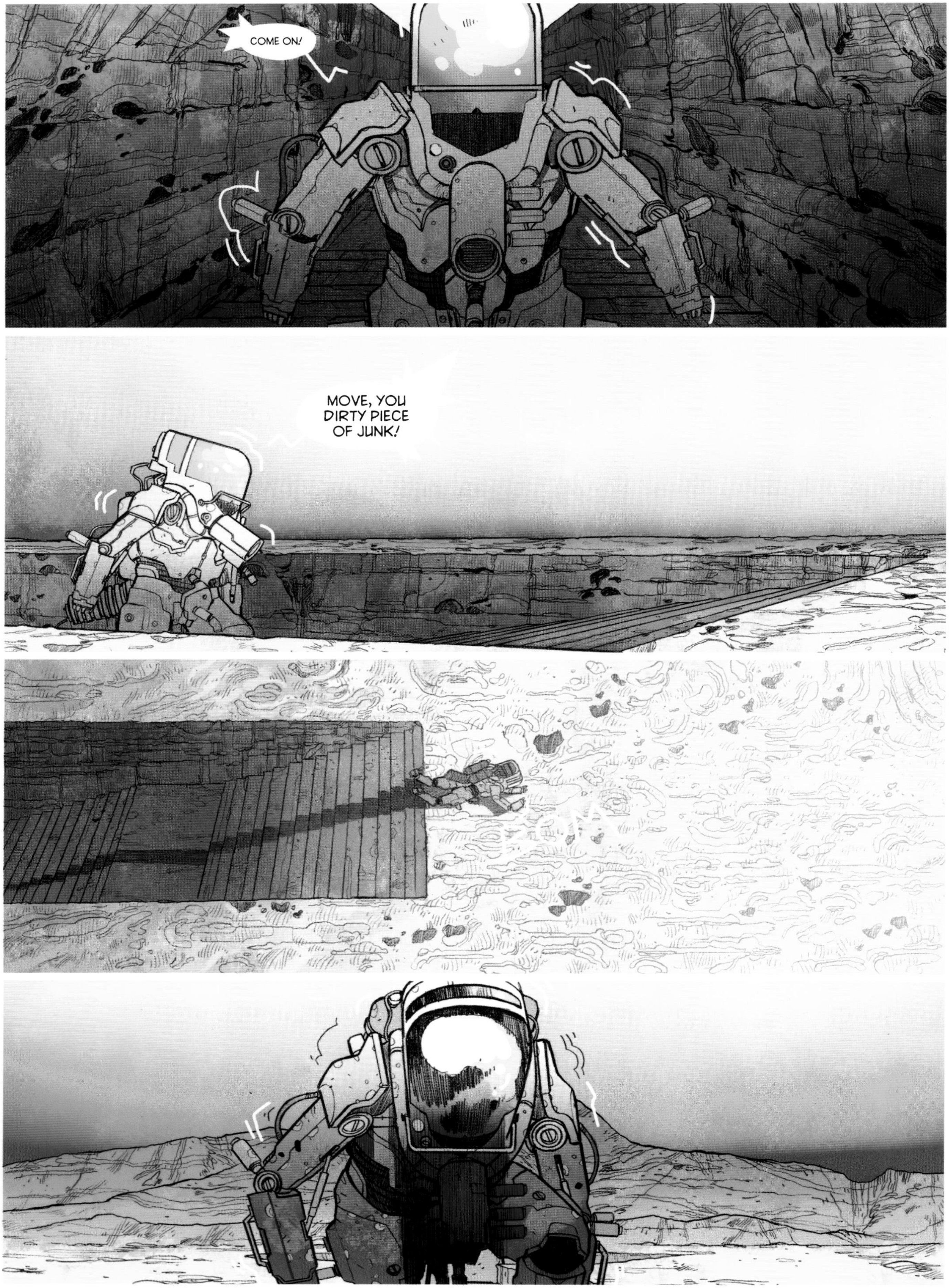
COME ON!
MOVE, YOU DIRTY PIECE OF JUNK!

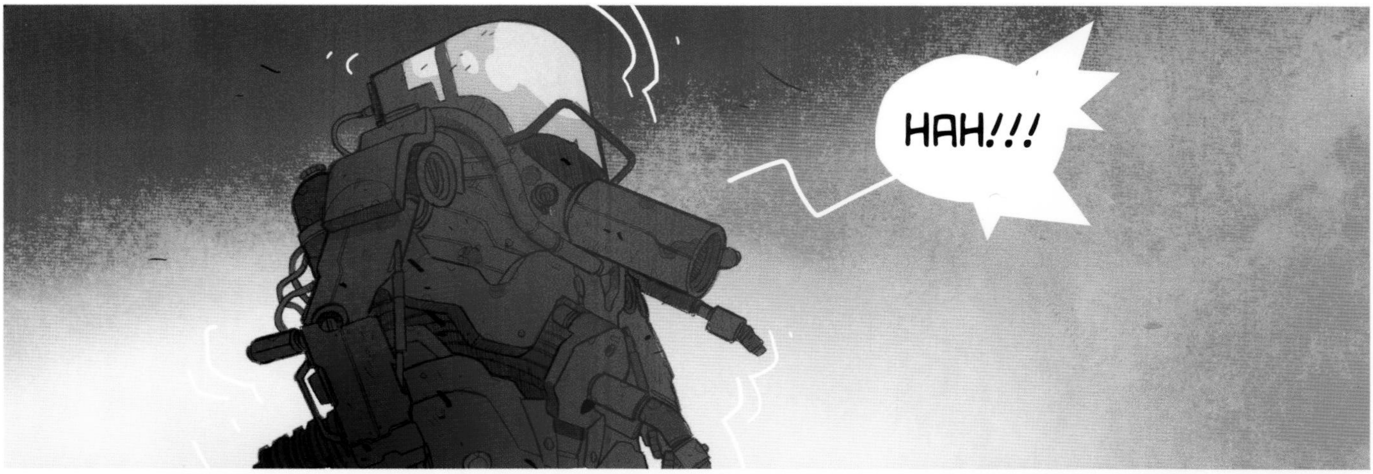
HAH!!!
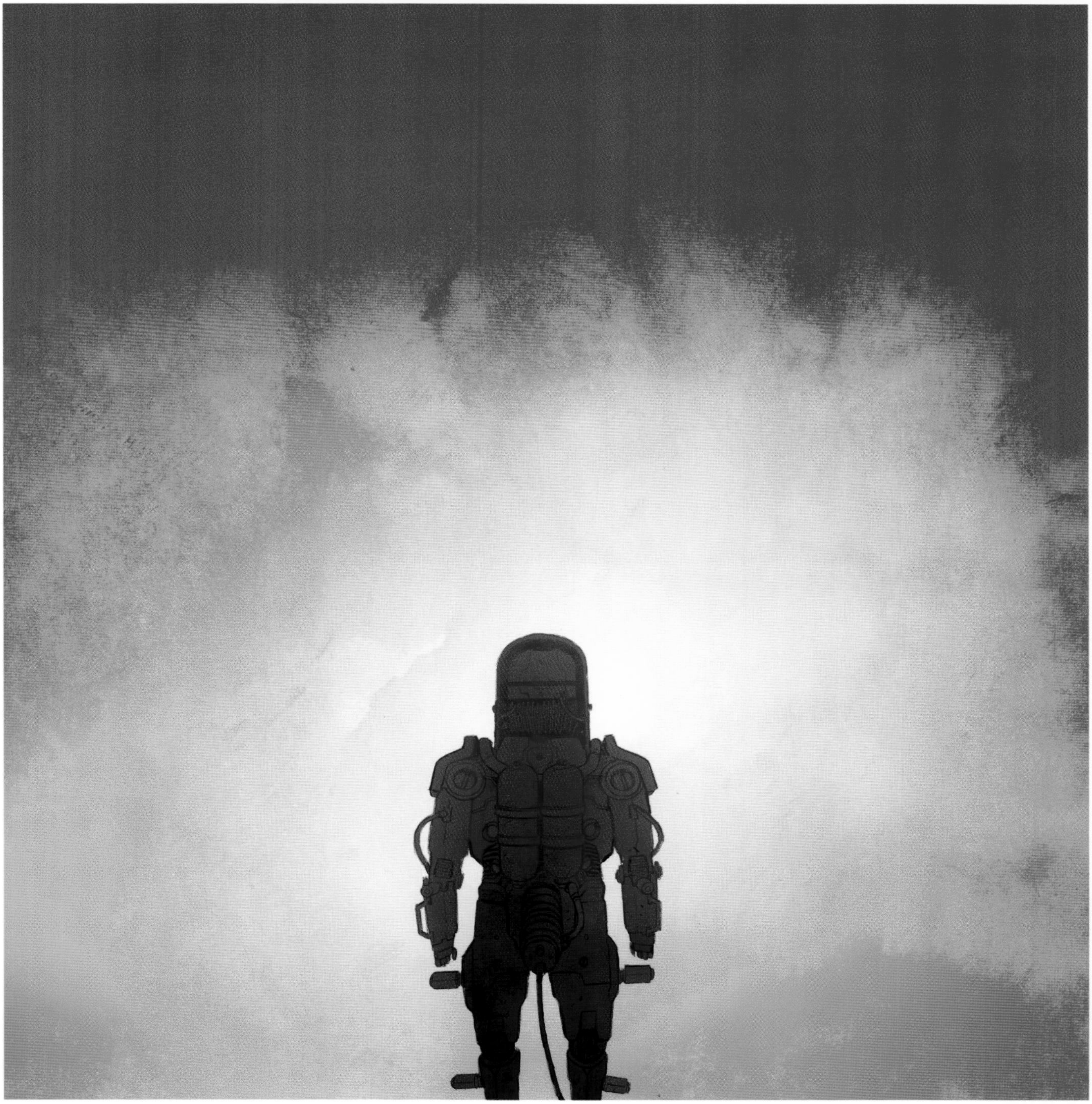

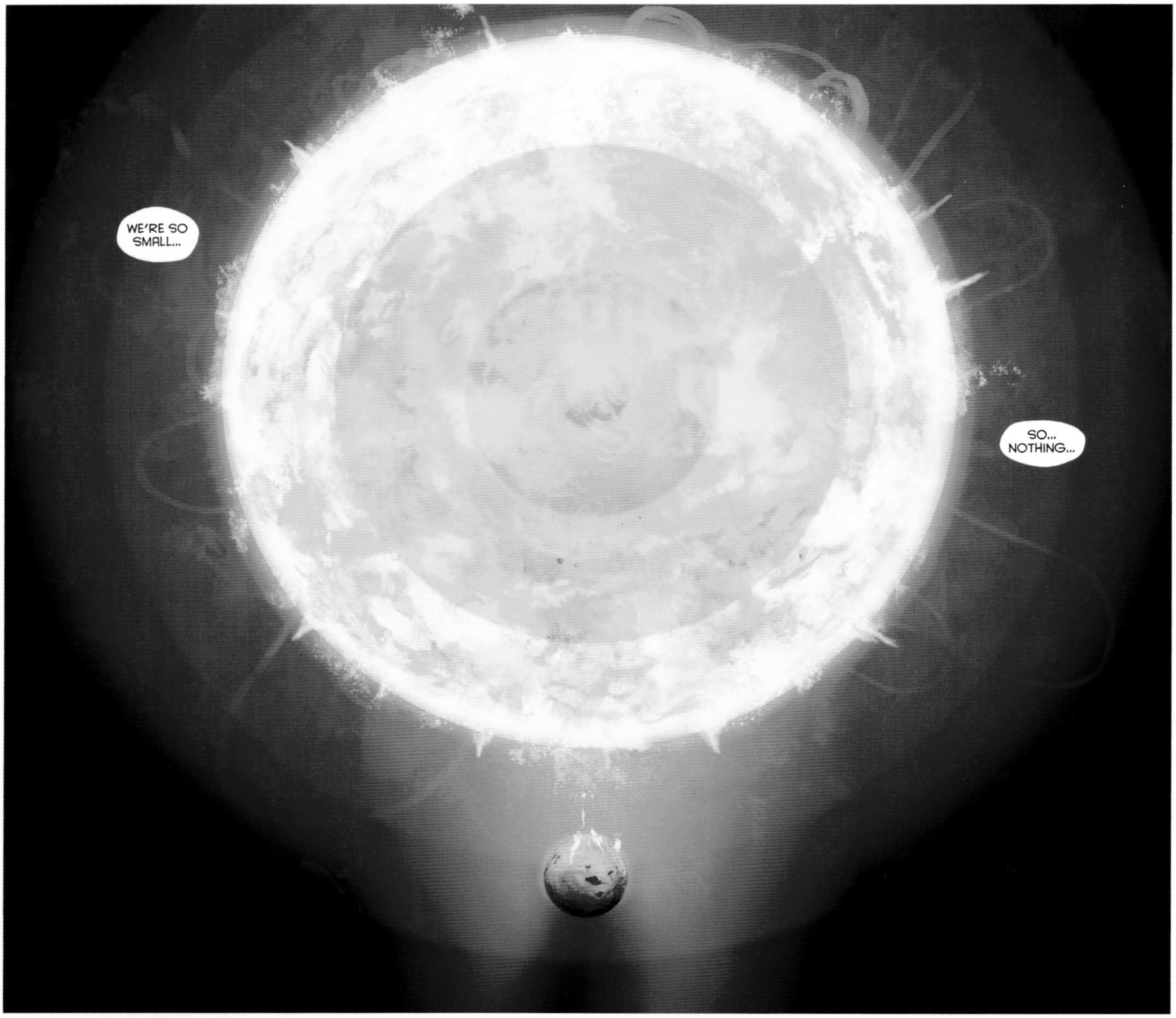
WE'RE SO SMALL...
SO... NOTHING...

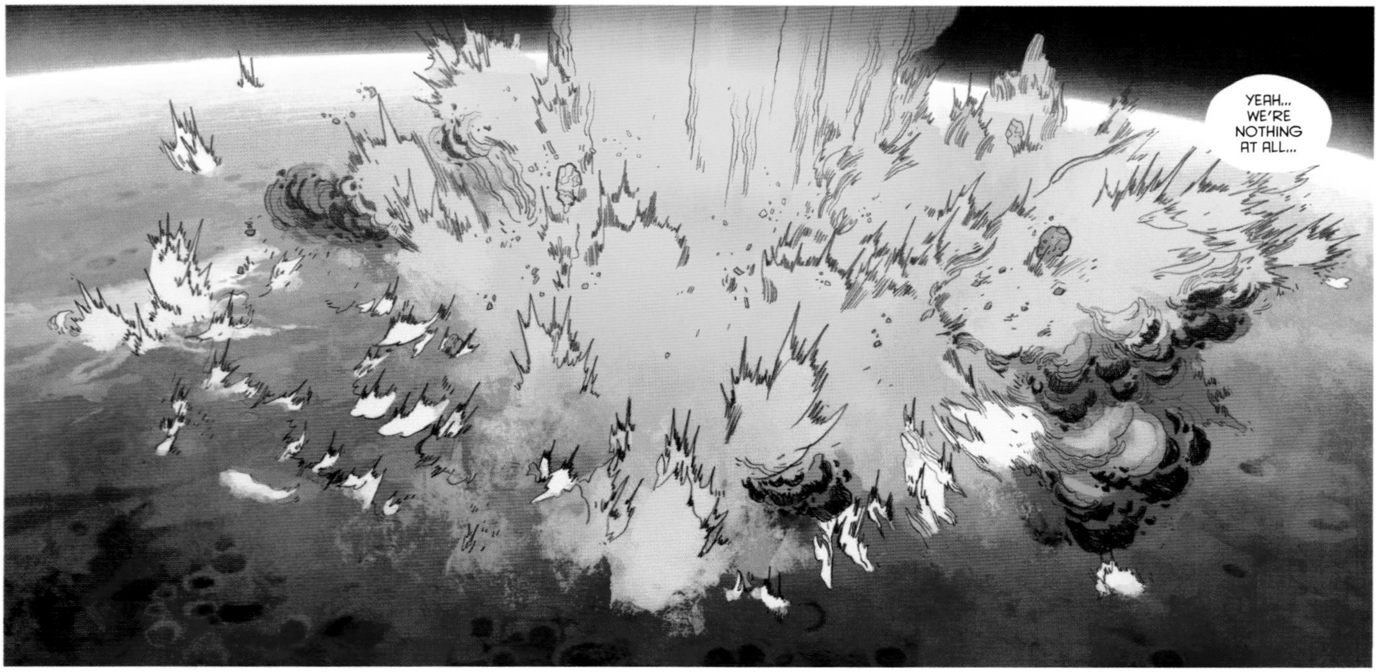
YEAH... WE'RE NOTHING AT ALL...

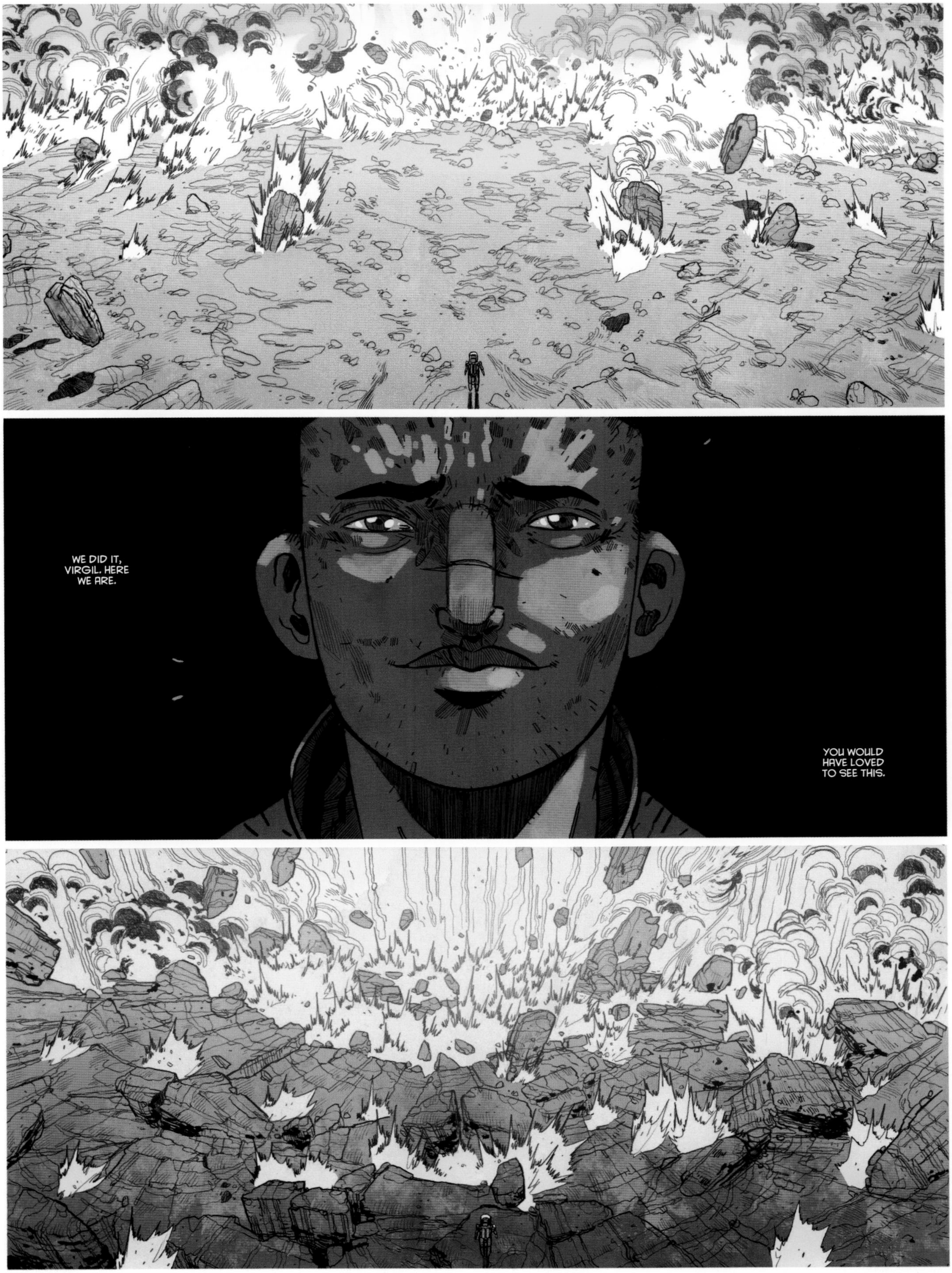
WE DID IT, VIRGIL. HERE WE ARE.
YOU WOULD HAVE LOVED TO SEE THIS.

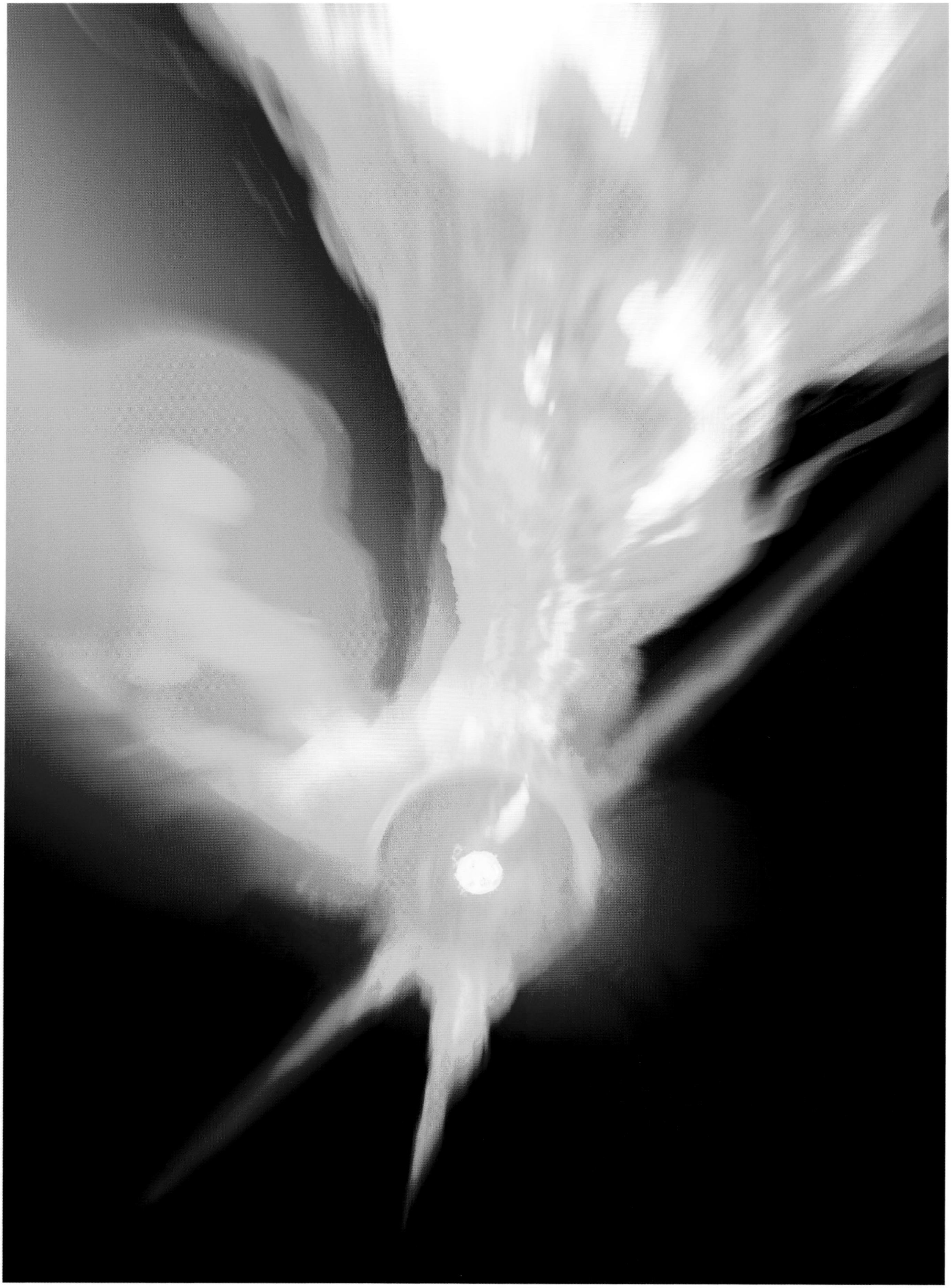

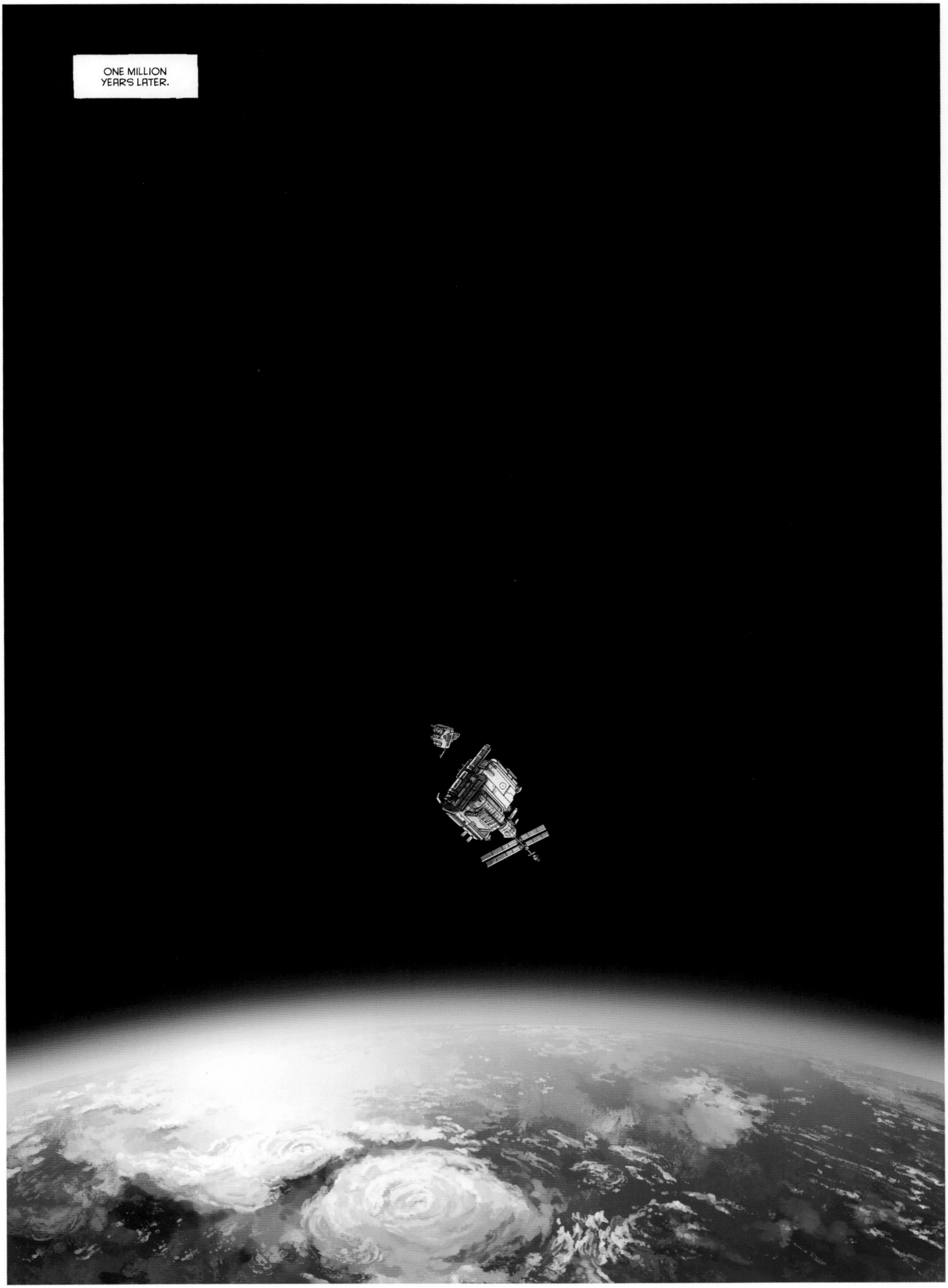
ONE MILLION
YEARS LATER.

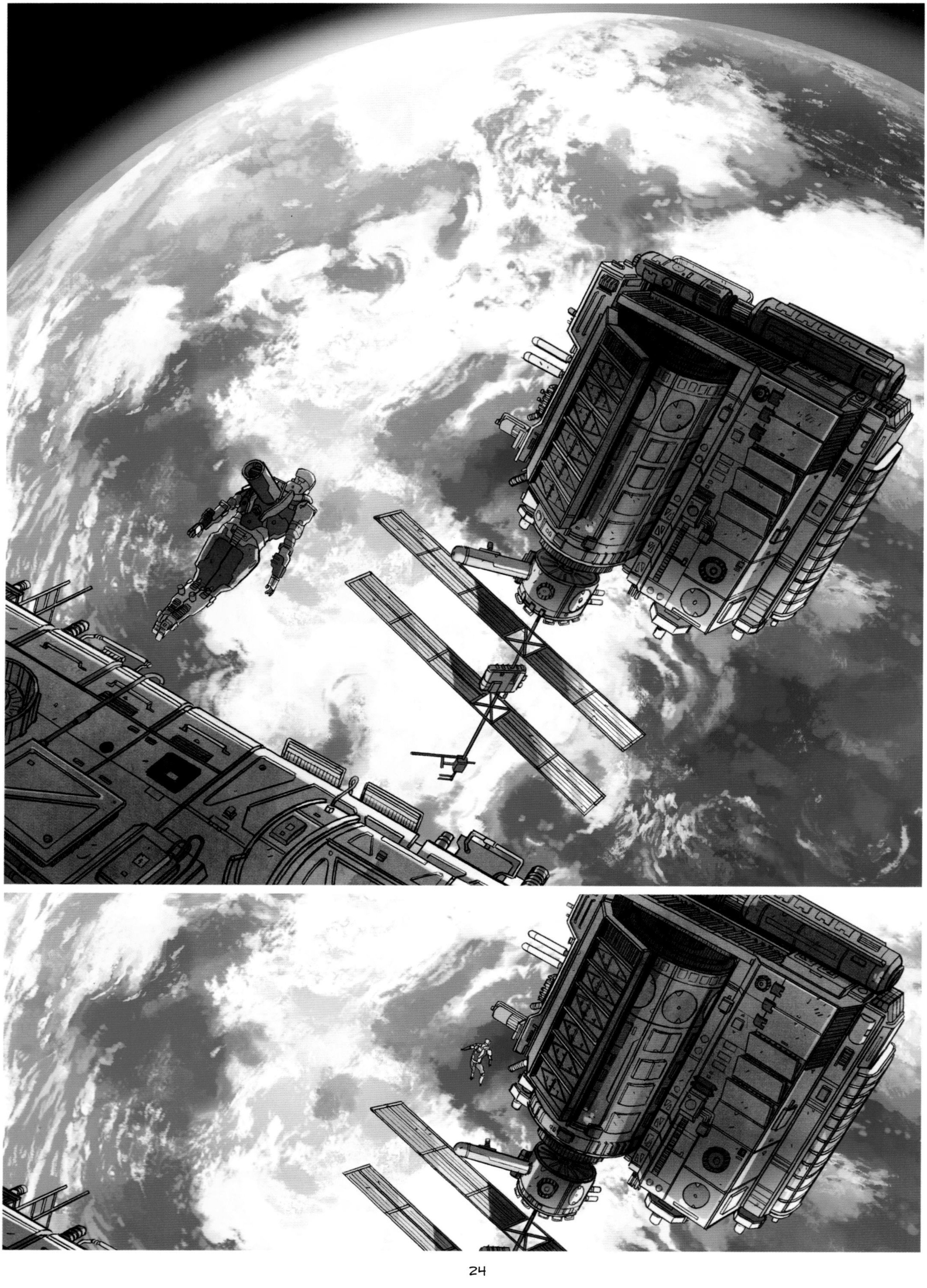

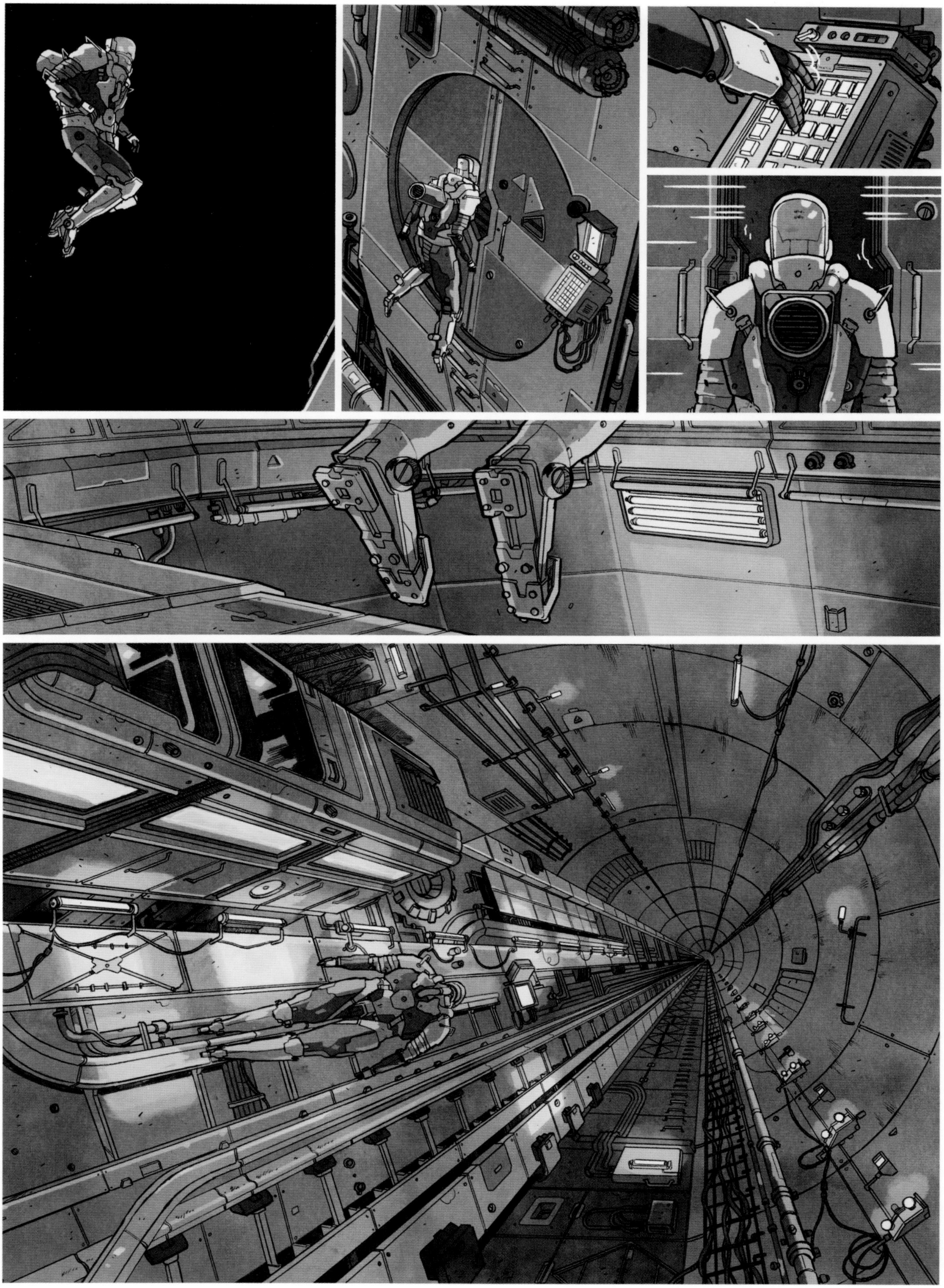

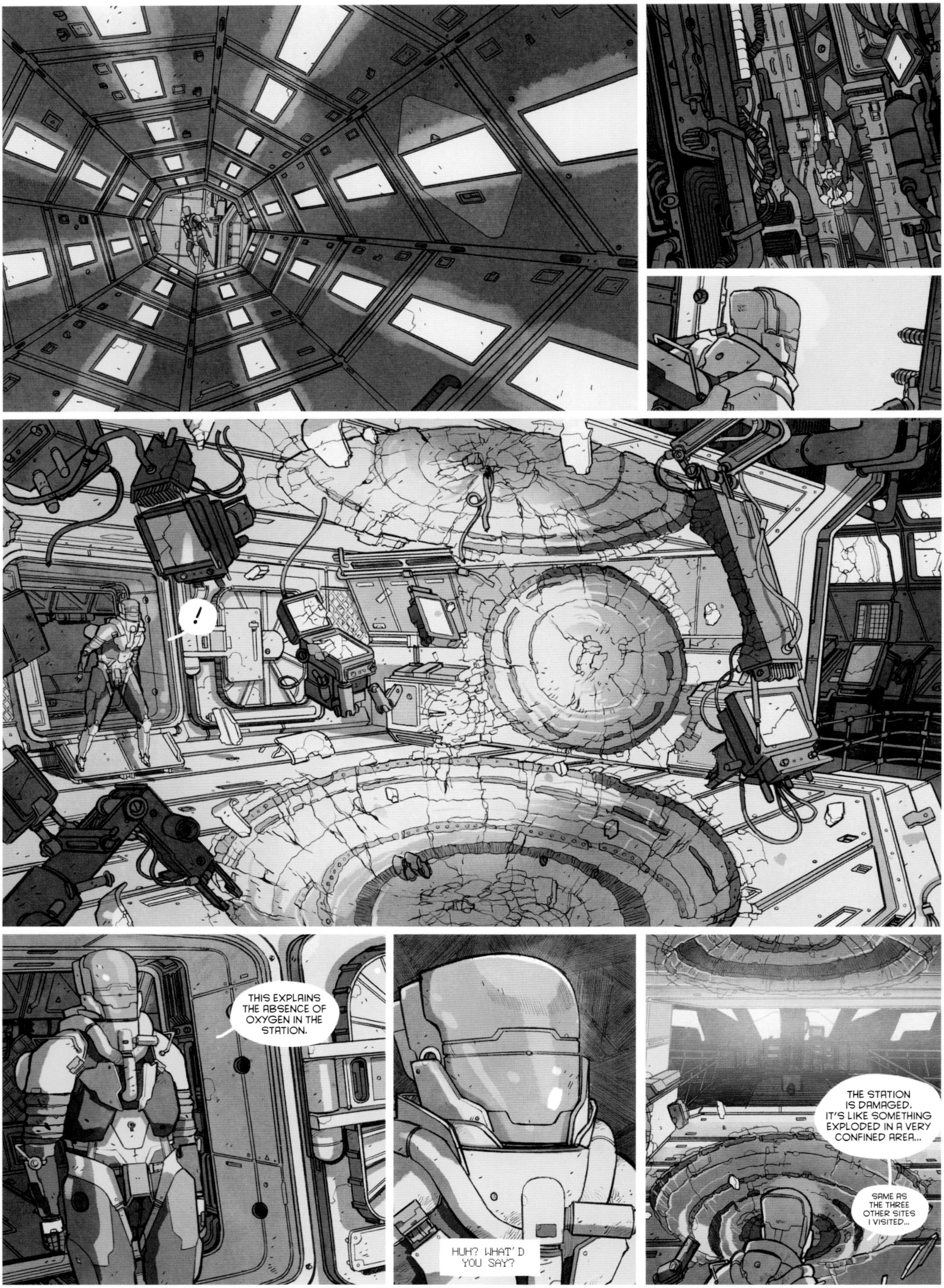
!
THIS EXPLAINS THE ABSENCE OF OXYGEN IN THE STATION.
HUH? WHAT'D YOU SAY?
THE STATION IS DAMAGED. IT'S LIKE SOMETHING EXPLODED IN A VERY CONFINED AREA...
SAME AS THE THREE OTHER SITES I VISITED...

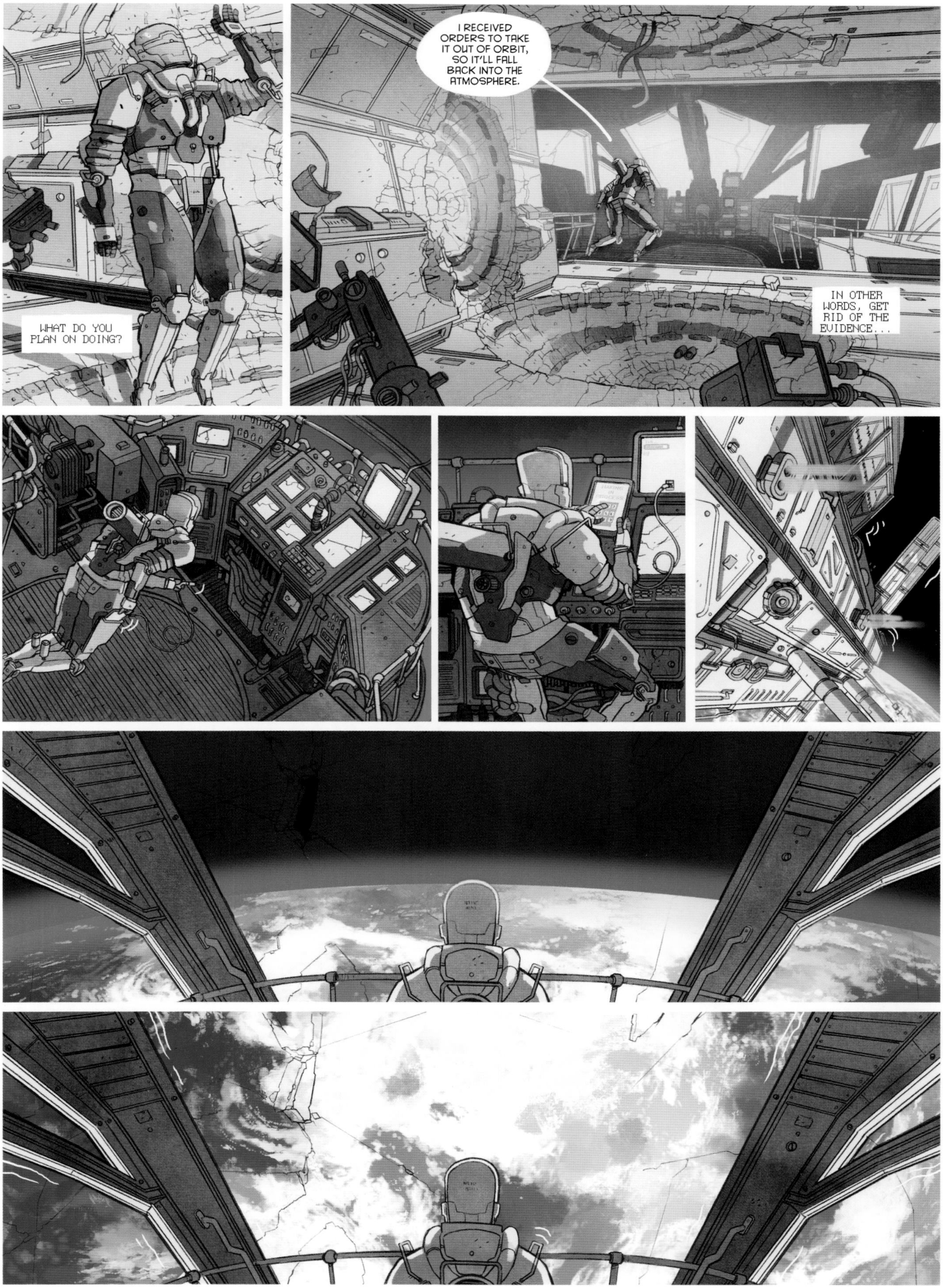
WHAT DO YOU PLAN ON DOING?
I RECEIVED ORDERS TO TAKE IT OUT OF ORBIT, SO IT'LL FALL BACK INTO THE ATMOSPHERE.
IN OTHER WORDS, GET RID OF THE EVIDENCE...

NOW I BETTER HURRY!
COME ON...
AH!
FASTER! FASTER!
DAMMIT! WHAT THE HELL ARE YOU DOING UP HERE?!

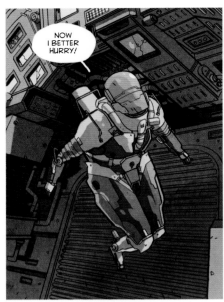

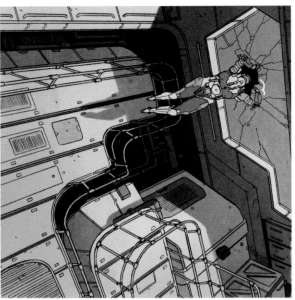

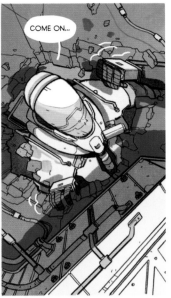

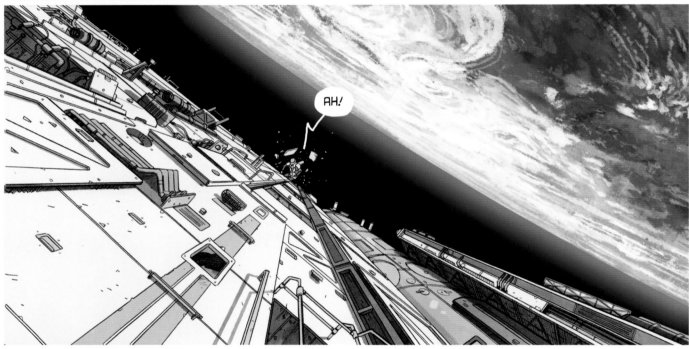

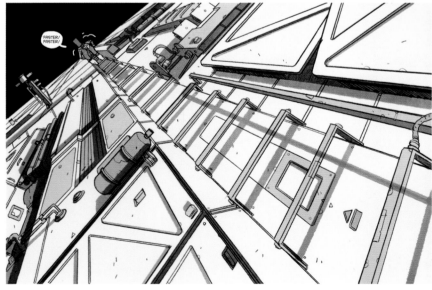

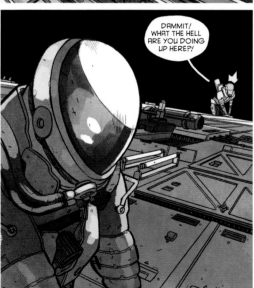

WHAT DOES IT LOOK LIKE? I'M SALVAGING GEAR! IT'S BEEN ABANDONED ANYWAY... I MIGHT AS WELL HELP MYSELF!
YEAH, WELL IT'S DANGEROUS, TOO! WE HAVE TO GET OUT OF HERE, PRONTO!
CLAC
PRESSURIZING AIRLOCK.
BRRRR RRRR RRRRR RRRRR
CLANG
CLANG
CLANG
IT WAS RECKLESS OF YOU TO COME, YOUNG LADY. A FEW MORE SECONDS, AND YOU WOULD HAVE PLUNGED BACK TO EARTH, TOO!

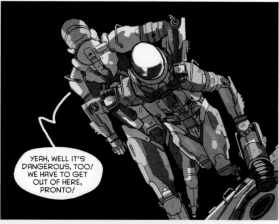

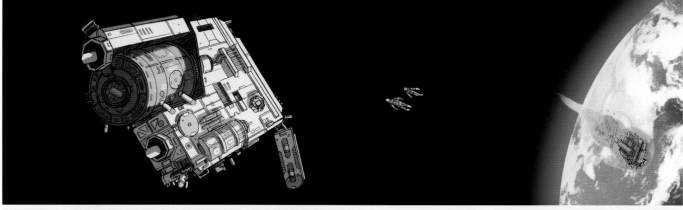

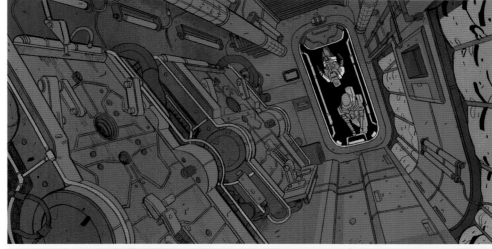

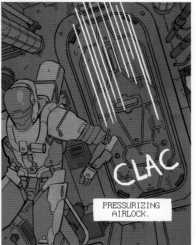

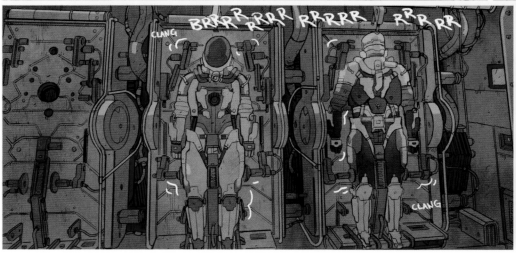

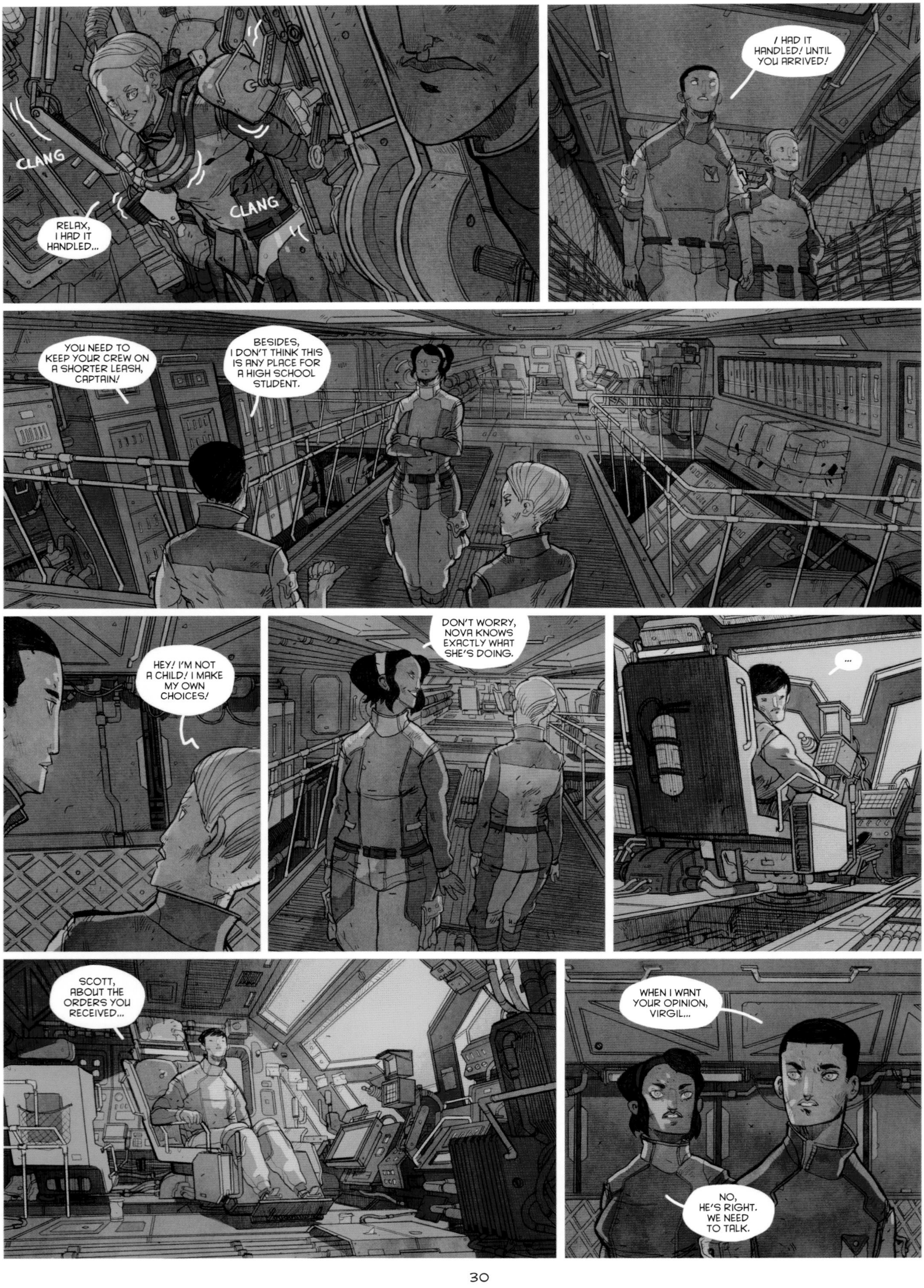
CLANG
CLANG
RELAX, I HAD IT HANDLED...
I HAD IT HANDLED! UNTIL YOU ARRIVED!
YOU NEED TO KEEP YOUR CREW ON A SHORTER LEASH, CAPTAIN!
BESIDES, I DON'T THINK THIS IS ANY PLACE FOR A HIGH SCHOOL STUDENT.
HEY! I'M NOT A CHILD! I MAKE MY OWN CHOICES!
DON'T WORRY, NOVA KNOWS EXACTLY WHAT SHE'S DOING.
...
SCOTT, ABOUT THE ORDERS YOU RECEIVED...
WHEN I WANT YOUR OPINION, VIRGIL...
NO, HE'S RIGHT. WE NEED TO TALK.

I DON'T BELIEVE THIS! DON'T YOU FIND IT STRANGE THAT YOU'RE GIVEN ORDERS TO INVESTIGATE UNEXPLAINED PHENOMENA IN THESE *ATOMIC RESEARCH* LABS, AND THEN SYSTEMATICALLY DESTROY ANY AND ALL PROOF THAT THE PHENOMENA IN QUESTION EVER EXISTED?

...

IF *TIANZHU ENTERPRISES* ASKS ME NOT TO DISCLOSE INFORMATION ABOUT THE SITUATION...

...THEN THEY MUST HAVE A GOOD REASON TO DO SO. I DON'T SEE WHY THEY'D WANT TO CREATE MASS PANIC. THESE EXPLOSIONS MIGHT BE NOTHING AT ALL.

SO, YOU CAN'T DEDUCE ANYTHING FROM WHAT YOU'VE SEEN?

NOTHING I CAN TALK ABOUT, NO.

DAMN IT, SCOTT! AS THE CAPTAIN OF THE DELACROIX, I DEMAND THAT YOU KEEP ME INFORMED ABOUT... HEY—DON'T WALK AWAY!

I DON'T WORK FOR YOU.

AÏCHA, ALLOW ME.

NOVA...

I'VE GOT THIS, DON'T WORRY.

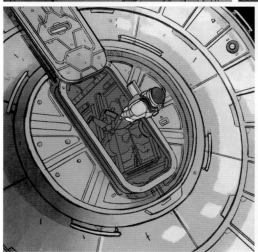

SCOTT?

31

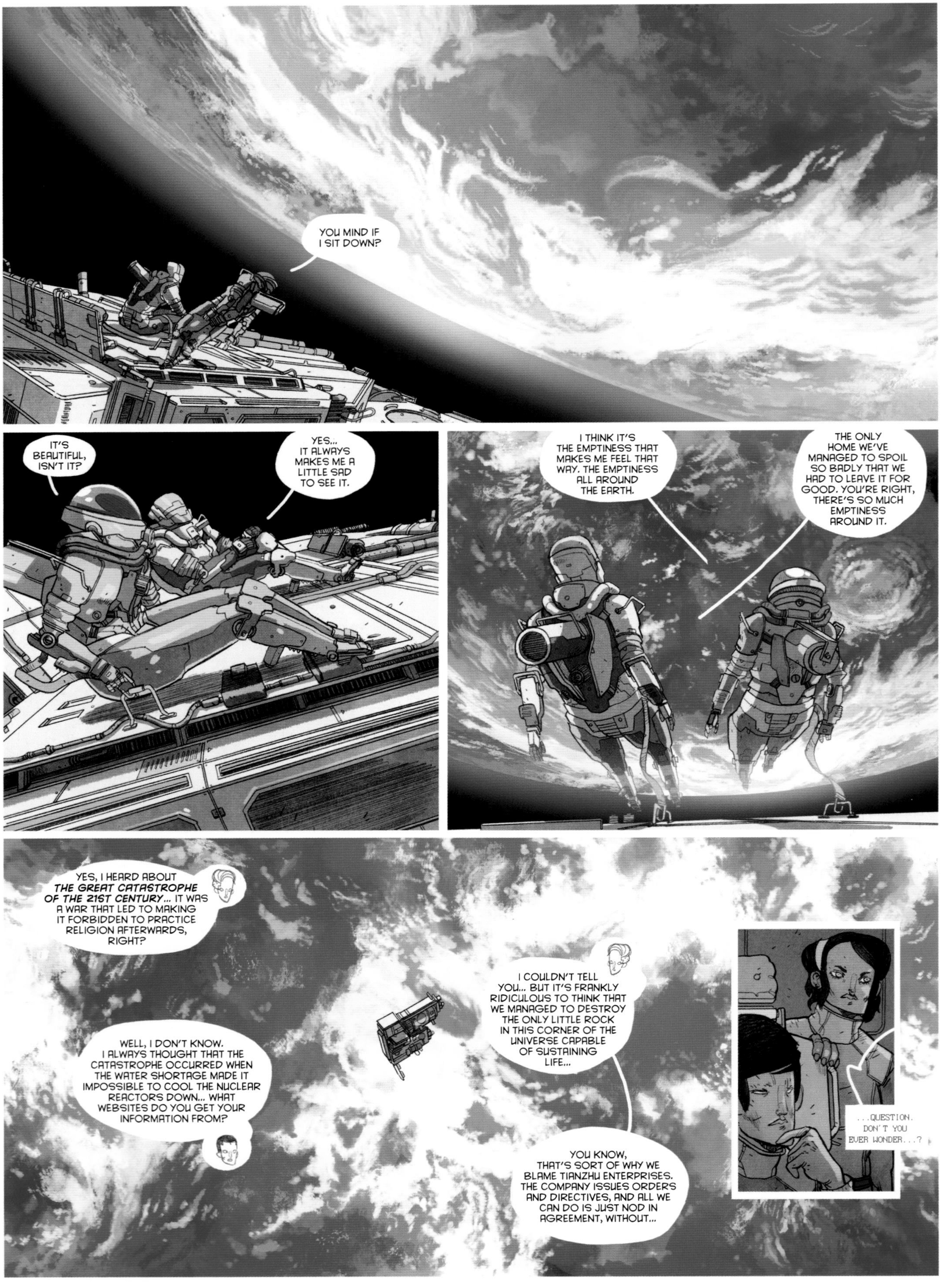
YOU MIND IF I SIT DOWN?
IT'S BEAUTIFUL, ISN'T IT?
YES... IT ALWAYS MAKES ME A LITTLE SAD TO SEE IT.
I THINK IT'S THE EMPTINESS THAT MAKES ME FEEL THAT WAY. THE EMPTINESS ALL AROUND THE EARTH.
THE ONLY HOME WE'VE MANAGED TO SPOIL SO BADLY THAT WE HAD TO LEAVE IT FOR GOOD. YOU'RE RIGHT, THERE'S SO MUCH EMPTINESS AROUND IT.
YES, I HEARD ABOUT *THE GREAT CATASTROPHE OF THE 21ST CENTURY*... IT WAS A WAR THAT LED TO MAKING IT FORBIDDEN TO PRACTICE RELIGION AFTERWARDS, RIGHT?
WELL, I DON'T KNOW. I ALWAYS THOUGHT THAT THE CATASTROPHE OCCURRED WHEN THE WATER SHORTAGE MADE IT IMPOSSIBLE TO COOL THE NUCLEAR REACTORS DOWN... WHAT WEBSITES DO YOU GET YOUR INFORMATION FROM?
I COULDN'T TELL YOU... BUT IT'S FRANKLY RIDICULOUS TO THINK THAT WE MANAGED TO DESTROY THE ONLY LITTLE ROCK IN THIS CORNER OF THE UNIVERSE CAPABLE OF SUSTAINING LIFE...
YOU KNOW, THAT'S SORT OF WHY WE BLAME TIANZHU ENTERPRISES. THE COMPANY ISSUES ORDERS AND DIRECTIVES, AND ALL WE CAN DO IS JUST NOD IN AGREEMENT, WITHOUT...
...QUESTION. DON'T YOU EVER WONDER...?

ARE YOU
A LITTLE
YOUNG TO BE SO
CURIOUS?

YOU THINK WE
DIDN'T QUESTION
ANYTHING WHEN WE
WERE YOUNGER?

AH, THE
INSOLENCE
OF YOUTH...

MAYBE WE'RE
MAKING OUR SHARE OF
MISTAKES NOW, TOO. BUT YOU KNOW,
WE'RE GOING TO HAVE TO LIVE WITH
THE CONSEQUENCES OF PREVIOUS
GENERATIONS' ERRORS. ARE WE
CONDEMNED TO MAKE THE SAME MISTAKES
OUR PARENTS DID, WHO MADE THE SAME
MISTAKES THEIR PARENTS DID? NONE OF
US CHOSE TO BE IN THIS SITUATION.
I JUST THINK THAT OUR GENERATION
ASKS ITSELF MORE QUESTIONS
THAN THE PREVIOUS ONE EVER
DID, THAT'S ALL.

ARE YOU
INSINUATING THAT
I'M TOO OLD TO
UNDERSTAND?

I THINK
THAT YOU'RE
ALREADY TOO
OLD TO WANT
TO CHANGE.

THE STRENGTH OF
ONE'S CONVICTIONS
ISN'T MEASURED
WITH AGE!

PUT ME
THROUGH
TO HER.

BUT SHE
TALKS TOO MUCH.
WE CAN'T TRUST
HER YET.

NOVA!
THAT'S
ENOUGH.

AH! I THINK
IT'S TIME TO
GO BACK
INSIDE.

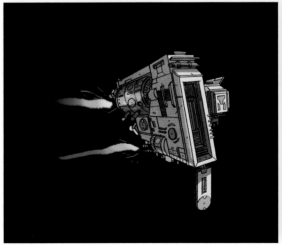

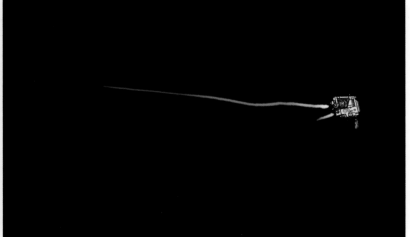

33

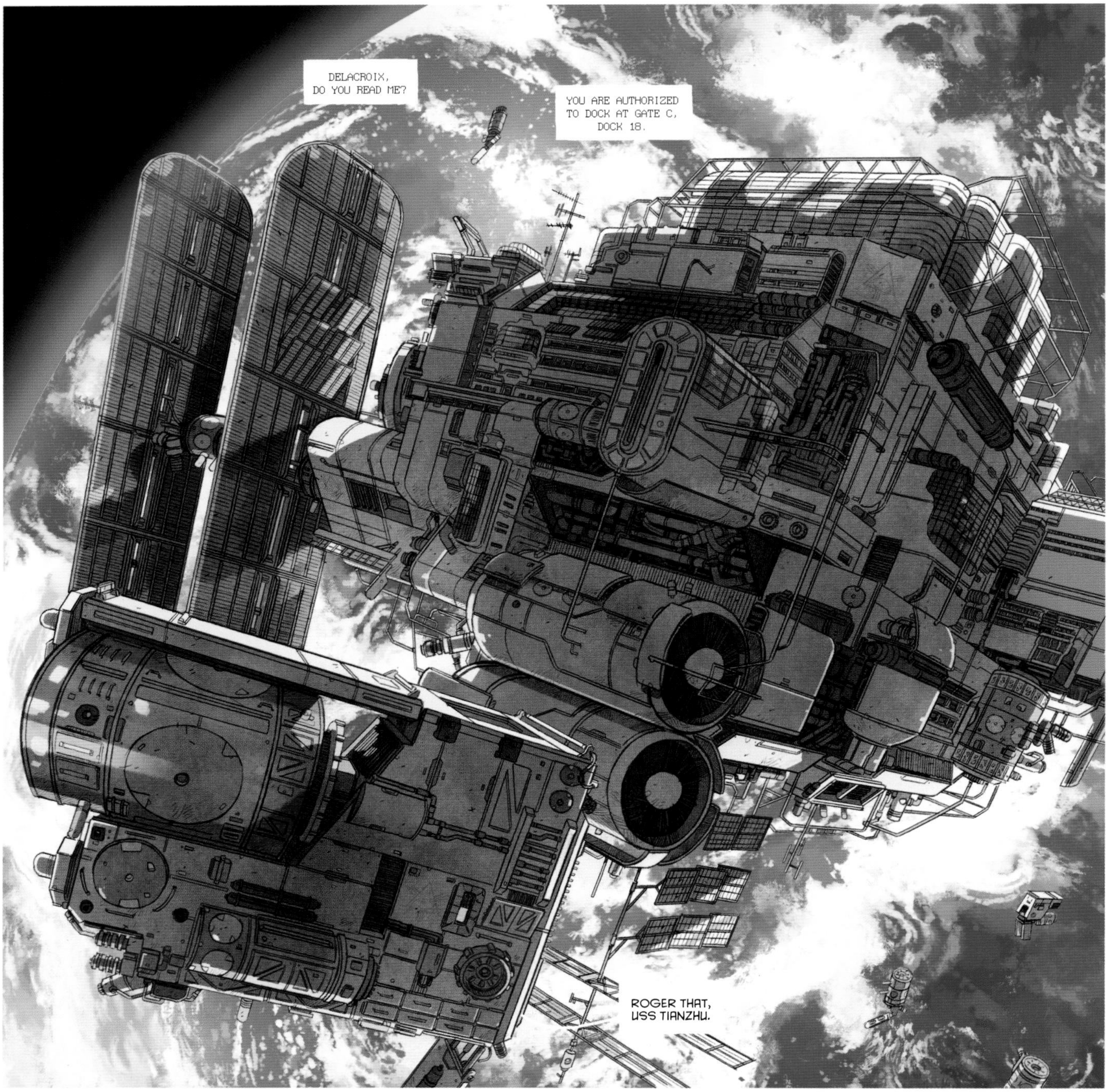
DELACROIX,
DO YOU READ ME?
YOU ARE AUTHORIZED
TO DOCK AT GATE C,
DOCK 18.
ROGER THAT,
USS TIANZHU.

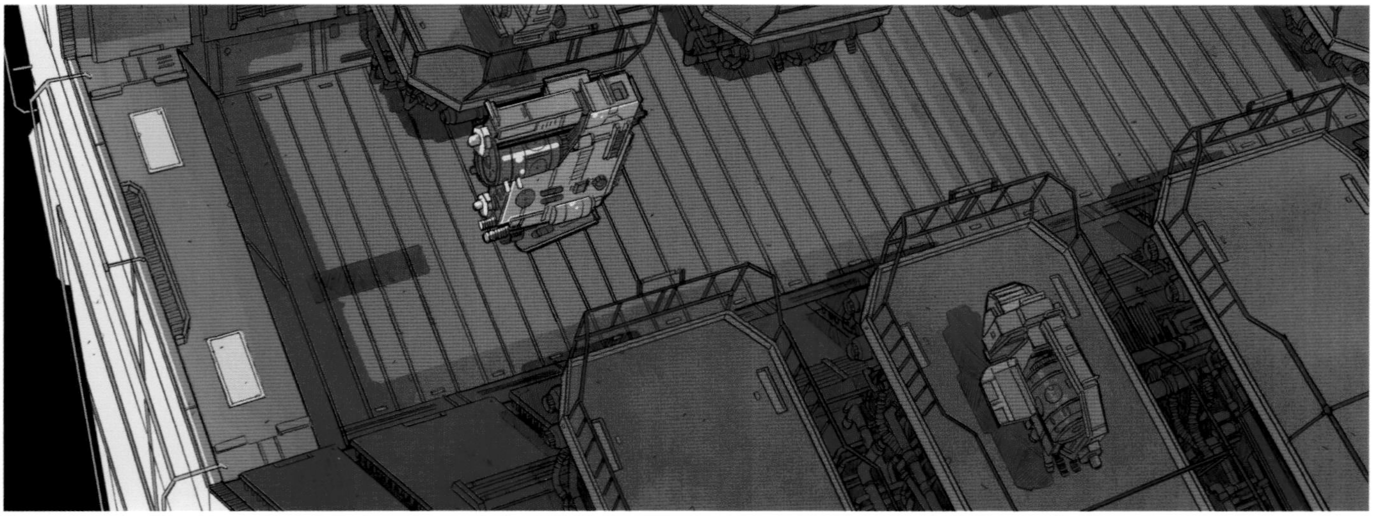

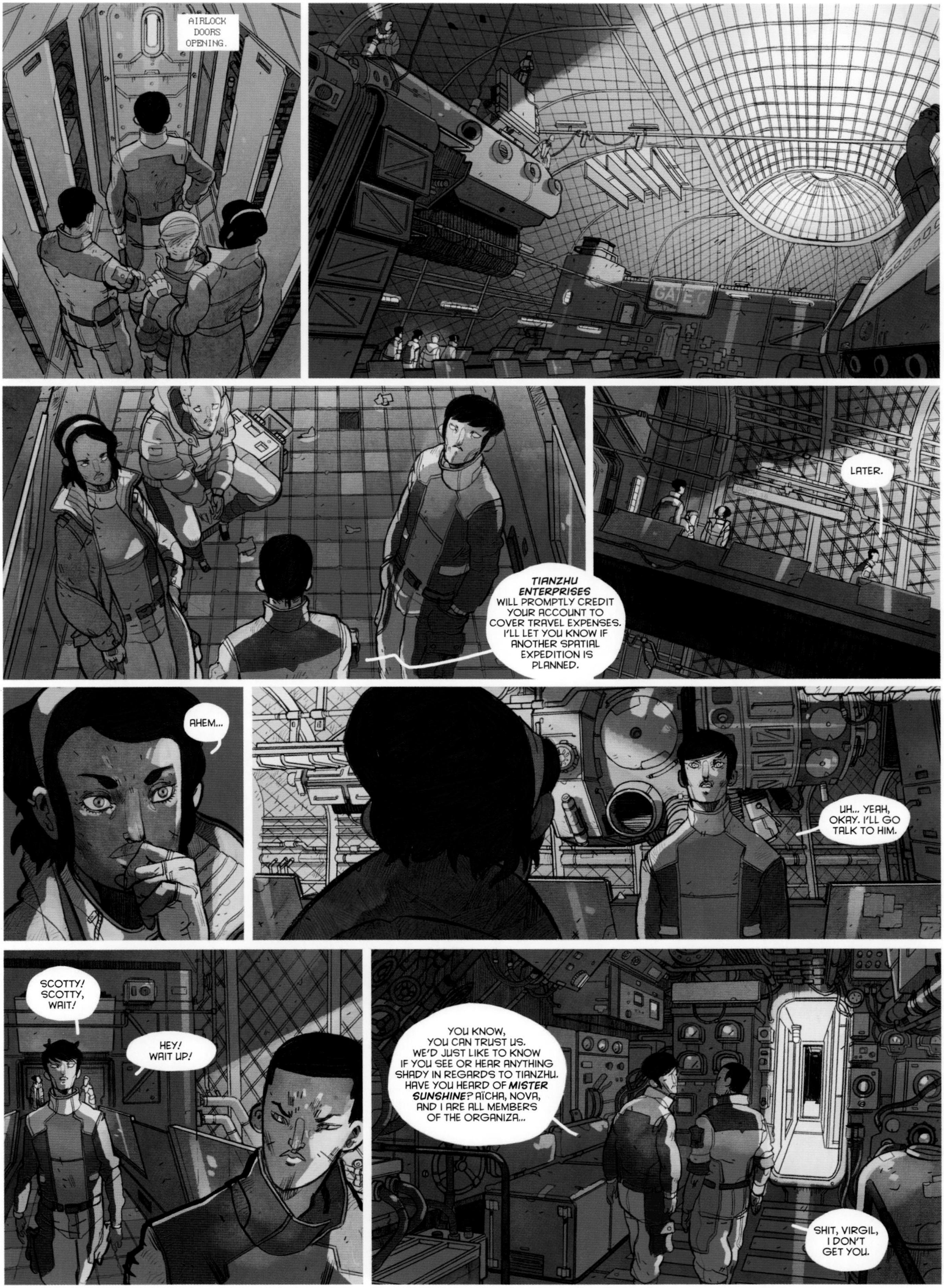
AIRLOCK DOORS OPENING.
LATER.
TIANZHU ENTERPRISES WILL PROMPTLY CREDIT YOUR ACCOUNT TO COVER TRAVEL EXPENSES. I'LL LET YOU KNOW IF ANOTHER SPATIAL EXPEDITION IS PLANNED.
AHEM...
UH... YEAH, OKAY. I'LL GO TALK TO HIM.
SCOTTY! SCOTTY, WAIT!
HEY! WAIT UP!
YOU KNOW, YOU CAN TRUST US. WE'D JUST LIKE TO KNOW IF YOU SEE OR HEAR ANYTHING SHADY IN REGARDS TO TIANZHU. HAVE YOU HEARD OF *MISTER SUNSHINE*? AÏCHA, NOVA, AND I ARE ALL MEMBERS OF THE ORGANIZA...
SHIT, VIRGIL, I DON'T GET YOU.

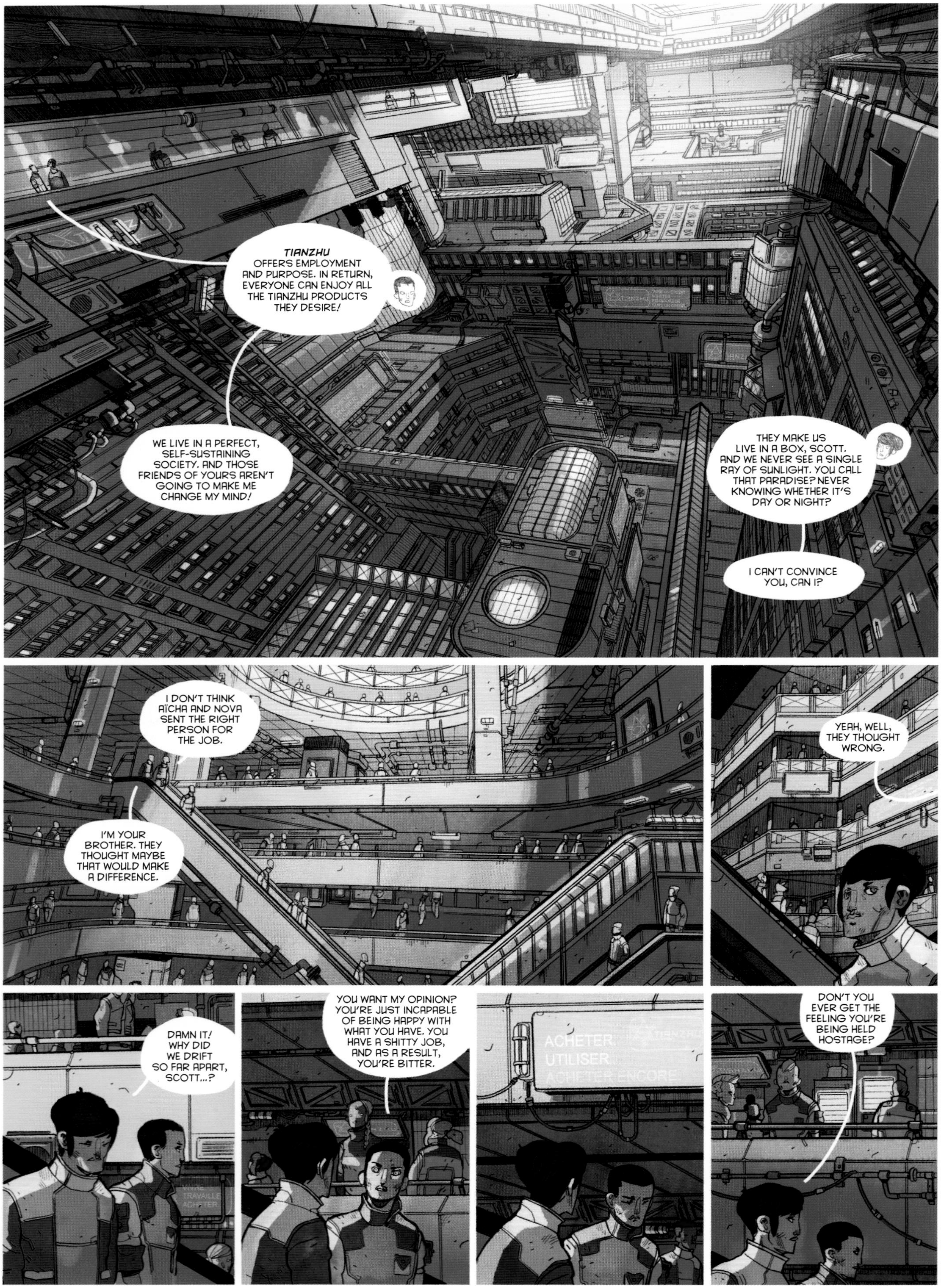
TIANZHU OFFERS EMPLOYMENT AND PURPOSE. IN RETURN, EVERYONE CAN ENJOY ALL THE TIANZHU PRODUCTS THEY DESIRE!
WE LIVE IN A PERFECT, SELF-SUSTAINING SOCIETY. AND THOSE FRIENDS OF YOURS AREN'T GOING TO MAKE ME CHANGE MY MIND!
THEY MAKE US LIVE IN A BOX, SCOTT. AND WE NEVER SEE A SINGLE RAY OF SUNLIGHT. YOU CALL THAT PARADISE? NEVER KNOWING WHETHER IT'S DAY OR NIGHT?
I CAN'T CONVINCE YOU, CAN I?
I DON'T THINK AÏCHA AND NOVA SENT THE RIGHT PERSON FOR THE JOB.
I'M YOUR BROTHER. THEY THOUGHT MAYBE THAT WOULD MAKE A DIFFERENCE.
YEAH, WELL, THEY THOUGHT WRONG.
DAMN IT! WHY DID WE DRIFT SO FAR APART, SCOTT...?
YOU WANT MY OPINION? YOU'RE JUST INCAPABLE OF BEING HAPPY WITH WHAT YOU HAVE. YOU HAVE A SHITTY JOB, AND AS A RESULT, YOU'RE BITTER.
ACHETER.
UTILISER.
ACHETER ENCORE
DON'T YOU EVER GET THE FEELING YOU'RE BEING HELD HOSTAGE?

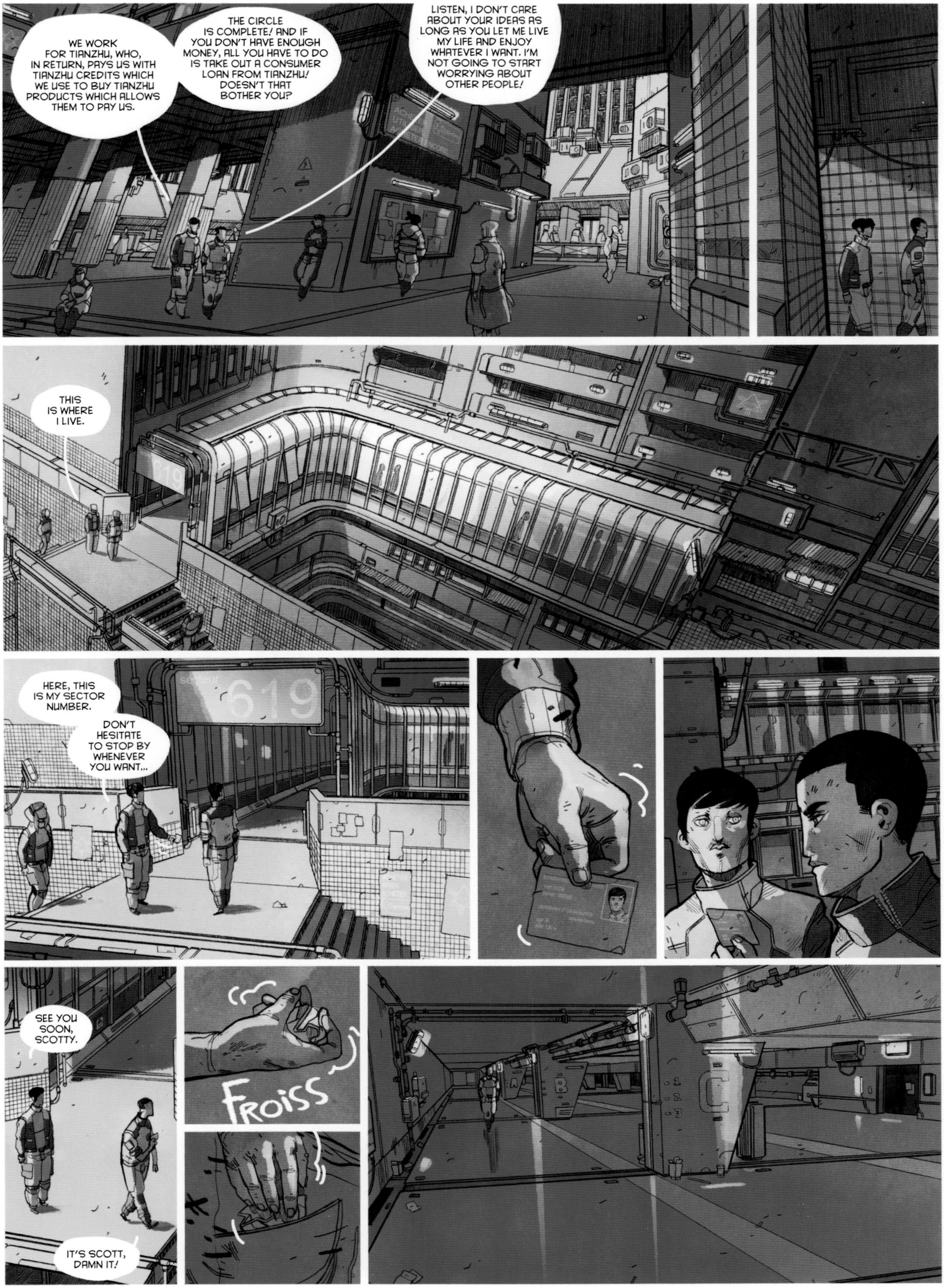
WE WORK FOR TIANZHU, WHO, IN RETURN, PAYS US WITH TIANZHU CREDITS WHICH WE USE TO BUY TIANZHU PRODUCTS WHICH ALLOWS THEM TO PAY US.
THE CIRCLE IS COMPLETE! AND IF YOU DON'T HAVE ENOUGH MONEY, ALL YOU HAVE TO DO IS TAKE OUT A CONSUMER LOAN FROM TIANZHU! DOESN'T THAT BOTHER YOU?
LISTEN, I DON'T CARE ABOUT YOUR IDEAS AS LONG AS YOU LET ME LIVE MY LIFE AND ENJOY WHATEVER I WANT. I'M NOT GOING TO START WORRYING ABOUT OTHER PEOPLE!
THIS IS WHERE I LIVE.
HERE, THIS IS MY SECTOR NUMBER.
DON'T HESITATE TO STOP BY WHENEVER YOU WANT...
SEE YOU SOON, SCOTTY.
IT'S SCOTT, DAMN IT!
FROISS

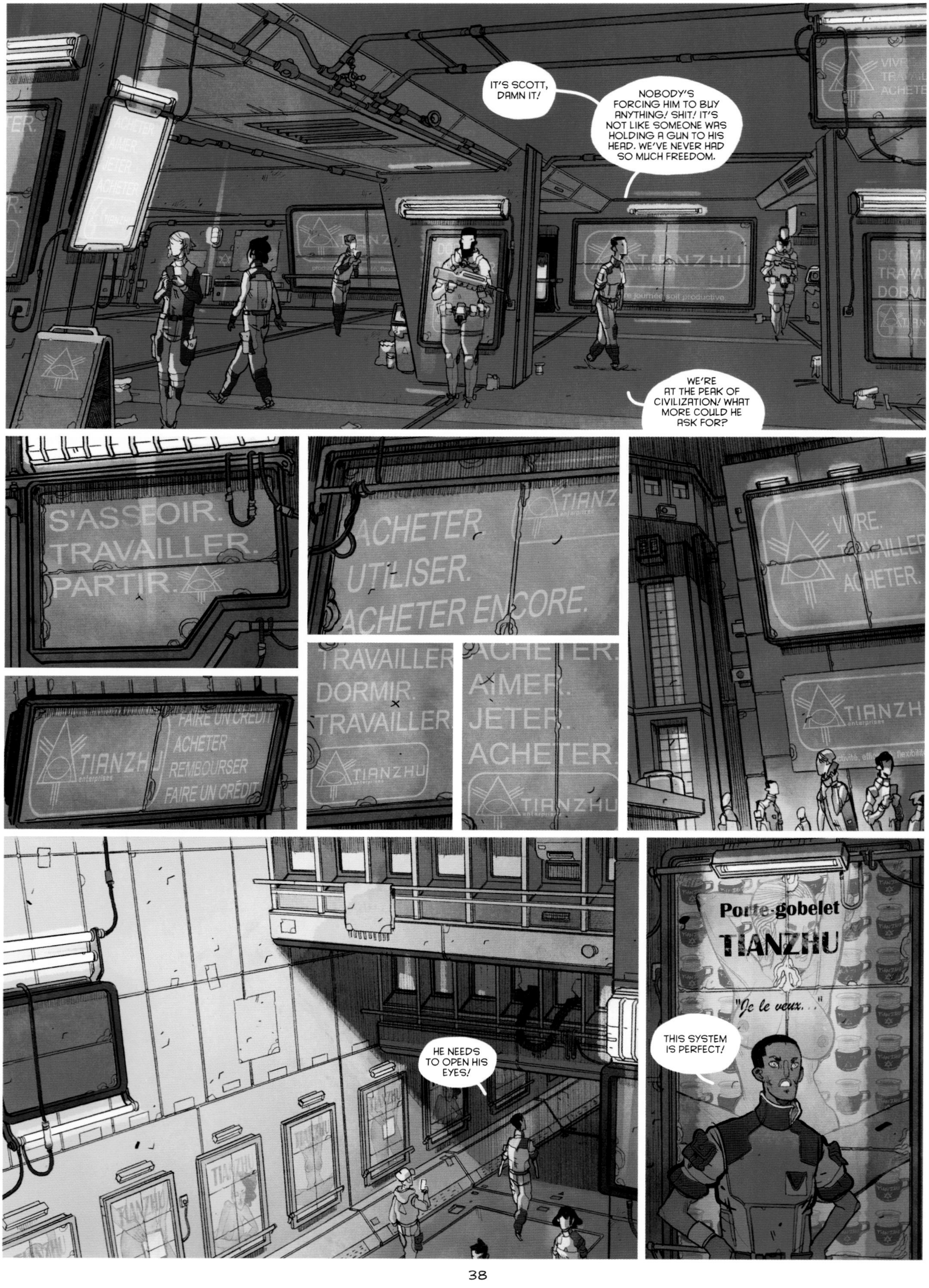

IT'S SCOTT, DAMN IT!
NOBODY'S FORCING HIM TO BUY ANYTHING! SHIT! IT'S NOT LIKE SOMEONE WAS HOLDING A GUN TO HIS HEAD. WE'VE NEVER HAD SO MUCH FREEDOM.
WE'RE AT THE PEAK OF CIVILIZATION! WHAT MORE COULD HE ASK FOR?
S'ASSEOIR. TRAVAILLER. PARTIR.
ACHETER. UTILISER. ACHETER ENCORE.
VIVRE. TRAVAILLER. ACHETER.
TIANZHU enterprises
FAIRE UN CRÉDIT ACHETER REMBOURSER FAIRE UN CRÉDIT
TRAVAILLER. DORMIR. TRAVAILLER.
ACHETER. AIMER. JETER. ACHETER.
Porte-gobelet TIANZHU
"Je le veux..."
HE NEEDS TO OPEN HIS EYES!
THIS SYSTEM IS PERFECT!

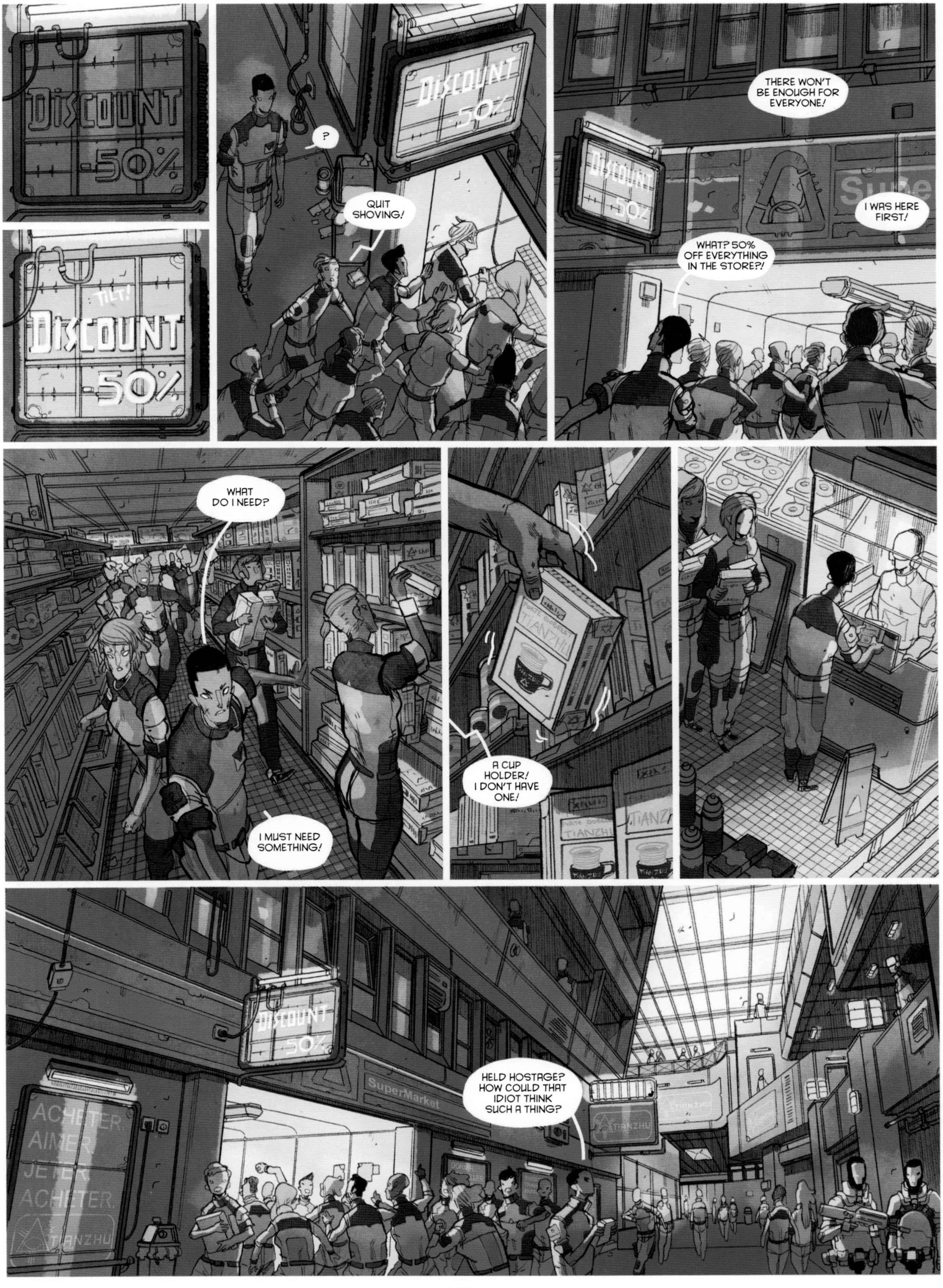
DISCOUNT -50%
TILT!
DISCOUNT -50%
DISCOUNT -50%
?
QUIT SHOVING!
THERE WON'T BE ENOUGH FOR EVERYONE!
DISCOUNT -50%
I WAS HERE FIRST!
WHAT? 50% OFF EVERYTHING IN THE STORE?!
WHAT DO I NEED?
I MUST NEED SOMETHING!
TIANZHU
A CUP HOLDER! I DON'T HAVE ONE!
TIANZHU
DISCOUNT -50%
SuperMarket
ACHETER.
AIMER.
JETER.
ACHETER.
TIANZHU
HELD HOSTAGE? HOW COULD THAT IDIOT THINK SUCH A THING?
TIANZHU

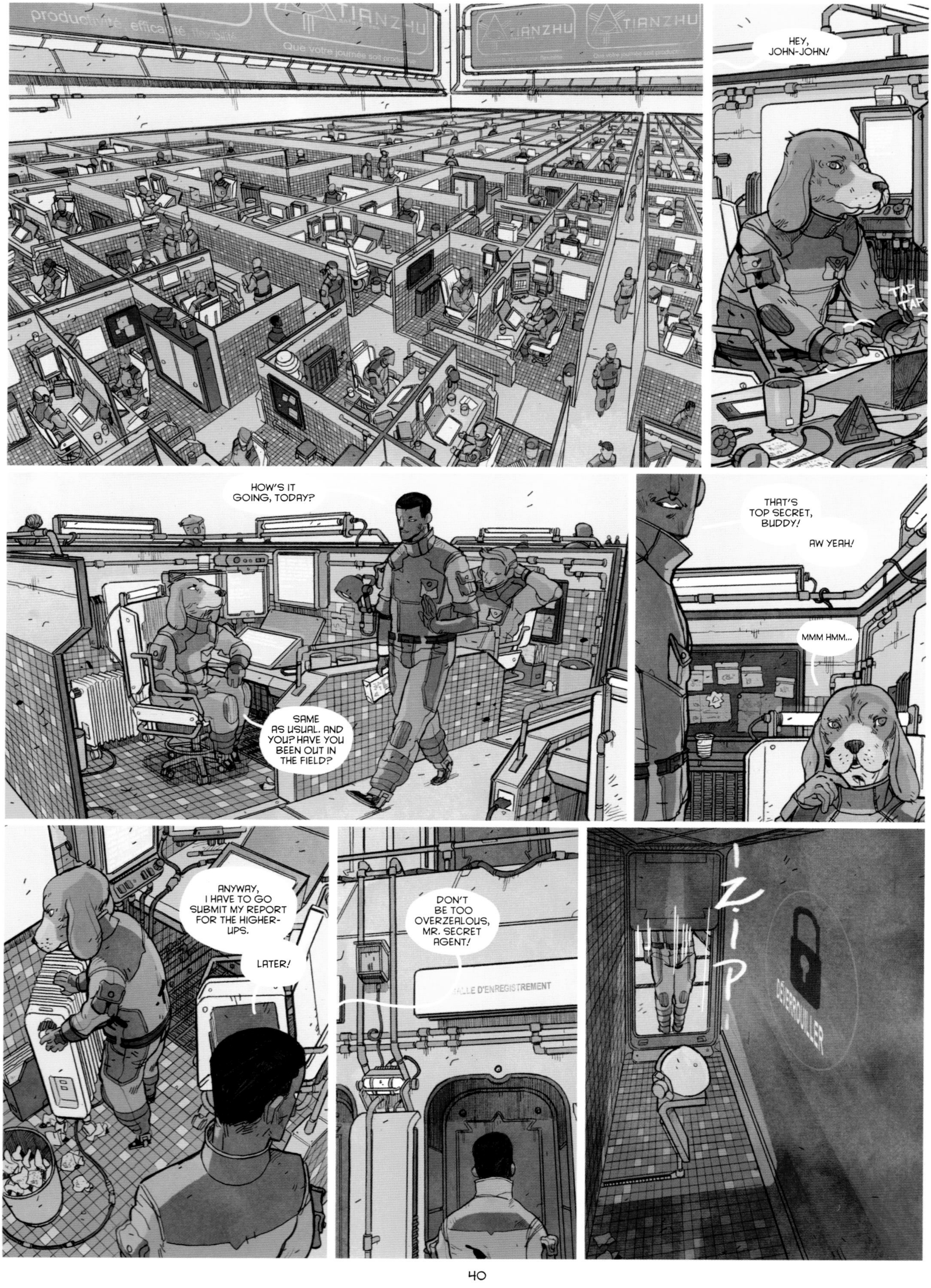
productivité
TIANZHU
TIANZHU
TIANZHU
HEY, JOHN-JOHN!
TAP TAP
HOW'S IT GOING, TODAY?
SAME AS USUAL. AND YOU? HAVE YOU BEEN OUT IN THE FIELD?
THAT'S TOP SECRET, BUDDY!
AW YEAH!
MMM HMM...
ANYWAY, I HAVE TO GO SUBMIT MY REPORT FOR THE HIGHER-UPS.
LATER!
DON'T BE TOO OVERZEALOUS, MR. SECRET AGENT!
SALLE D'ENREGISTREMENT
ZIP
DÉVERROUILLER

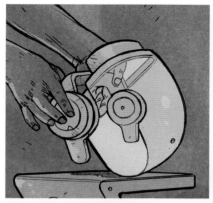

TIANZHU GLASS. *ACTIVATE.*

SLIDE

RECORD

DIVERS

REPORT DATE: NOVEMBER 6TH.

OBSERVATION...

DISCOVERY OF A SINGULARITY IN *TIANZHU ATOMIC RESEARCH STATION NO. 017.*

AS PREVIOUSLY OBSERVED, A SPHERICAL EXPLOSION, DISPLAYING NO SIGNS OF COMBUSTION...

RECORD

DIVERS

● REC
03:12:06 /
deskshop/record/061145

HEY JOHNNY-BOY!

...WAS DETECTED...

WE GOT A PRESENT FOR YOU!

HI, GUYS. I'M A LITTLE BUSY, HERE.

THIS WON'T TAKE LONG. LOOK WHAT WE FOUND!

IT WAS IN THE BACKROOM OF THIS SHABBY OLD SHOP THAT WAS AROUND BEFORE THE STATION. THE GUY GAVE IT TO US FOR FREE.

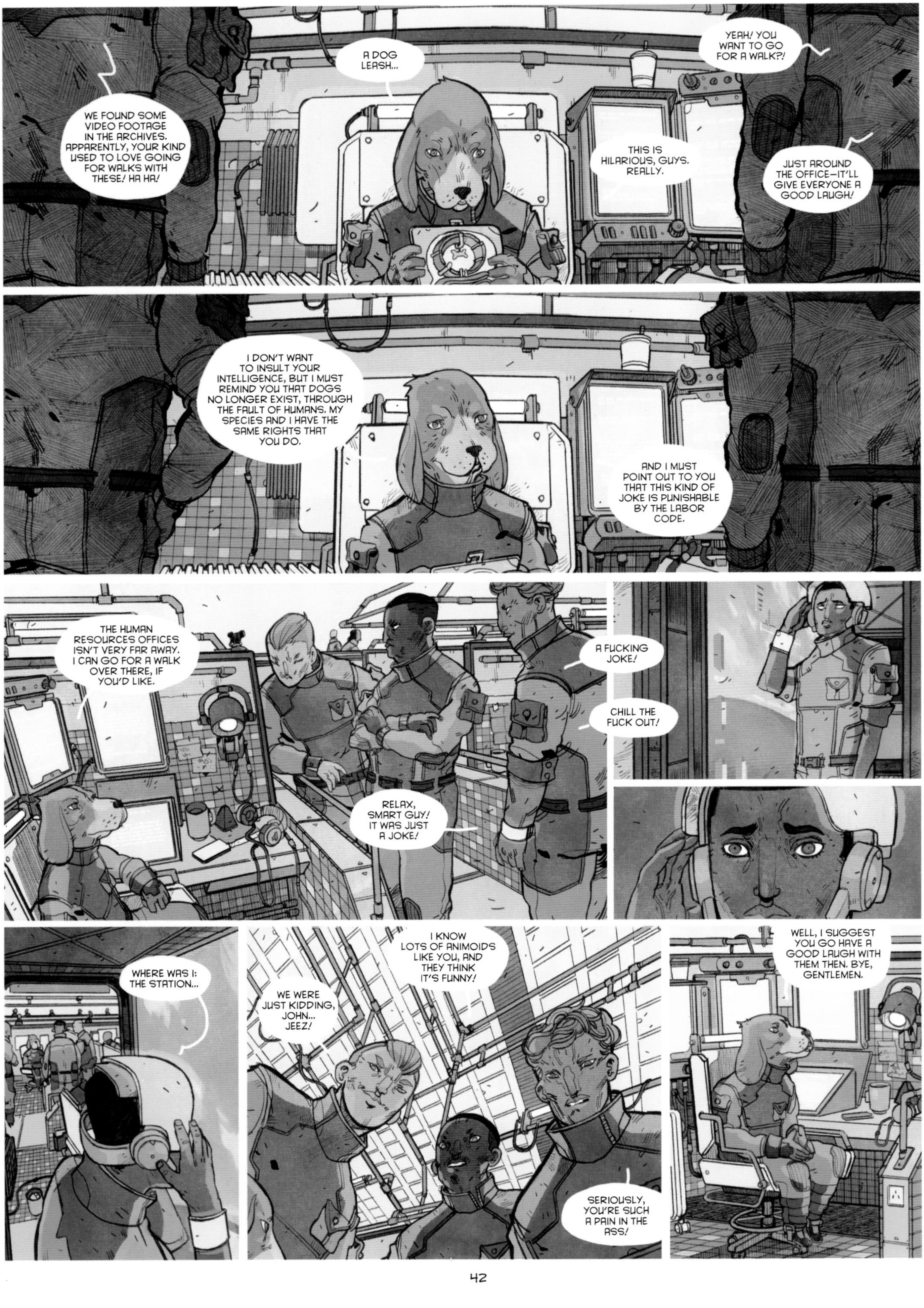

WE FOUND SOME VIDEO FOOTAGE IN THE ARCHIVES. APPARENTLY, YOUR KIND USED TO LOVE GOING FOR WALKS WITH THESE! HA HA!
A DOG LEASH...
YEAH! YOU WANT TO GO FOR A WALK?!
THIS IS HILARIOUS, GUYS. REALLY.
JUST AROUND THE OFFICE—IT'LL GIVE EVERYONE A GOOD LAUGH!
I DON'T WANT TO INSULT YOUR INTELLIGENCE, BUT I MUST REMIND YOU THAT DOGS NO LONGER EXIST, THROUGH THE FAULT OF HUMANS. MY SPECIES AND I HAVE THE SAME RIGHTS THAT YOU DO.
AND I MUST POINT OUT TO YOU THAT THIS KIND OF JOKE IS PUNISHABLE BY THE LABOR CODE.
THE HUMAN RESOURCES OFFICES ISN'T VERY FAR AWAY. I CAN GO FOR A WALK OVER THERE, IF YOU'D LIKE.
A FUCKING JOKE!
CHILL THE FUCK OUT!
RELAX, SMART GUY! IT WAS JUST A JOKE!
WHERE WAS I: THE STATION...
WE WERE JUST KIDDING, JOHN... JEEZ!
I KNOW LOTS OF ANIMOIDS LIKE YOU, AND THEY THINK IT'S FUNNY!
SERIOUSLY, YOU'RE SUCH A PAIN IN THE ASS!
WELL, I SUGGEST YOU GO HAVE A GOOD LAUGH WITH THEM THEN. BYE, GENTLEMEN.

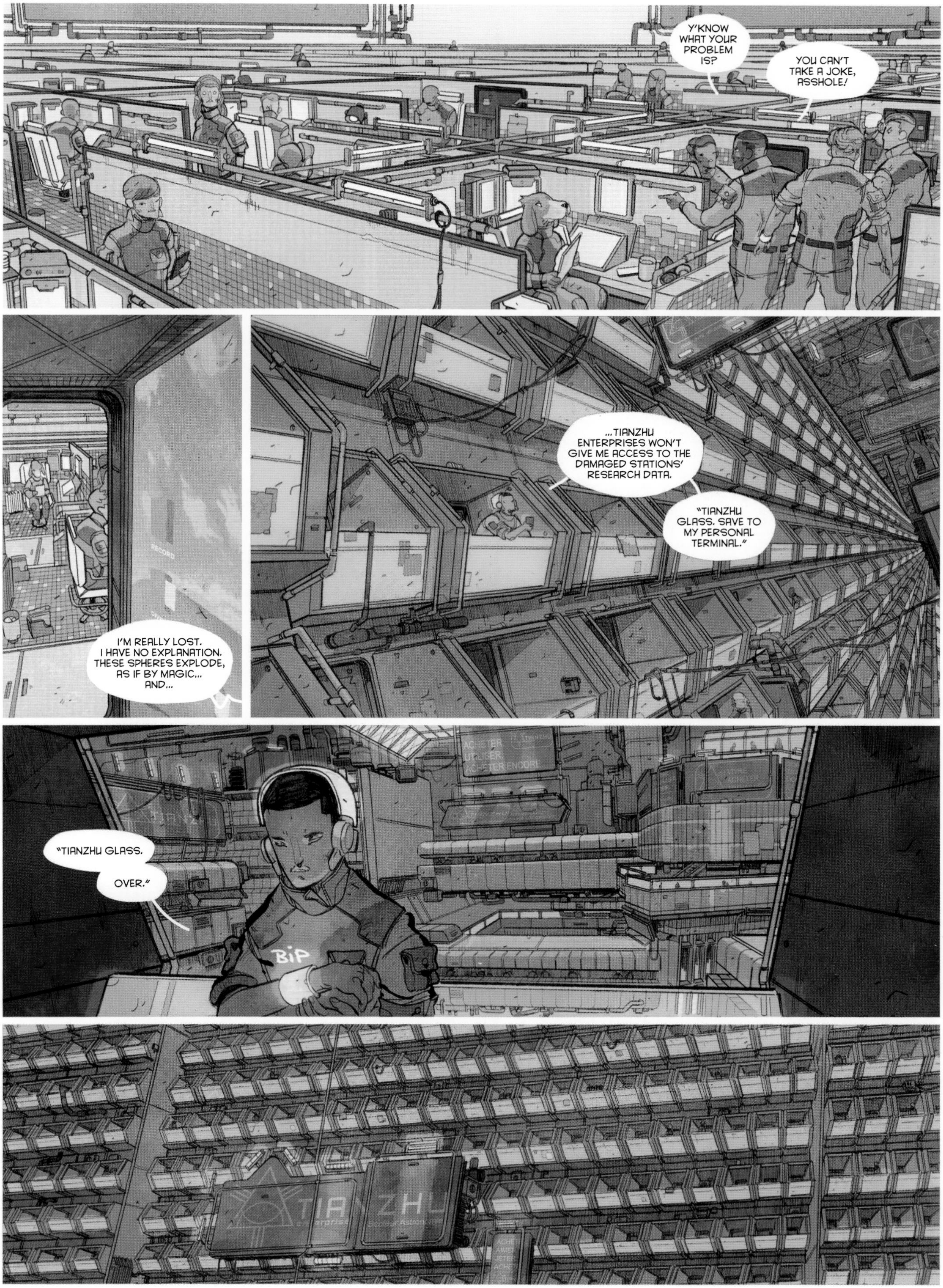
Y'KNOW WHAT YOUR PROBLEM IS?
YOU CAN'T TAKE A JOKE, ASSHOLE!
I'M REALLY LOST. I HAVE NO EXPLANATION. THESE SPHERES EXPLODE, AS IF BY MAGIC... AND...
...TIANZHU ENTERPRISES WON'T GIVE ME ACCESS TO THE DAMAGED STATIONS' RESEARCH DATA.
"TIANZHU GLASS. SAVE TO MY PERSONAL TERMINAL."
"TIANZHU GLASS.
OVER."
BIP
TIANZHU

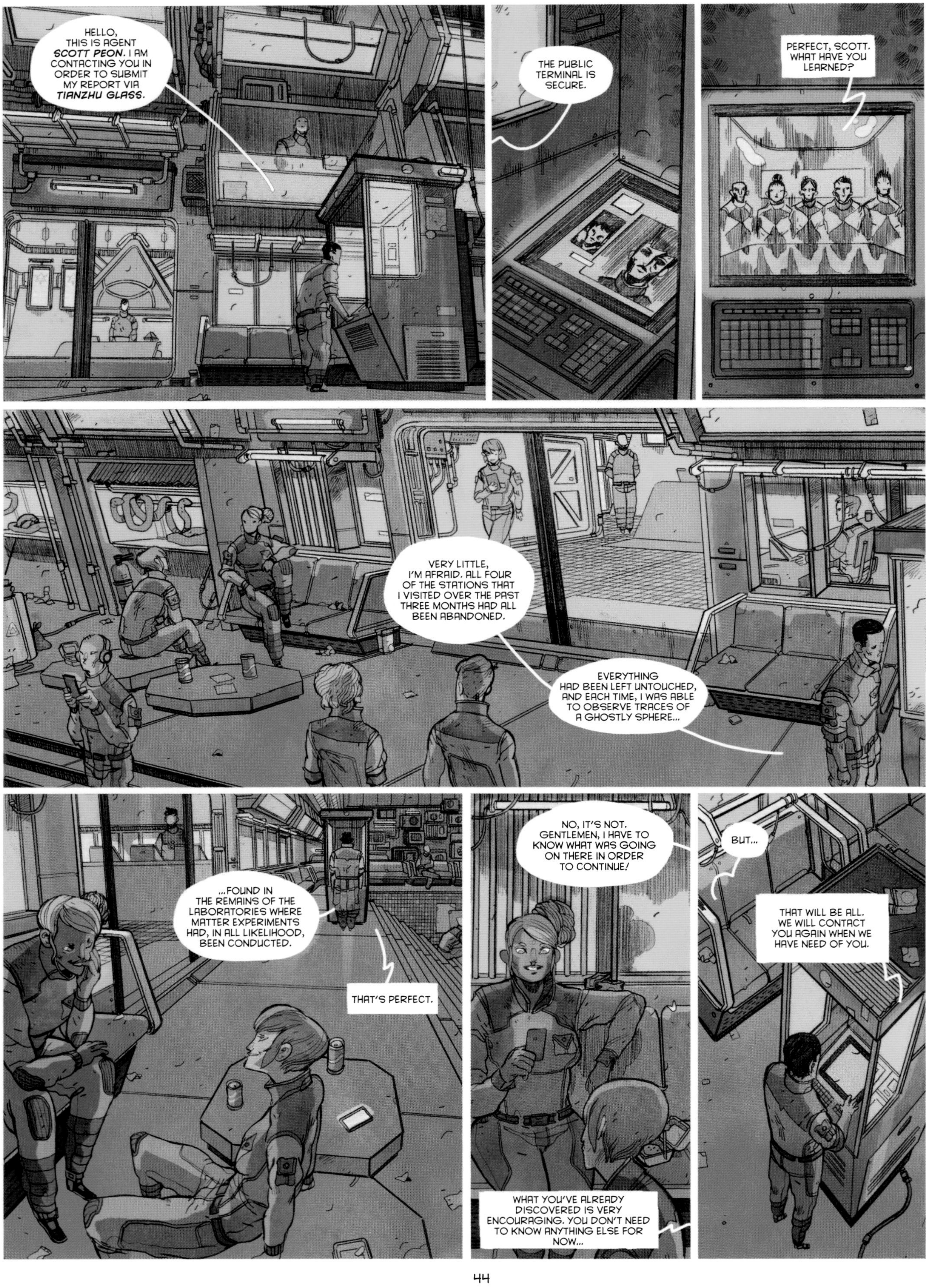
HELLO, THIS IS AGENT **SCOTT PEON**. I AM CONTACTING YOU IN ORDER TO SUBMIT MY REPORT VIA ***TIANZHU GLASS***.
THE PUBLIC TERMINAL IS SECURE.
PERFECT, SCOTT. WHAT HAVE YOU LEARNED?
VERY LITTLE, I'M AFRAID. ALL FOUR OF THE STATIONS THAT I VISITED OVER THE PAST THREE MONTHS HAD ALL BEEN ABANDONED.
EVERYTHING HAD BEEN LEFT UNTOUCHED, AND EACH TIME, I WAS ABLE TO OBSERVE TRACES OF A GHOSTLY SPHERE...
...FOUND IN THE REMAINS OF THE LABORATORIES WHERE MATTER EXPERIMENTS HAD, IN ALL LIKELIHOOD, BEEN CONDUCTED.
THAT'S PERFECT.
NO, IT'S NOT. GENTLEMEN, I HAVE TO KNOW WHAT WAS GOING ON THERE IN ORDER TO CONTINUE!
WHAT YOU'VE ALREADY DISCOVERED IS VERY ENCOURAGING. YOU DON'T NEED TO KNOW ANYTHING ELSE FOR NOW...
BUT...
THAT WILL BE ALL. WE WILL CONTACT YOU AGAIN WHEN WE HAVE NEED OF YOU.

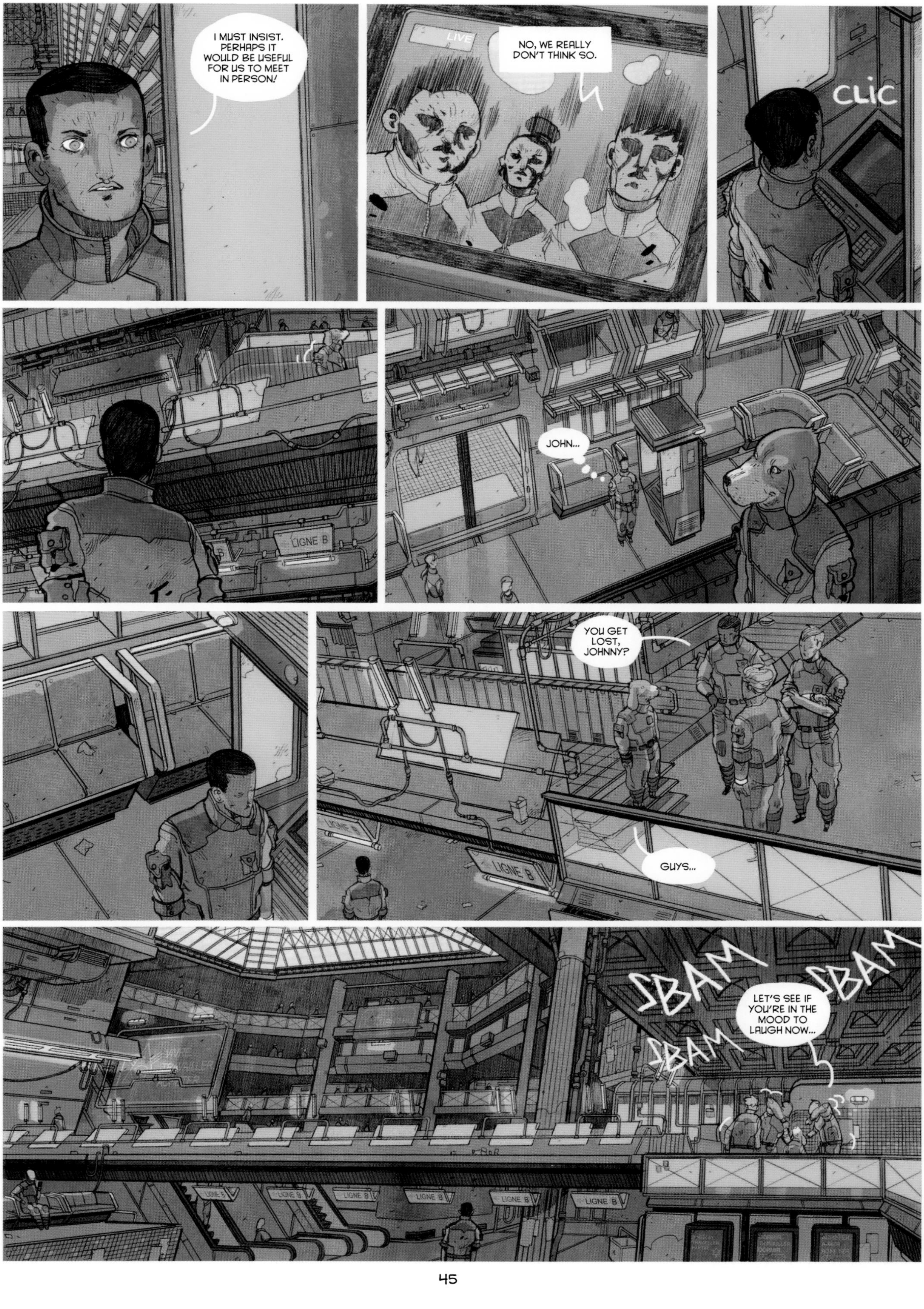
I MUST INSIST. PERHAPS IT WOULD BE USEFUL FOR US TO MEET IN PERSON!
LIVE
NO, WE REALLY DON'T THINK SO.
CLIC
LIGNE B
JOHN...
YOU GET LOST, JOHNNY?
GUYS...
LIGNE B
SBAM
SBAM
SBAM
LET'S SEE IF YOU'RE IN THE MOOD TO LAUGH NOW...
LIGNE B

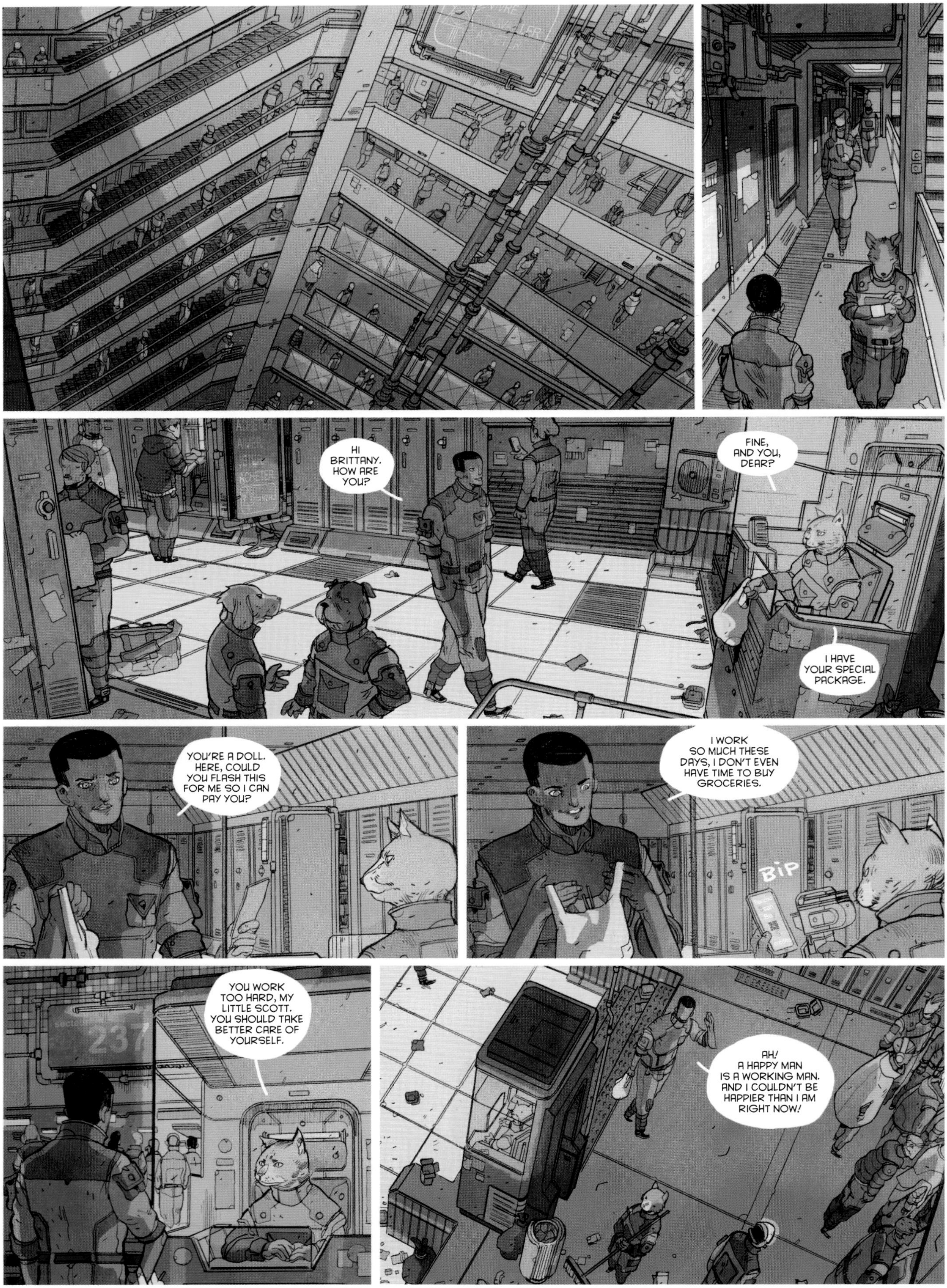
ACHETER
AIMER
JETER
ACHETER
HI BRITTANY. HOW ARE YOU?
FINE, AND YOU, DEAR?
I HAVE YOUR SPECIAL PACKAGE.
YOU'RE A DOLL. HERE, COULD YOU FLASH THIS FOR ME SO I CAN PAY YOU?
I WORK SO MUCH THESE DAYS, I DON'T EVEN HAVE TIME TO BUY GROCERIES.
BIP
237
YOU WORK TOO HARD, MY LITTLE SCOTT. YOU SHOULD TAKE BETTER CARE OF YOURSELF.
AH! A HAPPY MAN IS A WORKING MAN. AND I COULDN'T BE HAPPIER THAN I AM RIGHT NOW!

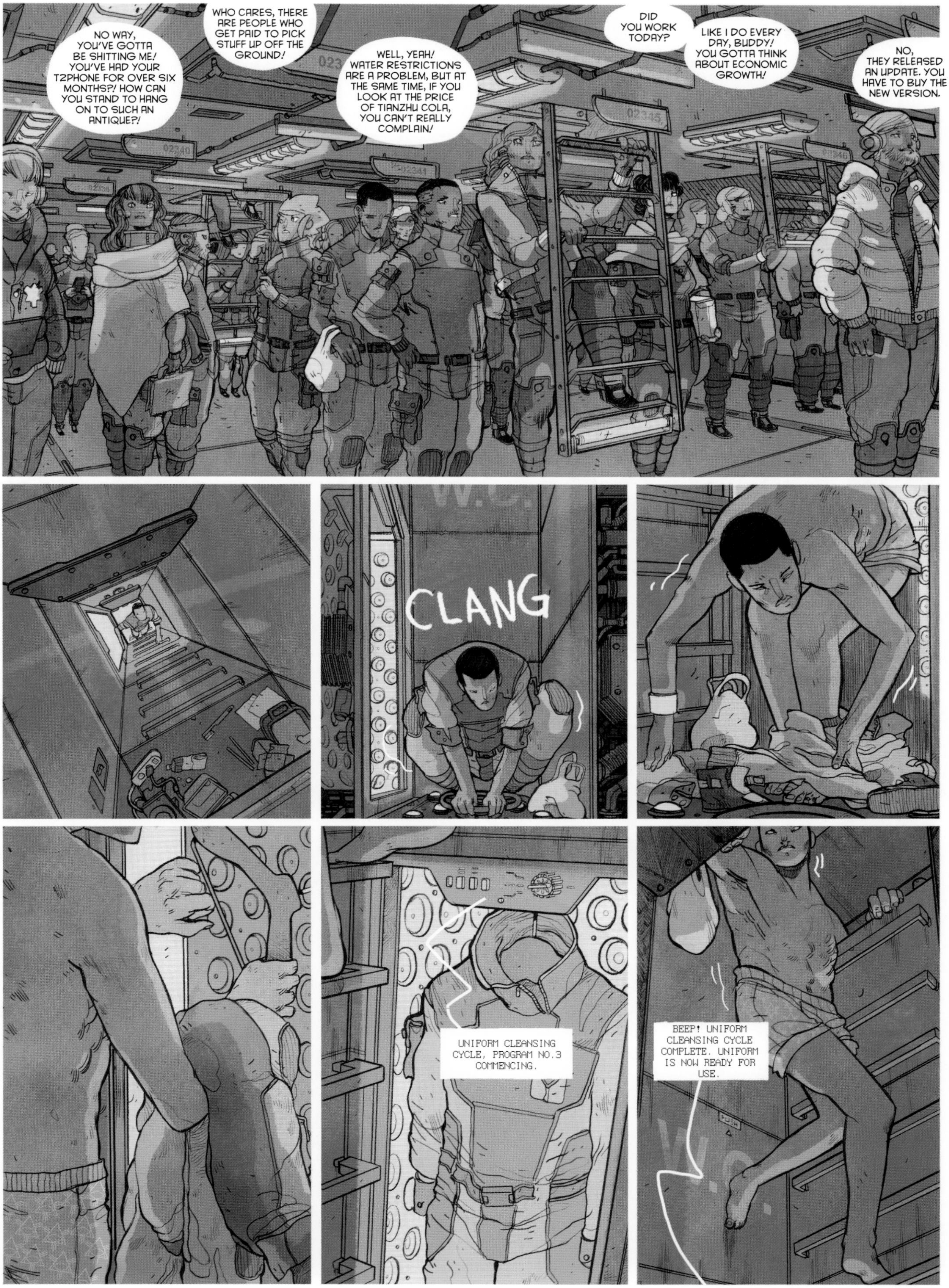
NO WAY, YOU'VE GOTTA BE SHITTING ME! YOU'VE HAD YOUR T2PHONE FOR OVER SIX MONTHS?! HOW CAN YOU STAND TO HANG ON TO SUCH AN ANTIQUE?!
WHO CARES, THERE ARE PEOPLE WHO GET PAID TO PICK STUFF UP OFF THE GROUND!
WELL, YEAH! WATER RESTRICTIONS ARE A PROBLEM, BUT AT THE SAME TIME, IF YOU LOOK AT THE PRICE OF TIANZHU COLA, YOU CAN'T REALLY COMPLAIN!
DID YOU WORK TODAY?
LIKE I DO EVERY DAY, BUDDY! YOU GOTTA THINK ABOUT ECONOMIC GROWTH!
NO, THEY RELEASED AN UPDATE. YOU HAVE TO BUY THE NEW VERSION.
CLANG
UNIFORM CLEANSING CYCLE, PROGRAM NO.3 COMMENCING.
BEEP! UNIFORM CLEANSING CYCLE COMPLETE. UNIFORM IS NOW READY FOR USE.

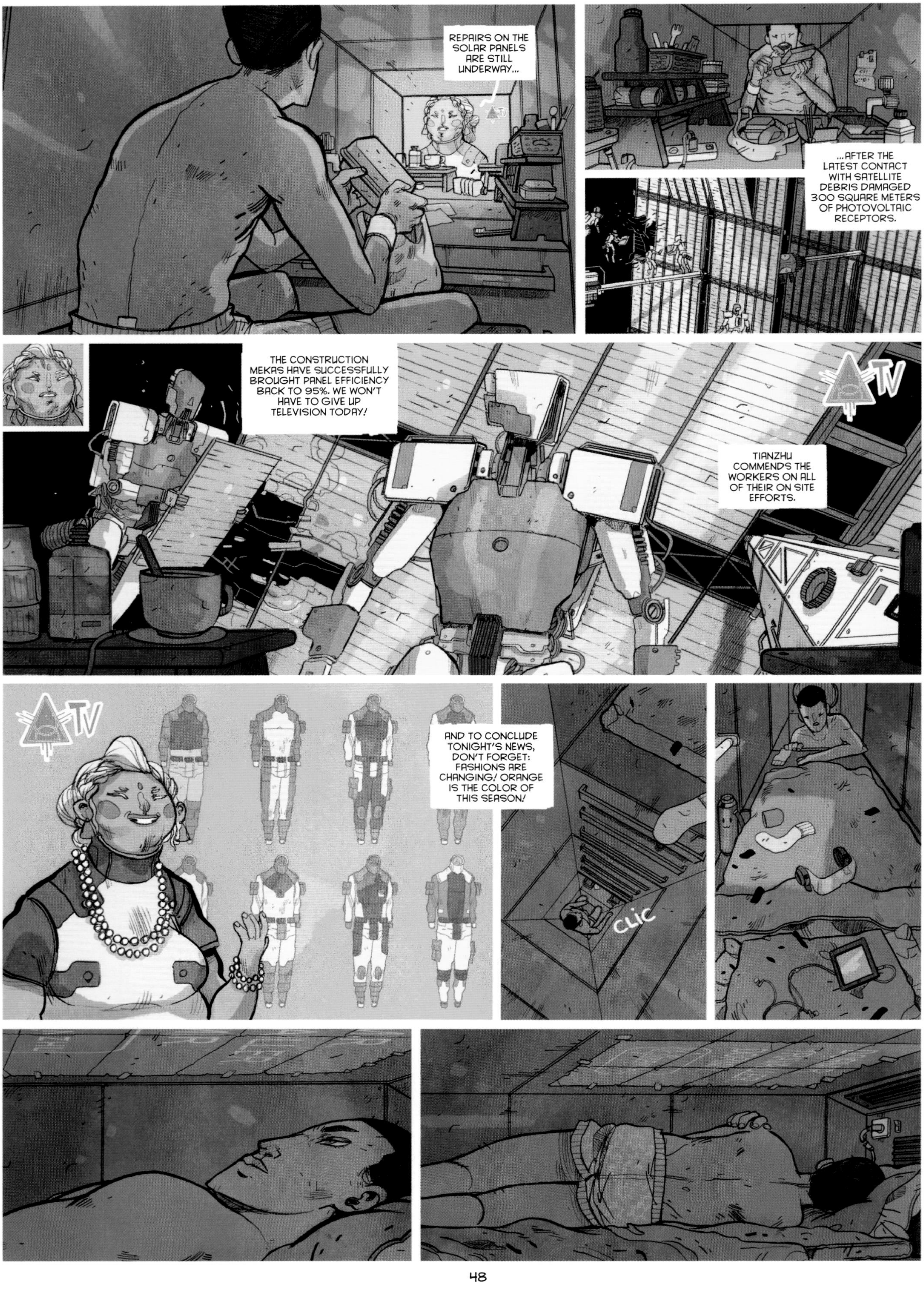
REPAIRS ON THE SOLAR PANELS ARE STILL UNDERWAY...
...AFTER THE LATEST CONTACT WITH SATELLITE DEBRIS DAMAGED 300 SQUARE METERS OF PHOTOVOLTAIC RECEPTORS.
TV
THE CONSTRUCTION MEKAS HAVE SUCCESSFULLY BROUGHT PANEL EFFICIENCY BACK TO 95%. WE WON'T HAVE TO GIVE UP TELEVISION TODAY!
TIANZHU COMMENDS THE WORKERS ON ALL OF THEIR ON SITE EFFORTS.
TV
AND TO CONCLUDE TONIGHT'S NEWS, DON'T FORGET: FASHIONS ARE CHANGING! ORANGE IS THE COLOR OF THIS SEASON!
CLIC

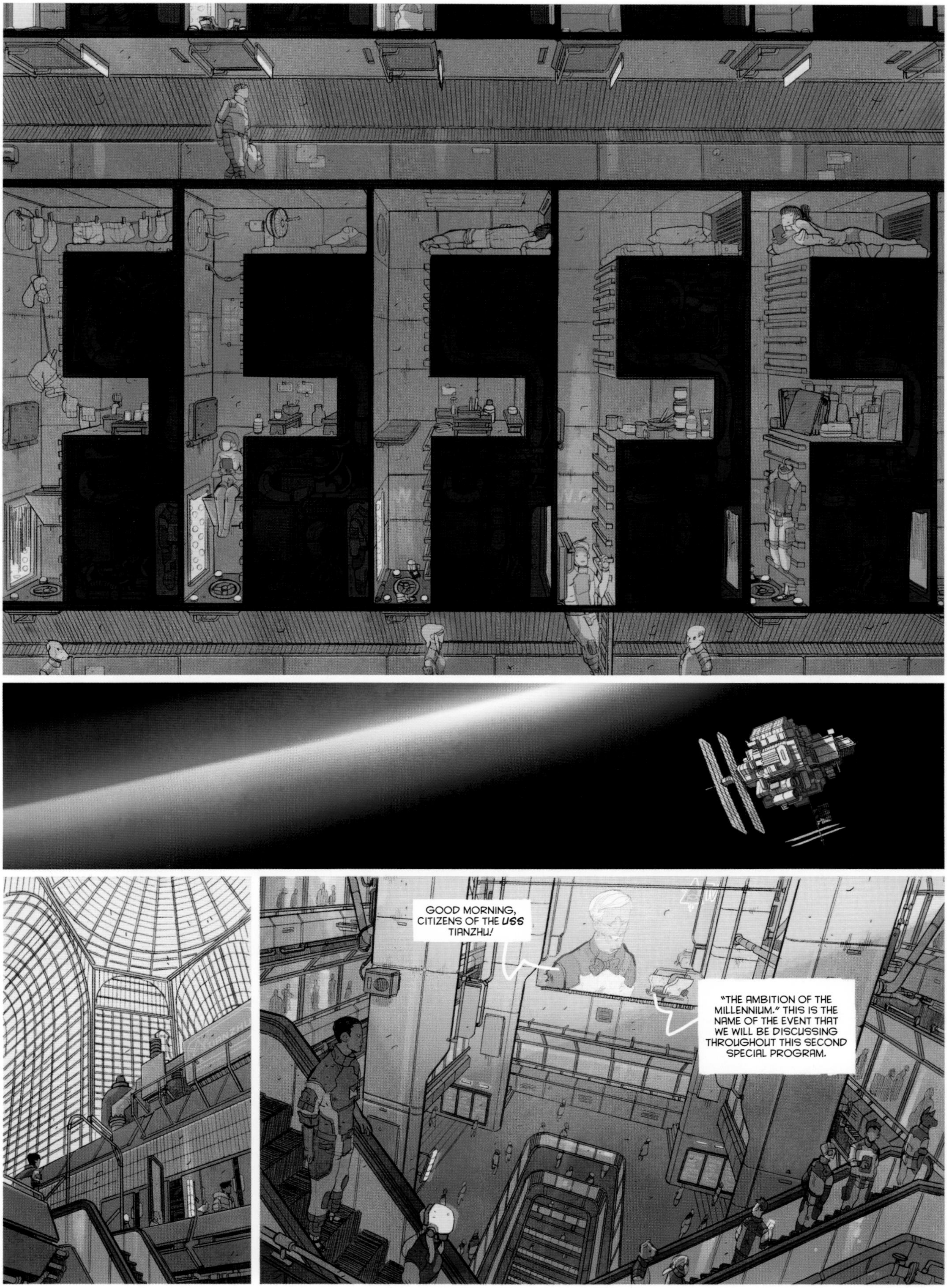
GOOD MORNING, CITIZENS OF THE USS TIANZHU!
"THE AMBITION OF THE MILLENNIUM." THIS IS THE NAME OF THE EVENT THAT WE WILL BE DISCUSSING THROUGHOUT THIS SECOND SPECIAL PROGRAM.

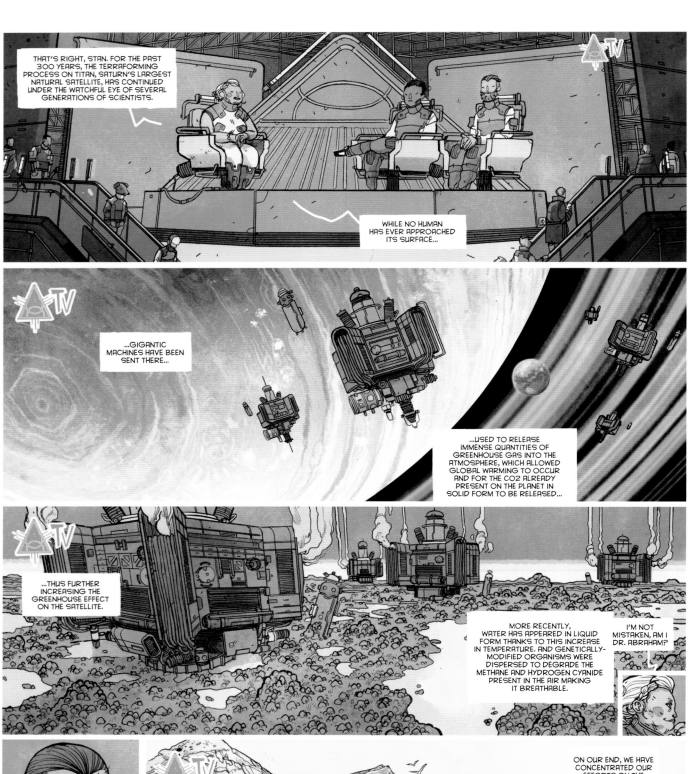

THAT'S RIGHT, STAN. FOR THE PAST 300 YEARS, THE TERRAFORMING PROCESS ON TITAN, SATURN'S LARGEST NATURAL SATELLITE, HAS CONTINUED UNDER THE WATCHFUL EYE OF SEVERAL GENERATIONS OF SCIENTISTS.

WHILE NO HUMAN HAS EVER APPROACHED ITS SURFACE...

...GIGANTIC MACHINES HAVE BEEN SENT THERE...

...USED TO RELEASE IMMENSE QUANTITIES OF GREENHOUSE GAS INTO THE ATMOSPHERE, WHICH ALLOWED GLOBAL WARMING TO OCCUR AND FOR THE CO_2 ALREADY PRESENT ON THE PLANET IN SOLID FORM TO BE RELEASED...

...THUS FURTHER INCREASING THE GREENHOUSE EFFECT ON THE SATELLITE.

MORE RECENTLY, WATER HAS APPEARED IN LIQUID FORM THANKS TO THIS INCREASE IN TEMPERATURE. AND GENETICALLY-MODIFIED ORGANISMS WERE DISPERSED TO DEGRADE THE METHANE AND HYDROGEN CYANIDE PRESENT IN THE AIR MAKING IT BREATHABLE.

I'M NOT MISTAKEN, AM I DR. ABRAHAM?

ON OUR END, WE HAVE CONCENTRATED OUR EFFORTS ON THE PROLIFERATION OF FLORA AND FAUNA IN THIS NEW HABITAT.

NO, YOU'RE QUITE RIGHT. MUCH OF THE WORK WAS CARRIED OUT BY OUR PREDECESSORS.

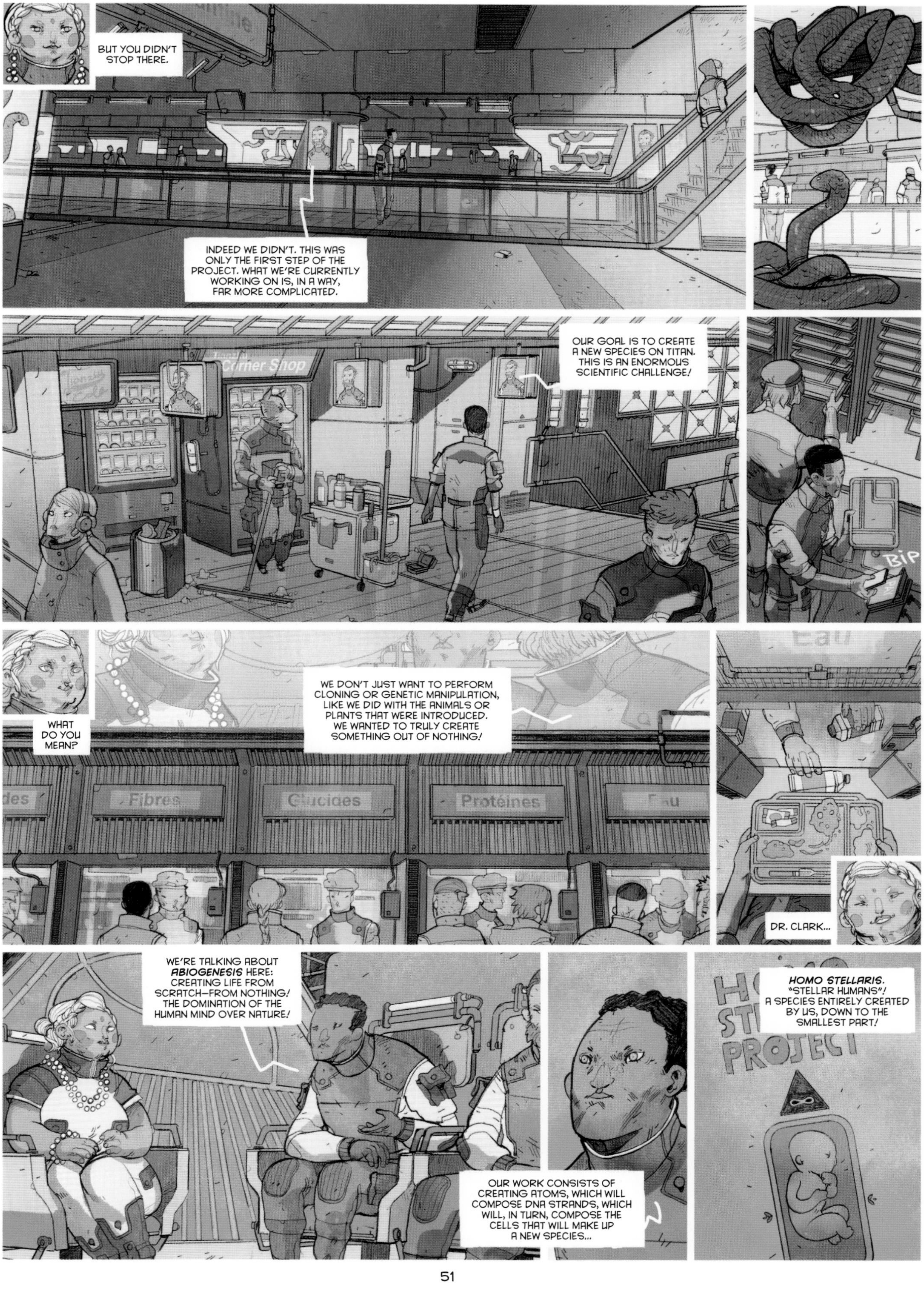
BUT YOU DIDN'T STOP THERE.
INDEED WE DIDN'T. THIS WAS ONLY THE FIRST STEP OF THE PROJECT. WHAT WE'RE CURRENTLY WORKING ON IS, IN A WAY, FAR MORE COMPLICATED.
Corner Shop
OUR GOAL IS TO CREATE A NEW SPECIES ON TITAN. THIS IS AN ENORMOUS SCIENTIFIC CHALLENGE!
BIP
WHAT DO YOU MEAN?
WE DON'T JUST WANT TO PERFORM CLONING OR GENETIC MANIPULATION, LIKE WE DID WITH THE ANIMALS OR PLANTS THAT WERE INTRODUCED. WE WANTED TO TRULY CREATE SOMETHING OUT OF NOTHING!
Fibres
Glucides
Protéines
Eau
DR. CLARK...
WE'RE TALKING ABOUT *ABIOGENESIS* HERE: CREATING LIFE FROM SCRATCH—FROM NOTHING! THE DOMINATION OF THE HUMAN MIND OVER NATURE!
OUR WORK CONSISTS OF CREATING ATOMS, WHICH WILL COMPOSE DNA STRANDS, WHICH WILL, IN TURN, COMPOSE THE CELLS THAT WILL MAKE UP A NEW SPECIES...
HOMO STELLARIS. "STELLAR HUMANS"! A SPECIES ENTIRELY CREATED BY US, DOWN TO THE SMALLEST PART!
PROJECT

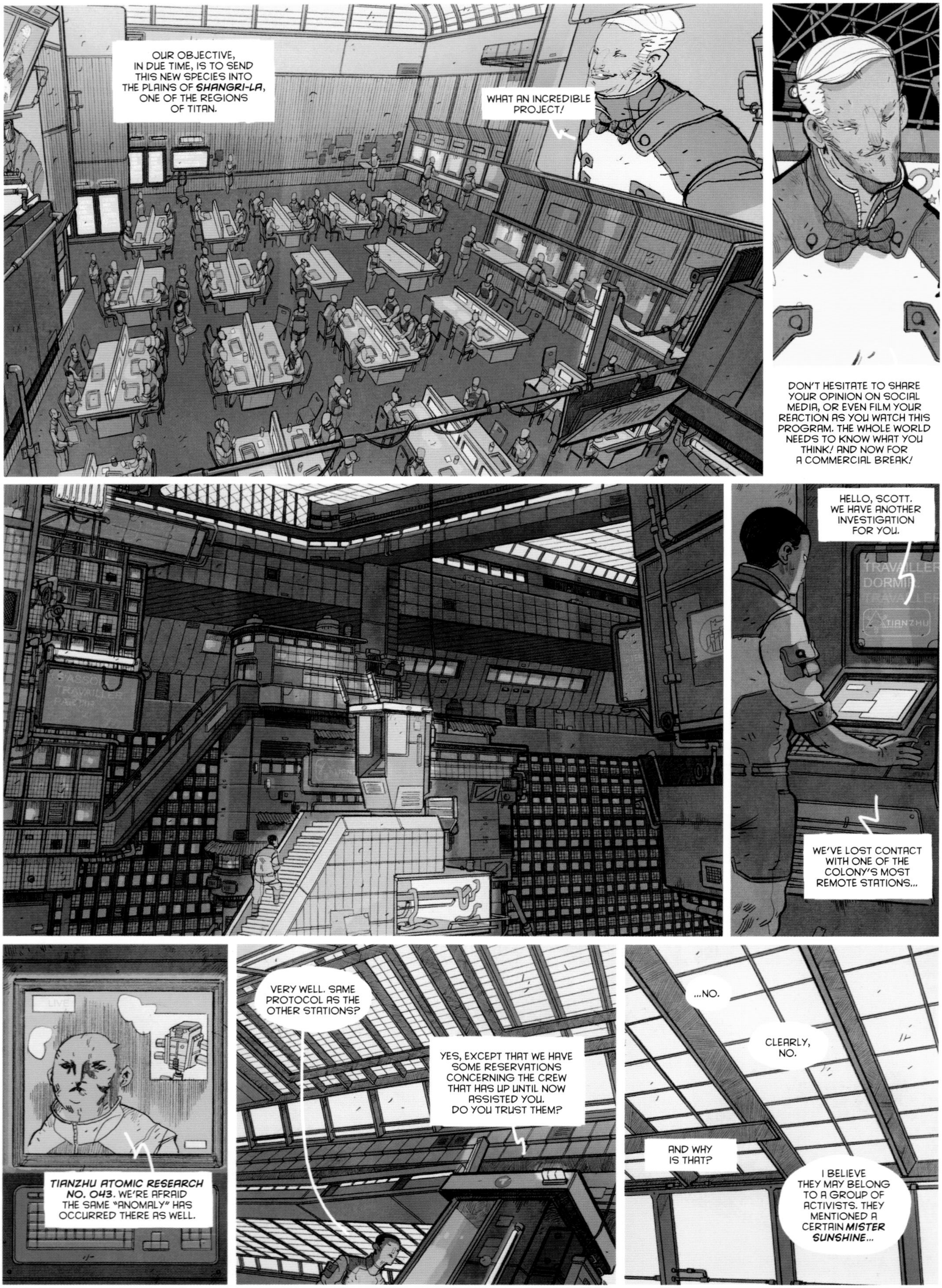
OUR OBJECTIVE, IN DUE TIME, IS TO SEND THIS NEW SPECIES INTO THE PLAINS OF **SHANGRI-LA**, ONE OF THE REGIONS OF TITAN.
WHAT AN INCREDIBLE PROJECT!
DON'T HESITATE TO SHARE YOUR OPINION ON SOCIAL MEDIA, OR EVEN FILM YOUR REACTION AS YOU WATCH THIS PROGRAM. THE WHOLE WORLD NEEDS TO KNOW WHAT YOU THINK! AND NOW FOR A COMMERCIAL BREAK!
HELLO, SCOTT. WE HAVE ANOTHER INVESTIGATION FOR YOU.
WE'VE LOST CONTACT WITH ONE OF THE COLONY'S MOST REMOTE STATIONS...
TIANZHU ATOMIC RESEARCH NO. 043. WE'RE AFRAID THE SAME "ANOMALY" HAS OCCURRED THERE AS WELL.
VERY WELL. SAME PROTOCOL AS THE OTHER STATIONS?
YES, EXCEPT THAT WE HAVE SOME RESERVATIONS CONCERNING THE CREW THAT HAS UP UNTIL NOW ASSISTED YOU. DO YOU TRUST THEM?
...NO.
CLEARLY, NO.
AND WHY IS THAT?
I BELIEVE THEY MAY BELONG TO A GROUP OF ACTIVISTS. THEY MENTIONED A CERTAIN ***MISTER SUNSHINE***...

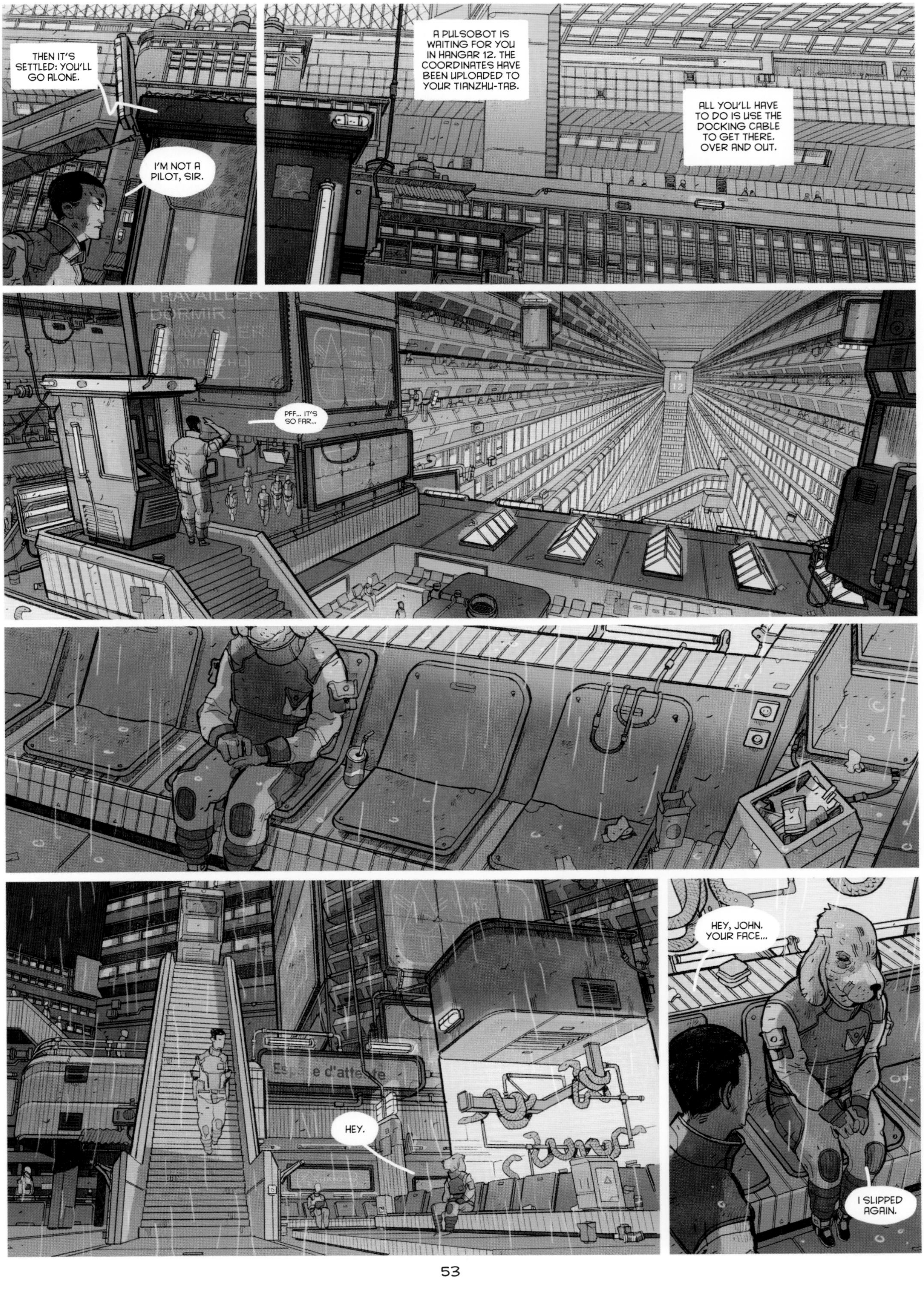
THEN IT'S SETTLED: YOU'LL GO ALONE.
I'M NOT A PILOT, SIR.
A PULSOBOT IS WAITING FOR YOU IN HANGAR 12. THE COORDINATES HAVE BEEN UPLOADED TO YOUR TIANZHU-TAB.
ALL YOU'LL HAVE TO DO IS USE THE DOCKING CABLE TO GET THERE. OVER AND OUT.
PFF... IT'S SO FAR...
HEY.
HEY, JOHN. YOUR FACE...
I SLIPPED AGAIN.

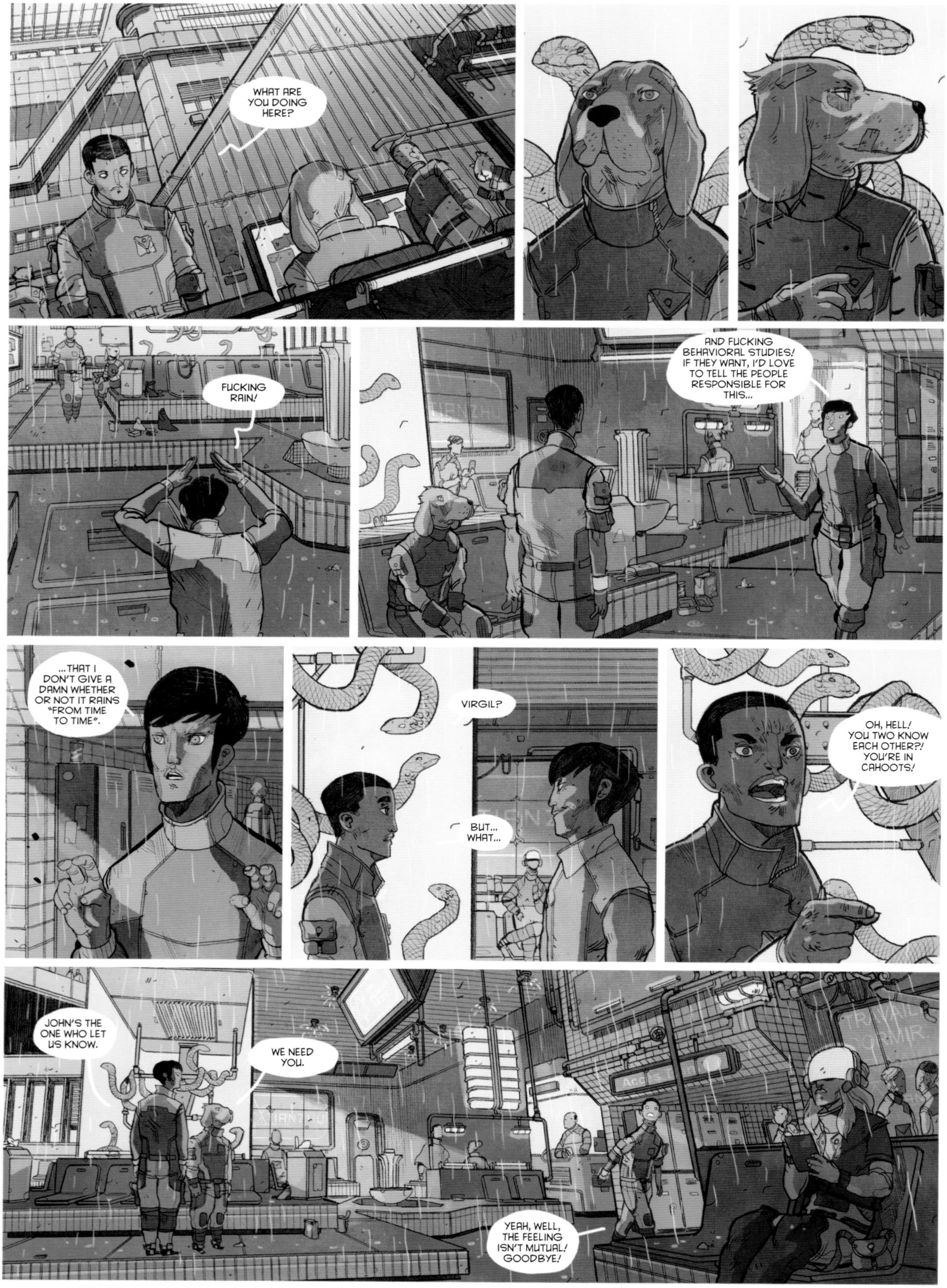
WHAT ARE YOU DOING HERE?
FUCKING RAIN!
AND FUCKING BEHAVIORAL STUDIES! IF THEY WANT, I'D LOVE TO TELL THE PEOPLE RESPONSIBLE FOR THIS...
...THAT I DON'T GIVE A DAMN WHETHER OR NOT IT RAINS "FROM TIME TO TIME".
VIRGIL?
BUT... WHAT...
OH, HELL! YOU TWO KNOW EACH OTHER?! YOU'RE IN CAHOOTS!
JOHN'S THE ONE WHO LET US KNOW.
WE NEED YOU.
YEAH, WELL, THE FEELING ISN'T MUTUAL! GOODBYE!

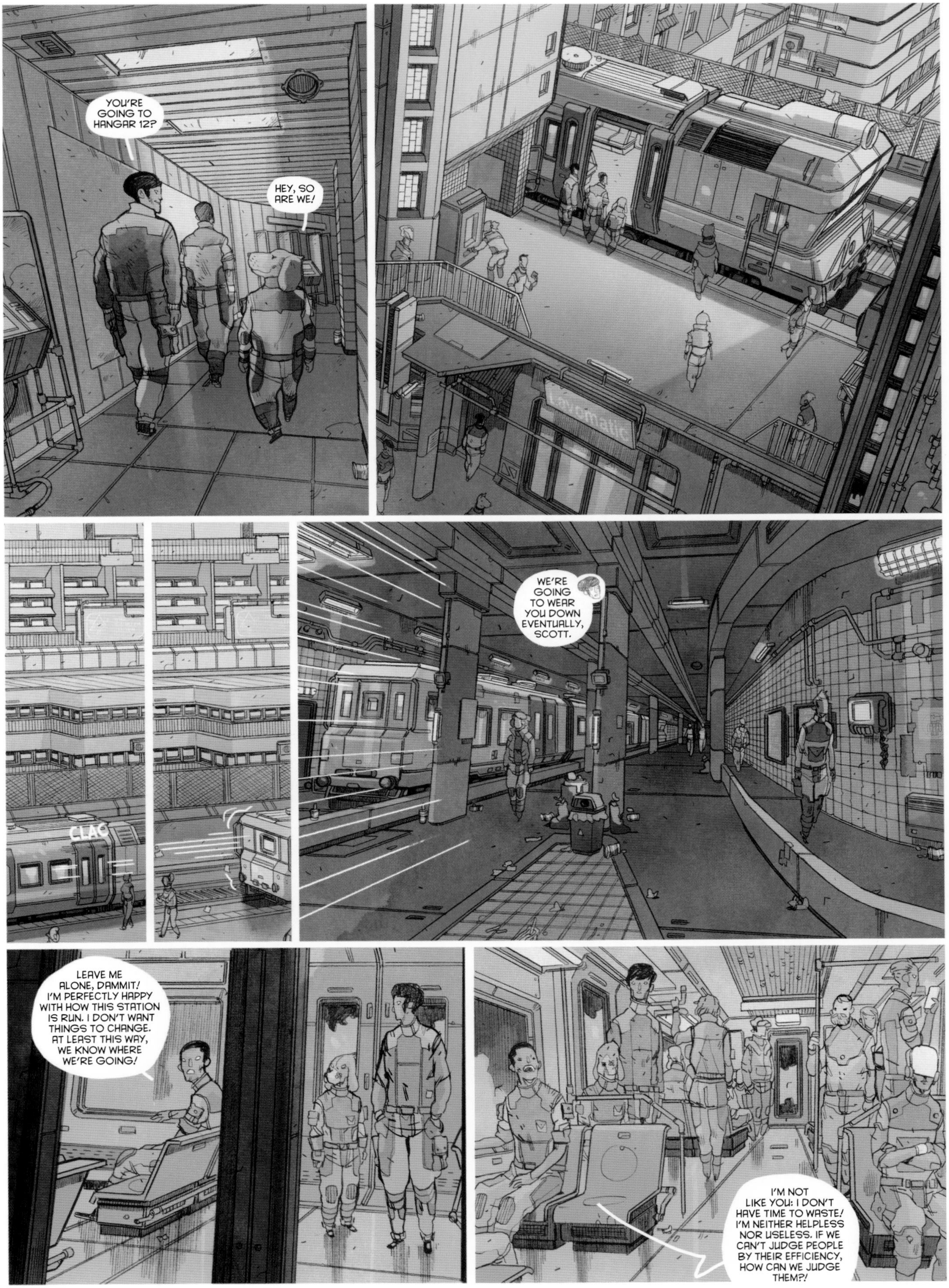
YOU'RE GOING TO HANGAR 12?
HEY, SO ARE WE!
Lavomatic
CLAC
WE'RE GOING TO WEAR YOU DOWN EVENTUALLY, SCOTT.
LEAVE ME ALONE, DAMMIT! I'M PERFECTLY HAPPY WITH HOW THIS STATION IS RUN. I DON'T WANT THINGS TO CHANGE. AT LEAST THIS WAY, WE KNOW WHERE WE'RE GOING!
I'M NOT LIKE YOU: I DON'T HAVE TIME TO WASTE! I'M NEITHER HELPLESS NOR USELESS. IF WE CAN'T JUDGE PEOPLE BY THEIR EFFICIENCY, HOW CAN WE JUDGE THEM?!

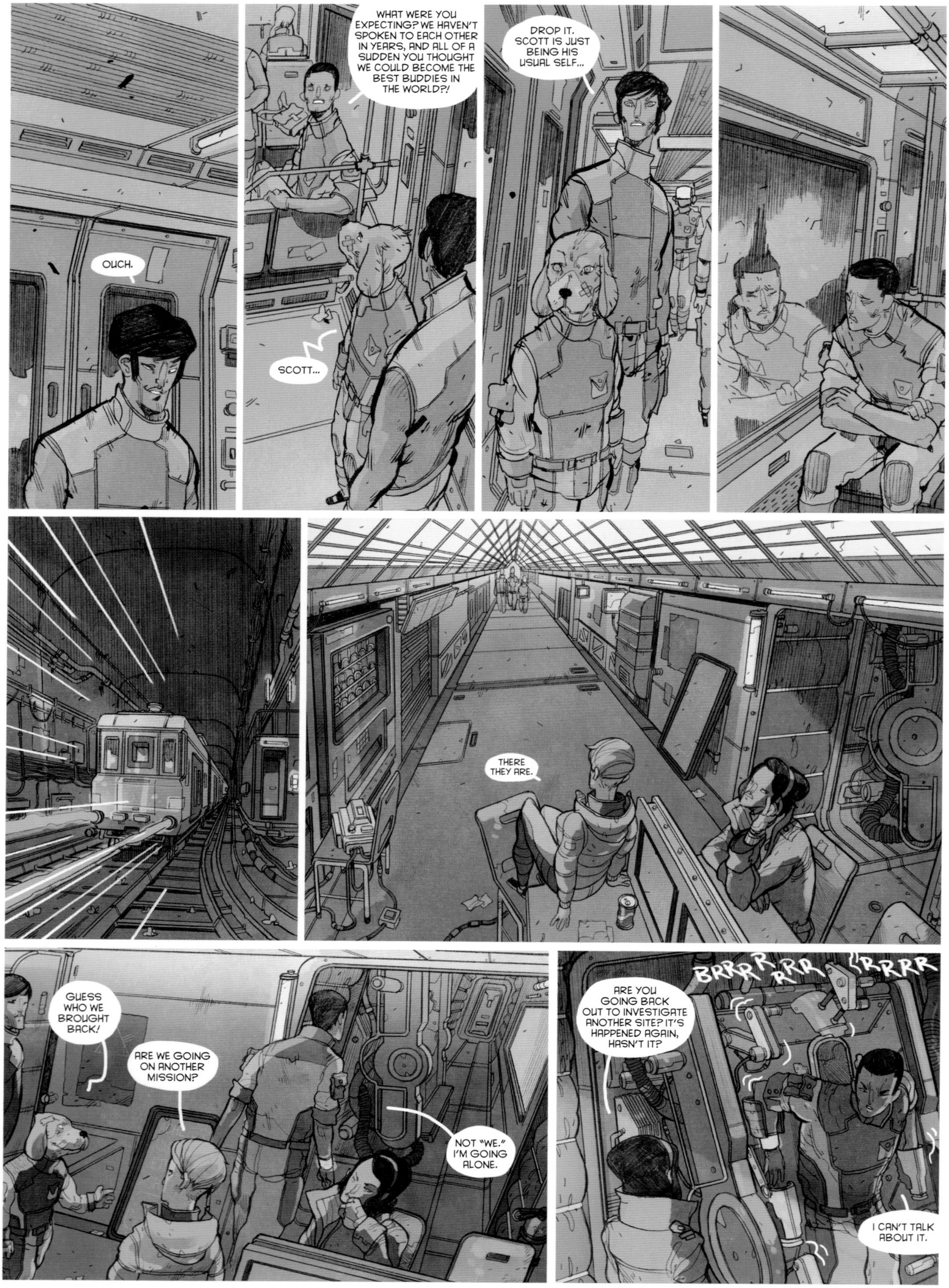
OUCH.
WHAT WERE YOU EXPECTING? WE HAVEN'T SPOKEN TO EACH OTHER IN YEARS, AND ALL OF A SUDDEN YOU THOUGHT WE COULD BECOME THE BEST BUDDIES IN THE WORLD?!
SCOTT...
DROP IT. SCOTT IS JUST BEING HIS USUAL SELF...
THERE THEY ARE.
GUESS WHO WE BROUGHT BACK!
ARE WE GOING ON ANOTHER MISSION?
NOT "WE." I'M GOING ALONE.
BRRRRRRRRRRRR
ARE YOU GOING BACK OUT TO INVESTIGATE ANOTHER SITE? IT'S HAPPENED AGAIN, HASN'T IT?
I CAN'T TALK ABOUT IT.

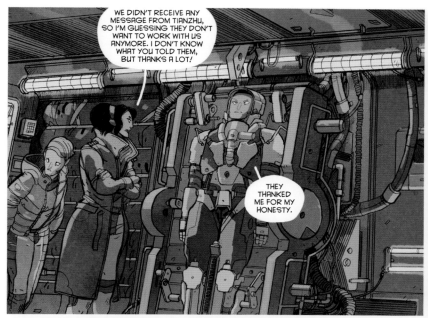

WE DIDN'T RECEIVE ANY MESSAGE FROM TIANZHU, SO I'M GUESSING THEY DON'T WANT TO WORK WITH US ANYMORE. I DON'T KNOW WHAT YOU TOLD THEM, BUT THANKS A LOT!

THEY THANKED ME FOR MY HONESTY.

WE'RE COMING WITH YOU. THEY'RE HIDING SOMETHING FROM US, AND THE COLONY HAS THE RIGHT TO KNOW!

SCOTT! OPEN YOUR EYES!

I TRUST THEM.

WE WANT TO KNOW!

57

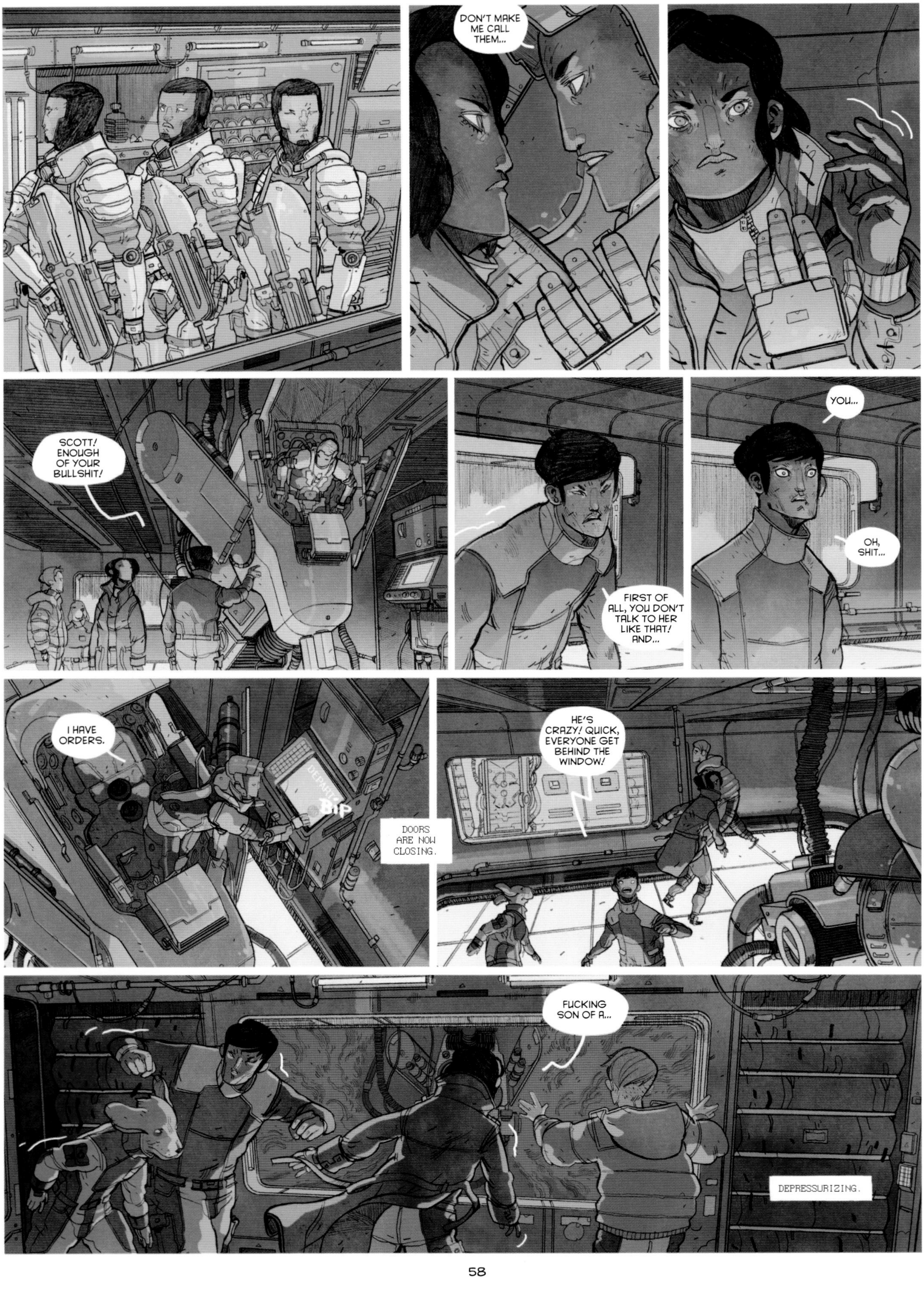

DON'T MAKE ME CALL THEM...
SCOTT! ENOUGH OF YOUR BULLSHIT!
FIRST OF ALL, YOU DON'T TALK TO HER LIKE THAT! AND...
YOU...
OH, SHIT...
I HAVE ORDERS.
DEPART
BIP
DOORS ARE NOW CLOSING.
HE'S CRAZY! QUICK, EVERYONE GET BEHIND THE WINDOW!
FUCKING SON OF A...
DEPRESSURIZING.

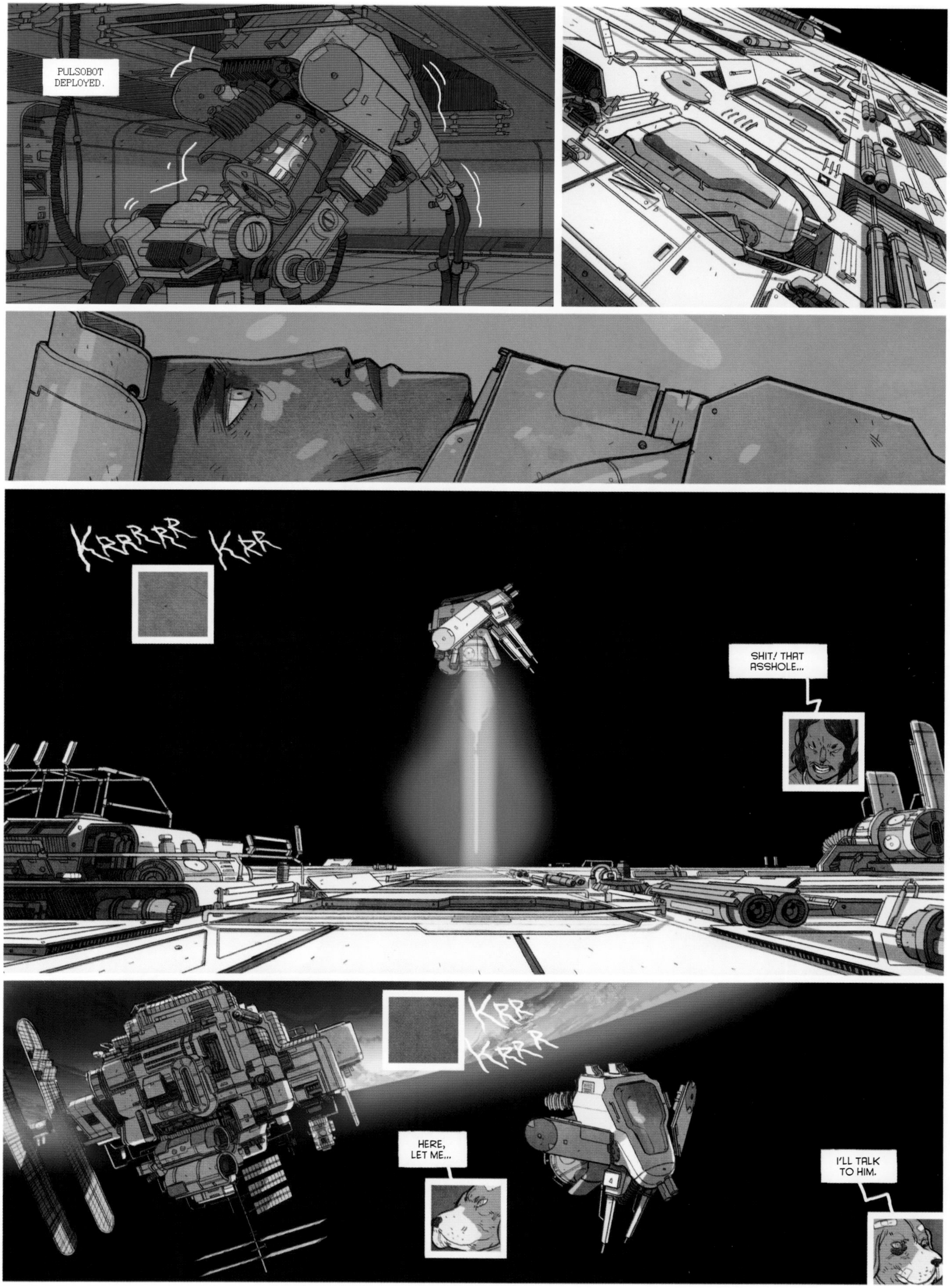
PULSOBOT DEPLOYED.
KRRRRR KRR
SHIT! THAT ASSHOLE...
KRR KRRR
HERE, LET ME...
I'LL TALK TO HIM.

SCOTT? IF WE CAN'T COME WITH YOU, CAN WE AT LEAST MAINTAIN RADIO CONTACT?

JUST WITH YOU, THEN.

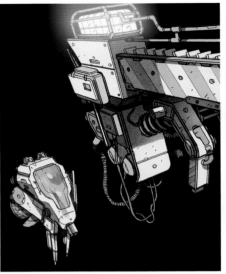

SCOTT?

MMH?

YOU NEED TO SEE THIS. IT'S ON *TIANZHU TV* RIGHT NOW.

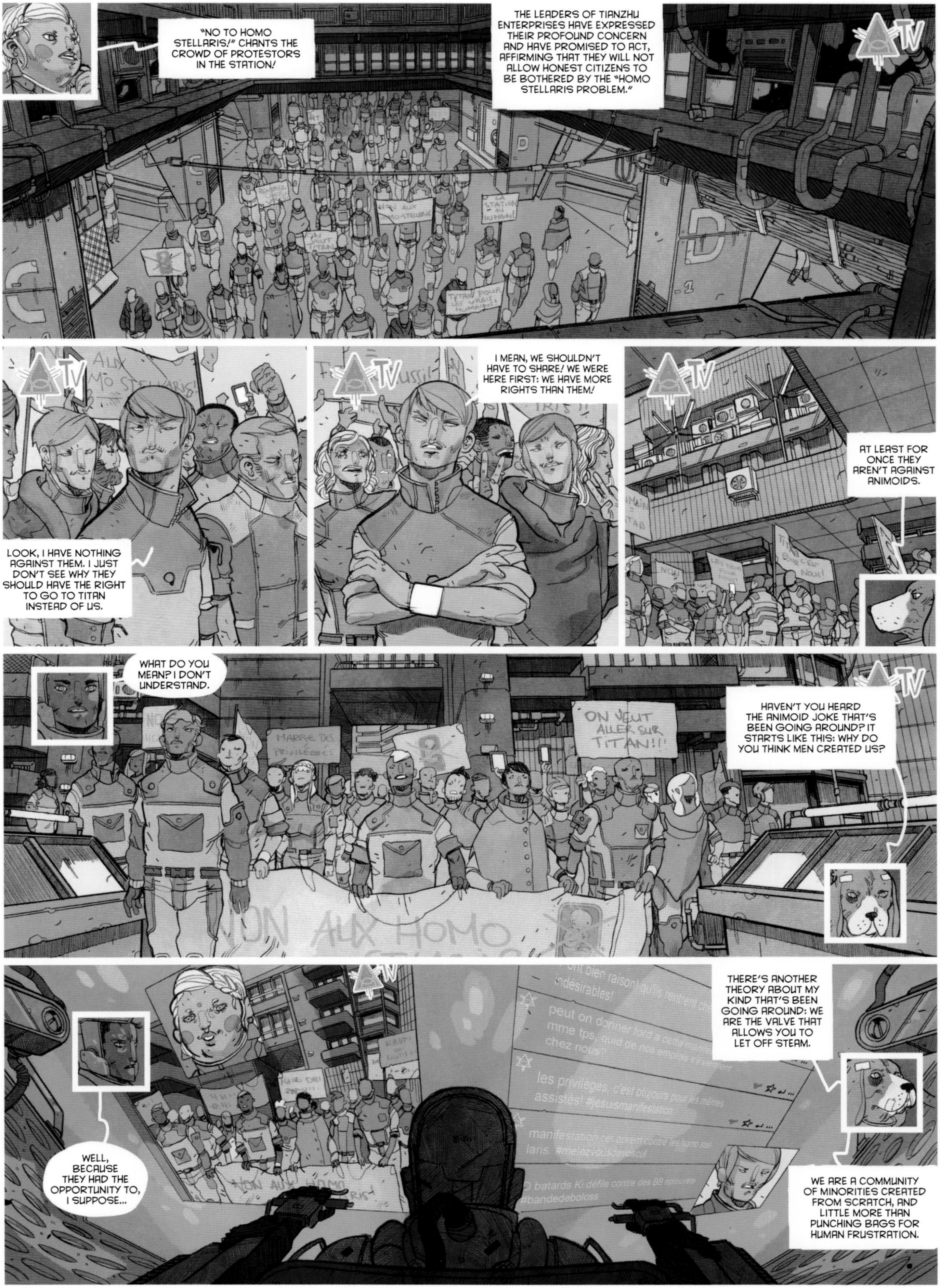

"NO TO HOMO STELLARIS!" CHANTS THE CROWD OF PROTESTORS IN THE STATION!
THE LEADERS OF TIANZHU ENTERPRISES HAVE EXPRESSED THEIR PROFOUND CONCERN AND HAVE PROMISED TO ACT, AFFIRMING THAT THEY WILL NOT ALLOW HONEST CITIZENS TO BE BOTHERED BY THE "HOMO STELLARIS PROBLEM."
TV
LOOK, I HAVE NOTHING AGAINST THEM. I JUST DON'T SEE WHY THEY SHOULD HAVE THE RIGHT TO GO TO TITAN INSTEAD OF US.
I MEAN, WE SHOULDN'T HAVE TO SHARE! WE WERE HERE FIRST: WE HAVE MORE RIGHTS THAN THEM!
AT LEAST FOR ONCE THEY AREN'T AGAINST ANIMOIDS.
WHAT DO YOU MEAN? I DON'T UNDERSTAND.
ON VEUT ALLER SUR TITAN!!
HAVEN'T YOU HEARD THE ANIMOID JOKE THAT'S BEEN GOING AROUND? IT STARTS LIKE THIS: WHY DO YOU THINK MEN CREATED US?
NON AUX HOMO
THERE'S ANOTHER THEORY ABOUT MY KIND THAT'S BEEN GOING AROUND: WE ARE THE VALVE THAT ALLOWS YOU TO LET OFF STEAM.
WELL, BECAUSE THEY HAD THE OPPORTUNITY TO, I SUPPOSE...
WE ARE A COMMUNITY OF MINORITIES CREATED FROM SCRATCH, AND LITTLE MORE THAN PUNCHING BAGS FOR HUMAN FRUSTRATION.

WHICH IS IMPORTANT IN A STATION WHERE THERE ARE NEITHER FRONTIERS NOR FOREIGNERS, AND WHERE EVERYONE STEPS ON EACH OTHER'S TOES DUE TO LACK OF SPACE.
WHAT INFALLIBLE LOGIC!
TRAVAILLER
ACHETER
WELL? WHAT'S THE PUNCHLINE?
I NEVER SAID IT WAS FUNNY. THAT IS THE JOKE!
AH, I SEE YOU'VE ARRIVED.

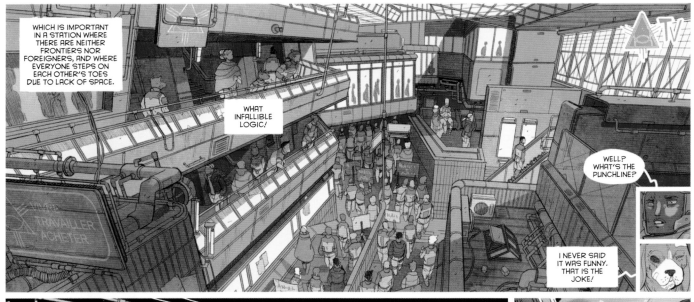

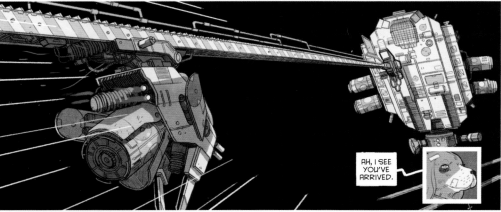

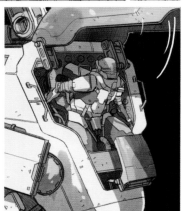

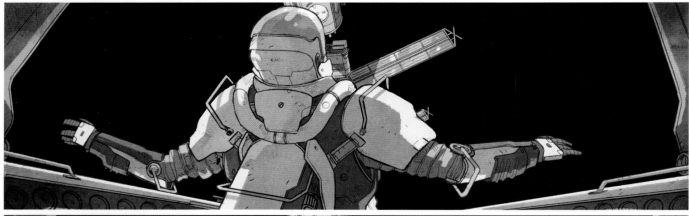

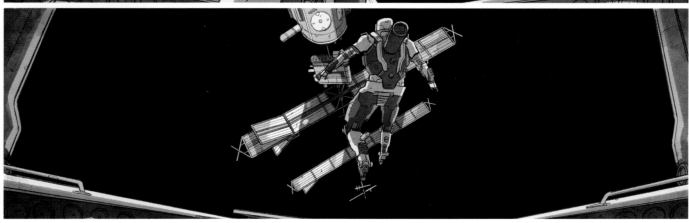

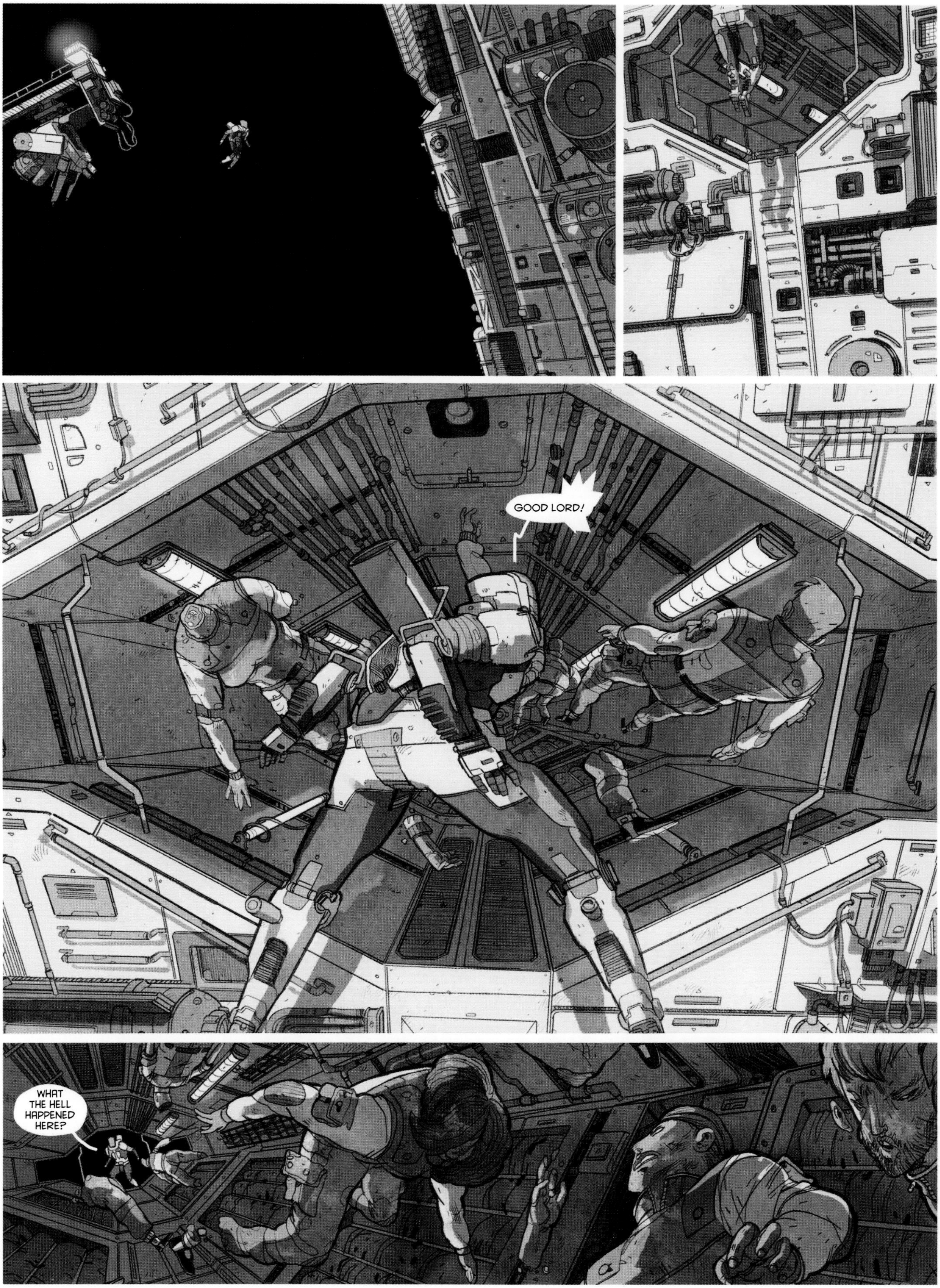
GOOD LORD!
WHAT THE HELL HAPPENED HERE?

LOCK
BIP
KRAK
PRESSURIZING AIRLOCK.
KRAK
KRAK
KRAK
TAK
TAK
KRAK
?
MA'AM?

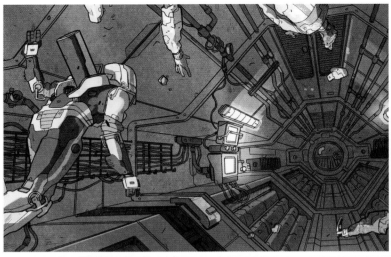

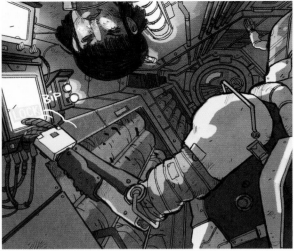

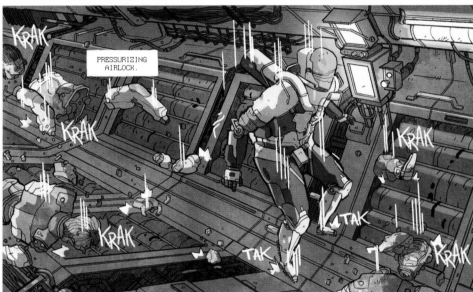

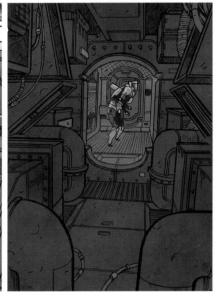

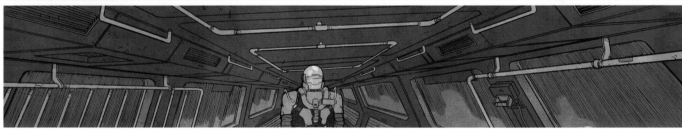

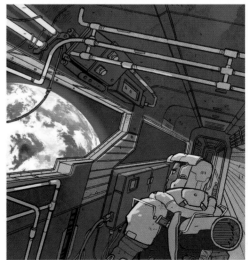

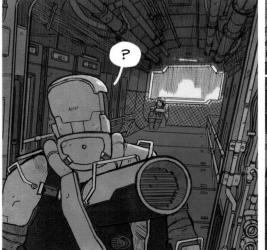

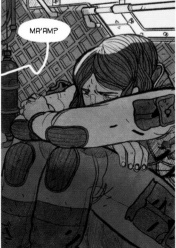

THERE WAS NOTHING I COULD DO. I... I TRIED, I SWEAR...

MA'AM, ARE YOU ALL RIGHT?

WHAT HAPPENED HERE? WHY WERE YOUR COLLEAGUES FLOATING OUT THERE?!

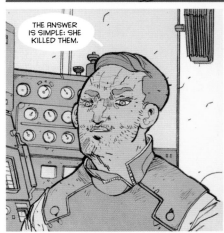

THE ANSWER IS SIMPLE: SHE KILLED THEM.

HUH?!

SHE'S COMPLETELY INSANE. WE HAD TO SEAL OURSELVES IN HERE TO ESCAPE FROM HER.

I'M NOT CRAZY... I'M NOT CRAZY...

I'M NOT CRAZY, I SWEAR!

I HAD NO CHOICE! YOU DON'T KNOW WHAT THEY DO HERE!

EXACTLY WHAT IS GOING ON HERE?!

WE ARE MEMBERS OF THE "AMBITION OF THE CENTURY" SCIENTIFIC TEAM. WE ARE AT THE TOP OF THE "HOMO STELLARIS" CHAIN.

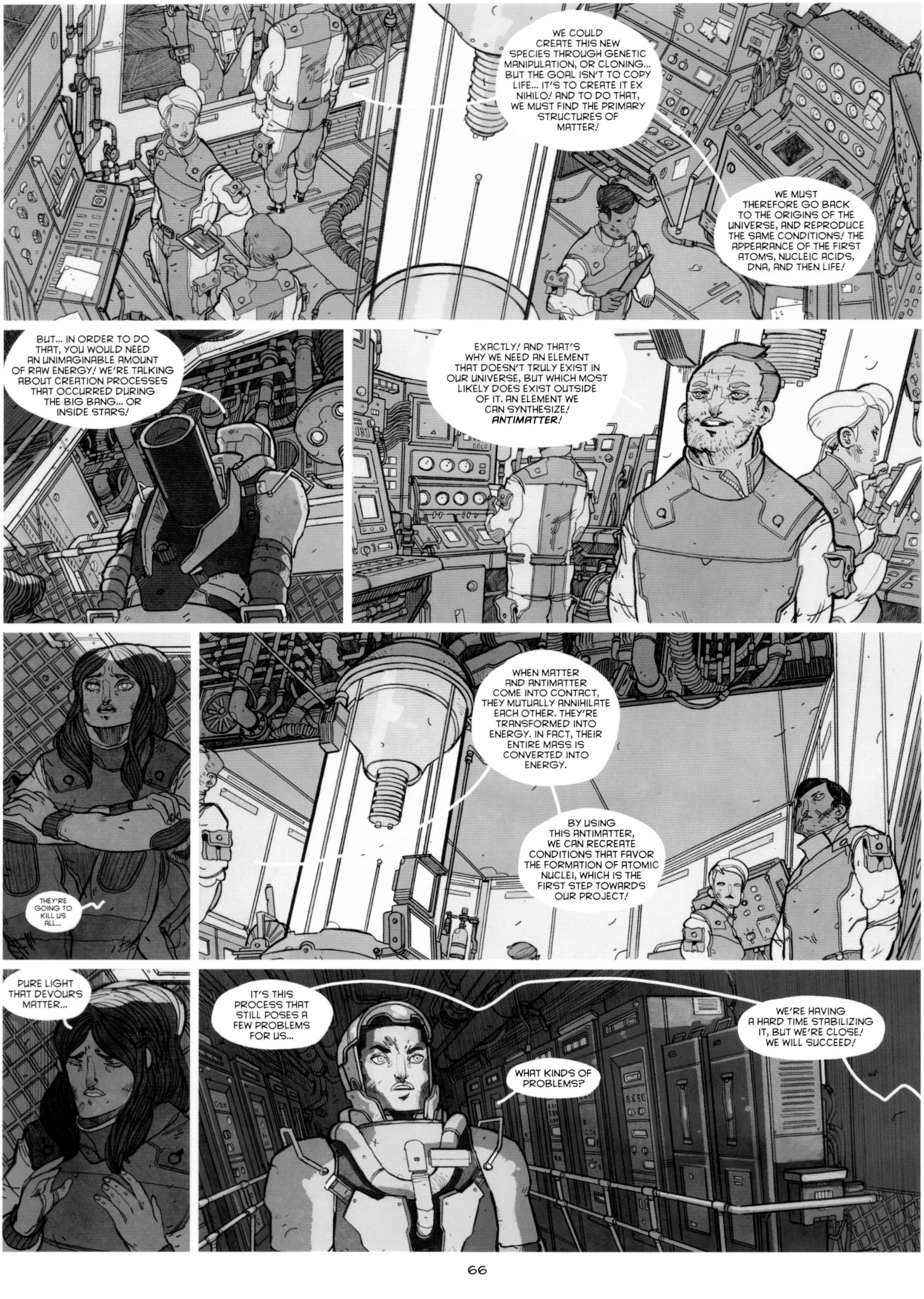
WE COULD CREATE THIS NEW SPECIES THROUGH GENETIC MANIPULATION, OR CLONING... BUT THE GOAL ISN'T TO COPY LIFE... IT'S TO CREATE IT EX NIHILO! AND TO DO THAT, WE MUST FIND THE PRIMARY STRUCTURES OF MATTER!
WE MUST THEREFORE GO BACK TO THE ORIGINS OF THE UNIVERSE, AND REPRODUCE THE SAME CONDITIONS! THE APPEARANCE OF THE FIRST ATOMS, NUCLEIC ACIDS, DNA, AND THEN LIFE!
BUT... IN ORDER TO DO THAT, YOU WOULD NEED AN UNIMAGINABLE AMOUNT OF RAW ENERGY! WE'RE TALKING ABOUT CREATION PROCESSES THAT OCCURRED DURING THE BIG BANG... OR INSIDE STARS!
EXACTLY! AND THAT'S WHY WE NEED AN ELEMENT THAT DOESN'T TRULY EXIST IN OUR UNIVERSE, BUT WHICH MOST LIKELY DOES EXIST OUTSIDE OF IT. AN ELEMENT WE CAN SYNTHESIZE! ANTIMATTER!
THEY'RE GOING TO KILL US ALL...
WHEN MATTER AND ANTIMATTER COME INTO CONTACT, THEY MUTUALLY ANNIHILATE EACH OTHER. THEY'RE TRANSFORMED INTO ENERGY. IN FACT, THEIR ENTIRE MASS IS CONVERTED INTO ENERGY.
BY USING THIS ANTIMATTER, WE CAN RECREATE CONDITIONS THAT FAVOR THE FORMATION OF ATOMIC NUCLEI, WHICH IS THE FIRST STEP TOWARDS OUR PROJECT!
PURE LIGHT THAT DEVOURS MATTER...
IT'S THIS PROCESS THAT STILL POSES A FEW PROBLEMS FOR US...
WE'RE HAVING A HARD TIME STABILIZING IT, BUT WE'RE CLOSE! WE WILL SUCCEED!
WHAT KINDS OF PROBLEMS?

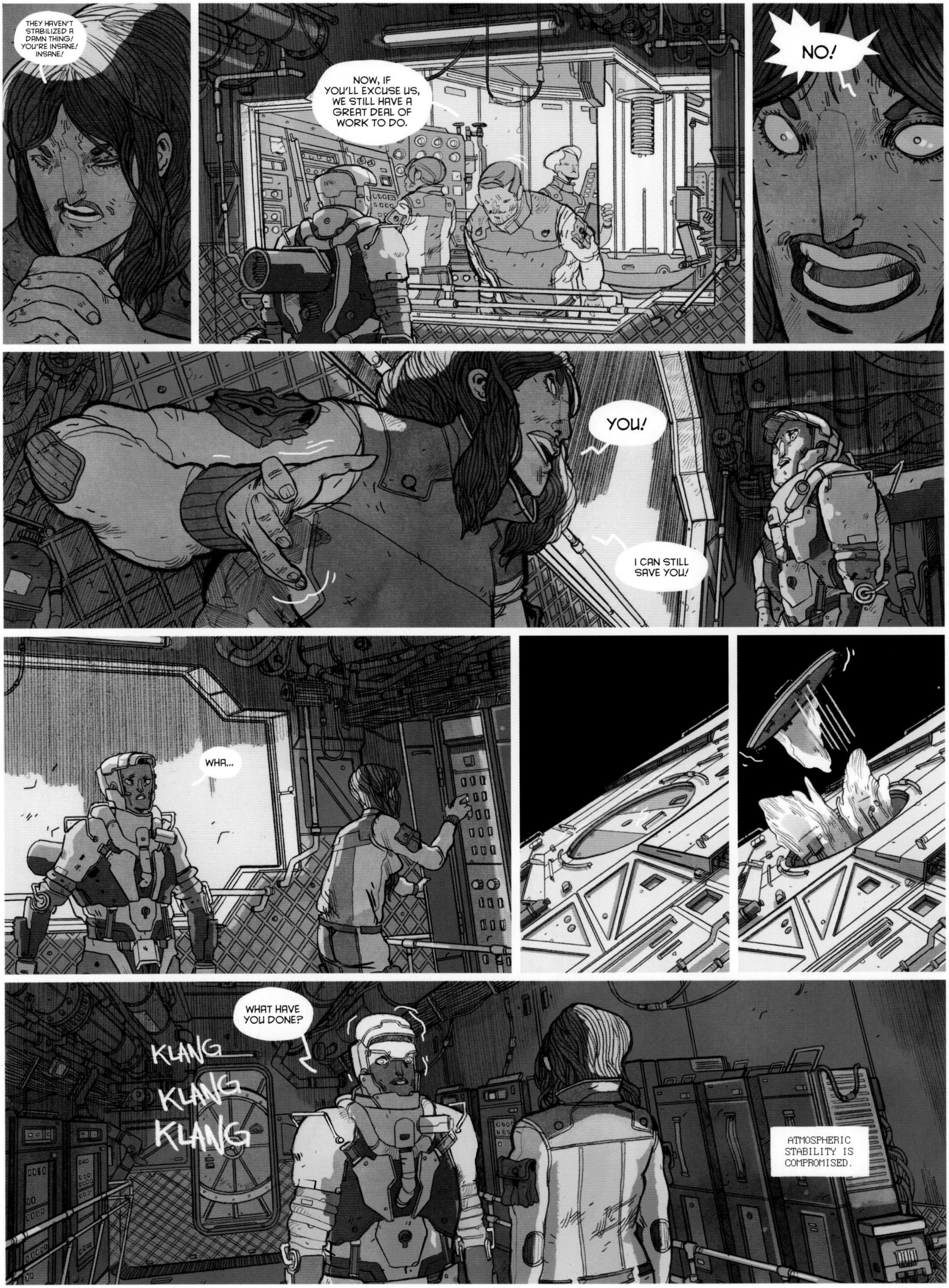
THEY HAVEN'T STABILIZED A DAMN THING! YOU'RE INSANE! INSANE!
NOW, IF YOU'LL EXCUSE US, WE STILL HAVE A GREAT DEAL OF WORK TO DO.
NO!
YOU!
I CAN STILL SAVE YOU!
WHA...
WHAT HAVE YOU DONE?
KLANG
KLANG
KLANG
ATMOSPHERIC STABILITY IS COMPROMISED.

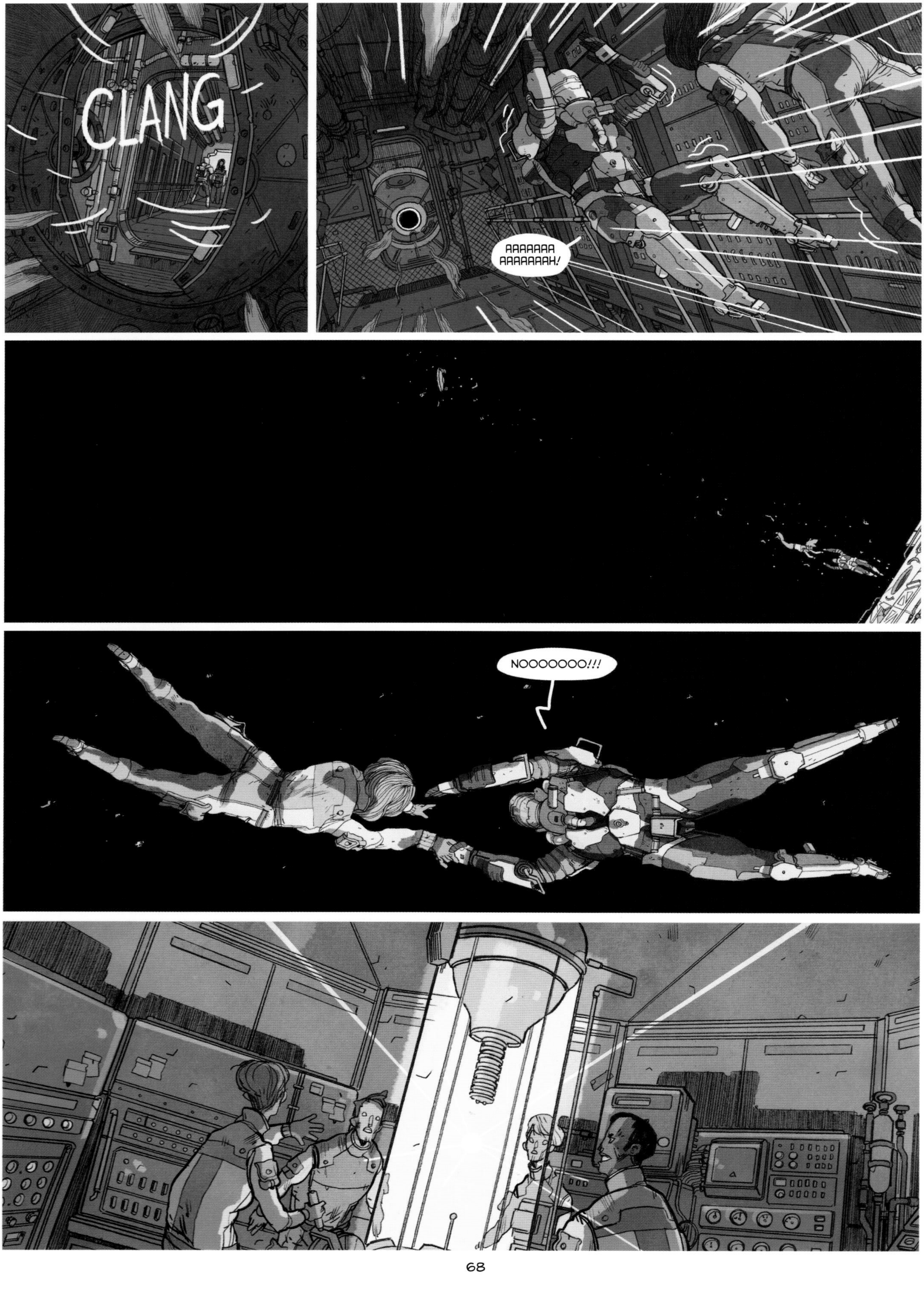
CLANG
AAAAAAA AAAAAAAH!
NOOOOOOO!!!

NO...

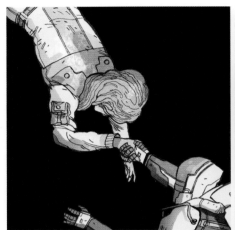

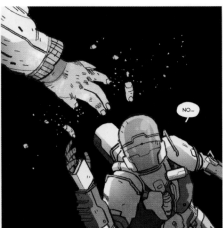

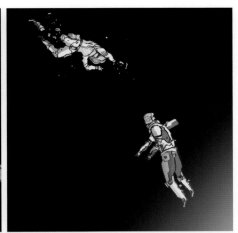

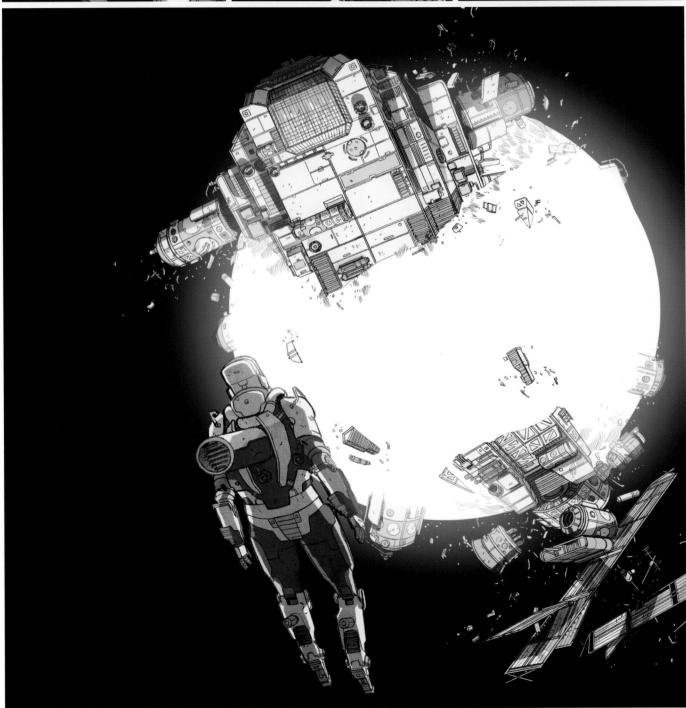

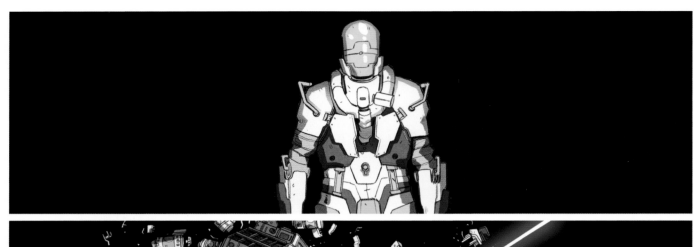

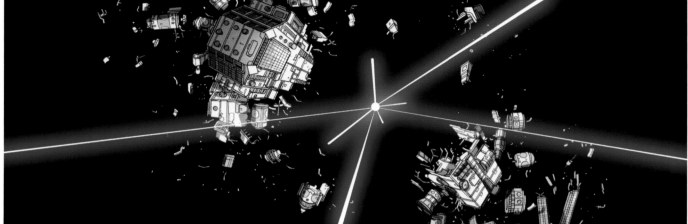

SCOTT... ARE YOU OKAY?

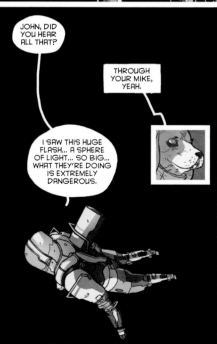

JOHN, DID YOU HEAR ALL THAT?

THROUGH YOUR MIKE, YEAH.

I SAW THIS HUGE FLASH... A SPHERE OF LIGHT... SO BIG... WHAT THEY'RE DOING IS EXTREMELY DANGEROUS.

YES, IT LOOKS THAT WAY.

THE SPHERES APPEAR TO BE LIMITED BY THE QUANTITY OF ANTIMATTER EMPLOYED. ONCE CONSUMED, THEY NO LONGER CREATE ANY ENERGY. THE SPHERES BURN OUT.

SCOTT, THIS WAS JUST AN ISOLATED LABORATORY. THE MAIN HOMO STELLARIS PRODUCTION LABS MUST BE ELSEWHERE. WHICH SURELY MEANS: MORE ANTIMATTER AND THEREFORE MORE RISKS.

WE HAVE TO NOTIFY TIANZHU H.Q.

I HAVE DOUBTS ABOUT WHAT THEY'LL DO WITH THIS INFORMATION. THIS IS BAD...

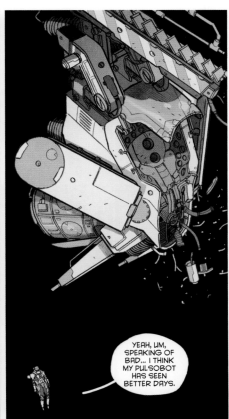

YEAH, UM, SPEAKING OF BAD... I THINK MY PULSOBOT HAS SEEN BETTER DAYS.

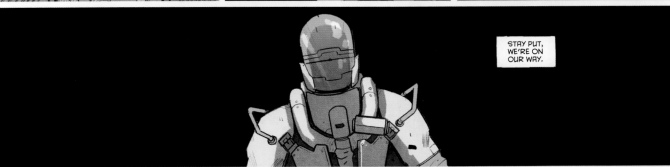

STAY PUT, WE'RE ON OUR WAY.

TAKE YOUR TIME...

71

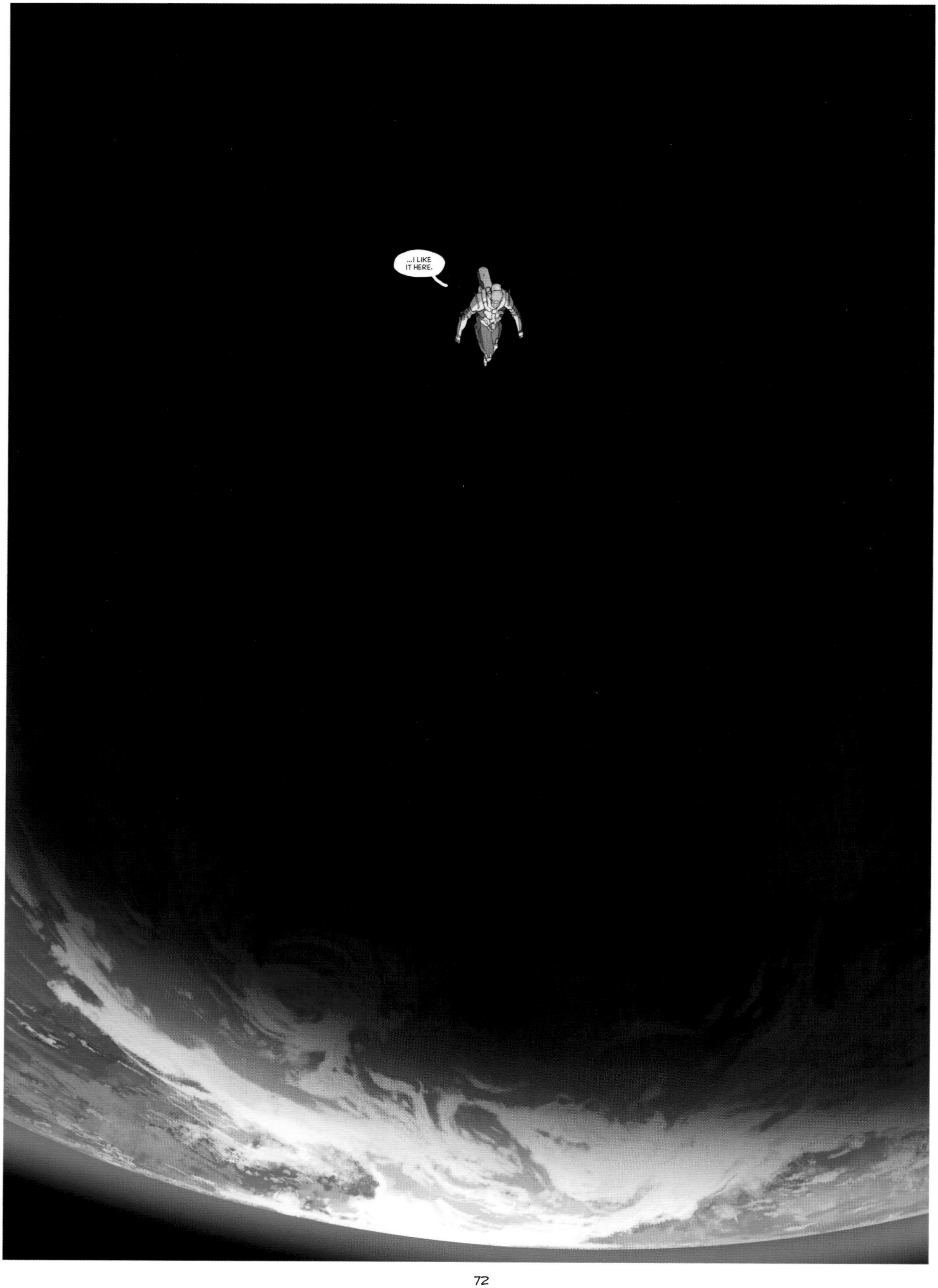
...I LIKE IT HERE.

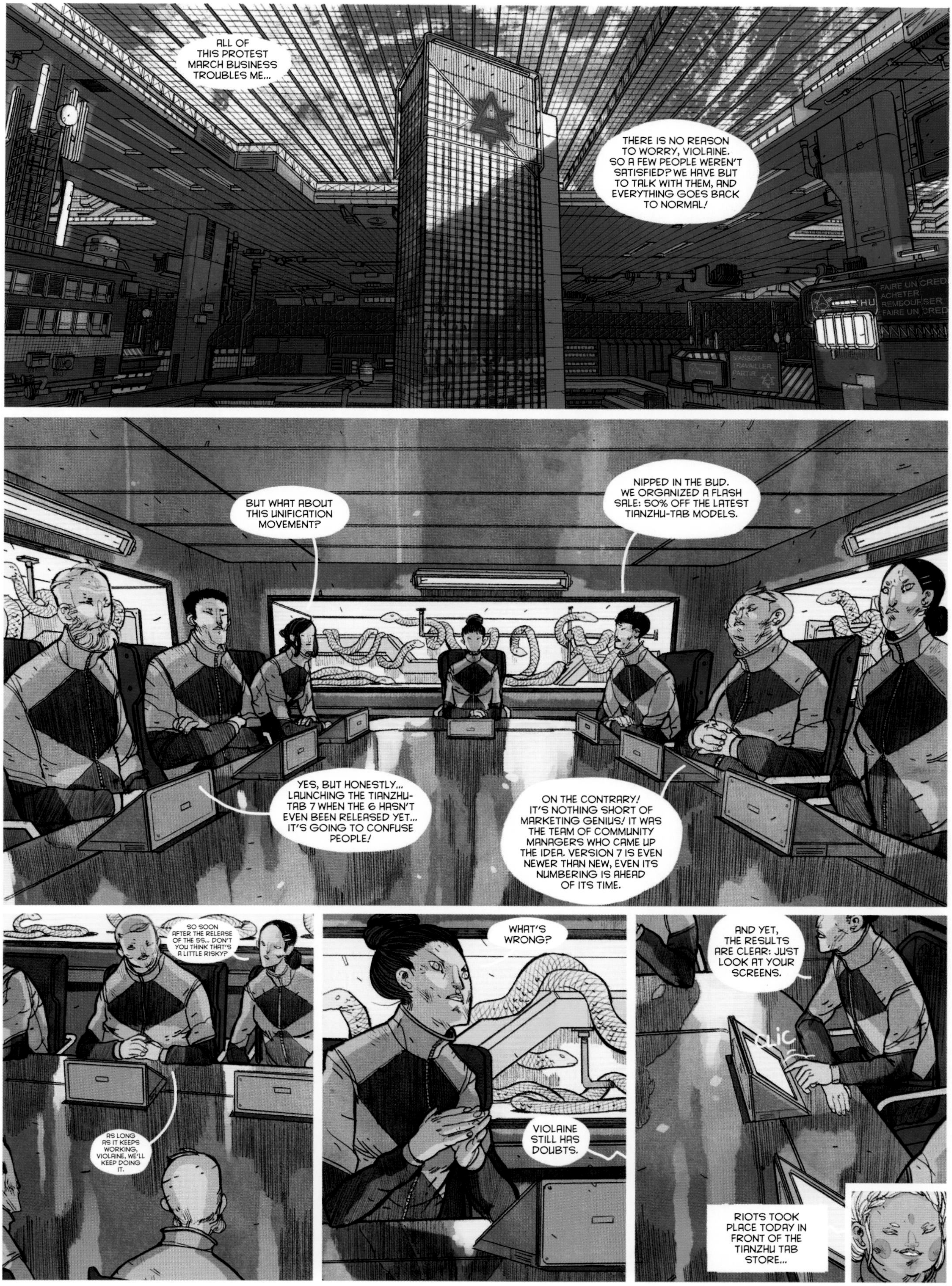
ALL OF THIS PROTEST MARCH BUSINESS TROUBLES ME...
THERE IS NO REASON TO WORRY, VIOLAINE. SO A FEW PEOPLE WEREN'T SATISFIED? WE HAVE BUT TO TALK WITH THEM, AND EVERYTHING GOES BACK TO NORMAL!
ACHETER
BUT WHAT ABOUT THIS UNIFICATION MOVEMENT?
NIPPED IN THE BUD. WE ORGANIZED A FLASH SALE: 50% OFF THE LATEST TIANZHU-TAB MODELS.
YES, BUT HONESTLY... LAUNCHING THE TIANZHU-TAB 7 WHEN THE 6 HASN'T EVEN BEEN RELEASED YET... IT'S GOING TO CONFUSE PEOPLE!
ON THE CONTRARY! IT'S NOTHING SHORT OF MARKETING GENIUS! IT WAS THE TEAM OF COMMUNITY MANAGERS WHO CAME UP THE IDEA. VERSION 7 IS EVEN NEWER THAN NEW, EVEN ITS NUMBERING IS AHEAD OF ITS TIME.
SO SOON AFTER THE RELEASE OF THE 5S... DON'T YOU THINK THAT'S A LITTLE RISKY?
AS LONG AS IT KEEPS WORKING, VIOLAINE, WE'LL KEEP DOING IT.
WHAT'S WRONG?
VIOLAINE STILL HAS DOUBTS.
AND YET, THE RESULTS ARE CLEAR: JUST LOOK AT YOUR SCREENS.
CLIC
RIOTS TOOK PLACE TODAY IN FRONT OF THE TIANZHU TAB STORE...

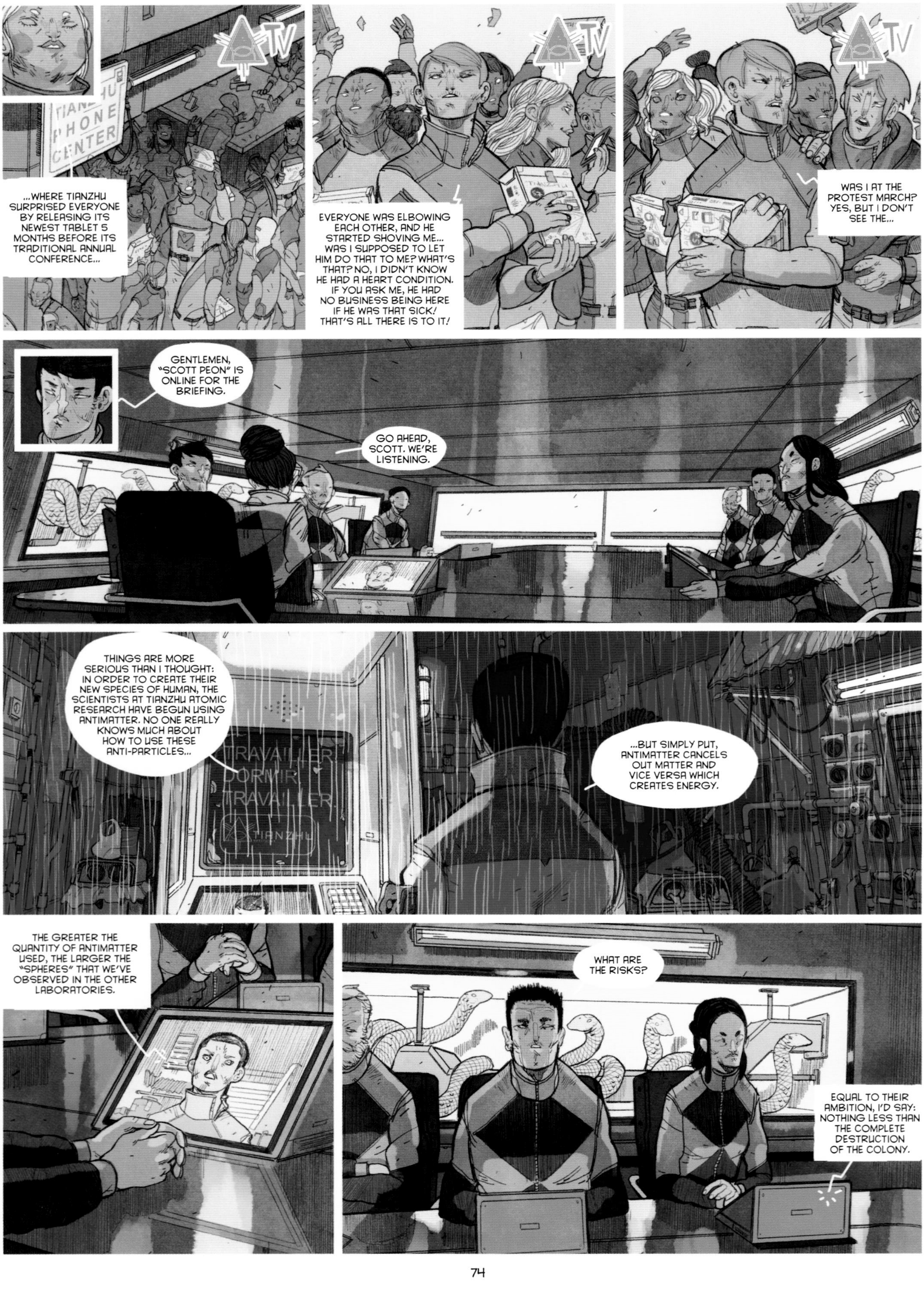

PHONE CENTER
...WHERE TIANZHU SURPRISED EVERYONE BY RELEASING ITS NEWEST TABLET 5 MONTHS BEFORE ITS TRADITIONAL ANNUAL CONFERENCE...
EVERYONE WAS ELBOWING EACH OTHER, AND HE STARTED SHOVING ME... WAS I SUPPOSED TO LET HIM DO THAT TO ME? WHAT'S THAT? NO, I DIDN'T KNOW HE HAD A HEART CONDITION. IF YOU ASK ME, HE HAD NO BUSINESS BEING HERE IF HE WAS THAT SICK! THAT'S ALL THERE IS TO IT!
WAS I AT THE PROTEST MARCH? YES, BUT I DON'T SEE THE...
GENTLEMEN, "SCOTT PEON" IS ONLINE FOR THE BRIEFING.
GO AHEAD, SCOTT. WE'RE LISTENING.
THINGS ARE MORE SERIOUS THAN I THOUGHT: IN ORDER TO CREATE THEIR NEW SPECIES OF HUMAN, THE SCIENTISTS AT TIANZHU ATOMIC RESEARCH HAVE BEGUN USING ANTIMATTER. NO ONE REALLY KNOWS MUCH ABOUT HOW TO USE THESE ANTI-PARTICLES...
TRAVAILLER
DORMIR
TRAVAILLER
TIANZHU
...BUT SIMPLY PUT, ANTIMATTER CANCELS OUT MATTER AND VICE VERSA WHICH CREATES ENERGY.
THE GREATER THE QUANTITY OF ANTIMATTER USED, THE LARGER THE "SPHERES" THAT WE'VE OBSERVED IN THE OTHER LABORATORIES.
WHAT ARE THE RISKS?
EQUAL TO THEIR AMBITION, I'D SAY: NOTHING LESS THAN THE COMPLETE DESTRUCTION OF THE COLONY.

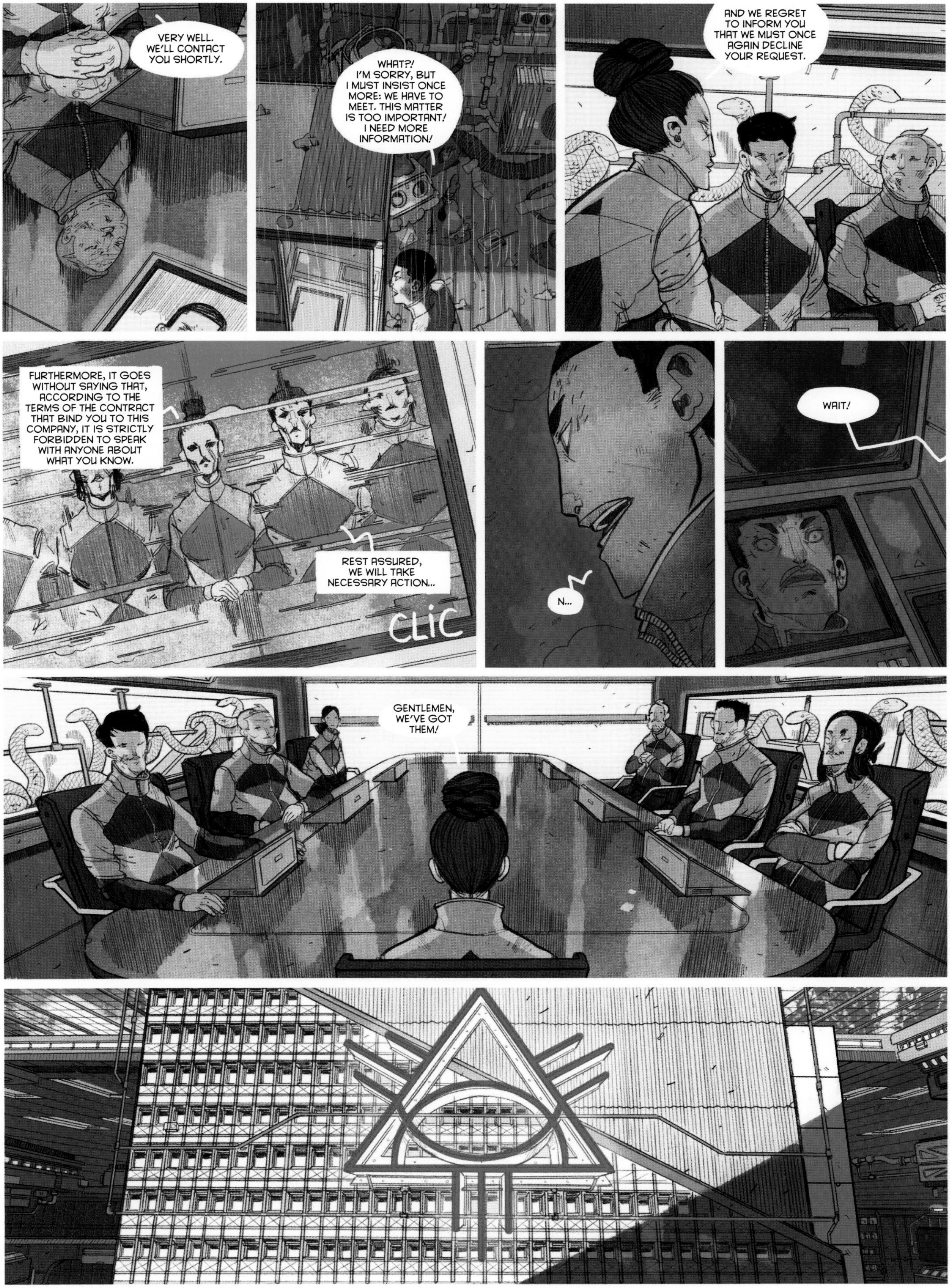
VERY WELL. WE'LL CONTACT YOU SHORTLY.
WHAT?! I'M SORRY, BUT I MUST INSIST ONCE MORE: WE HAVE TO MEET. THIS MATTER IS TOO IMPORTANT! I NEED MORE INFORMATION!
AND WE REGRET TO INFORM YOU THAT WE MUST ONCE AGAIN DECLINE YOUR REQUEST.
FURTHERMORE, IT GOES WITHOUT SAYING THAT, ACCORDING TO THE TERMS OF THE CONTRACT THAT BIND YOU TO THIS COMPANY, IT IS STRICTLY FORBIDDEN TO SPEAK WITH ANYONE ABOUT WHAT YOU KNOW.
REST ASSURED, WE WILL TAKE NECESSARY ACTION...
CLIC
N...
WAIT!
GENTLEMEN, WE'VE GOT THEM!

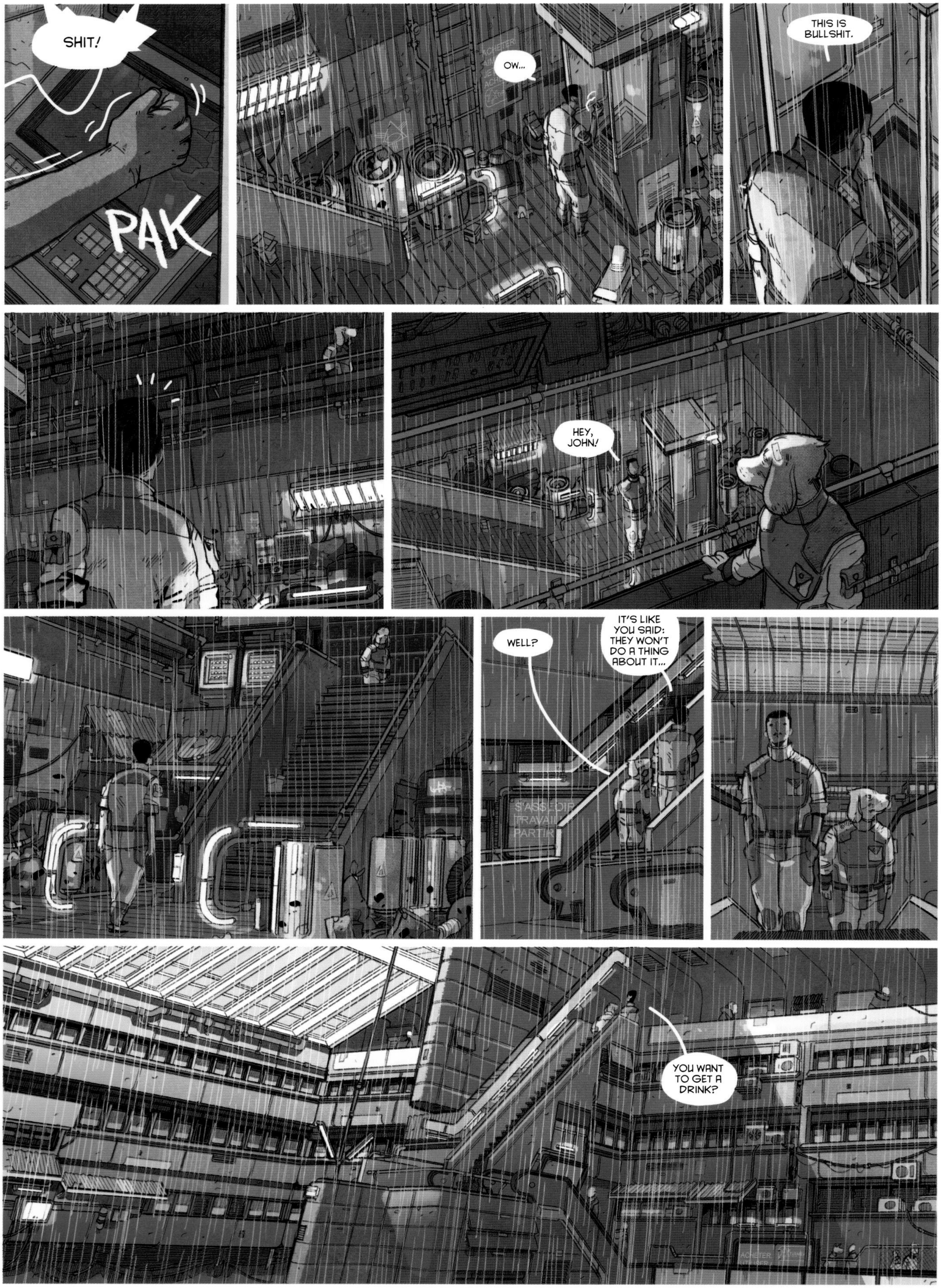
SHIT!
PAK
OW...
THIS IS BULLSHIT.
HEY, JOHN!
WELL?
IT'S LIKE YOU SAID: THEY WON'T DO A THING ABOUT IT...
YOU WANT TO GET A DRINK?
ACHETER

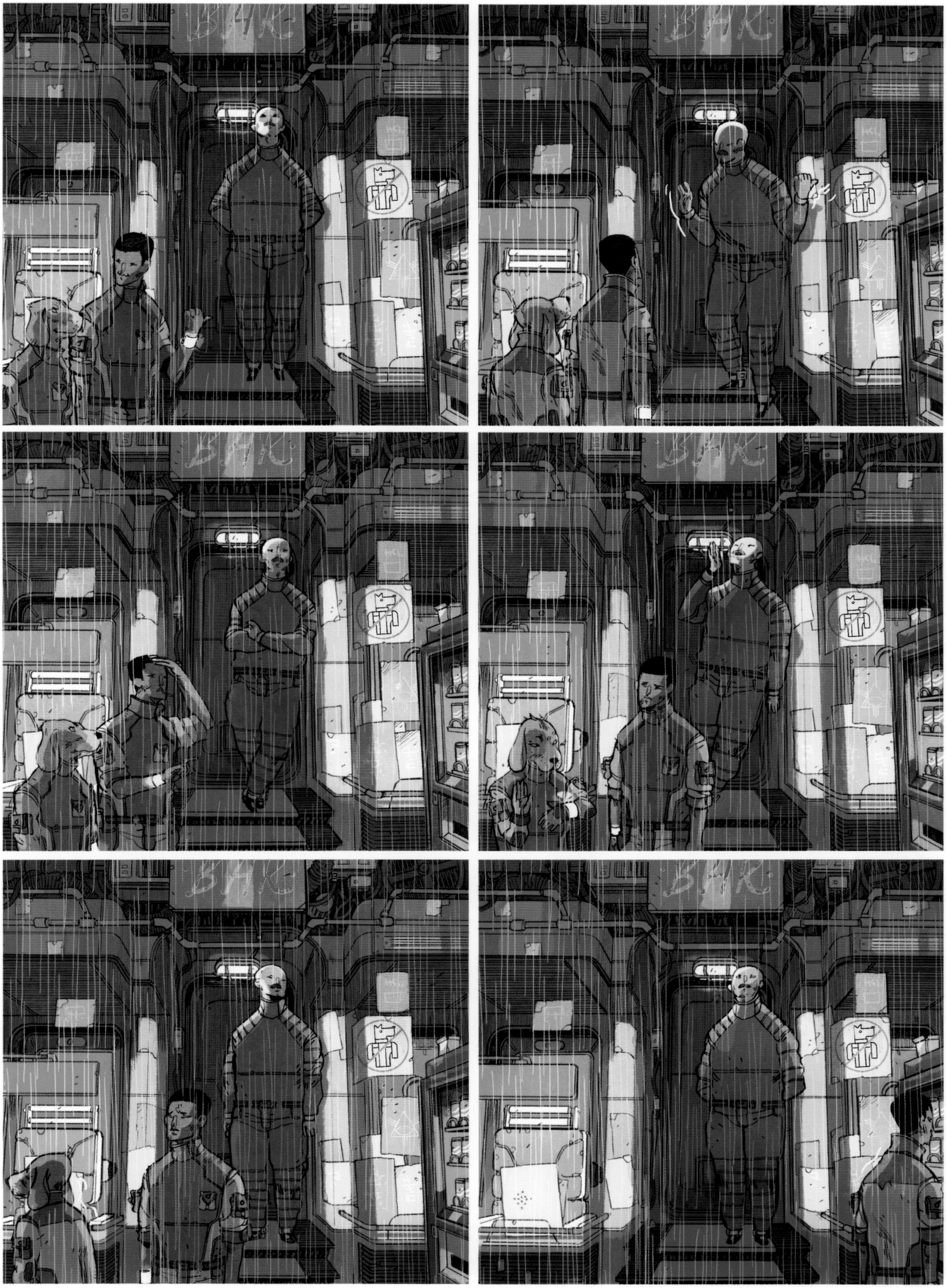
BAR

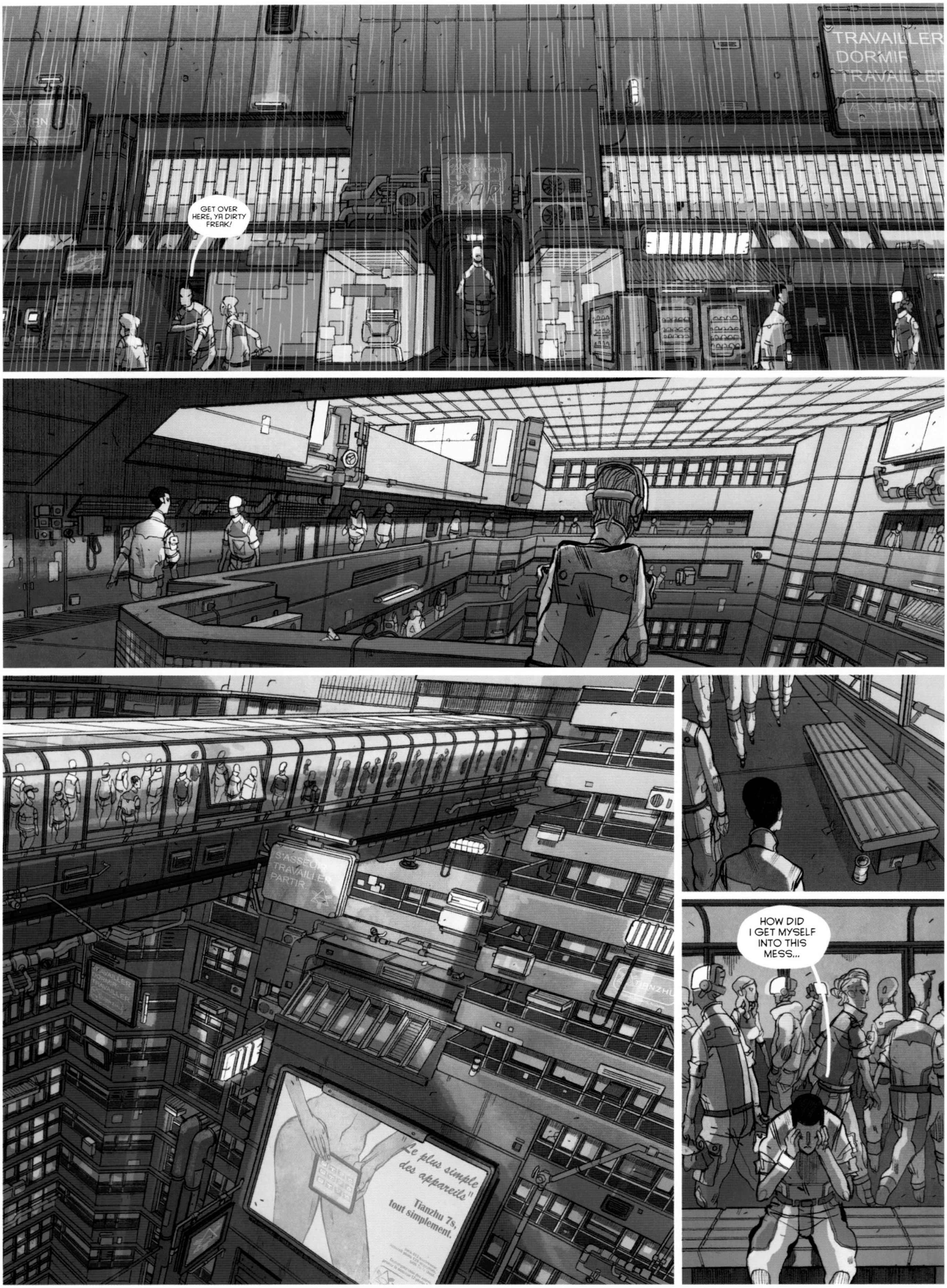
TRAVAILLER
DORMIR
TRAVAILLER
GET OVER HERE, YA DIRTY FREAK!
S'ASSEOIR
TRAVAILLER
PARTIR
"Le plus simple des appareils"
Tianzhu 7s, tout simplement.
HOW DID I GET MYSELF INTO THIS MESS...

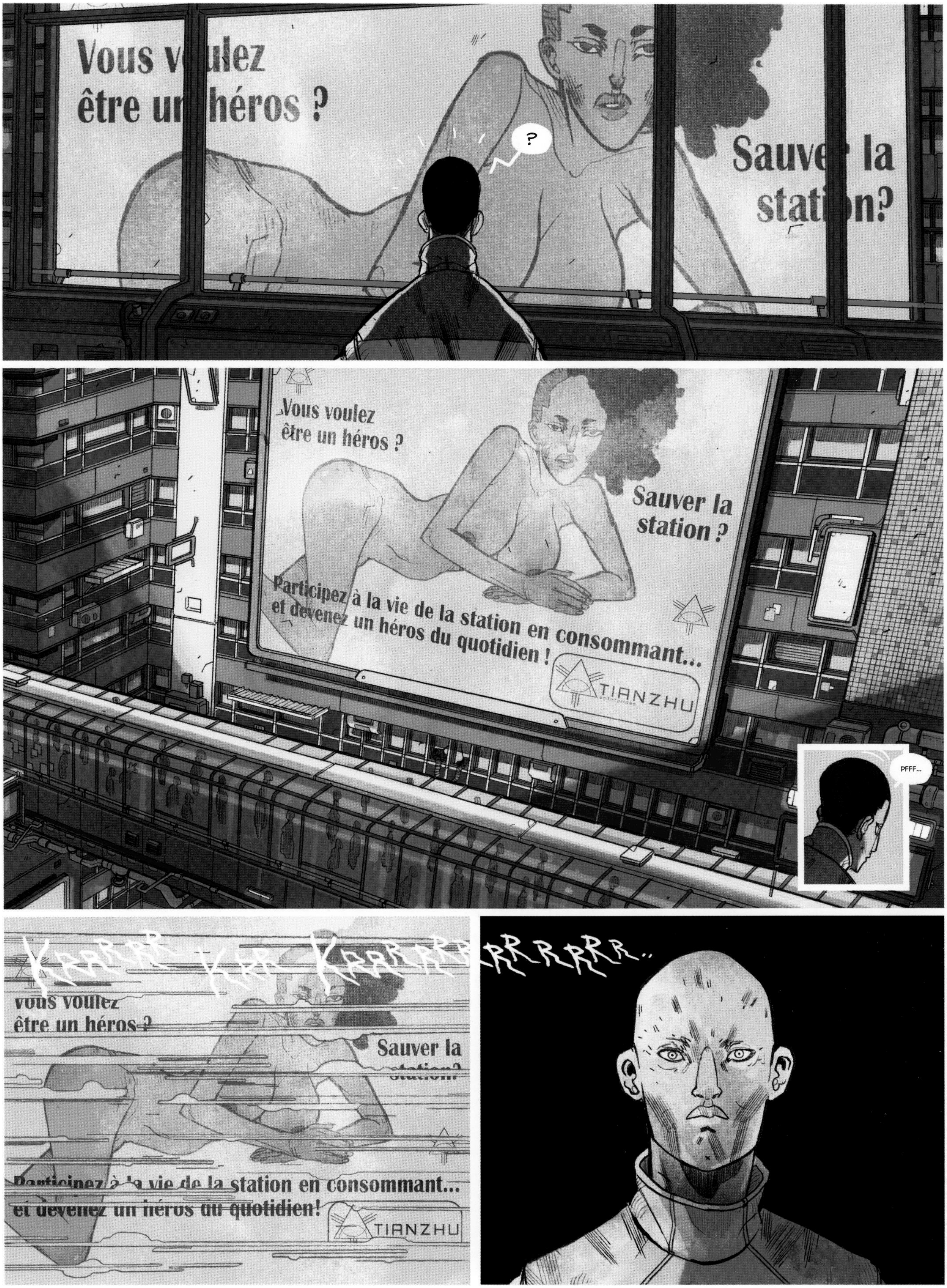

?
Vous voulez
être un héros ?
Sauver la
station ?
Participez à la vie de la station en consommant...
et devenez un héros du quotidien !
TIANZHU
PFFF...
KRRRRR KRR KRRRRRRRRRRRR..
Sauver la

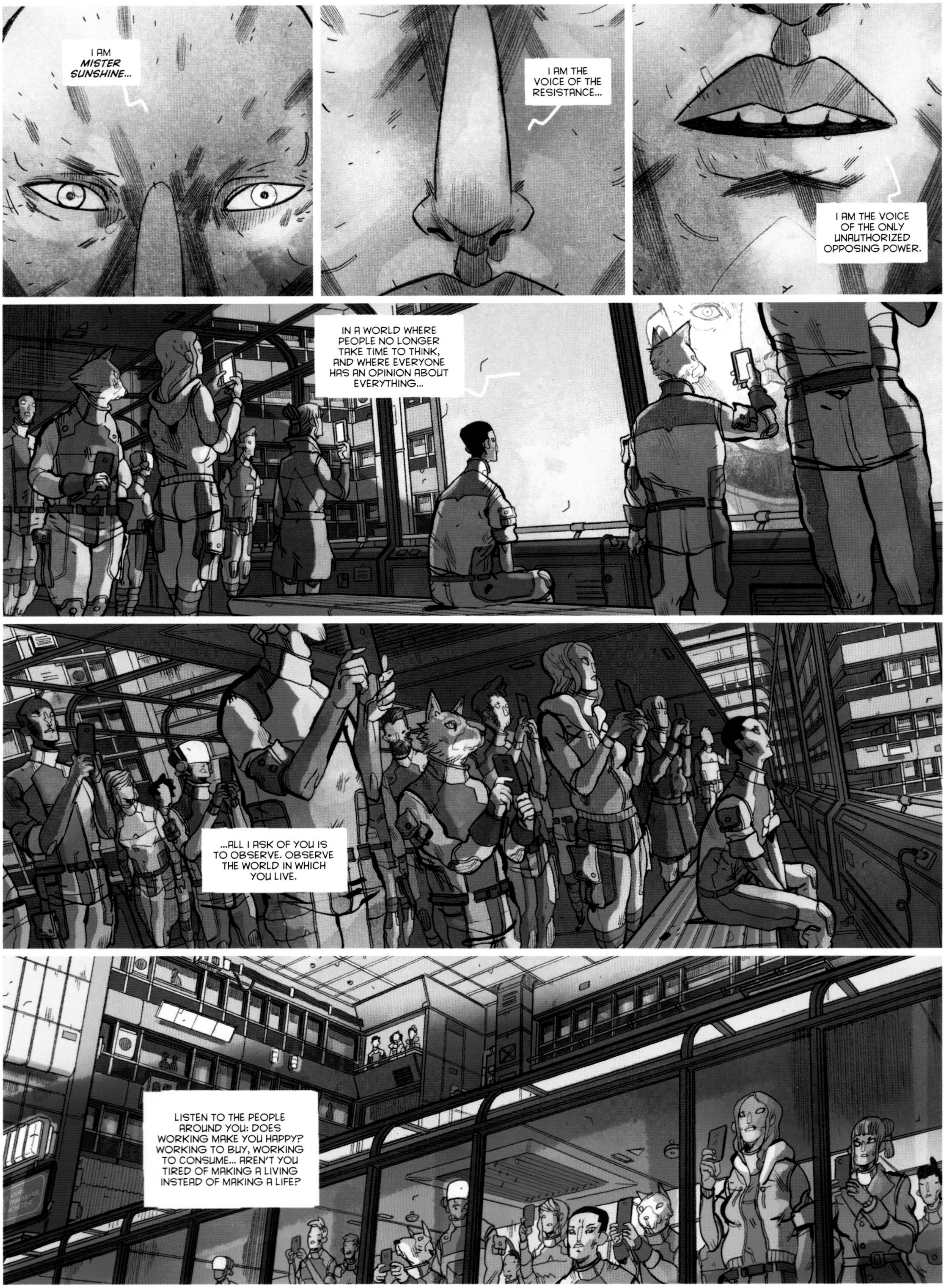
I AM MISTER SUNSHINE...
I AM THE VOICE OF THE RESISTANCE...
I AM THE VOICE OF THE ONLY UNAUTHORIZED OPPOSING POWER.
IN A WORLD WHERE PEOPLE NO LONGER TAKE TIME TO THINK, AND WHERE EVERYONE HAS AN OPINION ABOUT EVERYTHING...
...ALL I ASK OF YOU IS TO OBSERVE. OBSERVE THE WORLD IN WHICH YOU LIVE.
LISTEN TO THE PEOPLE AROUND YOU: DOES WORKING MAKE YOU HAPPY? WORKING TO BUY, WORKING TO CONSUME... AREN'T YOU TIRED OF MAKING A LIVING INSTEAD OF MAKING A LIFE?

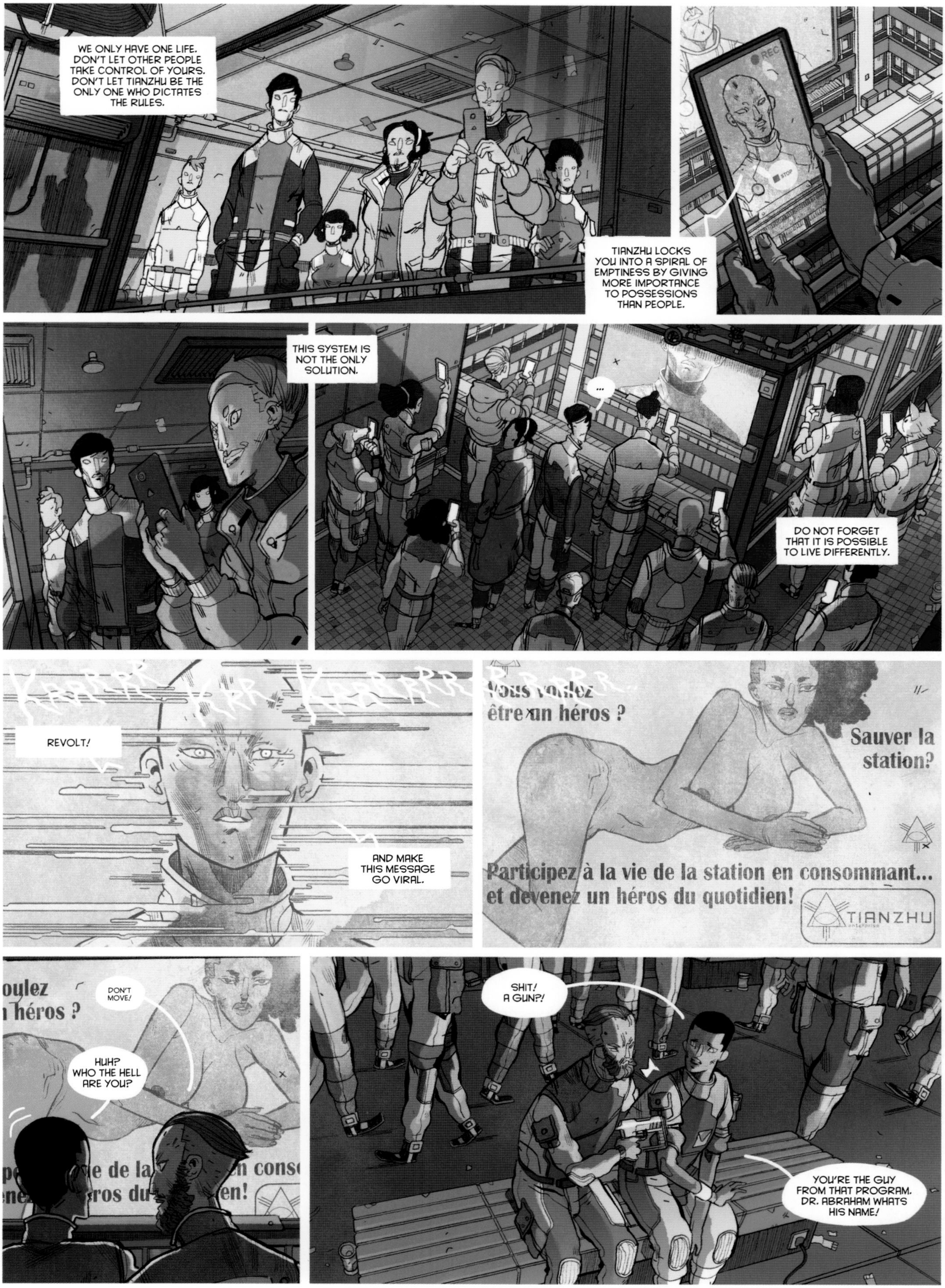
WE ONLY HAVE ONE LIFE. DON'T LET OTHER PEOPLE TAKE CONTROL OF YOURS. DON'T LET TIANZHU BE THE ONLY ONE WHO DICTATES THE RULES.
REC
STOP
TIANZHU LOCKS YOU INTO A SPIRAL OF EMPTINESS BY GIVING MORE IMPORTANCE TO POSSESSIONS THAN PEOPLE.
THIS SYSTEM IS NOT THE ONLY SOLUTION.
...
DO NOT FORGET THAT IT IS POSSIBLE TO LIVE DIFFERENTLY.
REVOLT!
AND MAKE THIS MESSAGE GO VIRAL.
ous voulez
être un héros ?
Sauver la station?
Participez à la vie de la station en consommant...
et devenez un héros du quotidien!
TIANZHU
DON'T MOVE!
HUH? WHO THE HELL ARE YOU?
SHIT! A GUN?!
YOU'RE THE GUY FROM THAT PROGRAM. DR. ABRAHAM WHATS HIS NAME!

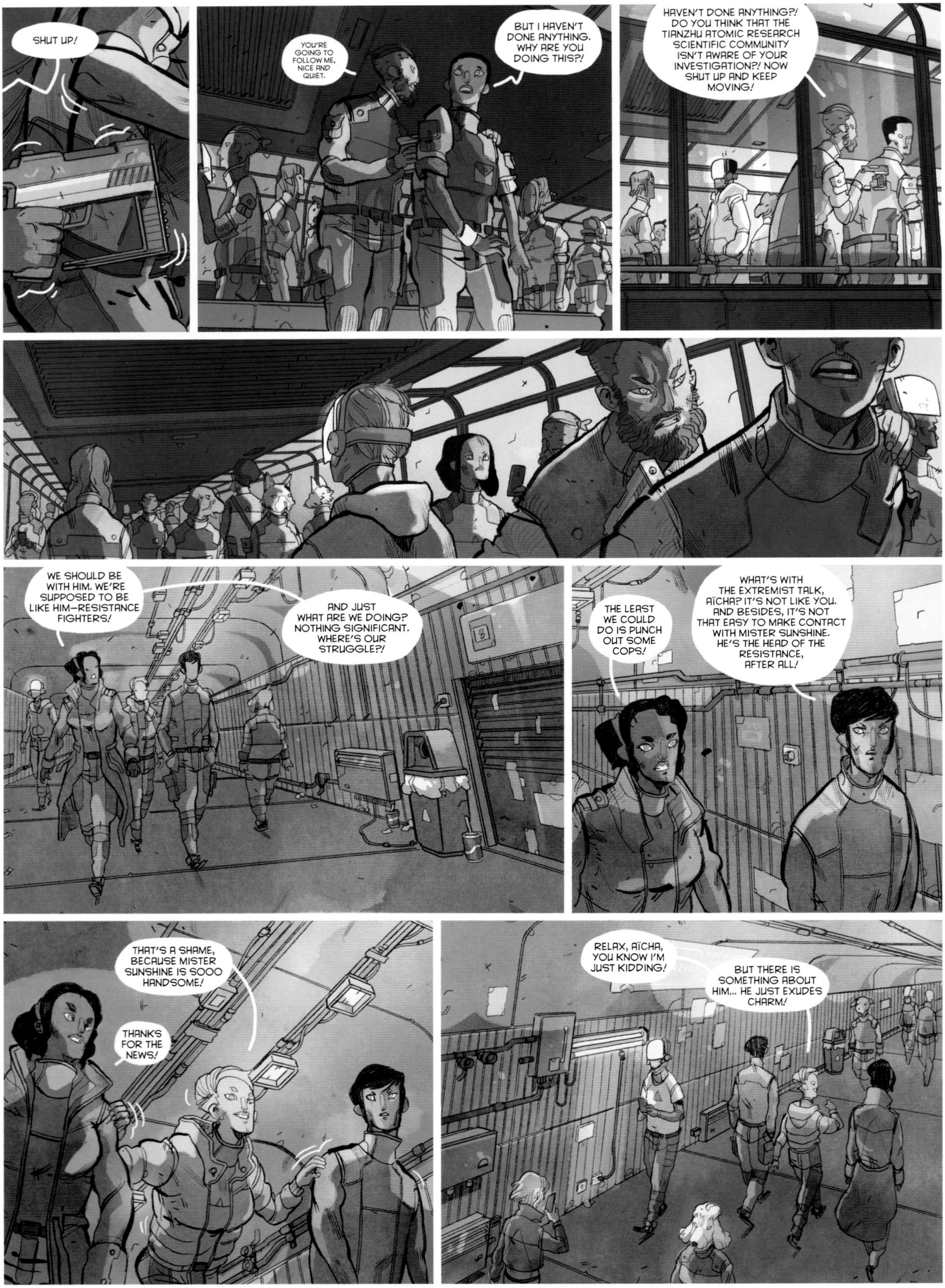
SHUT UP!
YOU'RE GOING TO FOLLOW ME, NICE AND QUIET.
BUT I HAVEN'T DONE ANYTHING. WHY ARE YOU DOING THIS?!
HAVEN'T DONE ANYTHING?! DO YOU THINK THAT THE TIANZHU ATOMIC RESEARCH SCIENTIFIC COMMUNITY ISN'T AWARE OF YOUR INVESTIGATION?! NOW SHUT UP AND KEEP MOVING!
WE SHOULD BE WITH HIM. WE'RE SUPPOSED TO BE LIKE HIM—RESISTANCE FIGHTERS!
AND JUST WHAT ARE WE DOING? NOTHING SIGNIFICANT. WHERE'S OUR STRUGGLE?!
THE LEAST WE COULD DO IS PUNCH OUT SOME COPS!
WHAT'S WITH THE EXTREMIST TALK, AÏCHA? IT'S NOT LIKE YOU. AND BESIDES, IT'S NOT THAT EASY TO MAKE CONTACT WITH MISTER SUNSHINE. HE'S THE HEAD OF THE RESISTANCE, AFTER ALL!
THAT'S A SHAME, BECAUSE MISTER SUNSHINE IS SOOO HANDSOME!
THANKS FOR THE NEWS!
RELAX, AÏCHA, YOU KNOW I'M JUST KIDDING!
BUT THERE IS SOMETHING ABOUT HIM... HE JUST EXUDES CHARM!

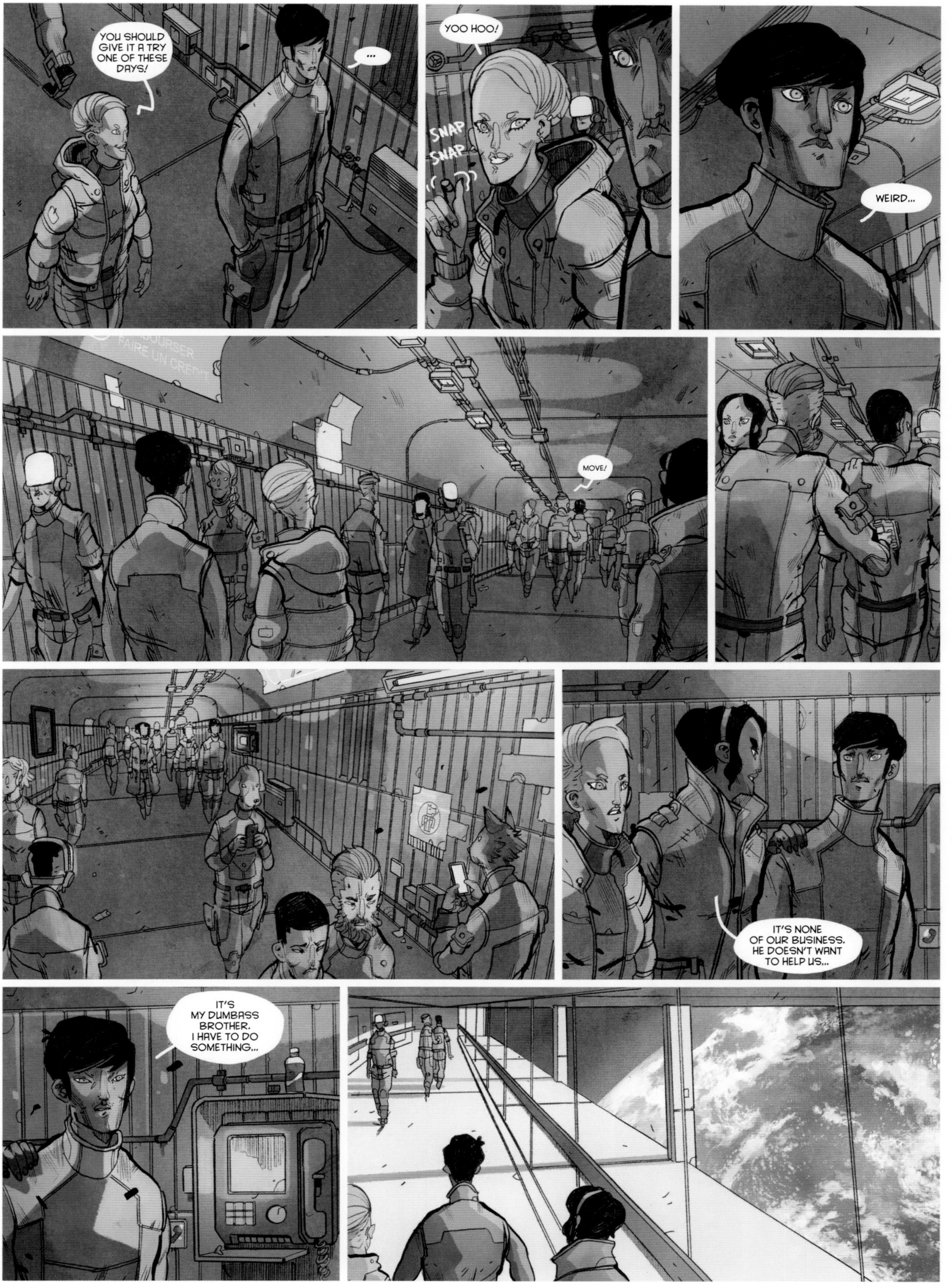
YOU SHOULD GIVE IT A TRY ONE OF THESE DAYS!
...
YOO HOO!
SNAP
SNAP
WEIRD...
MOVE!
IT'S NONE OF OUR BUSINESS. HE DOESN'T WANT TO HELP US...
IT'S MY DUMBASS BROTHER. I HAVE TO DO SOMETHING...

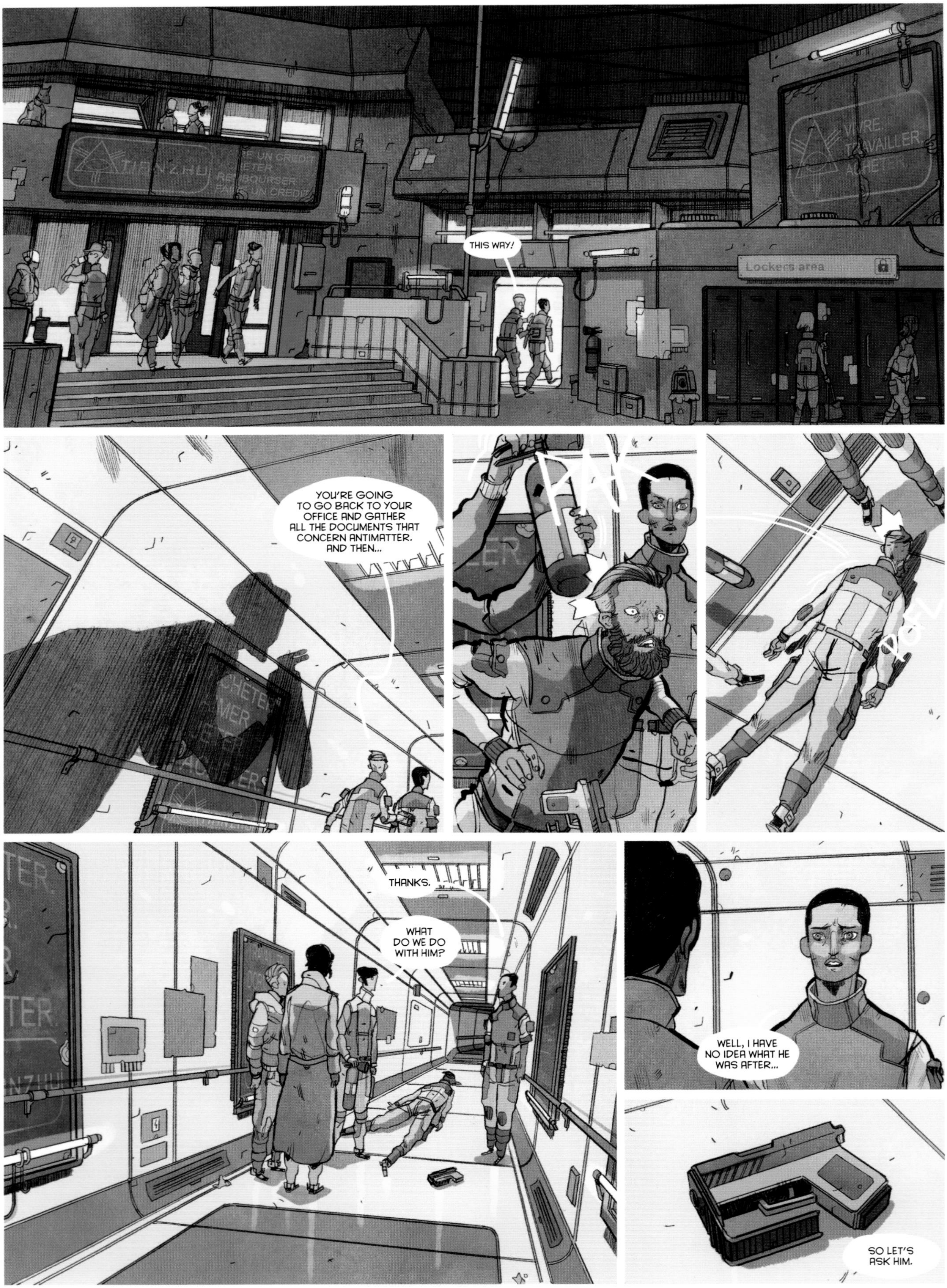
REMBOURSER
VIVRE TRAVAILLER ACHETER
Lockers area
THIS WAY!
YOU'RE GOING TO GO BACK TO YOUR OFFICE AND GATHER ALL THE DOCUMENTS THAT CONCERN ANTIMATTER. AND THEN...
THANKS.
WHAT DO WE DO WITH HIM?
WELL, I HAVE NO IDEA WHAT HE WAS AFTER...
SO LET'S ASK HIM.

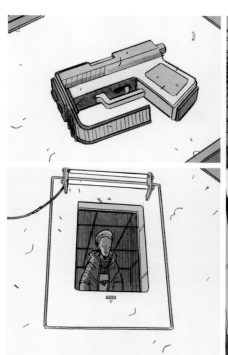

WELL?

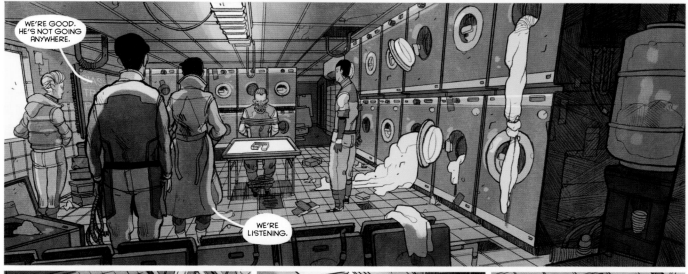

WE'RE GOOD. HE'S NOT GOING ANYWHERE.

WE'RE LISTENING.

I'M NOT A VIOLENT PERSON. IN FACT, I LOATHE VIOLENCE. THIS IS THE FIRST TIME I'VE EVER HELD A WEAPON.

IT'S ALL HIS FAULT!

HUH?

OUR PROJECT IS MUCH TOO IMPORTANT TO ALLOW THIS MAN TO MEDDLE IN OUR AFFAIRS.

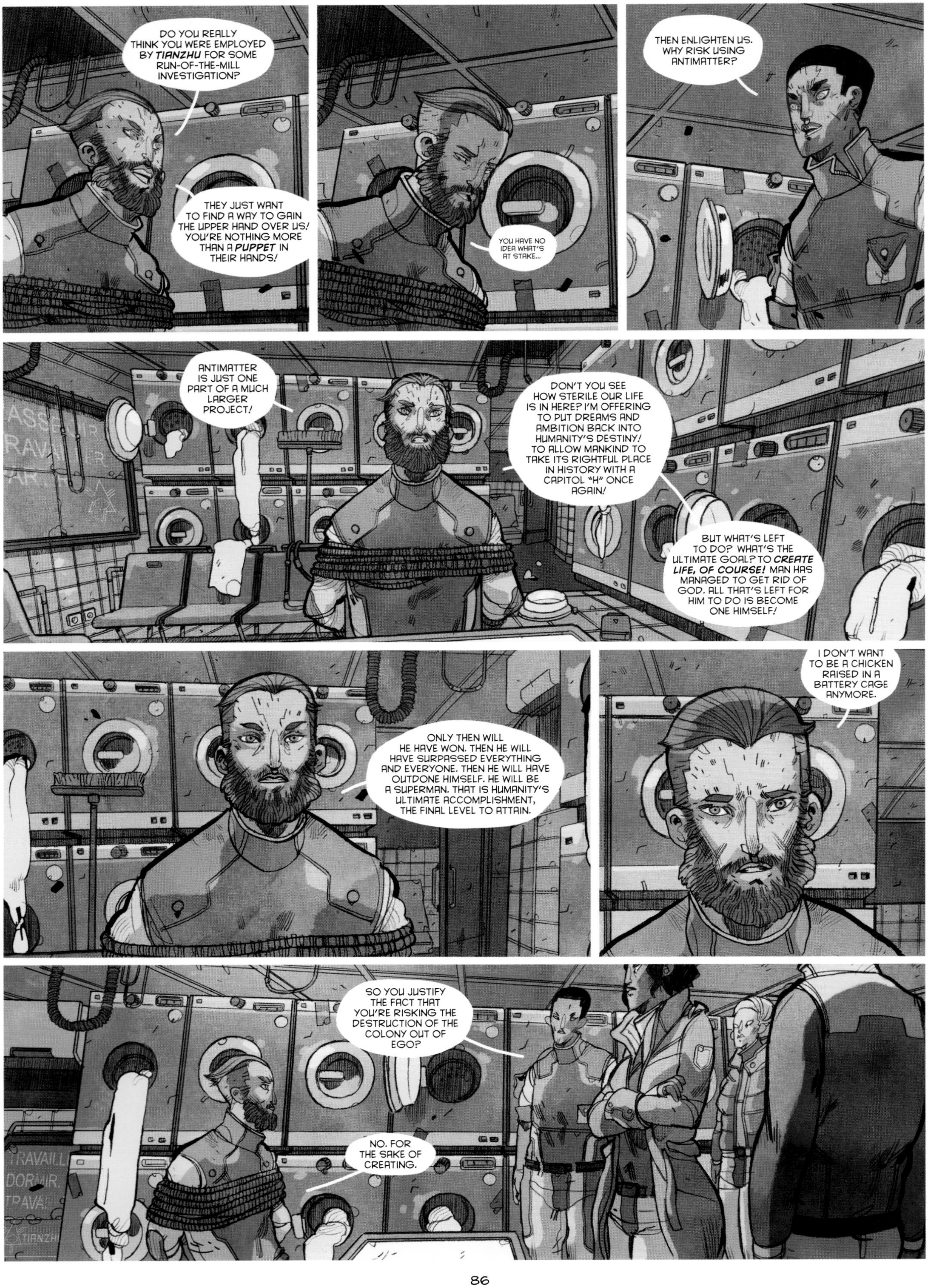
DO YOU REALLY THINK YOU WERE EMPLOYED BY **TIANZHU** FOR SOME RUN-OF-THE-MILL INVESTIGATION?
THEY JUST WANT TO FIND A WAY TO GAIN THE UPPER HAND OVER US! YOU'RE NOTHING MORE THAN A **PUPPET** IN THEIR HANDS!
YOU HAVE NO IDEA WHAT'S AT STAKE...
THEN ENLIGHTEN US. WHY RISK USING ANTIMATTER?
ANTIMATTER IS JUST ONE PART OF A MUCH LARGER PROJECT!
DON'T YOU SEE HOW STERILE OUR LIFE IS IN HERE? I'M OFFERING TO PUT DREAMS AND AMBITION BACK INTO HUMANITY'S DESTINY! TO ALLOW MANKIND TO TAKE ITS RIGHTFUL PLACE IN HISTORY WITH A CAPITOL "H" ONCE AGAIN!
BUT WHAT'S LEFT TO DO? WHAT'S THE ULTIMATE GOAL? TO **CREATE LIFE, OF COURSE!** MAN HAS MANAGED TO GET RID OF GOD. ALL THAT'S LEFT FOR HIM TO DO IS BECOME ONE HIMSELF!
ONLY THEN WILL HE HAVE WON. THEN HE WILL HAVE SURPASSED EVERYTHING AND EVERYONE. THEN HE WILL HAVE OUTDONE HIMSELF. HE WILL BE A SUPERMAN. THAT IS HUMANITY'S ULTIMATE ACCOMPLISHMENT, THE FINAL LEVEL TO ATTAIN.
I DON'T WANT TO BE A CHICKEN RAISED IN A BATTERY CAGE ANYMORE.
SO YOU JUSTIFY THE FACT THAT YOU'RE RISKING THE DESTRUCTION OF THE COLONY OUT OF EGO?
NO. FOR THE SAKE OF CREATING.

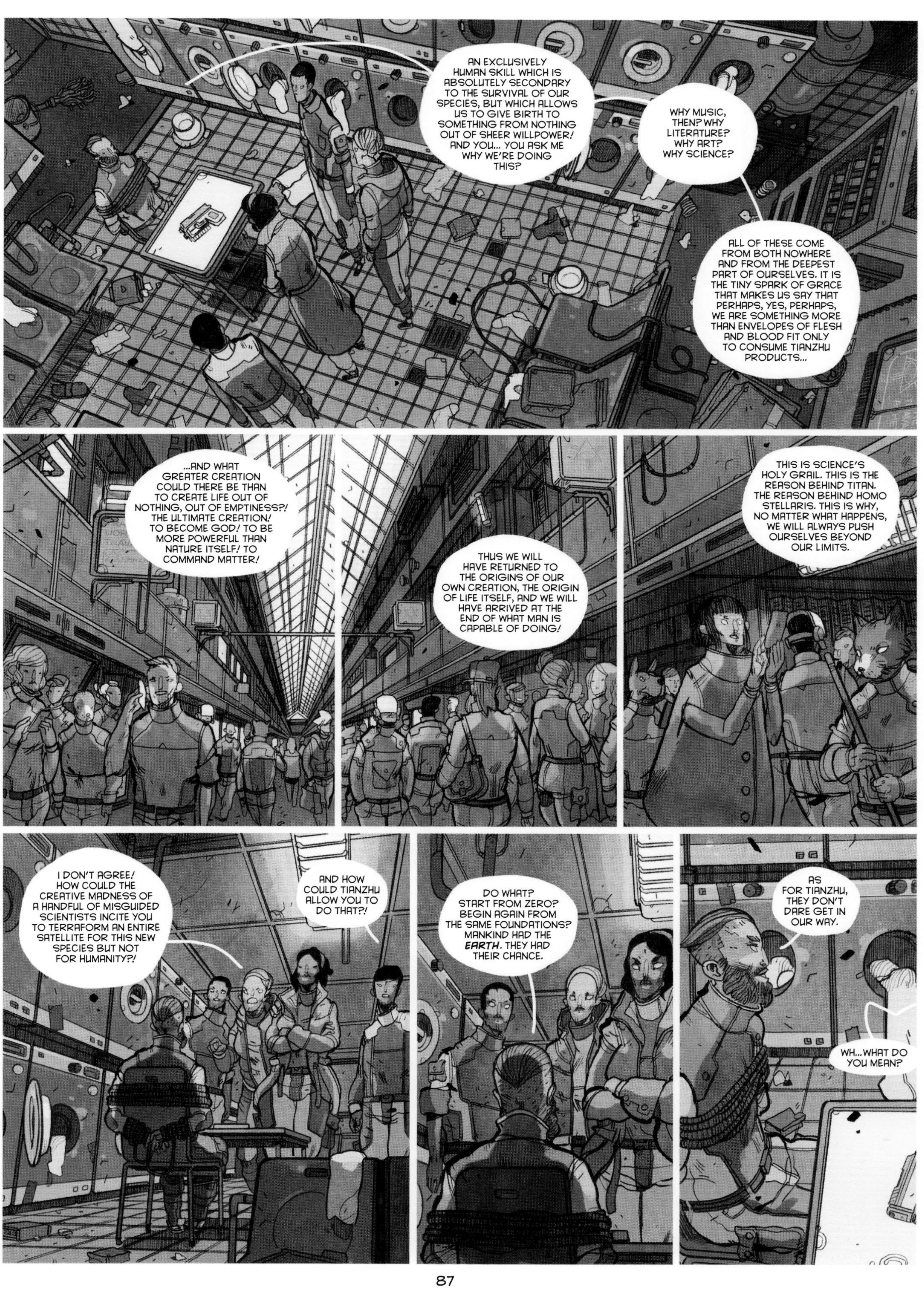

AN EXCLUSIVELY HUMAN SKILL WHICH IS ABSOLUTELY SECONDARY TO THE SURVIVAL OF OUR SPECIES, BUT WHICH ALLOWS US TO GIVE BIRTH TO SOMETHING FROM NOTHING OUT OF SHEER WILLPOWER! AND YOU... YOU ASK ME WHY WE'RE DOING THIS?
WHY MUSIC, THEN? WHY LITERATURE? WHY ART? WHY SCIENCE?
ALL OF THESE COME FROM BOTH NOWHERE AND FROM THE DEEPEST PART OF OURSELVES. IT IS THE TINY SPARK OF GRACE THAT MAKES US SAY THAT PERHAPS, YES, PERHAPS, WE ARE SOMETHING MORE THAN ENVELOPES OF FLESH AND BLOOD FIT ONLY TO CONSUME TIANZHU PRODUCTS...
...AND WHAT GREATER CREATION COULD THERE BE THAN TO CREATE LIFE OUT OF NOTHING, OUT OF EMPTINESS?! THE ULTIMATE CREATION! TO BECOME GOD! TO BE MORE POWERFUL THAN NATURE ITSELF! TO COMMAND MATTER!
THUS WE WILL HAVE RETURNED TO THE ORIGINS OF OUR OWN CREATION, THE ORIGIN OF LIFE ITSELF, AND WE WILL HAVE ARRIVED AT THE END OF WHAT MAN IS CAPABLE OF DOING!
THIS IS SCIENCE'S HOLY GRAIL. THIS IS THE REASON BEHIND TITAN. THE REASON BEHIND HOMO STELLARIS. THIS IS WHY, NO MATTER WHAT HAPPENS, WE WILL ALWAYS PUSH OURSELVES BEYOND OUR LIMITS.
I DON'T AGREE! HOW COULD THE CREATIVE MADNESS OF A HANDFUL OF MISGUIDED SCIENTISTS INCITE YOU TO TERRAFORM AN ENTIRE SATELLITE FOR THIS NEW SPECIES BUT NOT FOR HUMANITY?!
AND HOW COULD TIANZHU ALLOW YOU TO DO THAT?!
DO WHAT? START FROM ZERO? BEGIN AGAIN FROM THE SAME FOUNDATIONS? MANKIND HAD THE **EARTH**. THEY HAD THEIR CHANCE.
AS FOR TIANZHU, THEY DON'T DARE GET IN OUR WAY.
WH...WHAT DO YOU MEAN?

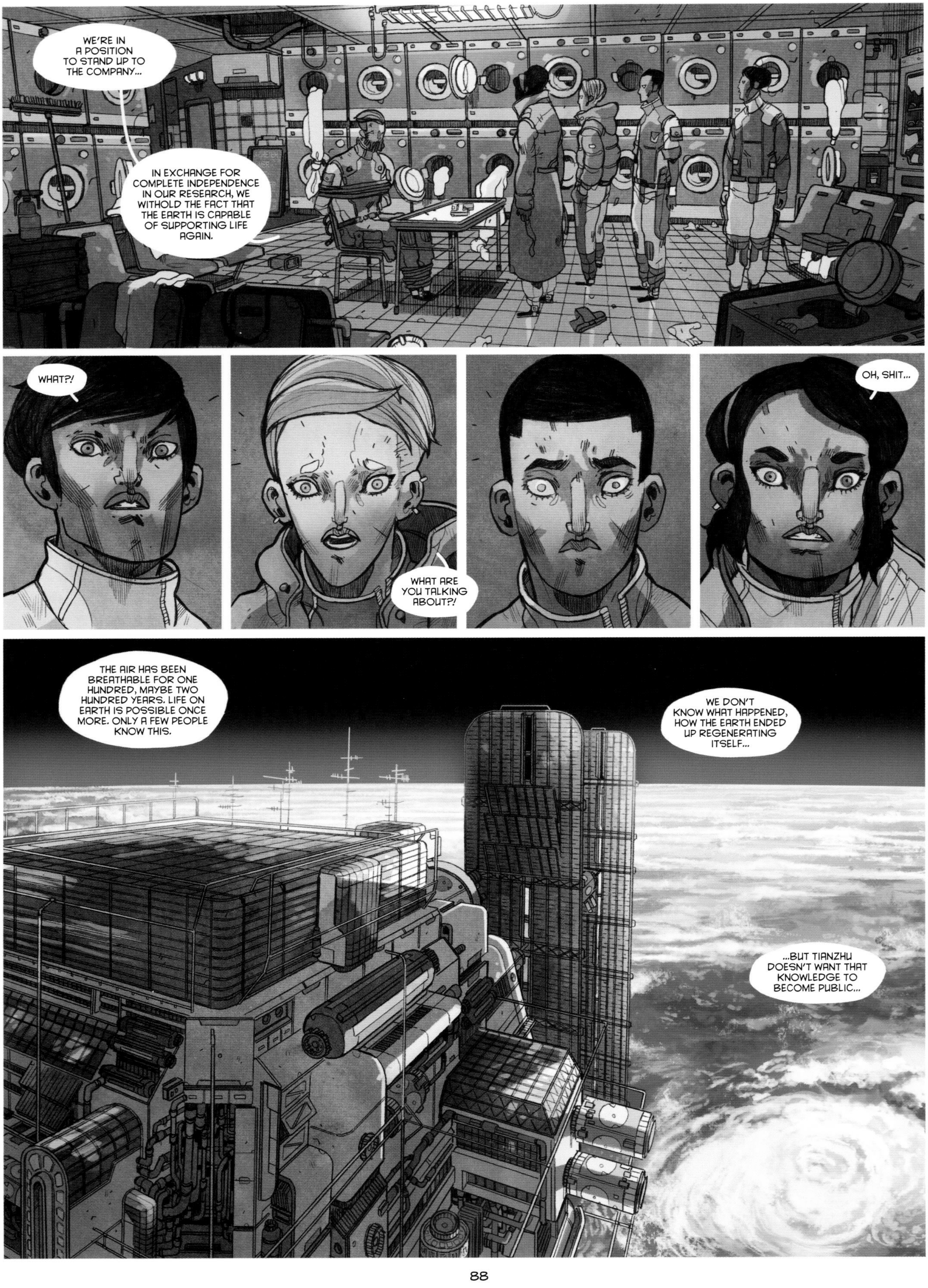
WE'RE IN A POSITION TO STAND UP TO THE COMPANY...
IN EXCHANGE FOR COMPLETE INDEPENDENCE IN OUR RESEARCH, WE WITHOLD THE FACT THAT THE EARTH IS CAPABLE OF SUPPORTING LIFE AGAIN.
WHAT?!
WHAT ARE YOU TALKING ABOUT?!
OH, SHIT...
THE AIR HAS BEEN BREATHABLE FOR ONE HUNDRED, MAYBE TWO HUNDRED YEARS. LIFE ON EARTH IS POSSIBLE ONCE MORE. ONLY A FEW PEOPLE KNOW THIS.
WE DON'T KNOW WHAT HAPPENED, HOW THE EARTH ENDED UP REGENERATING ITSELF...
...BUT TIANZHU DOESN'T WANT THAT KNOWLEDGE TO BECOME PUBLIC...

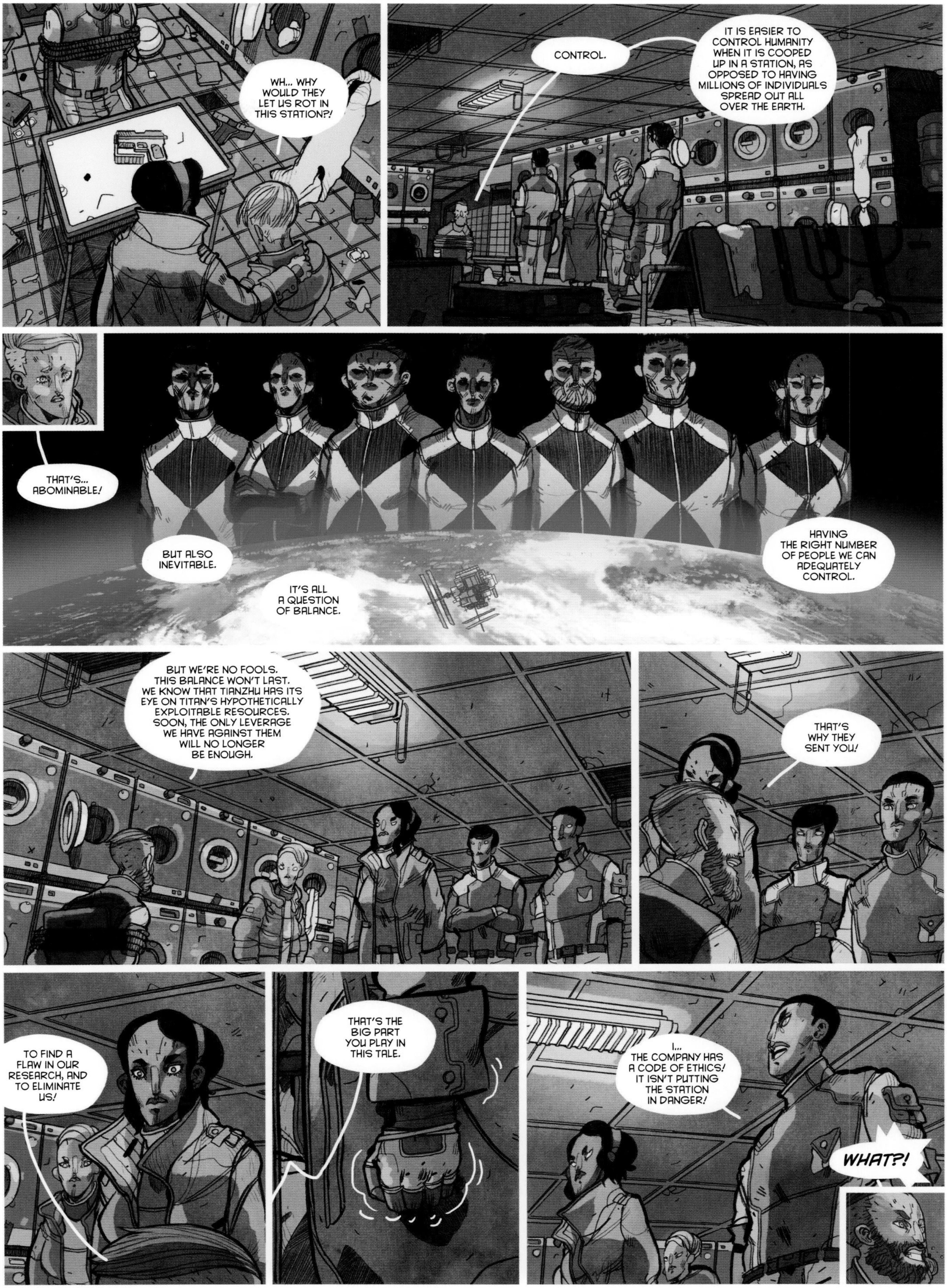
WH... WHY WOULD THEY LET US ROT IN THIS STATION?!
CONTROL.
IT IS EASIER TO CONTROL HUMANITY WHEN IT IS COOPED UP IN A STATION, AS OPPOSED TO HAVING MILLIONS OF INDIVIDUALS SPREAD OUT ALL OVER THE EARTH.
THAT'S... ABOMINABLE!
BUT ALSO INEVITABLE.
IT'S ALL A QUESTION OF BALANCE.
HAVING THE RIGHT NUMBER OF PEOPLE WE CAN ADEQUATELY CONTROL.
BUT WE'RE NO FOOLS. THIS BALANCE WON'T LAST. WE KNOW THAT TIANZHU HAS ITS EYE ON TITAN'S HYPOTHETICALLY EXPLOITABLE RESOURCES. SOON, THE ONLY LEVERAGE WE HAVE AGAINST THEM WILL NO LONGER BE ENOUGH.
THAT'S WHY THEY SENT YOU!
TO FIND A FLAW IN OUR RESEARCH, AND TO ELIMINATE US!
THAT'S THE BIG PART YOU PLAY IN THIS TALE.
I... THE COMPANY HAS A CODE OF ETHICS! IT ISN'T PUTTING THE STATION IN DANGER!
WHAT?!

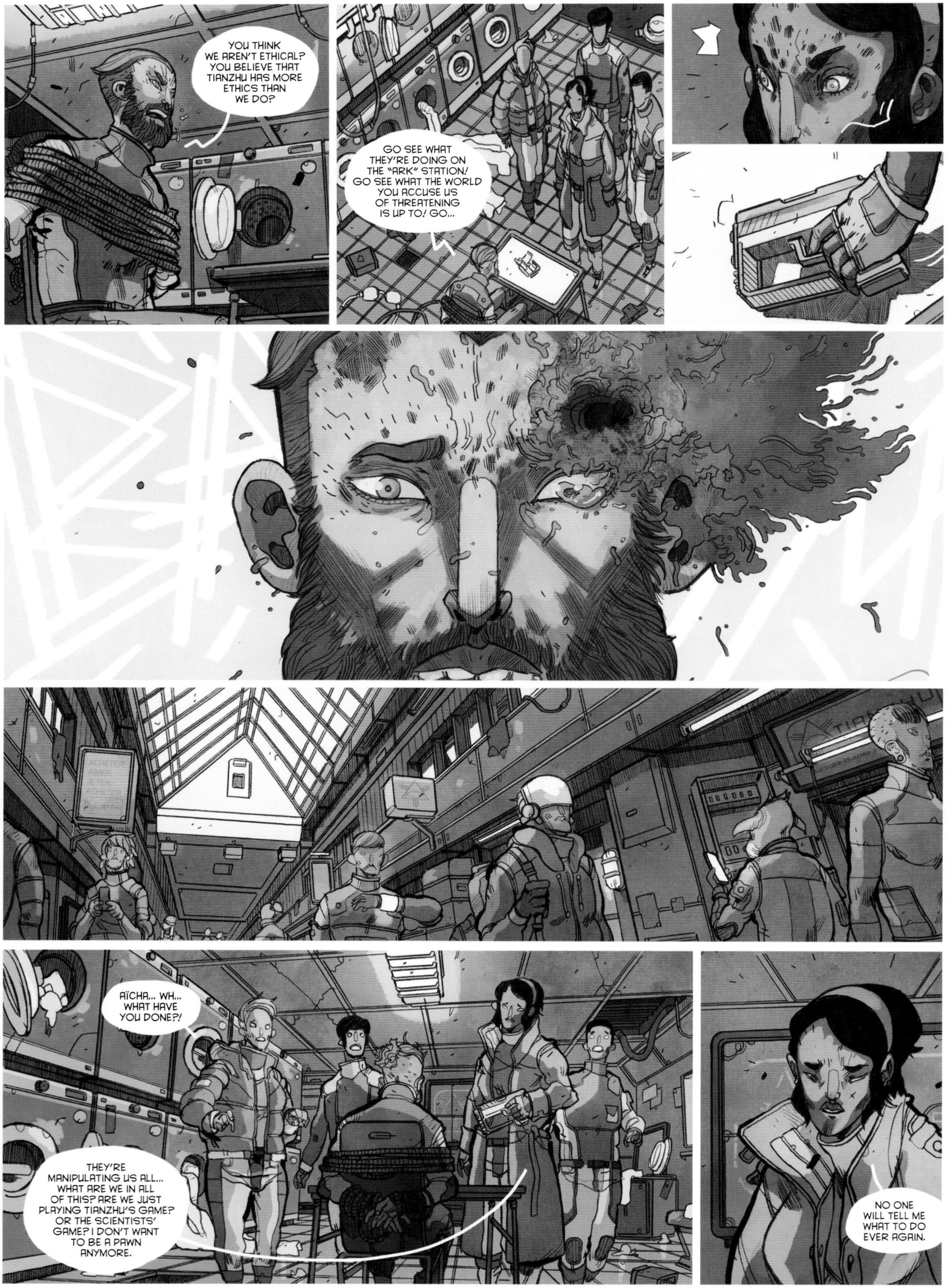

YOU THINK WE AREN'T ETHICAL? YOU BELIEVE THAT TIANZHU HAS MORE ETHICS THAN WE DO?
GO SEE WHAT THEY'RE DOING ON THE "ARK" STATION! GO SEE WHAT THE WORLD YOU ACCUSE US OF THREATENING IS UP TO! GO...
AÏCHA... WH... WHAT HAVE YOU DONE?!
THEY'RE MANIPULATING US ALL... WHAT ARE WE IN ALL OF THIS? ARE WE JUST PLAYING TIANZHU'S GAME? OR THE SCIENTISTS' GAME? I DON'T WANT TO BE A PAWN ANYMORE.
NO ONE WILL TELL ME WHAT TO DO EVER AGAIN.

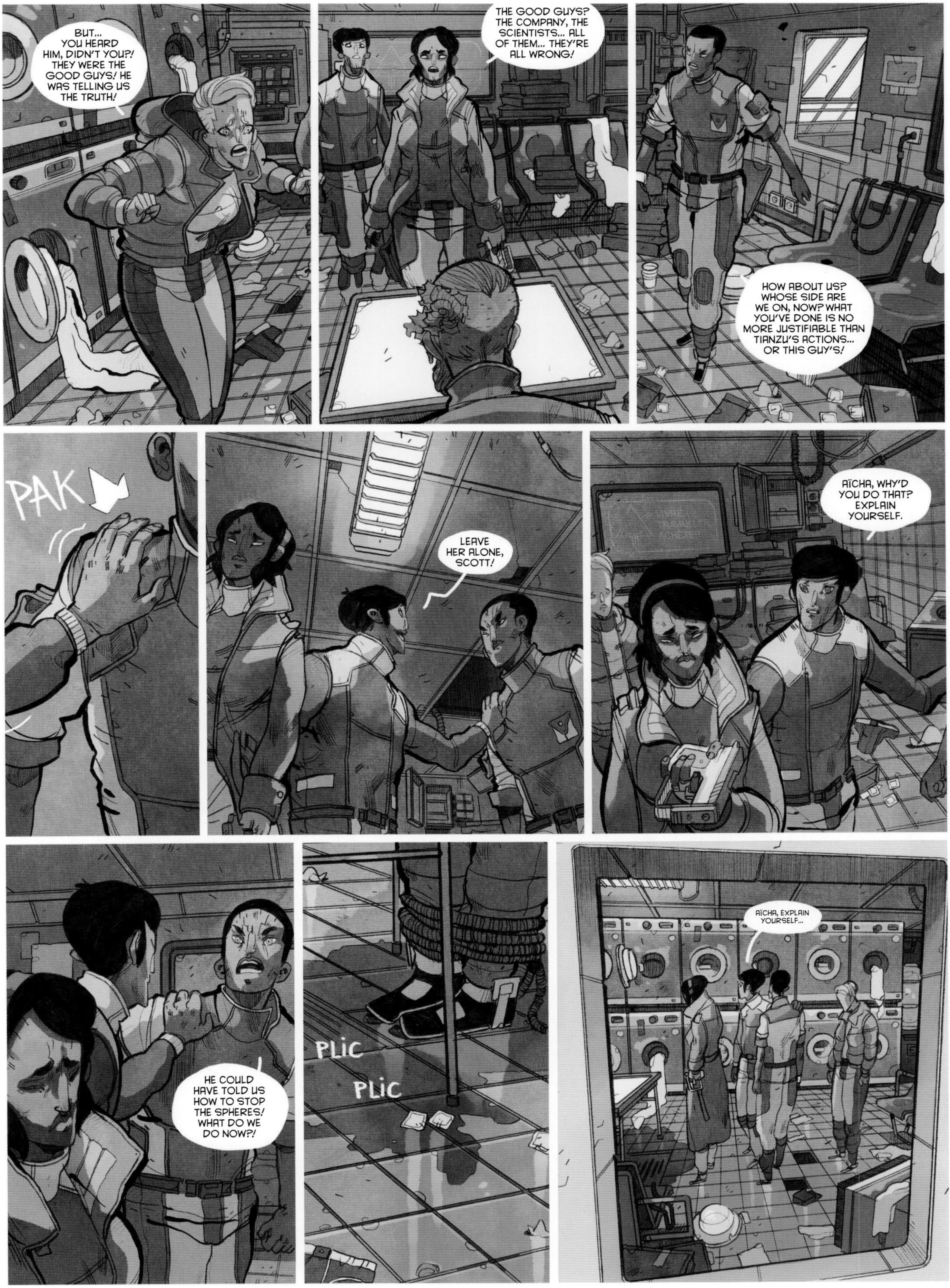
BUT... YOU HEARD HIM, DIDN'T YOU?! THEY WERE THE GOOD GUYS! HE WAS TELLING US THE TRUTH!
THE GOOD GUYS? THE COMPANY, THE SCIENTISTS... ALL OF THEM... THEY'RE ALL WRONG!
HOW ABOUT US? WHOSE SIDE ARE WE ON, NOW? WHAT YOU'VE DONE IS NO MORE JUSTIFIABLE THAN TIANZU'S ACTIONS... OR THIS GUY'S!
PAK
LEAVE HER ALONE, SCOTT!
AÏCHA, WHY'D YOU DO THAT? EXPLAIN YOURSELF.
HE COULD HAVE TOLD US HOW TO STOP THE SPHERES! WHAT DO WE DO NOW?!
PLIC
PLIC
AÏCHA, EXPLAIN YOURSELF...

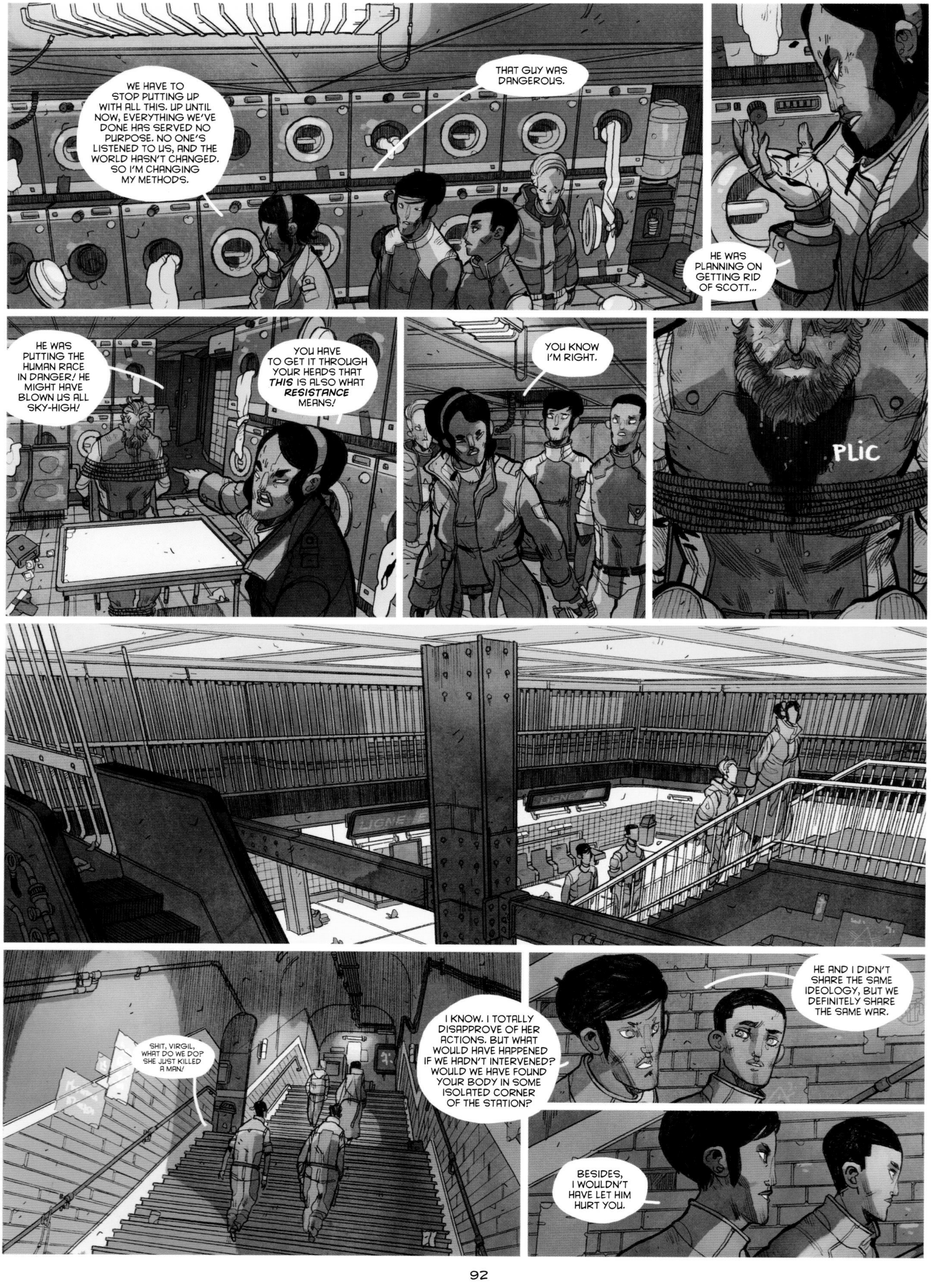
WE HAVE TO STOP PUTTING UP WITH ALL THIS. UP UNTIL NOW, EVERYTHING WE'VE DONE HAS SERVED NO PURPOSE. NO ONE'S LISTENED TO US, AND THE WORLD HASN'T CHANGED. SO I'M CHANGING MY METHODS.
THAT GUY WAS DANGEROUS.
HE WAS PLANNING ON GETTING RID OF SCOTT...
HE WAS PUTTING THE HUMAN RACE IN DANGER! HE MIGHT HAVE BLOWN US ALL SKY-HIGH!
YOU HAVE TO GET IT THROUGH YOUR HEADS THAT **THIS** IS ALSO WHAT ***RESISTANCE*** MEANS!
YOU KNOW I'M RIGHT.
PLIC
SHIT, VIRGIL, WHAT DO WE DO? SHE JUST KILLED A MAN!
I KNOW. I TOTALLY DISAPPROVE OF HER ACTIONS. BUT WHAT WOULD HAVE HAPPENED IF WE HADN'T INTERVENED? WOULD WE HAVE FOUND YOUR BODY IN SOME ISOLATED CORNER OF THE STATION?
HE AND I DIDN'T SHARE THE SAME IDEOLOGY, BUT WE DEFINITELY SHARE THE SAME WAR.
BESIDES, I WOULDN'T HAVE LET HIM HURT YOU.

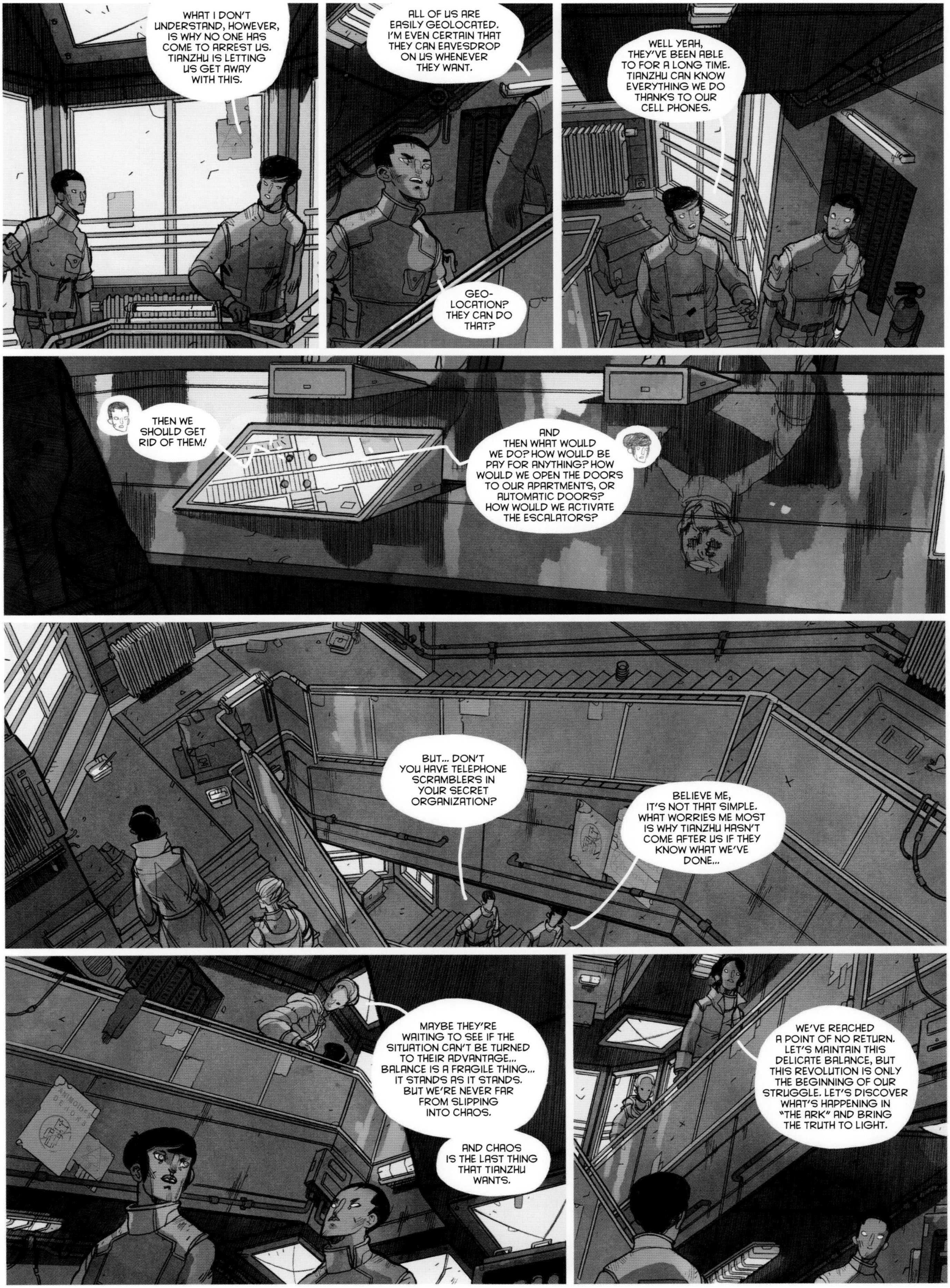
WHAT I DON'T UNDERSTAND, HOWEVER, IS WHY NO ONE HAS COME TO ARREST US. TIANZHU IS LETTING US GET AWAY WITH THIS.
ALL OF US ARE EASILY GEOLOCATED. I'M EVEN CERTAIN THAT THEY CAN EAVESDROP ON US WHENEVER THEY WANT.
GEO-LOCATION? THEY CAN DO THAT?
WELL YEAH, THEY'VE BEEN ABLE TO FOR A LONG TIME. TIANZHU CAN KNOW EVERYTHING WE DO THANKS TO OUR CELL PHONES.
THEN WE SHOULD GET RID OF THEM!
AND THEN WHAT WOULD WE DO? HOW WOULD BE PAY FOR ANYTHING? HOW WOULD WE OPEN THE DOORS TO OUR APARTMENTS, OR AUTOMATIC DOORS? HOW WOULD WE ACTIVATE THE ESCALATORS?
BUT... DON'T YOU HAVE TELEPHONE SCRAMBLERS IN YOUR SECRET ORGANIZATION?
BELIEVE ME, IT'S NOT THAT SIMPLE. WHAT WORRIES ME MOST IS WHY TIANZHU HASN'T COME AFTER US IF THEY KNOW WHAT WE'VE DONE...
MAYBE THEY'RE WAITING TO SEE IF THE SITUATION CAN'T BE TURNED TO THEIR ADVANTAGE... BALANCE IS A FRAGILE THING... IT STANDS AS IT STANDS. BUT WE'RE NEVER FAR FROM SLIPPING INTO CHAOS.
AND CHAOS IS THE LAST THING THAT TIANZHU WANTS.
WE'VE REACHED A POINT OF NO RETURN. LET'S MAINTAIN THIS DELICATE BALANCE, BUT THIS REVOLUTION IS ONLY THE BEGINNING OF OUR STRUGGLE. LET'S DISCOVER WHAT'S HAPPENING IN "THE ARK" AND BRING THE TRUTH TO LIGHT.

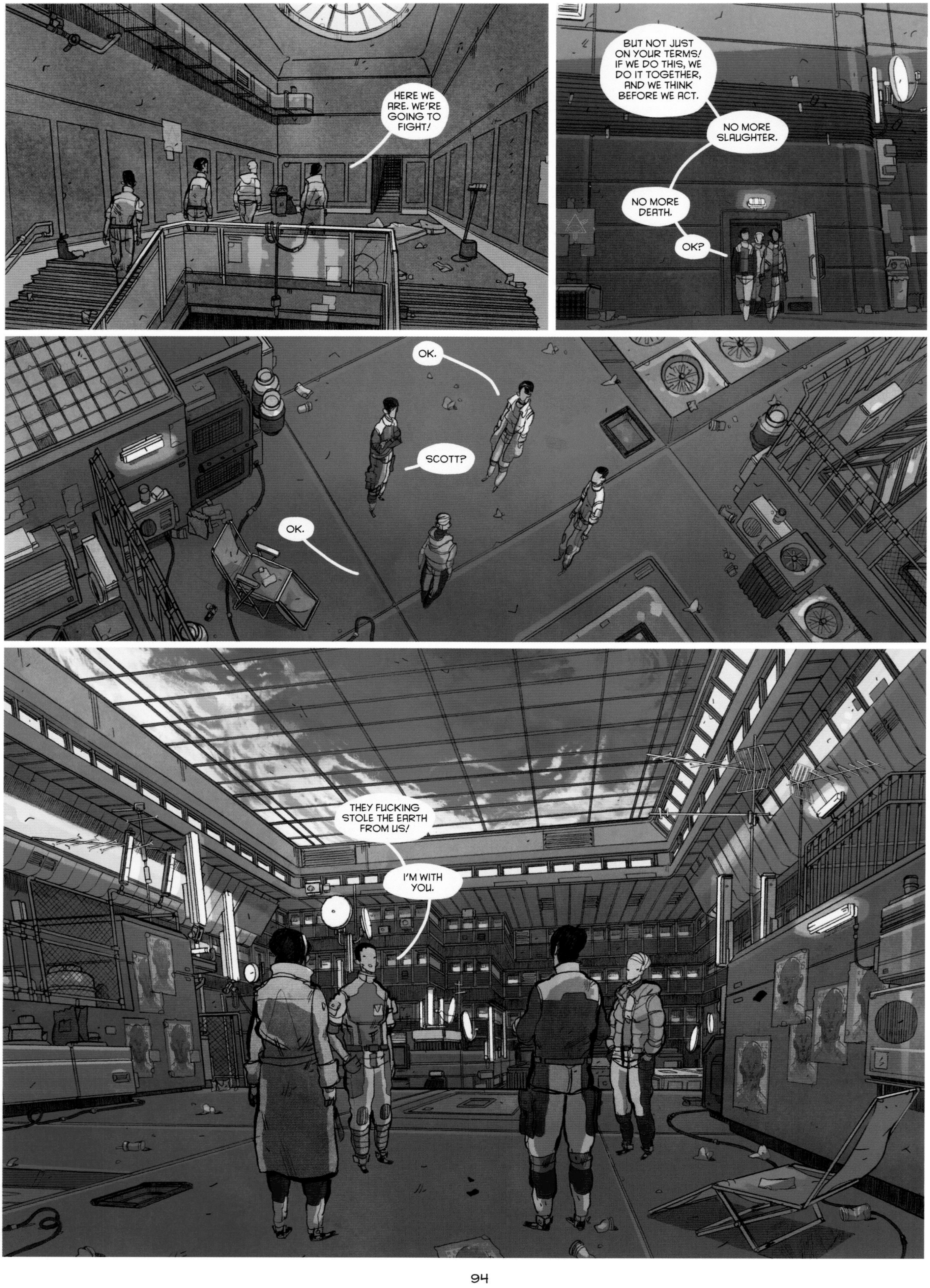
HERE WE ARE. WE'RE GOING TO FIGHT!
BUT NOT JUST ON YOUR TERMS! IF WE DO THIS, WE DO IT TOGETHER, AND WE THINK BEFORE WE ACT.
NO MORE SLAUGHTER.
NO MORE DEATH.
OK?
OK.
SCOTT?
OK.
THEY FUCKING STOLE THE EARTH FROM US!
I'M WITH YOU.

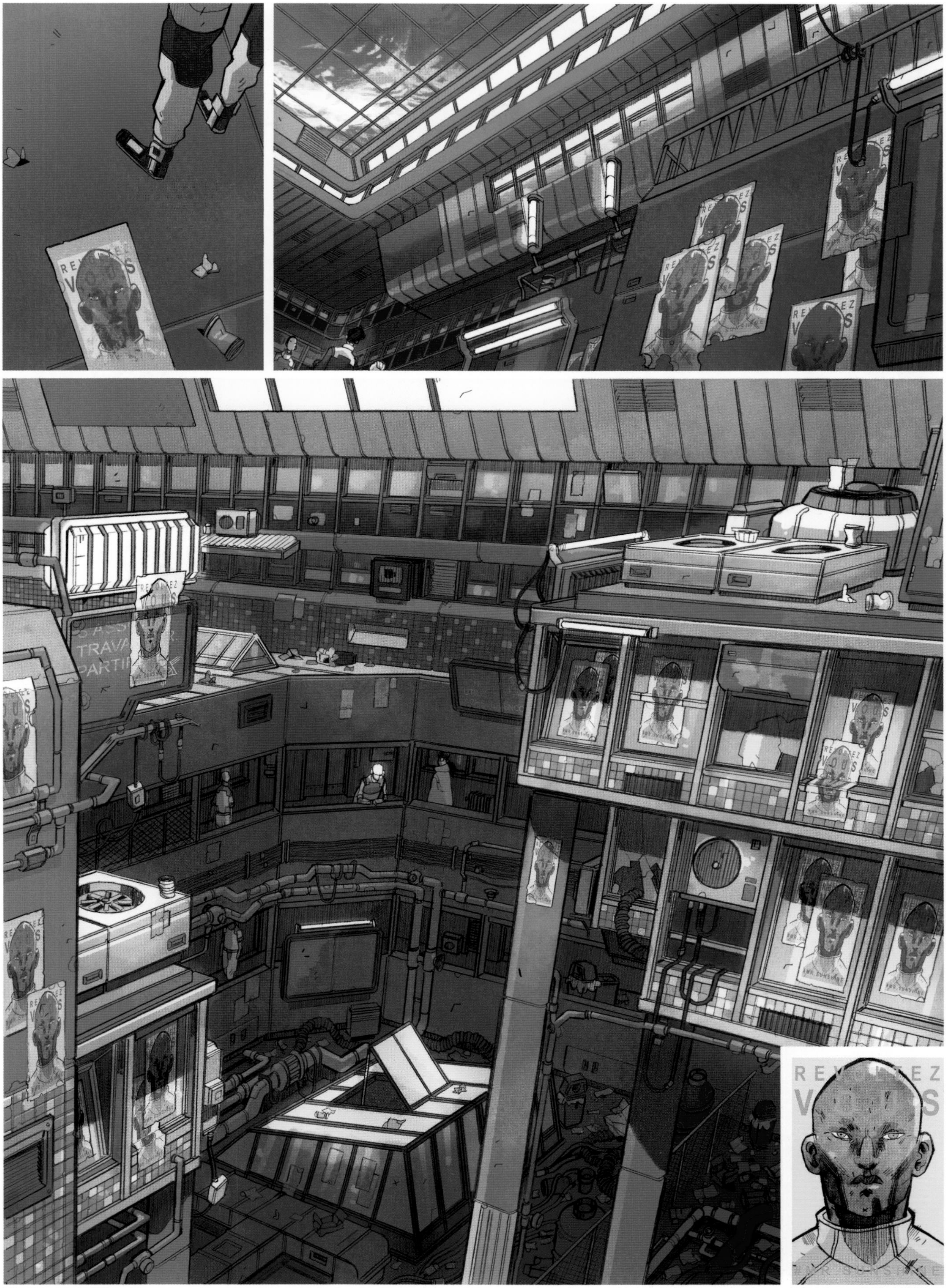
REVOLTEZ
VOUS
MR. SUNSHINE

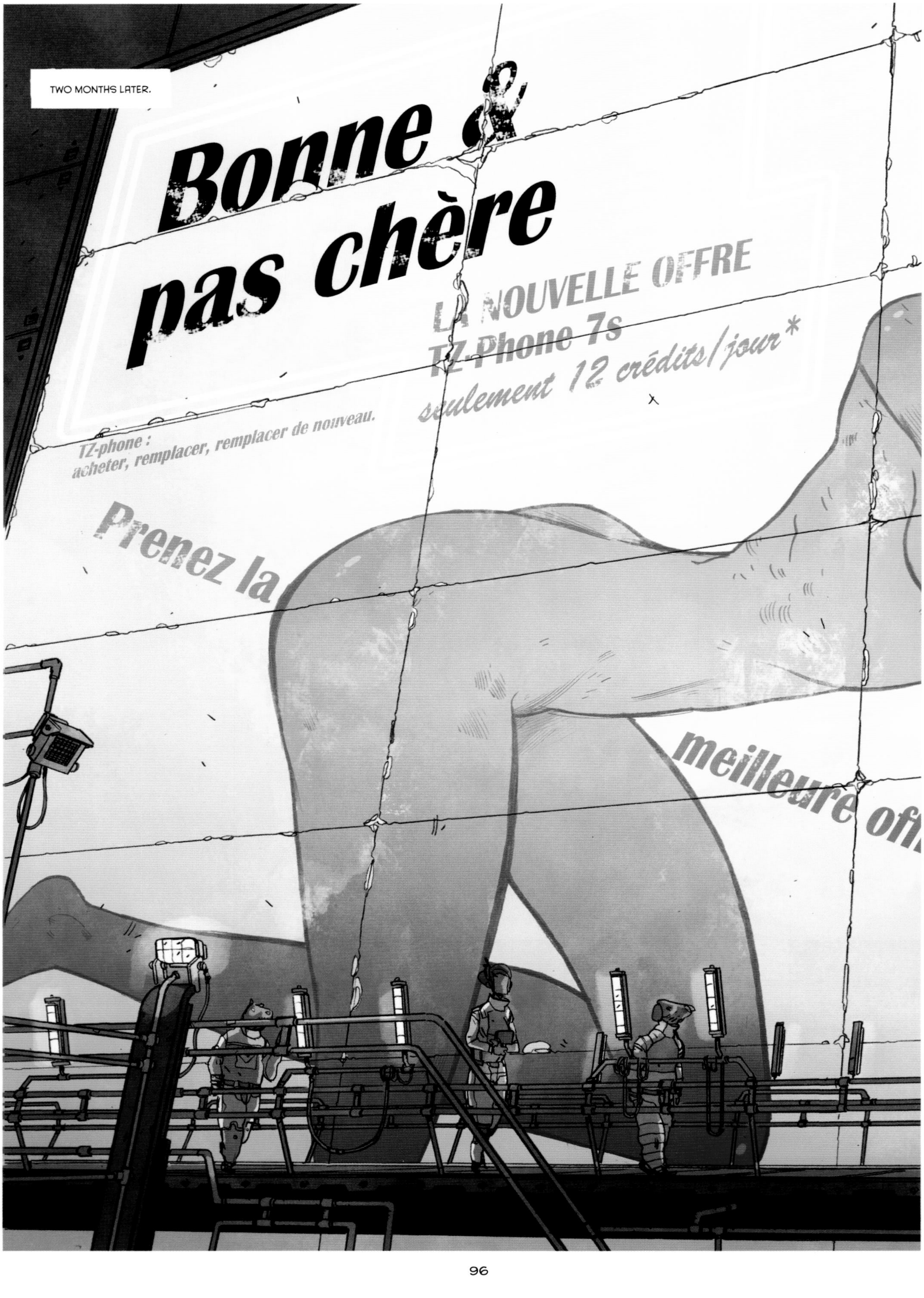
TWO MONTHS LATER.
Bonne &
pas chère
LA NOUVELLE OFFRE
TZ-Phone 7s
seulement 12 crédits/jour*
TZ-phone :
acheter, remplacer, remplacer de nouveau.
Prenez la
meilleure off

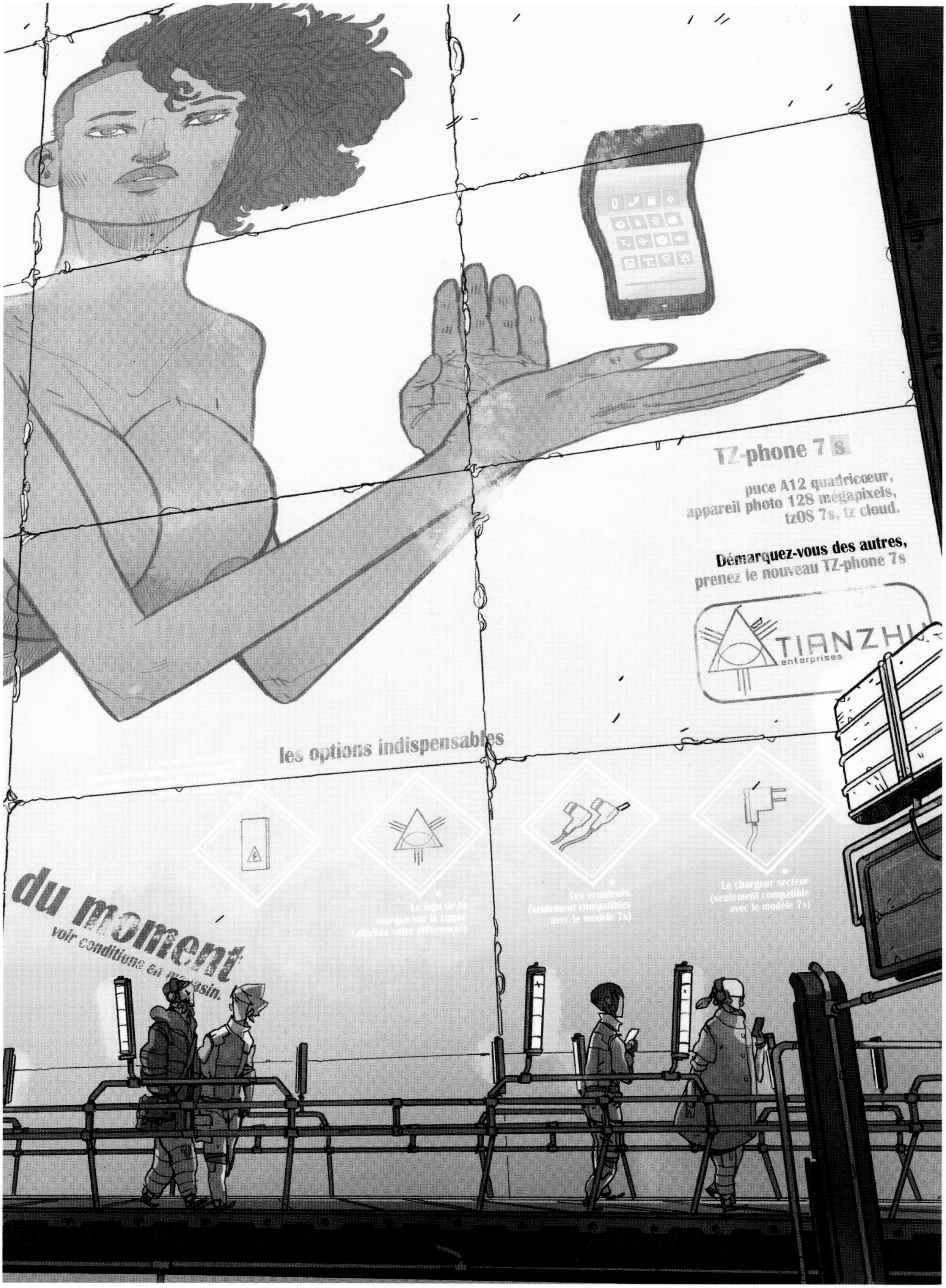
TZ-phone 7 s
puce A12 quadricoeur,
appareil photo 128 mégapixels,
tzOS 7s, tz cloud.
Démarquez-vous des autres,
prenez le nouveau TZ-phone 7s
TIANZHU enterprises
les options indispensables
Le logo de la marque sur la coque (affichez votre différence!)
Les écouteurs (seulement compatibles avec le modèle 7s)
Le chargeur secteur (seulement compatible avec le modèle 7s)
du moment
voir conditions en magasin.

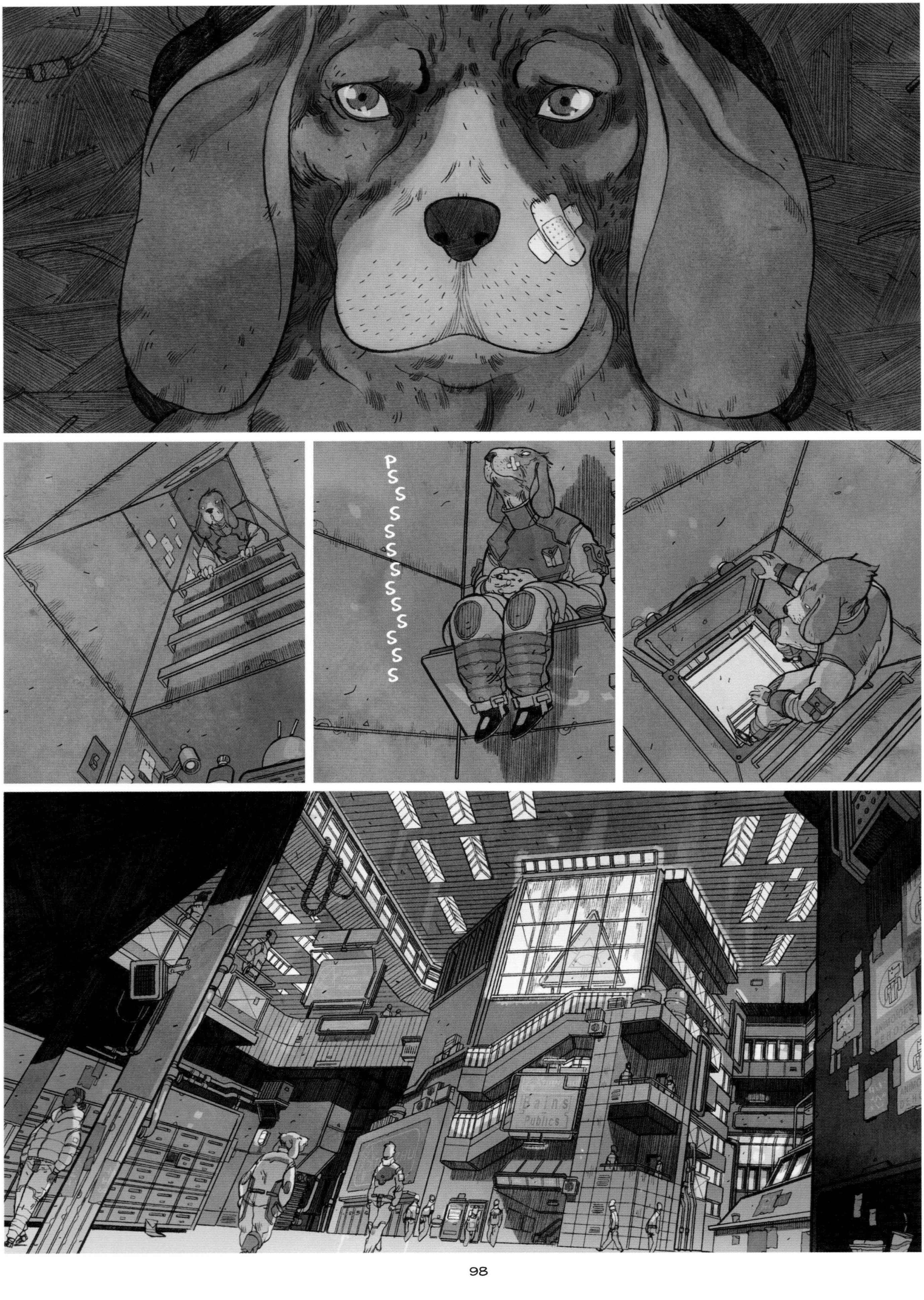
PSSSSSSSSSSSS
Bains
Publics
ANIMOÏDES
DEHORS

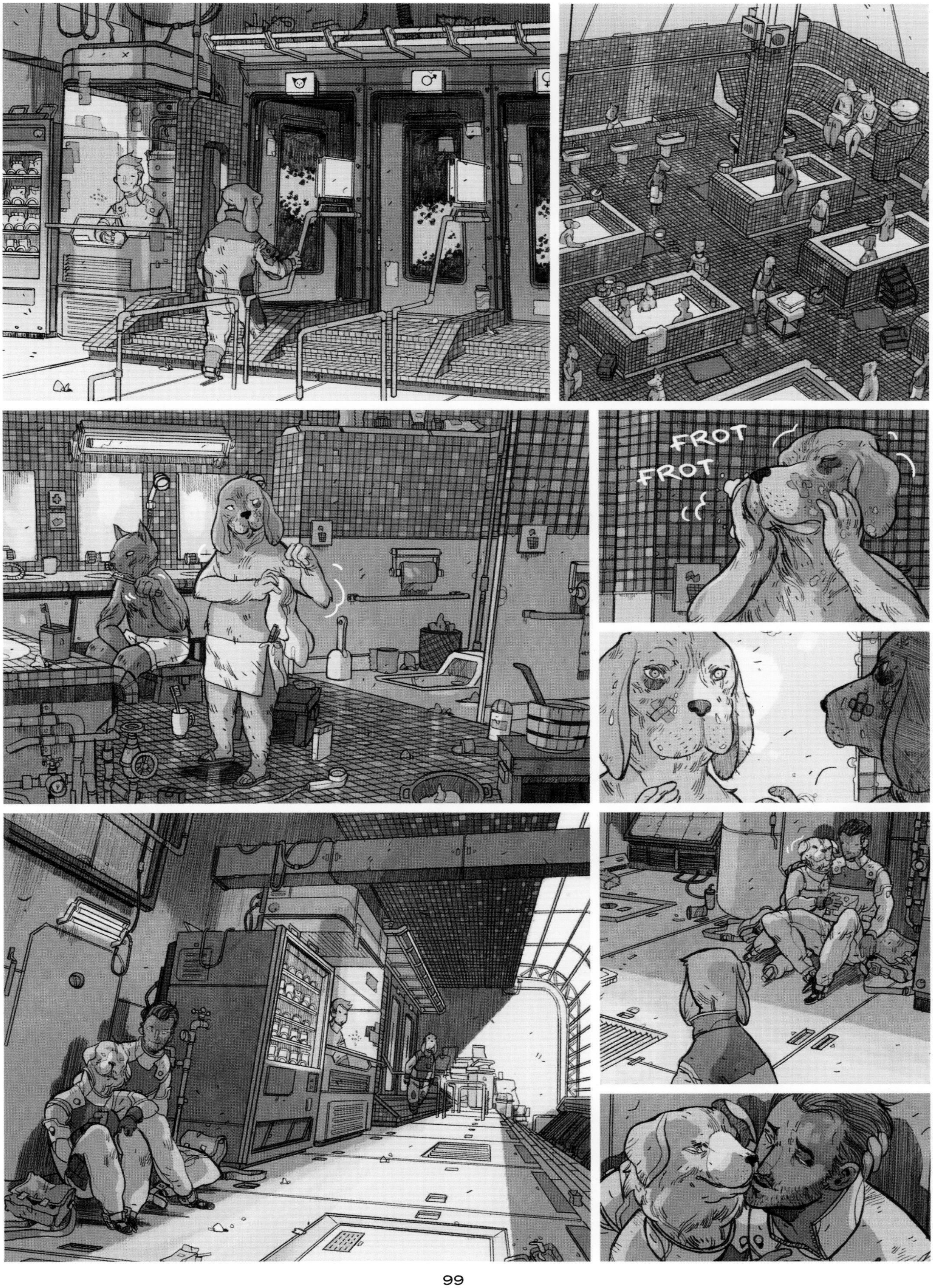
FROT
FROT

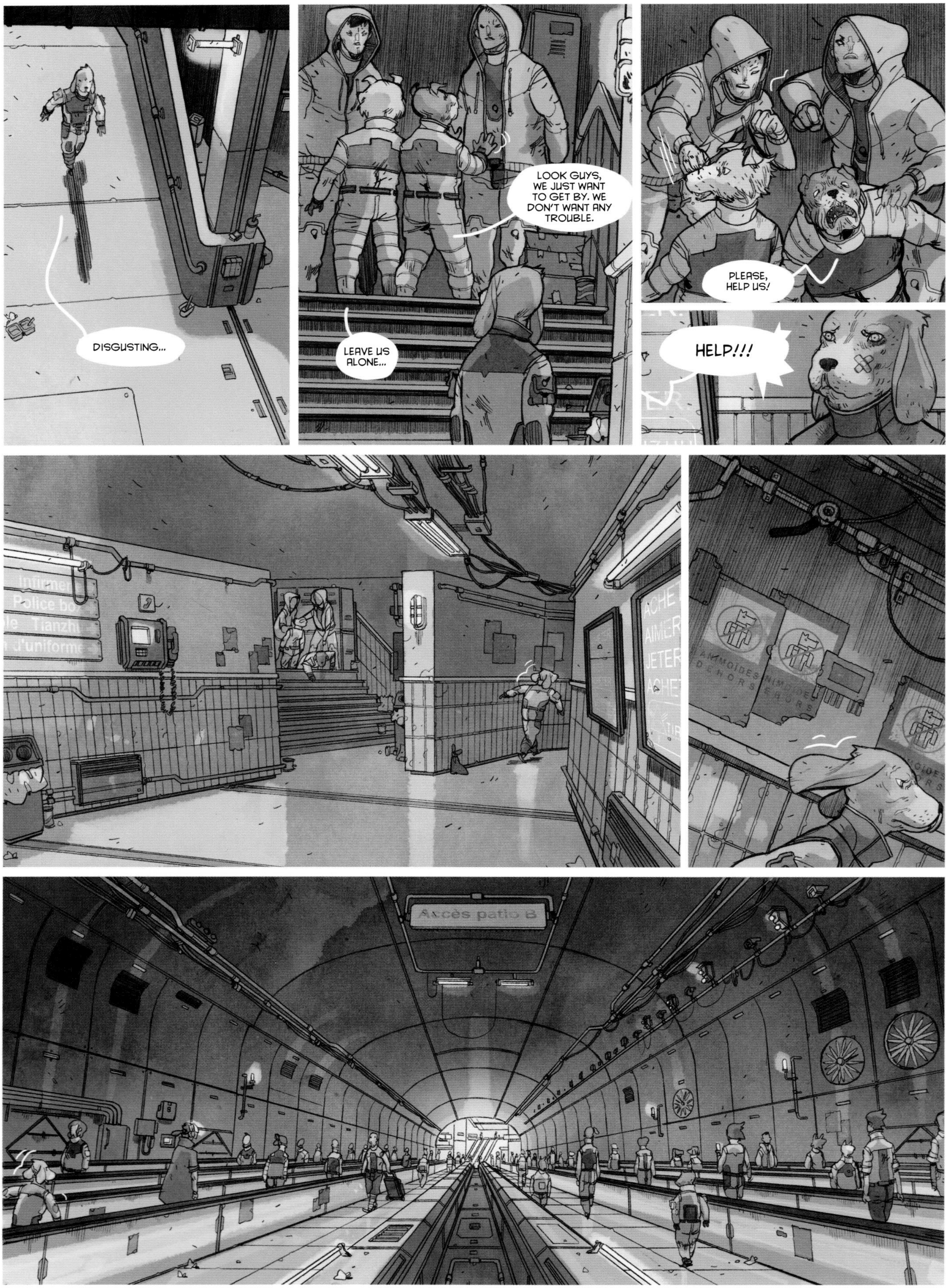
DISGUSTING...
LOOK GUYS, WE JUST WANT TO GET BY. WE DON'T WANT ANY TROUBLE.
LEAVE US ALONE...
PLEASE, HELP US!
HELP!!!
Accès patio B

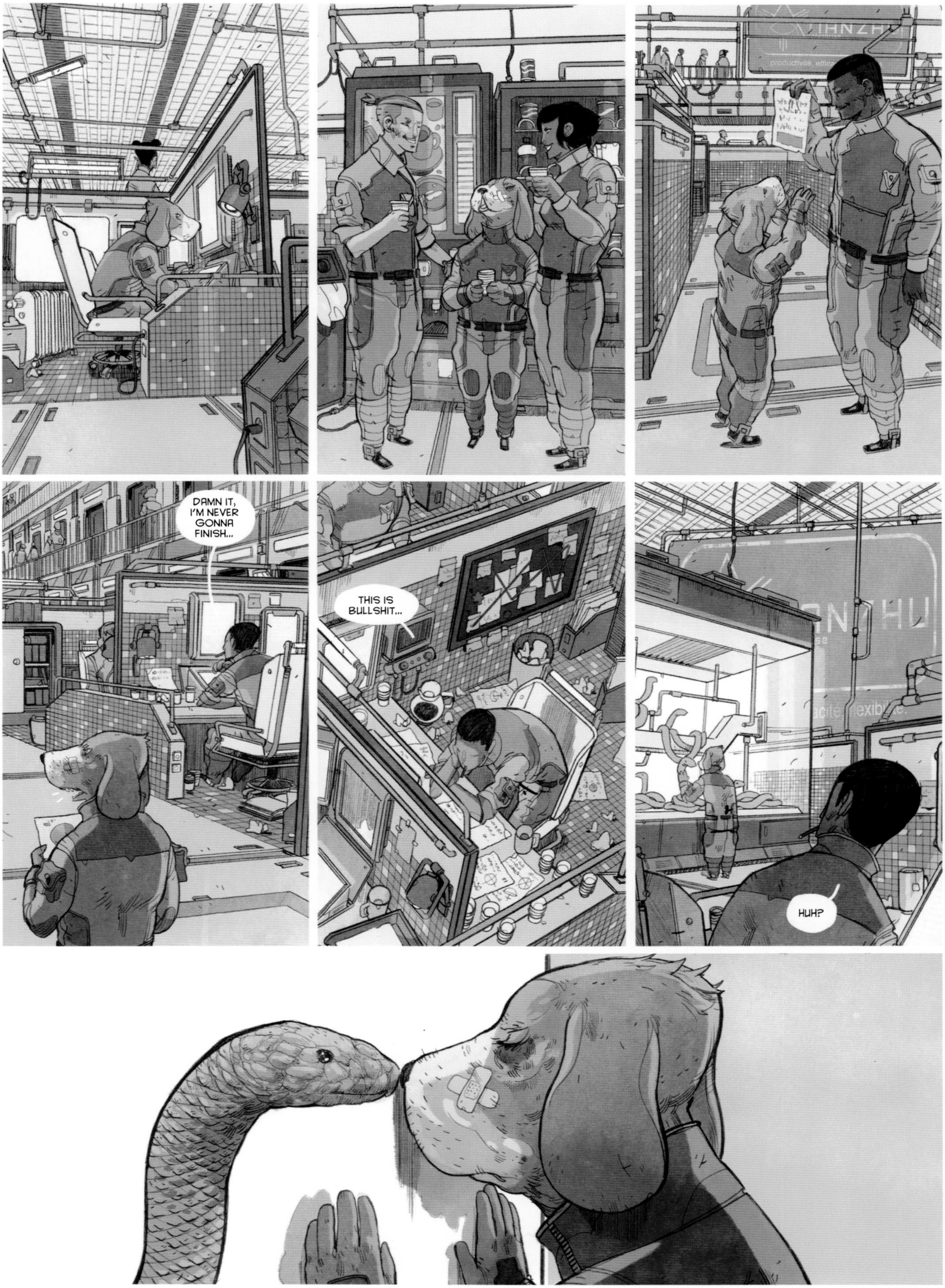
productivité, effic
DAMN IT, I'M NEVER GONNA FINISH...
THIS IS BULLSHIT...
HUH?

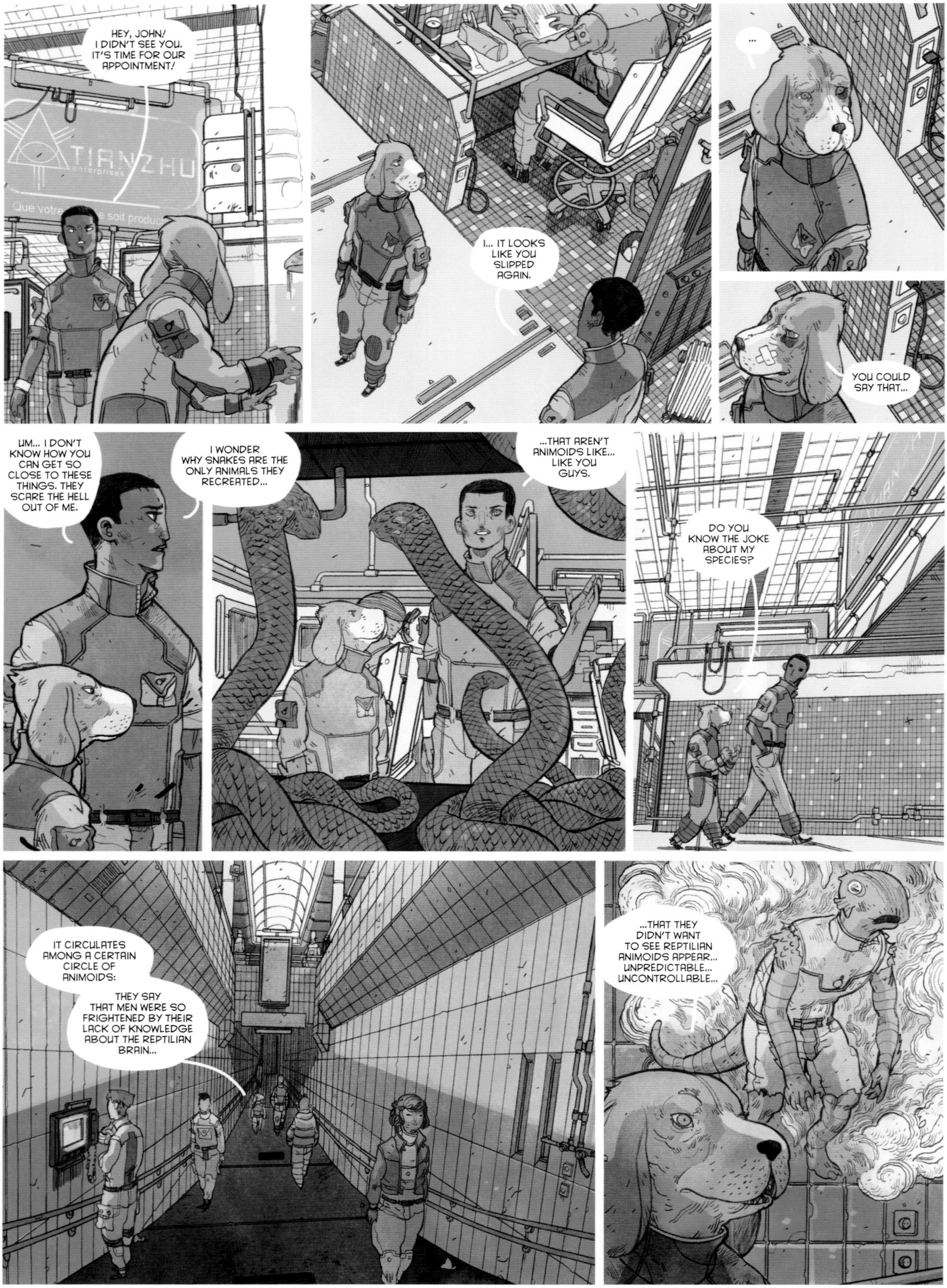
HEY, JOHN! I DIDN'T SEE YOU. IT'S TIME FOR OUR APPOINTMENT!
TIANZHU
enterprises
I... IT LOOKS LIKE YOU SLIPPED AGAIN.
...
YOU COULD SAY THAT...
UM... I DON'T KNOW HOW YOU CAN GET SO CLOSE TO THESE THINGS. THEY SCARE THE HELL OUT OF ME.
I WONDER WHY SNAKES ARE THE ONLY ANIMALS THEY RECREATED...
...THAT AREN'T ANIMOIDS LIKE... LIKE YOU GUYS.
DO YOU KNOW THE JOKE ABOUT MY SPECIES?
IT CIRCULATES AMONG A CERTAIN CIRCLE OF ANIMOIDS:
THEY SAY THAT MEN WERE SO FRIGHTENED BY THEIR LACK OF KNOWLEDGE ABOUT THE REPTILIAN BRAIN...
...THAT THEY DIDN'T WANT TO SEE REPTILIAN ANIMOIDS APPEAR... UNPREDICTABLE... UNCONTROLLABLE...

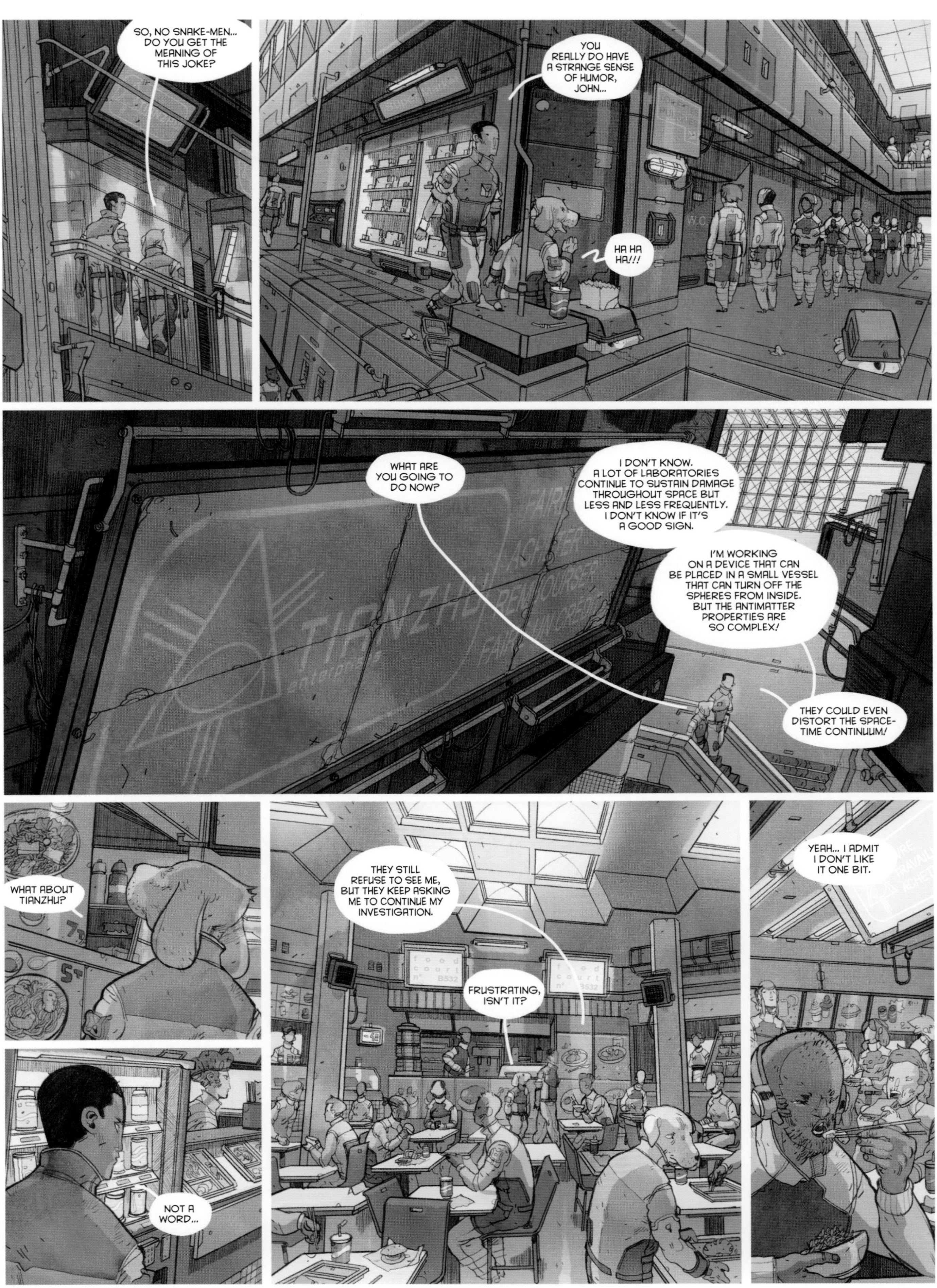

SO, NO SNAKE-MEN... DO YOU GET THE MEANING OF THIS JOKE?
YOU REALLY DO HAVE A STRANGE SENSE OF HUMOR, JOHN...
HA HA HA!!!
WHAT ARE YOU GOING TO DO NOW?
I DON'T KNOW. A LOT OF LABORATORIES CONTINUE TO SUSTAIN DAMAGE THROUGHOUT SPACE BUT LESS AND LESS FREQUENTLY. I DON'T KNOW IF IT'S A GOOD SIGN.
I'M WORKING ON A DEVICE THAT CAN BE PLACED IN A SMALL VESSEL THAT CAN TURN OFF THE SPHERES FROM INSIDE. BUT THE ANTIMATTER PROPERTIES ARE SO COMPLEX!
THEY COULD EVEN DISTORT THE SPACE-TIME CONTINUUM!
TIANZHU enterprises
WHAT ABOUT TIANZHU?
NOT A WORD...
THEY STILL REFUSE TO SEE ME, BUT THEY KEEP ASKING ME TO CONTINUE MY INVESTIGATION.
FRUSTRATING, ISN'T IT?
YEAH... I ADMIT I DON'T LIKE IT ONE BIT.

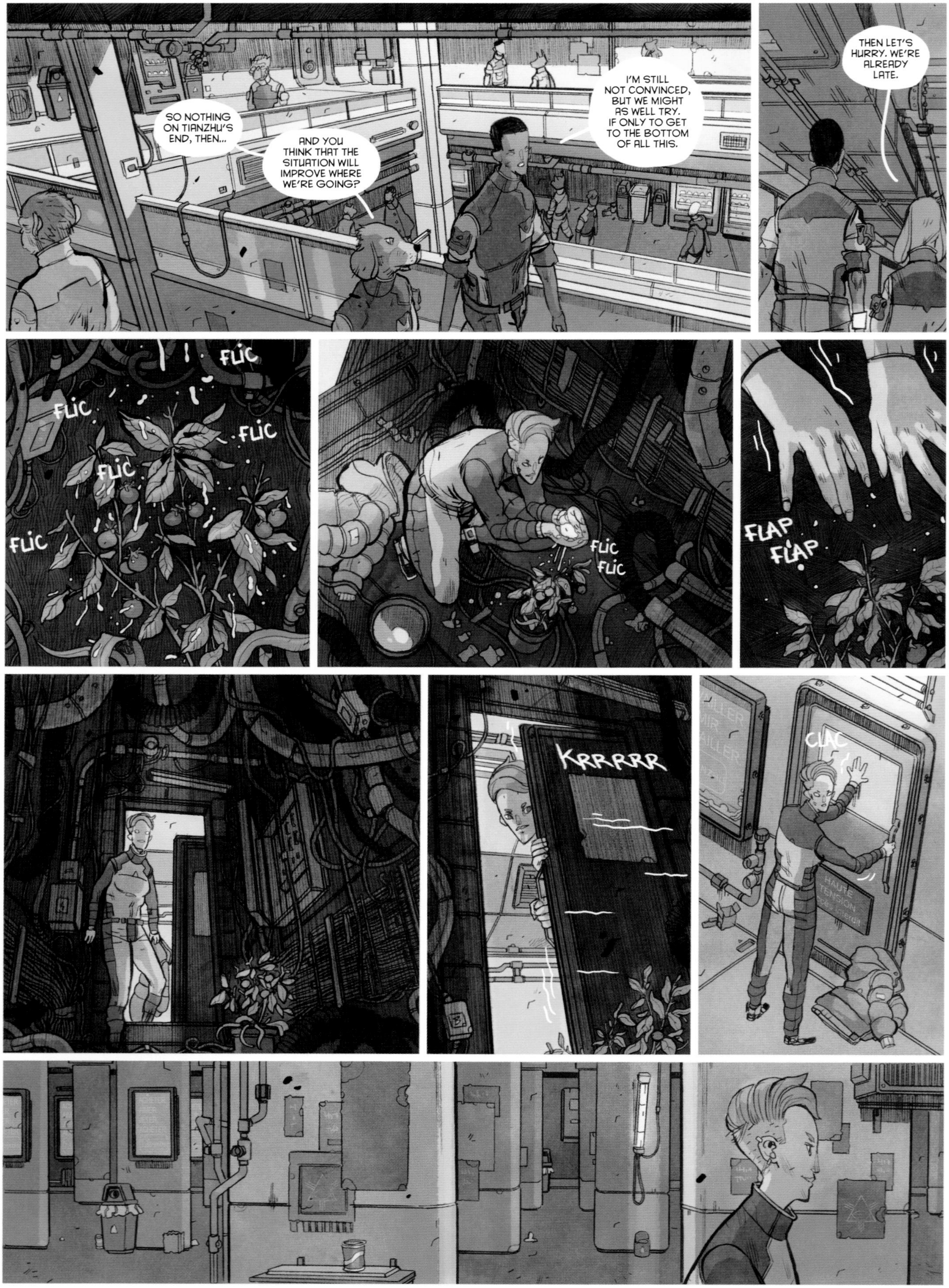

SO NOTHING ON TIANZHU'S END, THEN...
AND YOU THINK THAT THE SITUATION WILL IMPROVE WHERE WE'RE GOING?
I'M STILL NOT CONVINCED, BUT WE MIGHT AS WELL TRY. IF ONLY TO GET TO THE BOTTOM OF ALL THIS.
THEN LET'S HURRY. WE'RE ALREADY LATE.
FLIC
FLIC
FLIC
FLIC
FLIC
FLIC
FLIC
FLAP
FLAP
KRRRRR
CLAC
HAUTE TENSION

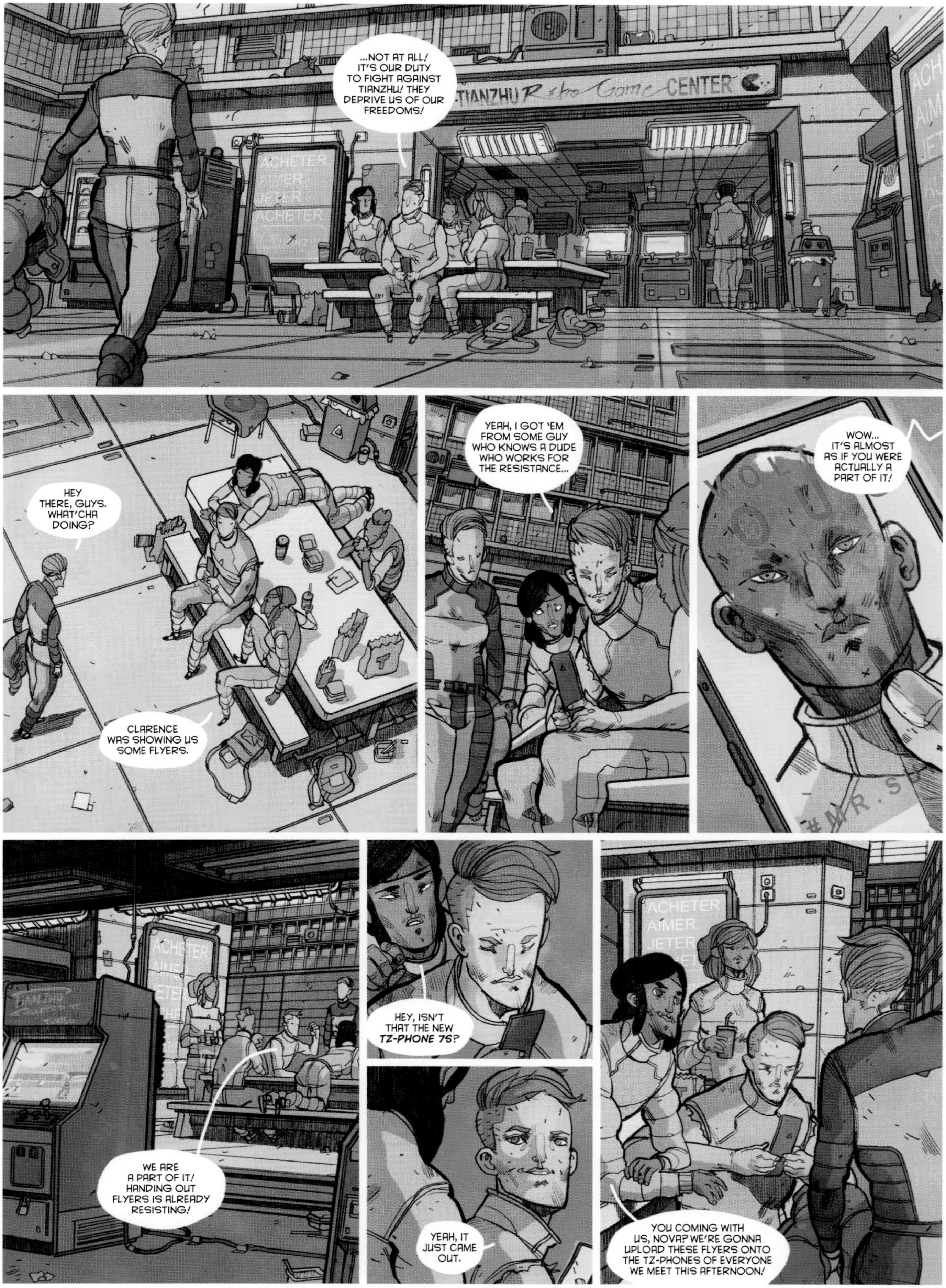
...NOT AT ALL! IT'S OUR DUTY TO FIGHT AGAINST TIANZHU! THEY DEPRIVE US OF OUR FREEDOMS!
TIANZHU Retro Game CENTER
ACHETER. AIMER. JETER. ACHETER.
HEY THERE, GUYS. WHAT'CHA DOING?
CLARENCE WAS SHOWING US SOME FLYERS.
YEAH, I GOT 'EM FROM SOME GUY WHO KNOWS A DUDE WHO WORKS FOR THE RESISTANCE...
WOW... IT'S ALMOST AS IF YOU WERE ACTUALLY A PART OF IT!
WE ARE A PART OF IT! HANDING OUT FLYERS IS ALREADY RESISTING!
HEY, ISN'T THAT THE NEW *TZ-PHONE 7S*?
YEAH, IT JUST CAME OUT.
ACHETER. AIMER. JETER.
YOU COMING WITH US, NOVA? WE'RE GONNA UPLOAD THESE FLYERS ONTO THE TZ-PHONES OF EVERYONE WE MEET THIS AFTERNOON!

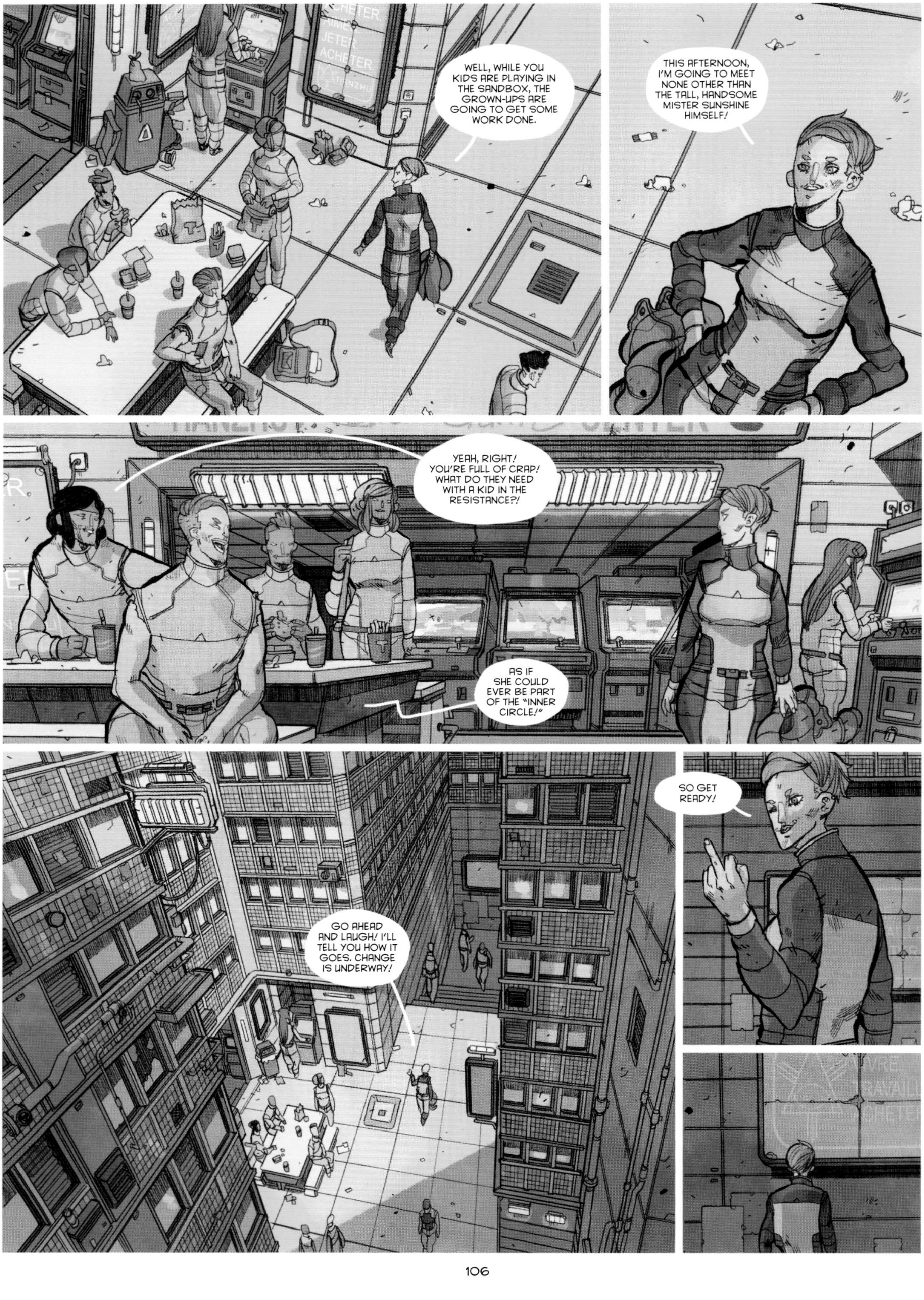
ACHETER.
AIMER.
JETER.
ACHETER.
WELL, WHILE YOU KIDS ARE PLAYING IN THE SANDBOX, THE GROWN-UPS ARE GOING TO GET SOME WORK DONE.
THIS AFTERNOON, I'M GOING TO MEET NONE OTHER THAN THE TALL, HANDSOME MISTER SUNSHINE HIMSELF!
YEAH, RIGHT! YOU'RE FULL OF CRAP! WHAT DO THEY NEED WITH A KID IN THE RESISTANCE?!
AS IF SHE COULD EVER BE PART OF THE "INNER CIRCLE!"
SO GET READY!
GO AHEAD AND LAUGH! I'LL TELL YOU HOW IT GOES. CHANGE IS UNDERWAY!
TRAVAILL
ACHETER

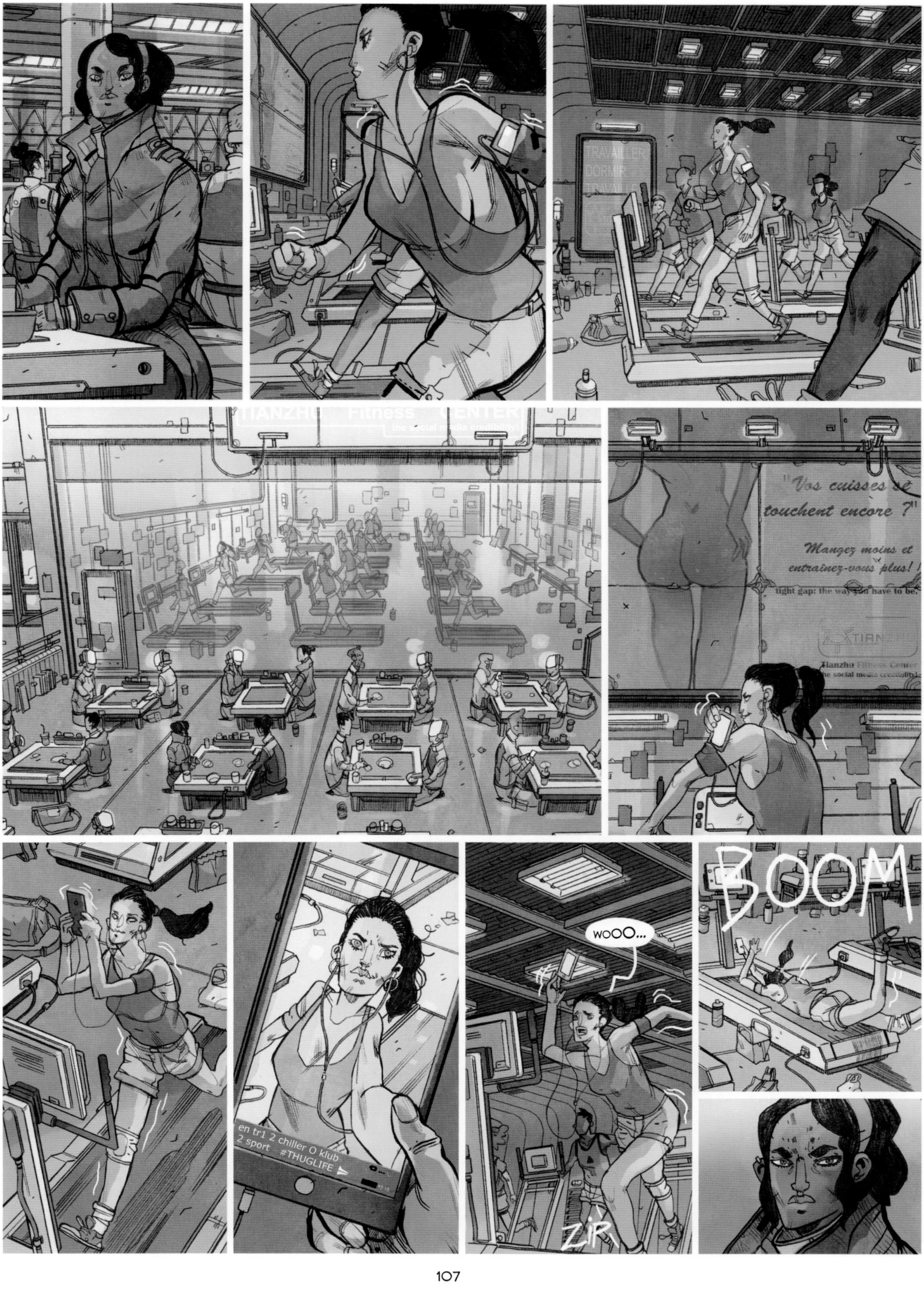
TRAVAILLER
DORMIR
TIANZHU Fitness CENTER
the social media credibility!
"Vos cuisses se touchent encore ?"
Mangez moins et entraînez-vous plus!
tight gap: the way you have to be.
Tianzhu Fitness Center
the social media credibility!
en tr1 2 chiller O klub 2 sport #THUGLIFE
WOOO...
ZIP
BOOM

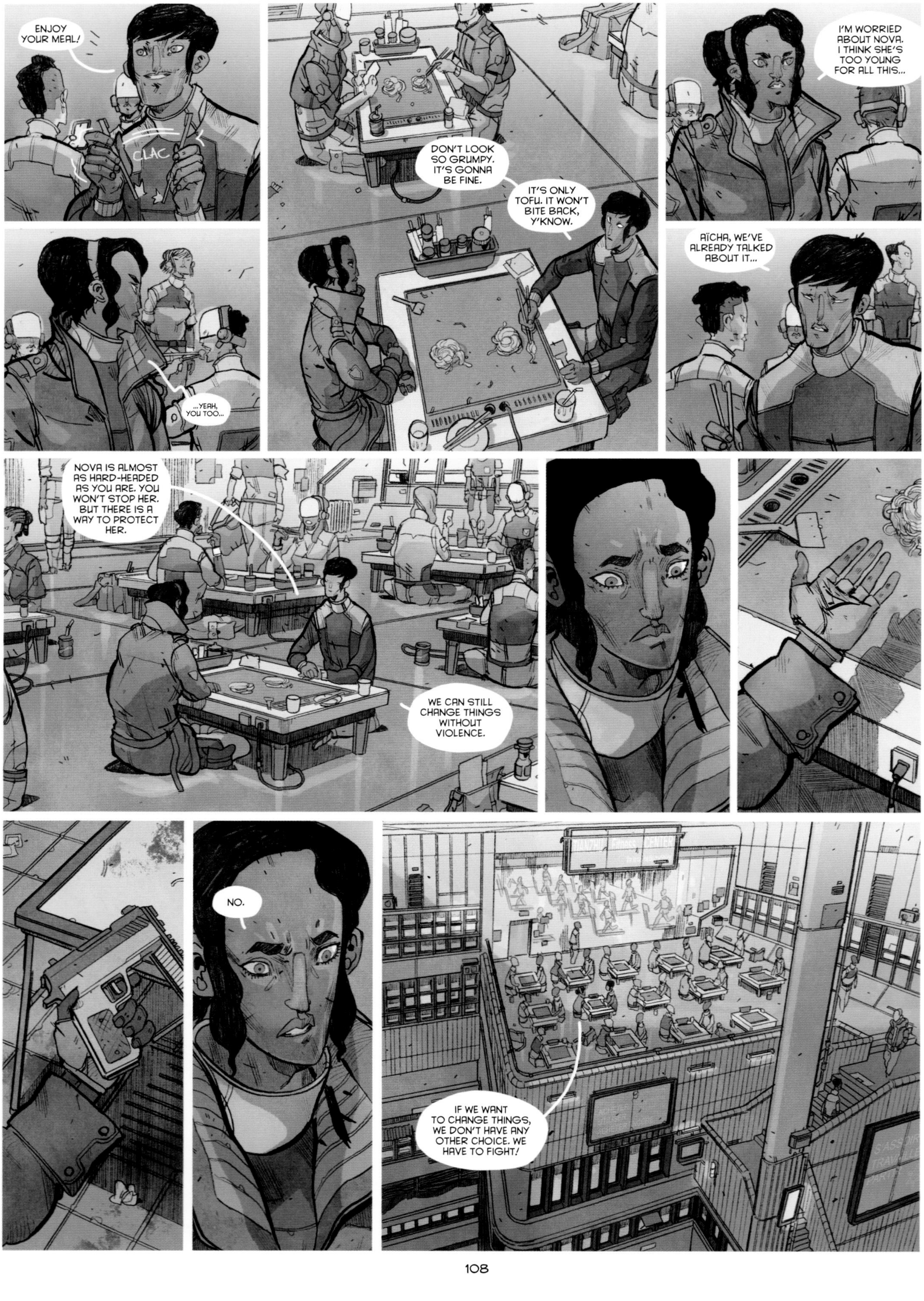
ENJOY YOUR MEAL!
CLAC
...YEAH, YOU TOO...
DON'T LOOK SO GRUMPY. IT'S GONNA BE FINE.
IT'S ONLY TOFU. IT WON'T BITE BACK, Y'KNOW.
I'M WORRIED ABOUT NOVA. I THINK SHE'S TOO YOUNG FOR ALL THIS...
AÏCHA, WE'VE ALREADY TALKED ABOUT IT...
NOVA IS ALMOST AS HARD-HEADED AS YOU ARE. YOU WON'T STOP HER. BUT THERE IS A WAY TO PROTECT HER.
WE CAN STILL CHANGE THINGS WITHOUT VIOLENCE.
NO.
IF WE WANT TO CHANGE THINGS, WE DON'T HAVE ANY OTHER CHOICE. WE HAVE TO FIGHT!

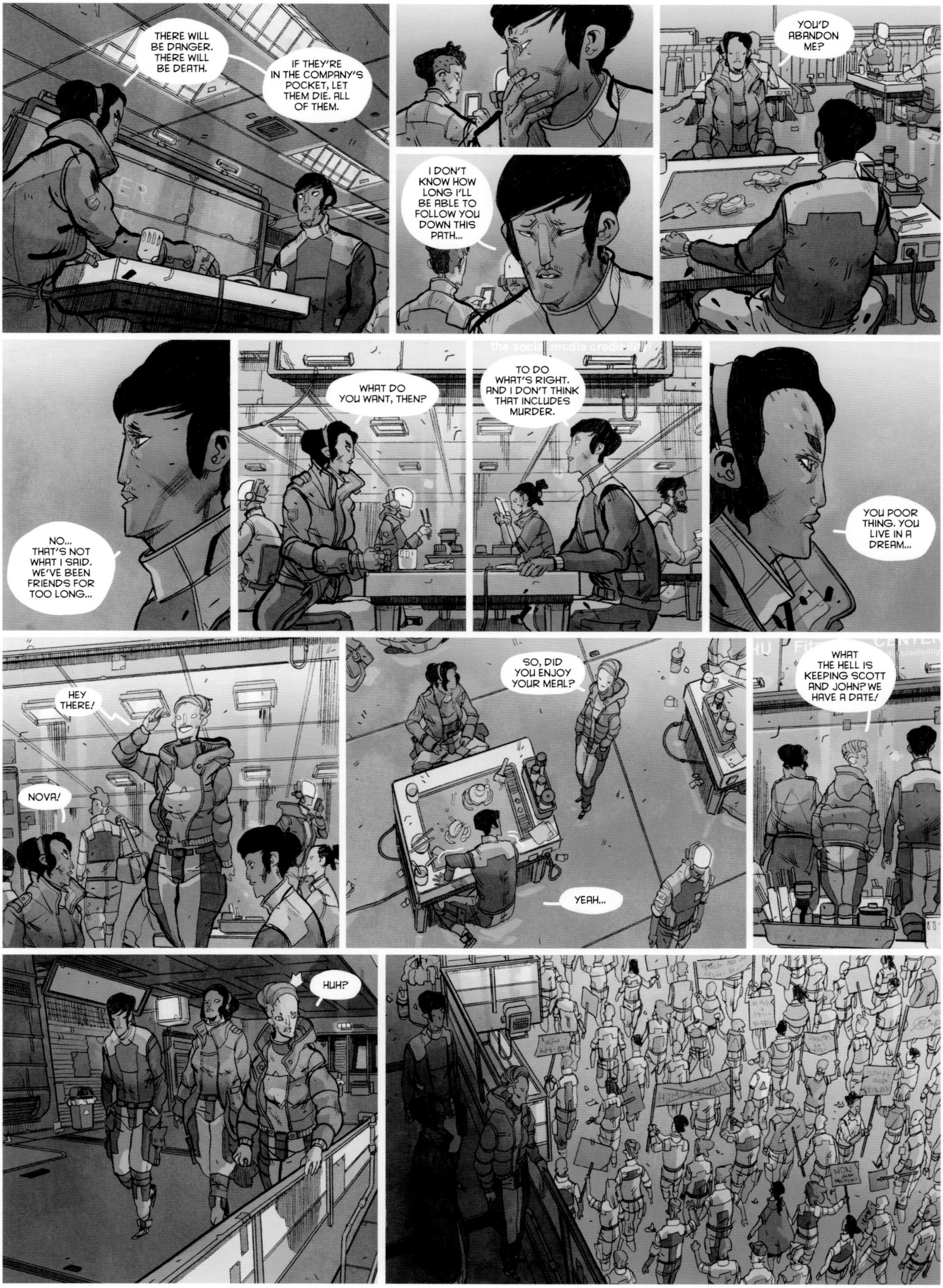
THERE WILL BE DANGER. THERE WILL BE DEATH.
IF THEY'RE IN THE COMPANY'S POCKET, LET THEM DIE. ALL OF THEM.
YOU'D ABANDON ME?
I DON'T KNOW HOW LONG I'LL BE ABLE TO FOLLOW YOU DOWN THIS PATH...
NO... THAT'S NOT WHAT I SAID. WE'VE BEEN FRIENDS FOR TOO LONG...
WHAT DO YOU WANT, THEN?
TO DO WHAT'S RIGHT. AND I DON'T THINK THAT INCLUDES MURDER.
YOU POOR THING. YOU LIVE IN A DREAM...
HEY THERE!
NOVA!
SO, DID YOU ENJOY YOUR MEAL?
YEAH...
WHAT THE HELL IS KEEPING SCOTT AND JOHN? WE HAVE A DATE!
HUH?

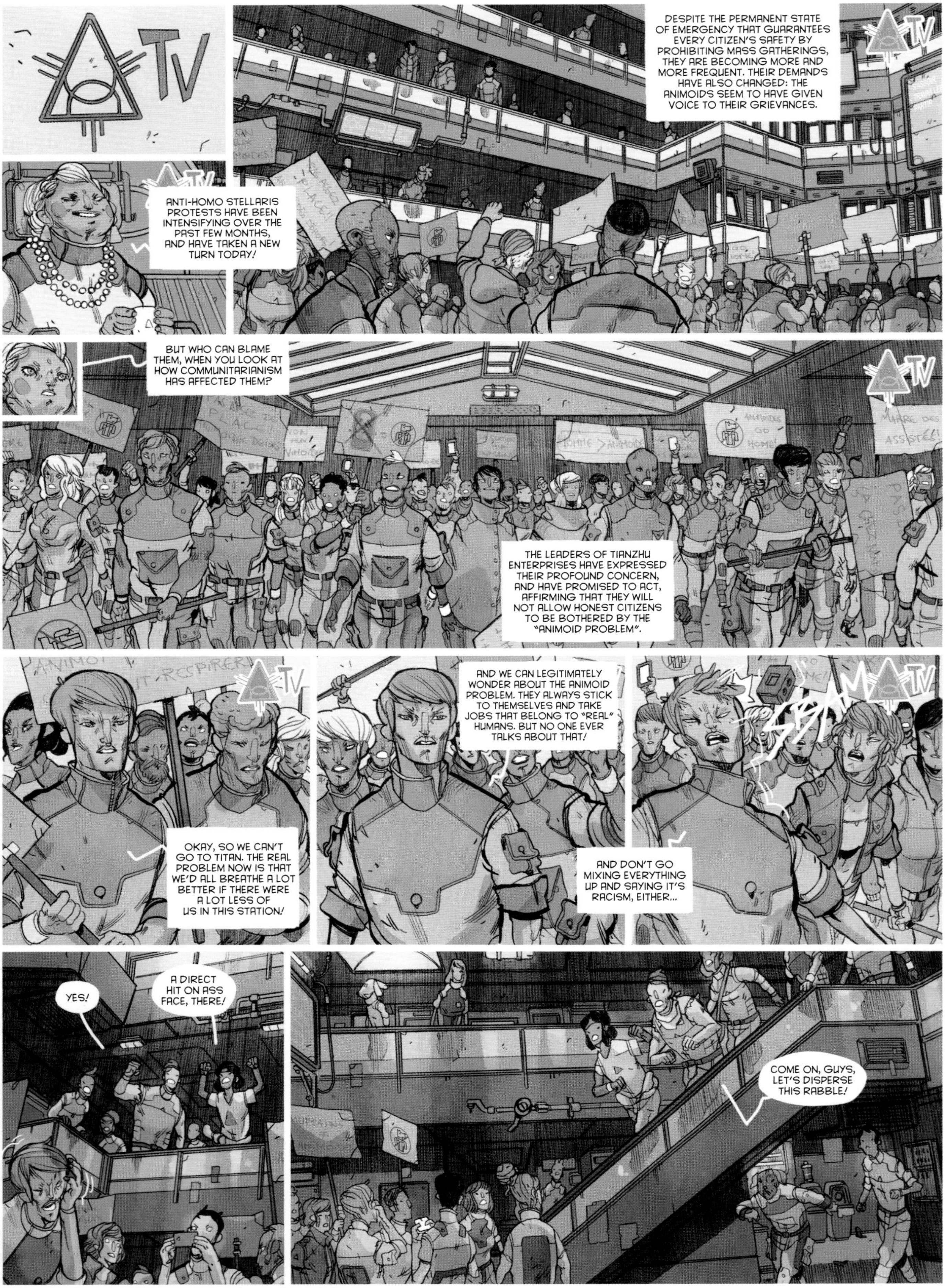
TV
DESPITE THE PERMANENT STATE OF EMERGENCY THAT GUARANTEES EVERY CITIZEN'S SAFETY BY PROHIBITING MASS GATHERINGS, THEY ARE BECOMING MORE AND MORE FREQUENT. THEIR DEMANDS HAVE ALSO CHANGED: THE ANIMOIDS SEEM TO HAVE GIVEN VOICE TO THEIR GRIEVANCES.
ANTI-HOMO STELLARIS PROTESTS HAVE BEEN INTENSIFYING OVER THE PAST FEW MONTHS, AND HAVE TAKEN A NEW TURN TODAY!
BUT WHO CAN BLAME THEM, WHEN YOU LOOK AT HOW COMMUNITARIANISM HAS AFFECTED THEM?
ANIMOIDES GO HOME!
HOMME > ANIMOIDE
MARRE DES ASSISTÉS!
THE LEADERS OF TIANZHU ENTERPRISES HAVE EXPRESSED THEIR PROFOUND CONCERN, AND HAVE PROMISED TO ACT, AFFIRMING THAT THEY WILL NOT ALLOW HONEST CITIZENS TO BE BOTHERED BY THE "ANIMOID PROBLEM".
OKAY, SO WE CAN'T GO TO TITAN. THE REAL PROBLEM NOW IS THAT WE'D ALL BREATHE A LOT BETTER IF THERE WERE A LOT LESS OF US IN THIS STATION!
AND WE CAN LEGITIMATELY WONDER ABOUT THE ANIMOID PROBLEM. THEY ALWAYS STICK TO THEMSELVES AND TAKE JOBS THAT BELONG TO "REAL" HUMANS. BUT NO ONE EVER TALKS ABOUT THAT!
AND DON'T GO MIXING EVERYTHING UP AND SAYING IT'S RACISM, EITHER...
SBAM
YES!
A DIRECT HIT ON ASS FACE, THERE!
COME ON, GUYS, LET'S DISPERSE THIS RABBLE!

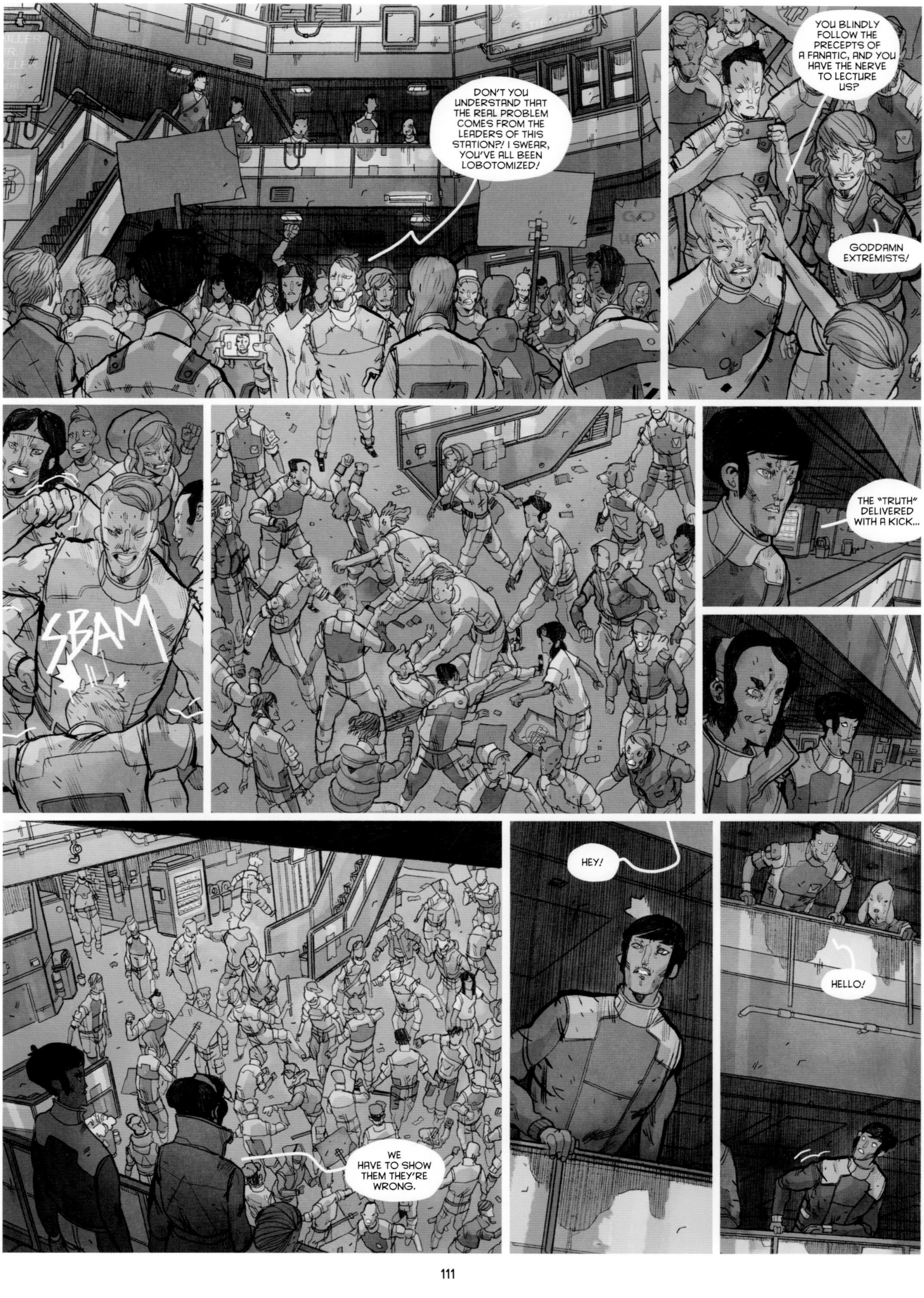
DON'T YOU UNDERSTAND THAT THE REAL PROBLEM COMES FROM THE LEADERS OF THIS STATION?! I SWEAR, YOU'VE ALL BEEN LOBOTOMIZED!
YOU BLINDLY FOLLOW THE PRECEPTS OF A FANATIC, AND YOU HAVE THE NERVE TO LECTURE US?
GODDAMN EXTREMISTS!
SBAM
THE "TRUTH" DELIVERED WITH A KICK...
WE HAVE TO SHOW THEM THEY'RE WRONG.
HEY!
HELLO!

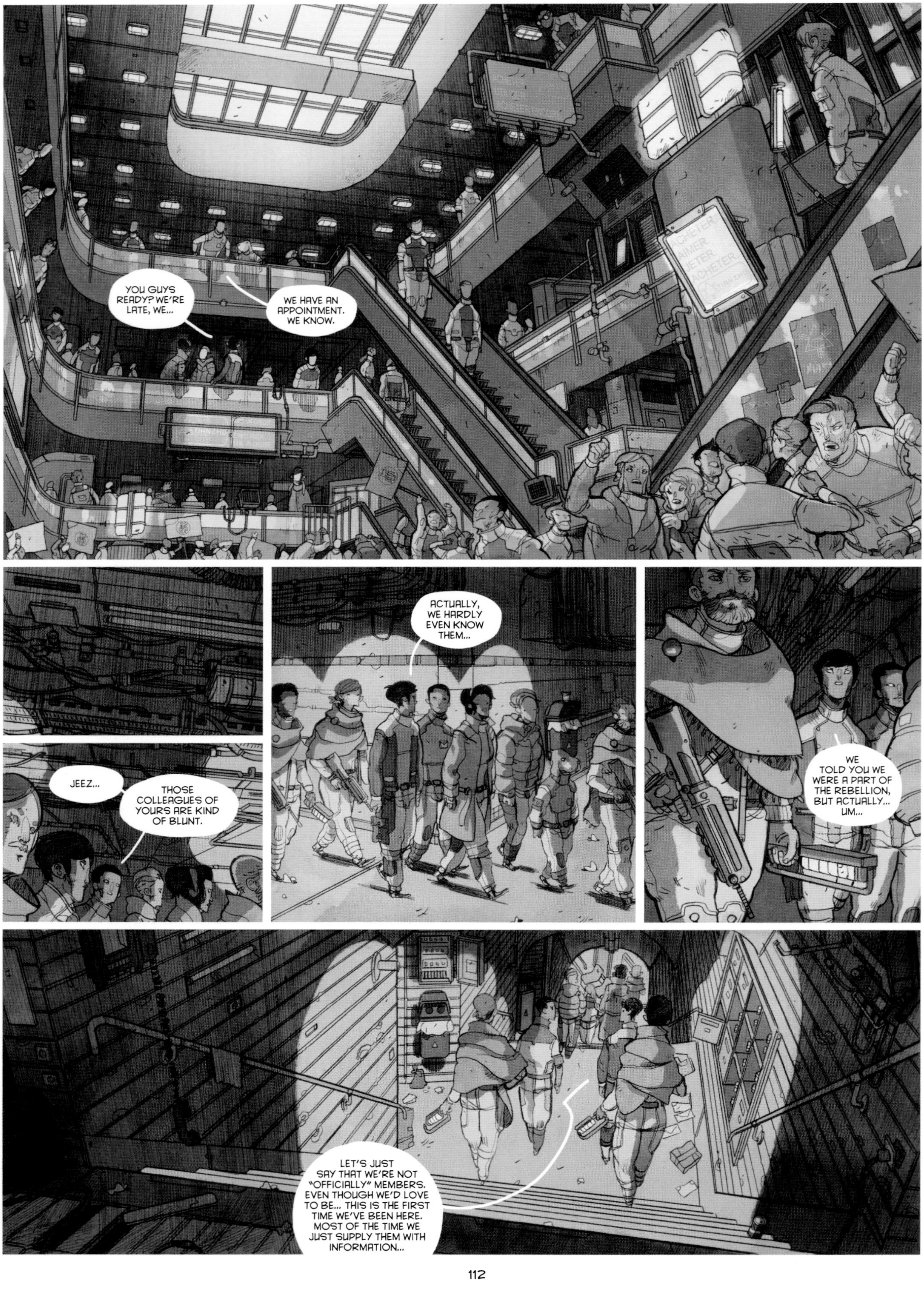
ACHETER. AIMER. JETER. ACHETER.
YOU GUYS READY? WE'RE LATE, WE...
WE HAVE AN APPOINTMENT. WE KNOW.
JEEZ...
THOSE COLLEAGUES OF YOURS ARE KIND OF BLUNT.
ACTUALLY, WE HARDLY EVEN KNOW THEM...
WE TOLD YOU WE WERE A PART OF THE REBELLION, BUT ACTUALLY... UM...
LET'S JUST SAY THAT WE'RE NOT "OFFICIALLY" MEMBERS. EVEN THOUGH WE'D LOVE TO BE... THIS IS THE FIRST TIME WE'VE BEEN HERE. MOST OF THE TIME WE JUST SUPPLY THEM WITH INFORMATION...

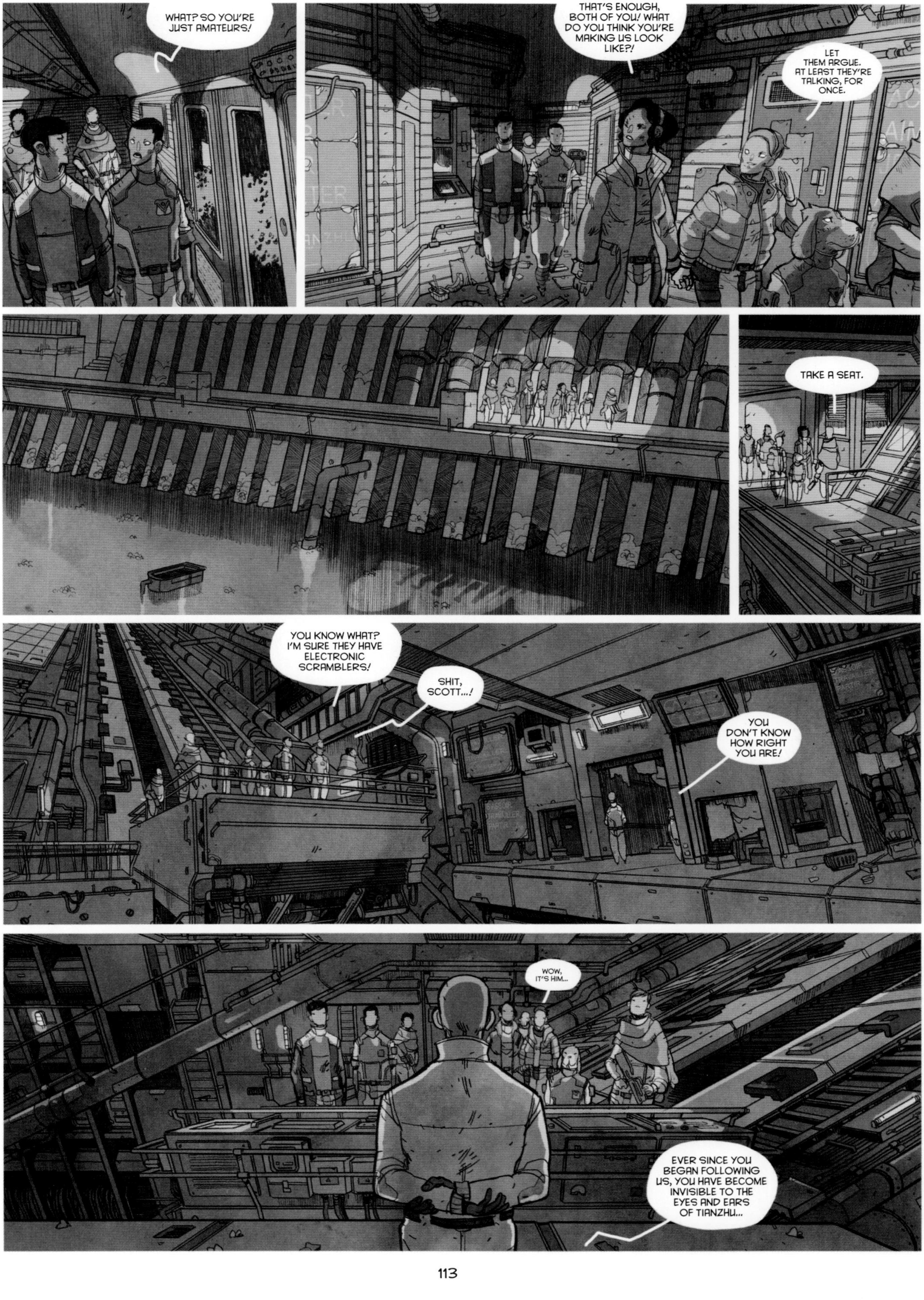
WHAT? SO YOU'RE JUST AMATEURS!
THAT'S ENOUGH, BOTH OF YOU! WHAT DO YOU THINK YOU'RE MAKING US LOOK LIKE?!
LET THEM ARGUE. AT LEAST THEY'RE TALKING, FOR ONCE.
TAKE A SEAT.
YOU KNOW WHAT? I'M SURE THEY HAVE ELECTRONIC SCRAMBLERS!
SHIT, SCOTT...!
YOU DON'T KNOW HOW RIGHT YOU ARE!
WOW, IT'S HIM...
EVER SINCE YOU BEGAN FOLLOWING US, YOU HAVE BECOME INVISIBLE TO THE EYES AND EARS OF TIANZHU...

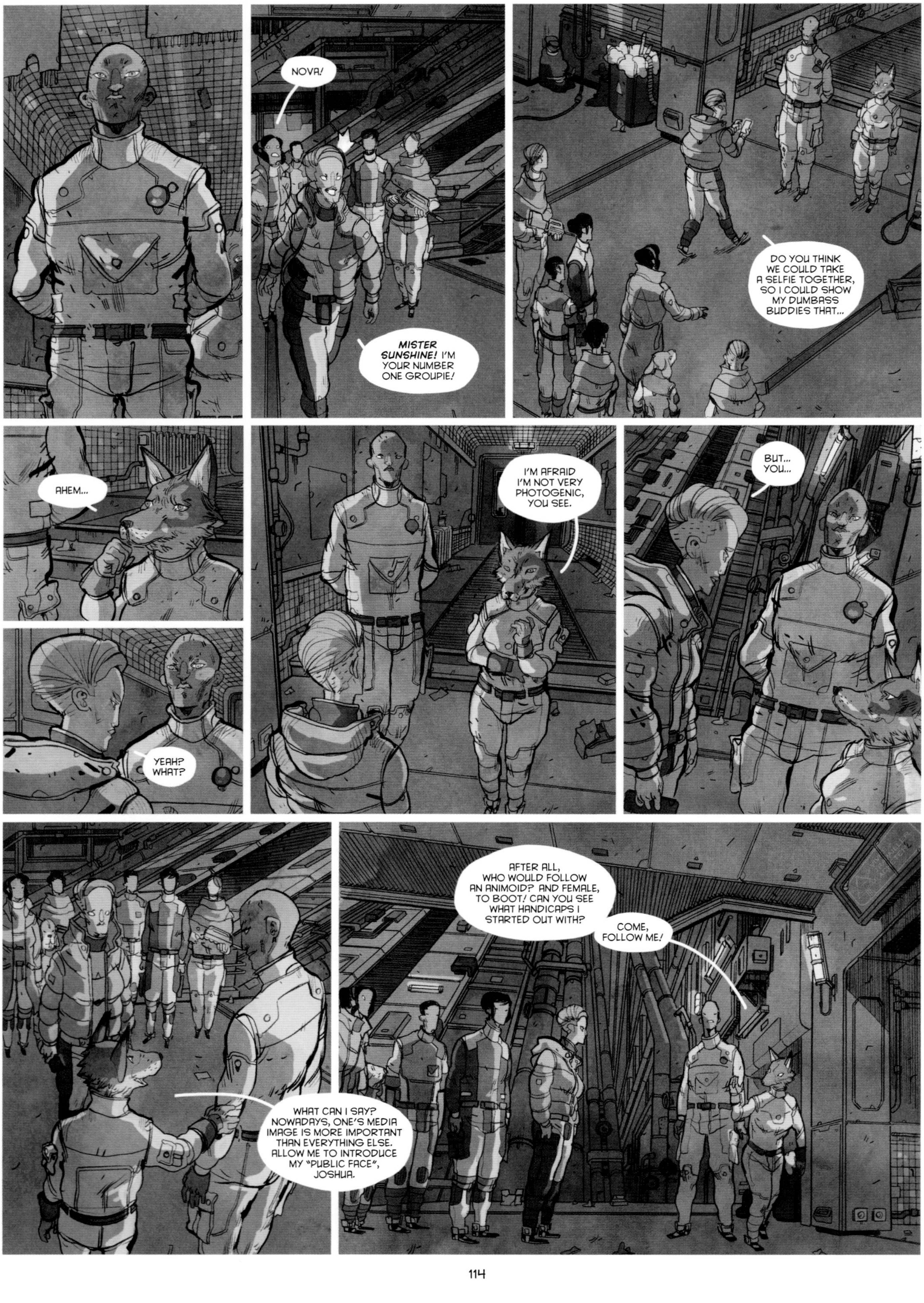
NOVA!
MISTER SUNSHINE! I'M YOUR NUMBER ONE GROUPIE!
DO YOU THINK WE COULD TAKE A SELFIE TOGETHER, SO I COULD SHOW MY DUMBASS BUDDIES THAT...
AHEM...
YEAH? WHAT?
I'M AFRAID I'M NOT VERY PHOTOGENIC, YOU SEE.
BUT... YOU...
WHAT CAN I SAY? NOWADAYS, ONE'S MEDIA IMAGE IS MORE IMPORTANT THAN EVERYTHING ELSE. ALLOW ME TO INTRODUCE MY "PUBLIC FACE", JOSHUA.
AFTER ALL, WHO WOULD FOLLOW AN ANIMOID? AND FEMALE, TO BOOT! CAN YOU SEE WHAT HANDICAPS I STARTED OUT WITH?
COME, FOLLOW ME!

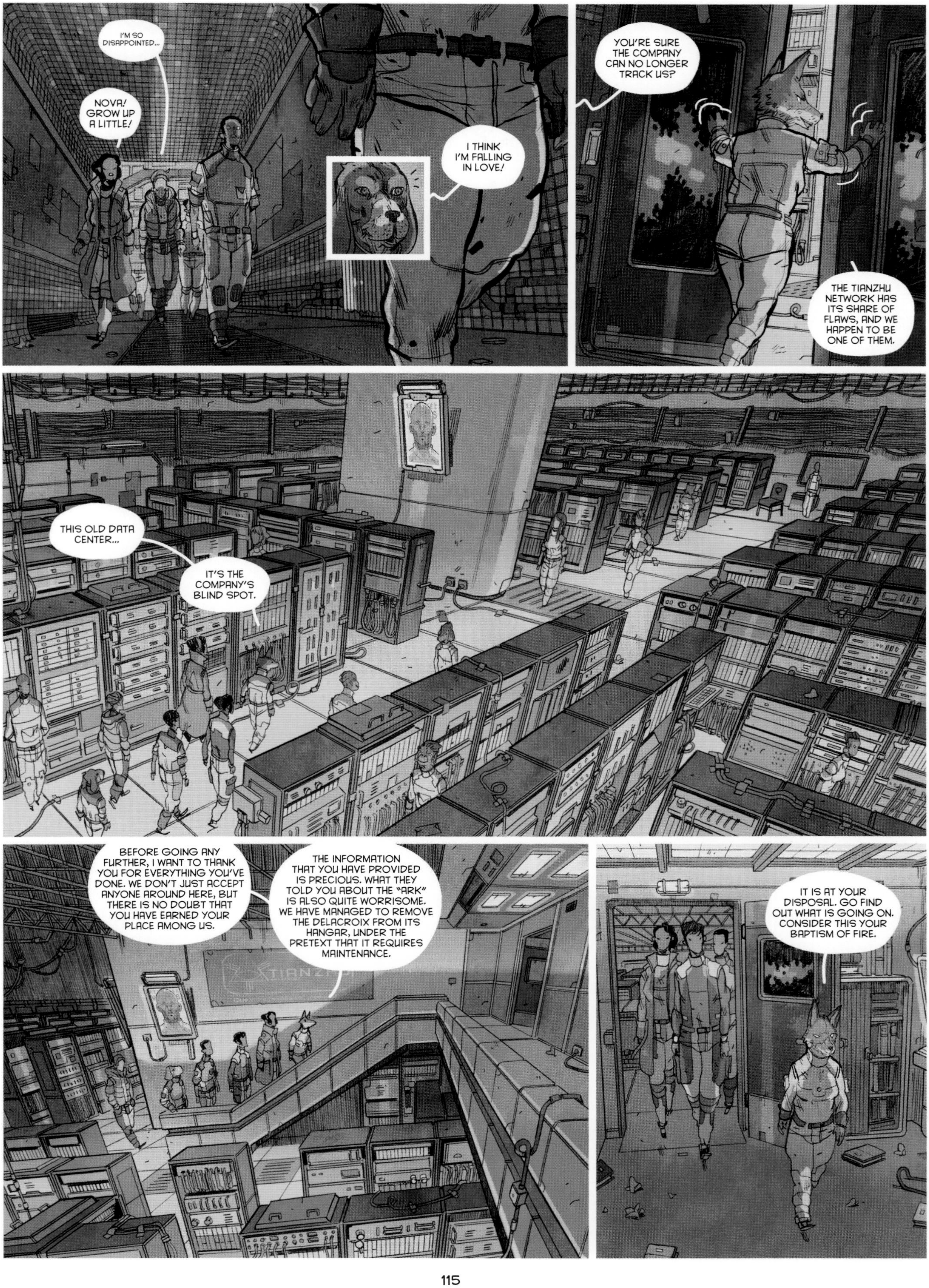
I'M SO DISAPPOINTED...
NOVA! GROW UP A LITTLE!
I THINK I'M FALLING IN LOVE!
YOU'RE SURE THE COMPANY CAN NO LONGER TRACK US?
THE TIANZHU NETWORK HAS ITS SHARE OF FLAWS, AND WE HAPPEN TO BE ONE OF THEM.
THIS OLD DATA CENTER...
IT'S THE COMPANY'S BLIND SPOT.
BEFORE GOING ANY FURTHER, I WANT TO THANK YOU FOR EVERYTHING YOU'VE DONE. WE DON'T JUST ACCEPT ANYONE AROUND HERE, BUT THERE IS NO DOUBT THAT YOU HAVE EARNED YOUR PLACE AMONG US.
THE INFORMATION THAT YOU HAVE PROVIDED IS PRECIOUS. WHAT THEY TOLD YOU ABOUT THE "ARK" IS ALSO QUITE WORRISOME. WE HAVE MANAGED TO REMOVE THE DELACROIX FROM ITS HANGAR, UNDER THE PRETEXT THAT IT REQUIRES MAINTENANCE.
IT IS AT YOUR DISPOSAL. GO FIND OUT WHAT IS GOING ON. CONSIDER THIS YOUR BAPTISM OF FIRE.

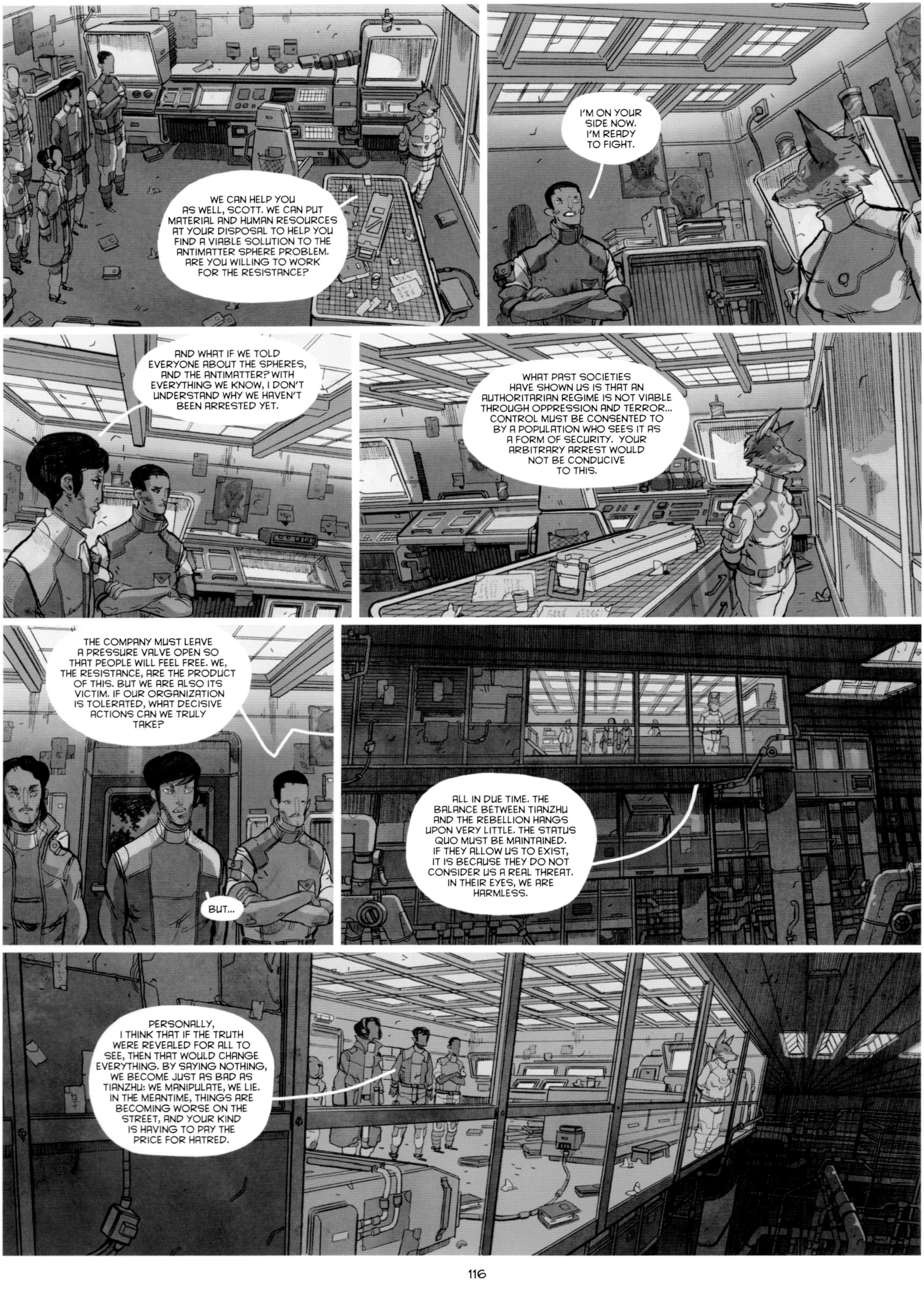

WE CAN HELP YOU AS WELL, SCOTT. WE CAN PUT MATERIAL AND HUMAN RESOURCES AT YOUR DISPOSAL TO HELP YOU FIND A VIABLE SOLUTION TO THE ANTIMATTER SPHERE PROBLEM. ARE YOU WILLING TO WORK FOR THE RESISTANCE?
I'M ON YOUR SIDE NOW. I'M READY TO FIGHT.
AND WHAT IF WE TOLD EVERYONE ABOUT THE SPHERES, AND THE ANTIMATTER? WITH EVERYTHING WE KNOW, I DON'T UNDERSTAND WHY WE HAVEN'T BEEN ARRESTED YET.
WHAT PAST SOCIETIES HAVE SHOWN US IS THAT AN AUTHORITARIAN REGIME IS NOT VIABLE THROUGH OPPRESSION AND TERROR... CONTROL MUST BE CONSENTED TO BY A POPULATION WHO SEES IT AS A FORM OF SECURITY. YOUR ARBITRARY ARREST WOULD NOT BE CONDUCIVE TO THIS.
THE COMPANY MUST LEAVE A PRESSURE VALVE OPEN SO THAT PEOPLE WILL FEEL FREE. WE, THE RESISTANCE, ARE THE PRODUCT OF THIS. BUT WE ARE ALSO ITS VICTIM. IF OUR ORGANIZATION IS TOLERATED, WHAT DECISIVE ACTIONS CAN WE TRULY TAKE?
BUT...
ALL IN DUE TIME. THE BALANCE BETWEEN TIANZHU AND THE REBELLION HANGS UPON VERY LITTLE. THE STATUS QUO MUST BE MAINTAINED. IF THEY ALLOW US TO EXIST, IT IS BECAUSE THEY DO NOT CONSIDER US A REAL THREAT. IN THEIR EYES, WE ARE HARMLESS.
PERSONALLY, I THINK THAT IF THE TRUTH WERE REVEALED FOR ALL TO SEE, THEN THAT WOULD CHANGE EVERYTHING. BY SAYING NOTHING, WE BECOME JUST AS BAD AS TIANZHU: WE MANIPULATE, WE LIE. IN THE MEANTIME, THINGS ARE BECOMING WORSE ON THE STREET, AND YOUR KIND IS HAVING TO PAY THE PRICE FOR HATRED.

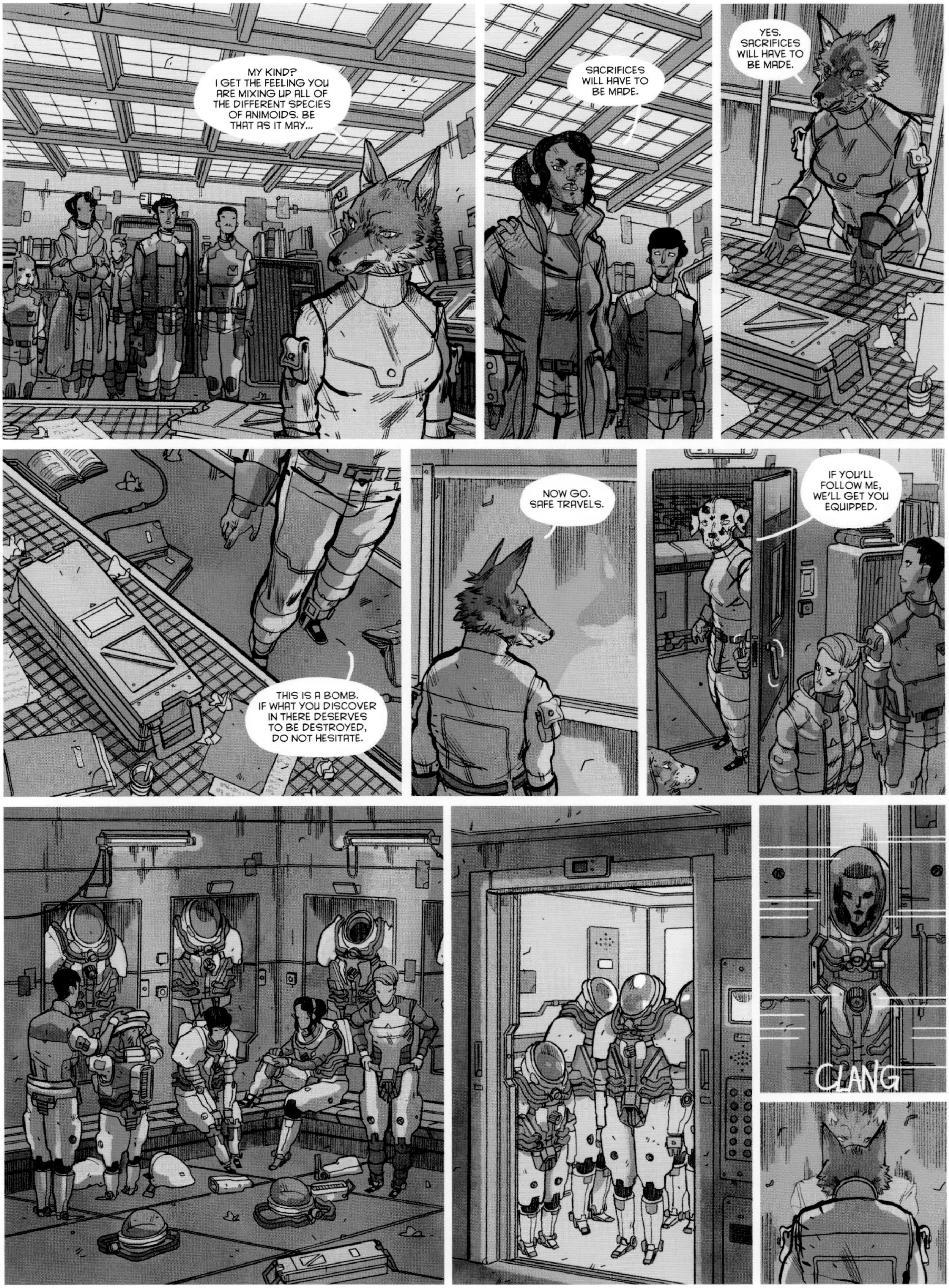
MY KIND? I GET THE FEELING YOU ARE MIXING UP ALL OF THE DIFFERENT SPECIES OF ANIMOIDS. BE THAT AS IT MAY...
SACRIFICES WILL HAVE TO BE MADE.
YES. SACRIFICES WILL HAVE TO BE MADE.
THIS IS A BOMB. IF WHAT YOU DISCOVER IN THERE DESERVES TO BE DESTROYED, DO NOT HESITATE.
NOW GO. SAFE TRAVELS.
IF YOU'LL FOLLOW ME, WE'LL GET YOU EQUIPPED.
CLANG

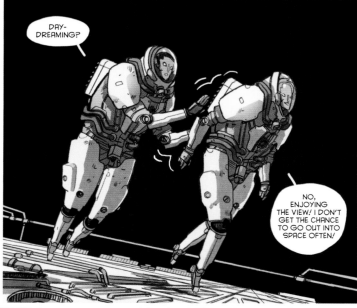

DAY-DREAMING?

NO, ENJOYING THE VIEW! I DON'T GET THE CHANCE TO GO OUT INTO SPACE OFTEN!

WHICH IS KIND OF IRONIC WITH A NAME LIKE YOURS!

HUH?

NOVA. DO YOU KNOW WHAT IT MEANS?

NO.

IT'S AN EXPLODING SUN, WHICH THE ANCIENTS BELIEVED WAS THE BIRTH OF A NEW STAR. THAT'S WHERE THE NAME COMES FROM. IT MEANS "NEW". IT'S A BEAUTIFUL NAME.

EVEN IF IT'S FULL OF IMAGERY, THEY WEREN'T COMPLETELY WRONG. SUPERNOVAE ARE STARS THAT EXPLODE WHEN THEY DIE, SPREADING THE MATTER THAT THEY CREATED DURING THEIR LONG LIVES ACROSS THE ENTIRE UNIVERSE. IT'S THIS COMPLEX MATTER TRAVELING THROUGHOUT THE UNIVERSE THAT CREATED PLANETS AND LIFE AT THE BEGINNING OF THE WORLD.

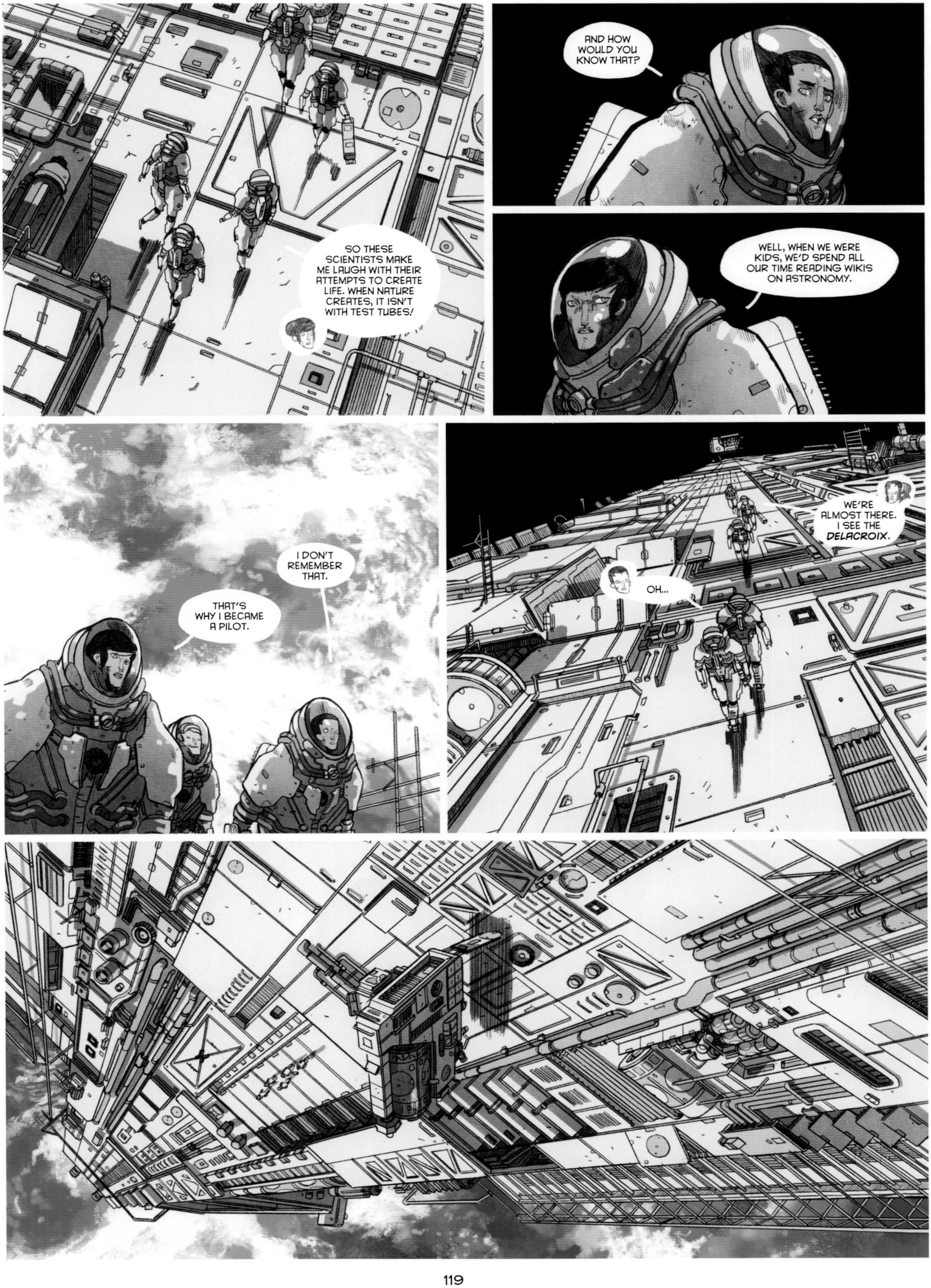
SO THESE SCIENTISTS MAKE ME LAUGH WITH THEIR ATTEMPTS TO CREATE LIFE. WHEN NATURE CREATES, IT ISN'T WITH TEST TUBES!
AND HOW WOULD YOU KNOW THAT?
WELL, WHEN WE WERE KIDS, WE'D SPEND ALL OUR TIME READING WIKIS ON ASTRONOMY.
I DON'T REMEMBER THAT.
THAT'S WHY I BECAME A PILOT.
WE'RE ALMOST THERE. I SEE THE *DELACROIX*.
OH...

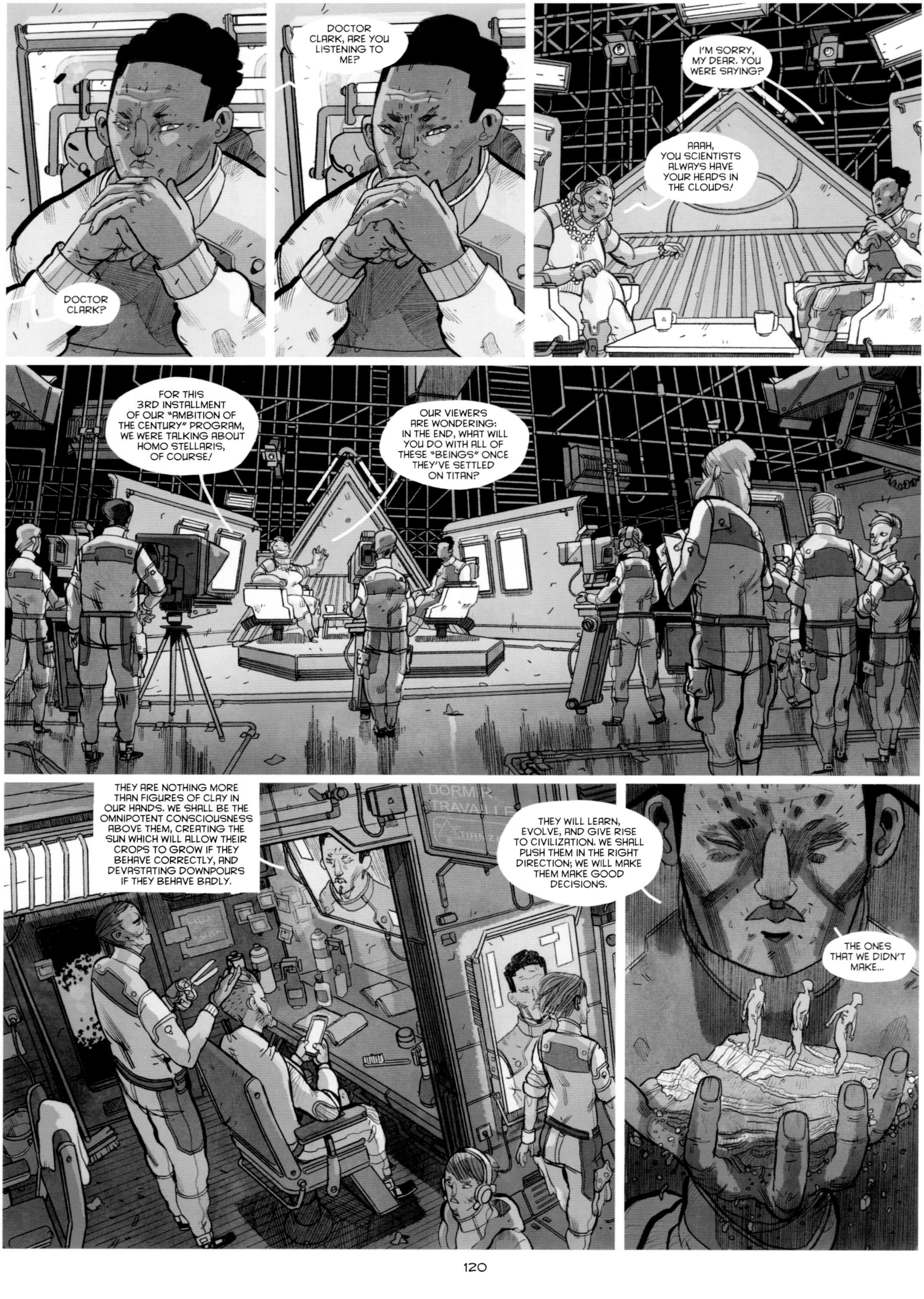
DOCTOR CLARK?
DOCTOR CLARK, ARE YOU LISTENING TO ME?
I'M SORRY, MY DEAR. YOU WERE SAYING?
AAAH, YOU SCIENTISTS ALWAYS HAVE YOUR HEADS IN THE CLOUDS!
FOR THIS 3RD INSTALLMENT OF OUR "AMBITION OF THE CENTURY" PROGRAM, WE WERE TALKING ABOUT HOMO STELLARIS, OF COURSE!
OUR VIEWERS ARE WONDERING: IN THE END, WHAT WILL YOU DO WITH ALL OF THESE "BEINGS" ONCE THEY'VE SETTLED ON TITAN?
THEY ARE NOTHING MORE THAN FIGURES OF CLAY IN OUR HANDS. WE SHALL BE THE OMNIPOTENT CONSCIOUSNESS ABOVE THEM, CREATING THE SUN WHICH WILL ALLOW THEIR CROPS TO GROW IF THEY BEHAVE CORRECTLY, AND DEVASTATING DOWNPOURS IF THEY BEHAVE BADLY.
THEY WILL LEARN, EVOLVE, AND GIVE RISE TO CIVILIZATION. WE SHALL PUSH THEM IN THE RIGHT DIRECTION; WE WILL MAKE THEM MAKE GOOD DECISIONS.
THE ONES THAT WE DIDN'T MAKE...

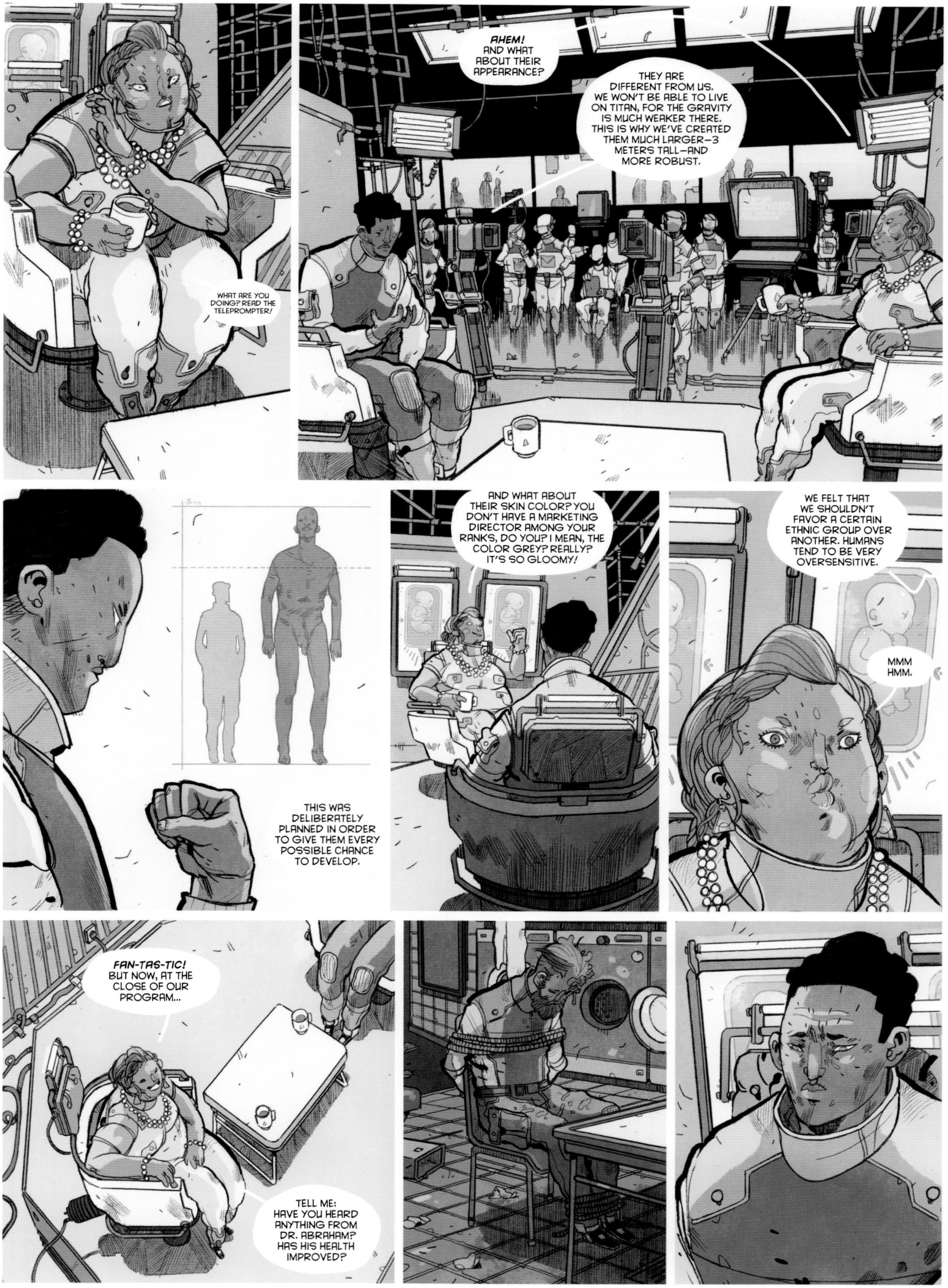
WHAT ARE YOU DOING? READ THE TELEPROMPTER!
AHEM! AND WHAT ABOUT THEIR APPEARANCE?
THEY ARE DIFFERENT FROM US. WE WON'T BE ABLE TO LIVE ON TITAN, FOR THE GRAVITY IS MUCH WEAKER THERE. THIS IS WHY WE'VE CREATED THEM MUCH LARGER—3 METERS TALL—AND MORE ROBUST.
THIS WAS DELIBERATELY PLANNED IN ORDER TO GIVE THEM EVERY POSSIBLE CHANCE TO DEVELOP.
AND WHAT ABOUT THEIR SKIN COLOR? YOU DON'T HAVE A MARKETING DIRECTOR AMONG YOUR RANKS, DO YOU? I MEAN, THE COLOR GREY? REALLY? IT'S SO GLOOMY!
WE FELT THAT WE SHOULDN'T FAVOR A CERTAIN ETHNIC GROUP OVER ANOTHER. HUMANS TEND TO BE VERY OVERSENSITIVE.
MMM HMM.
FAN-TAS-TIC! BUT NOW, AT THE CLOSE OF OUR PROGRAM...
TELL ME: HAVE YOU HEARD ANYTHING FROM DR. ABRAHAM? HAS HIS HEALTH IMPROVED?

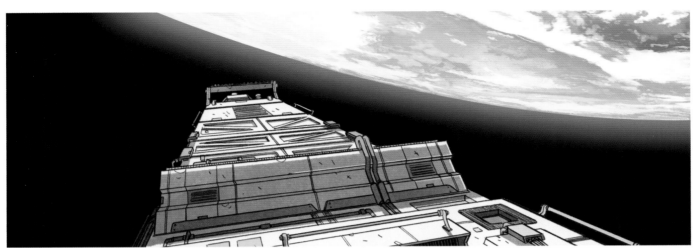

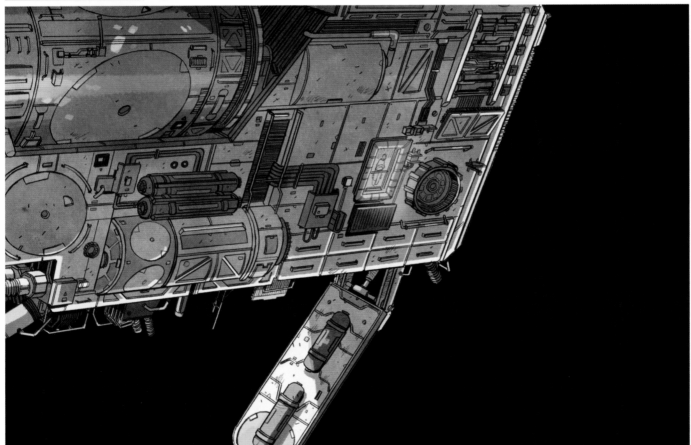

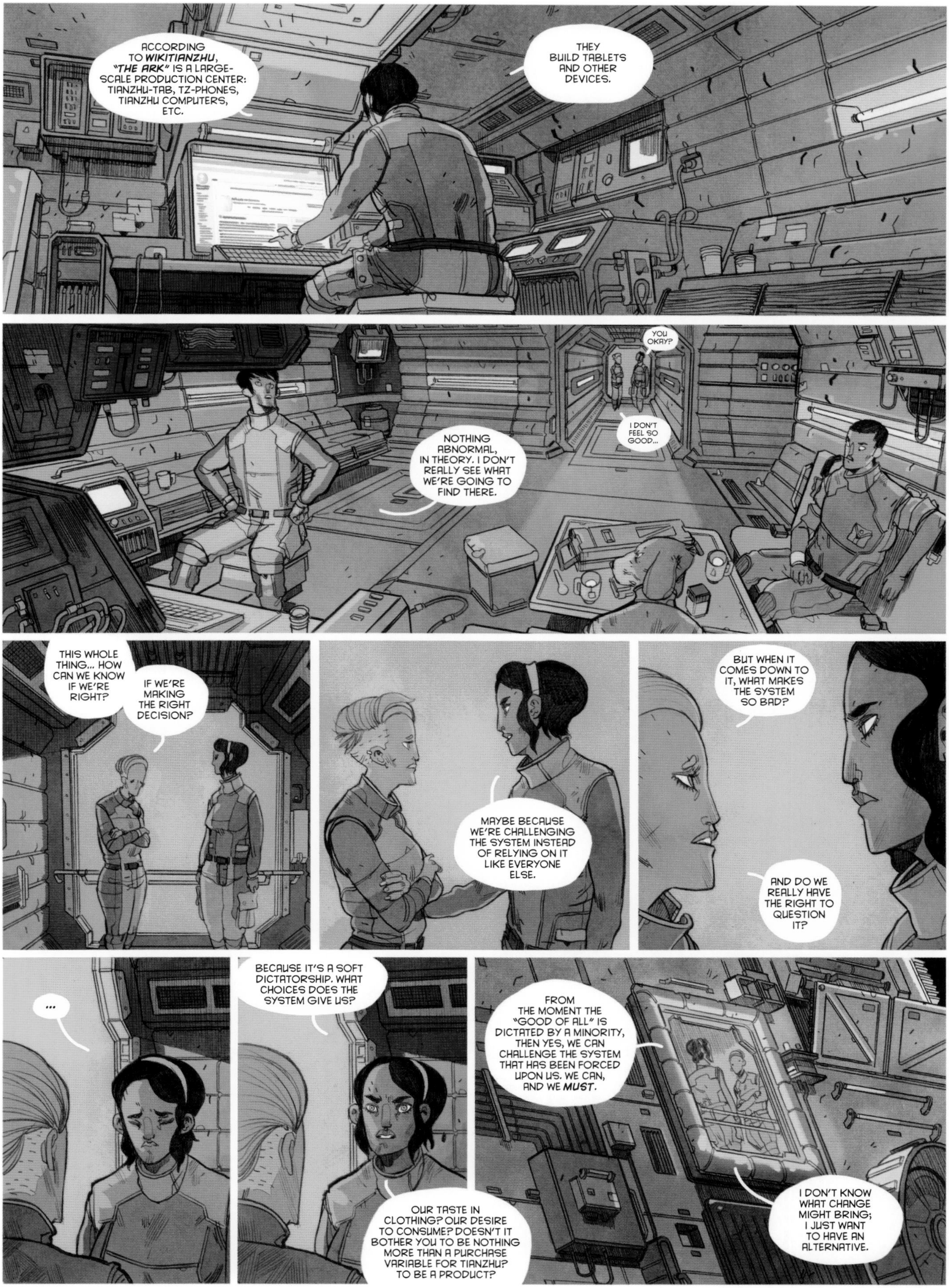

ACCORDING TO **WIKITIANZHU**, **"THE ARK"** IS A LARGE-SCALE PRODUCTION CENTER: TIANZHU-TAB, TZ-PHONES, TIANZHU COMPUTERS, ETC.
THEY BUILD TABLETS AND OTHER DEVICES.
NOTHING ABNORMAL, IN THEORY. I DON'T REALLY SEE WHAT WE'RE GOING TO FIND THERE.
YOU OKAY?
I DON'T FEEL SO GOOD...
THIS WHOLE THING... HOW CAN WE KNOW IF WE'RE RIGHT?
IF WE'RE MAKING THE RIGHT DECISION?
MAYBE BECAUSE WE'RE CHALLENGING THE SYSTEM INSTEAD OF RELYING ON IT LIKE EVERYONE ELSE.
BUT WHEN IT COMES DOWN TO IT, WHAT MAKES THE SYSTEM SO BAD?
AND DO WE REALLY HAVE THE RIGHT TO QUESTION IT?
...
BECAUSE IT'S A SOFT DICTATORSHIP. WHAT CHOICES DOES THE SYSTEM GIVE US?
OUR TASTE IN CLOTHING? OUR DESIRE TO CONSUME? DOESN'T IT BOTHER YOU TO BE NOTHING MORE THAN A PURCHASE VARIABLE FOR TIANZHU? TO BE A PRODUCT?
FROM THE MOMENT THE "GOOD OF ALL" IS DICTATED BY A MINORITY, THEN YES, WE CAN CHALLENGE THE SYSTEM THAT HAS BEEN FORCED UPON US. WE CAN, AND WE **MUST**.
I DON'T KNOW WHAT CHANGE MIGHT BRING; I JUST WANT TO HAVE AN ALTERNATIVE.

OKAY...
YOU'RE
RIGHT.

THANKS.

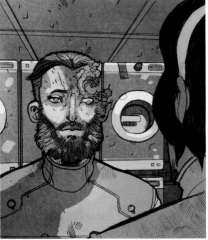

YEAH...
I SURE AM...

SERIOUSLY?
YOU DON'T KNOW
THE JOKE THAT'S
BEEN GOING AROUND
ABOUT MY KIND?!

UM,
NO...

THE REASON WHY THERE ARE
SO FEW *FELINE ANIMOIDS* IN
THE STATION, COMPARED TO
THE OTHER SPECIES, IS BECAUSE
MEN THOUGHT THAT THEY WOULD
DETHRONE THEM AND BECOME
THE MASTERS OF THE WORLD,
THANKS TO THEIR HYPNOTIC
POWERS!

A THIRD
OF THE INTERNET
WAS MADE UP OF
CAT VIDEOS!
PEOPLE WOULD
SPEND HOURS
WATCHING
THEM!

WHAT?!

HEH HEH!

INCREDIBLE...
BUT WHY?

WHO KNOWS?
HUMANS MUST
HAVE REVERED
THEM BACK
THEN!

GUYS...

WE STICK
TO THE PLAN. VIRGIL
AND I STAY ON BOARD
THE DELACROIX, IN CASE
WE'RE FORCED TO LEAVE
IN A HURRY. THE THREE
OF YOU WILL GO EXPLORE
THE STATION. WE ONLY
HAVE ONE WEAPON.
WHO WANTS IT?

ME.

I'LL
TAKE IT.

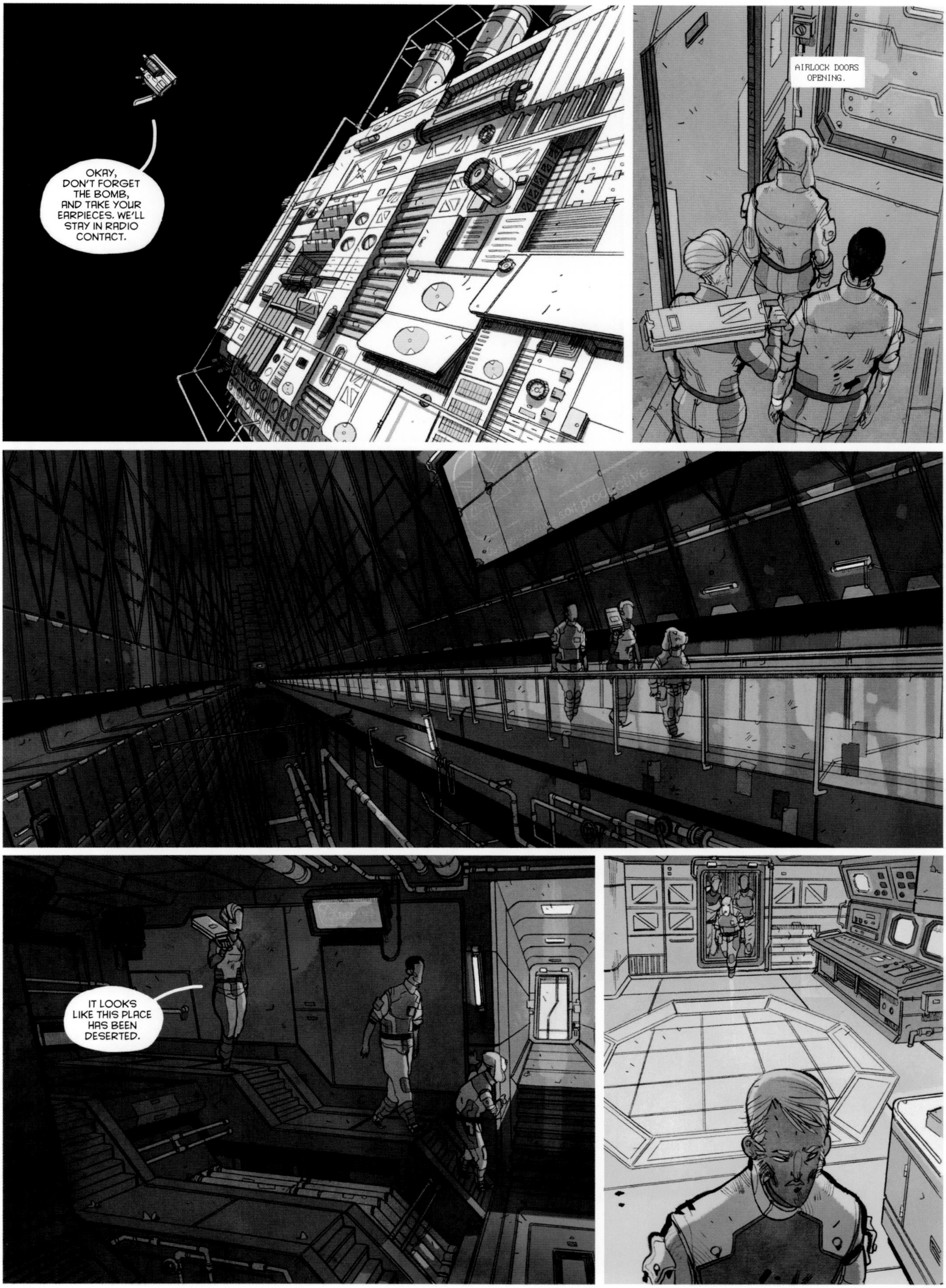
OKAY, DON'T FORGET THE BOMB, AND TAKE YOUR EARPIECES. WE'LL STAY IN RADIO CONTACT.
AIRLOCK DOORS OPENING.
IT LOOKS LIKE THIS PLACE HAS BEEN DESERTED.

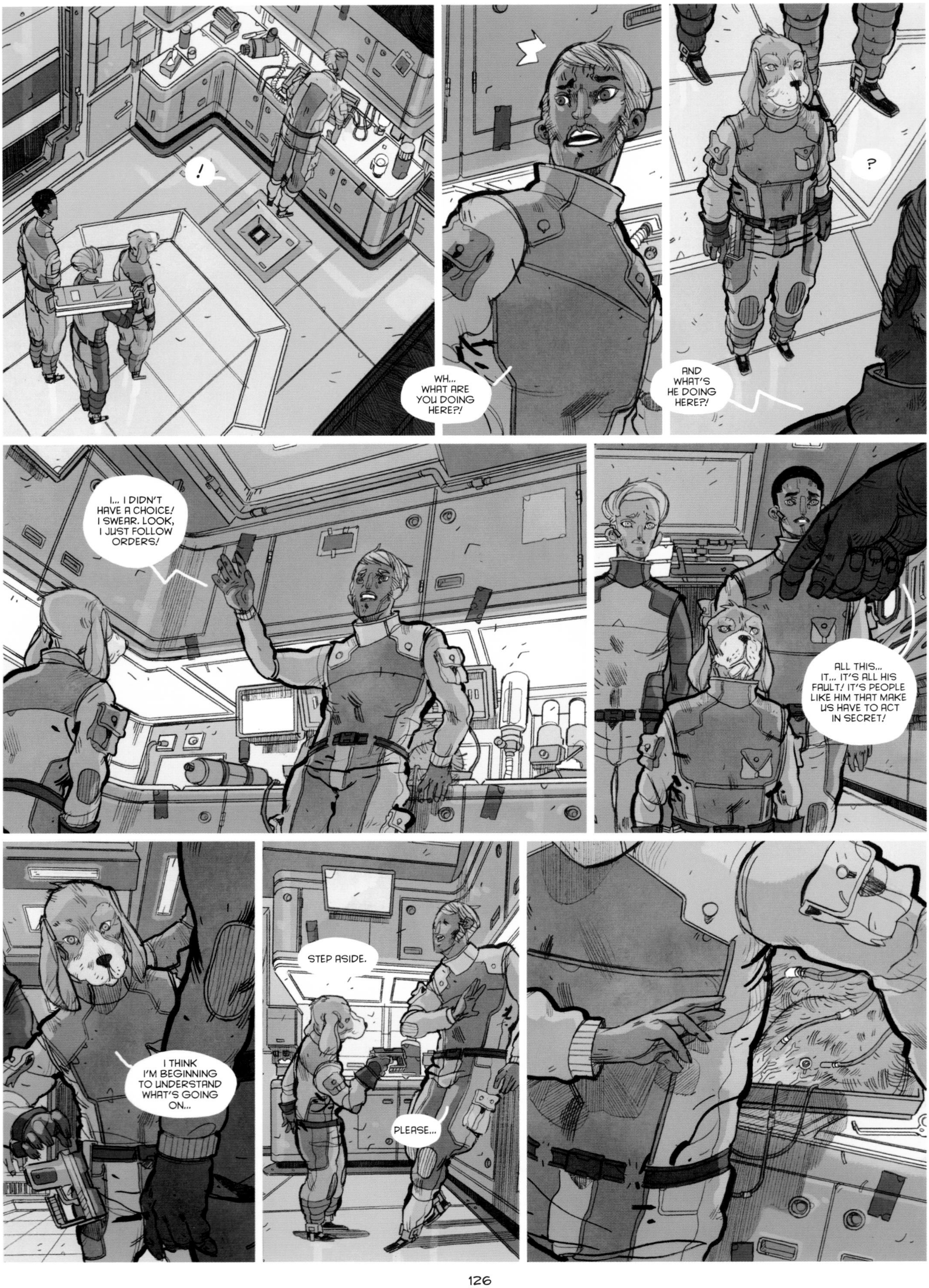
!
WH... WHAT ARE YOU DOING HERE?!
?
AND WHAT'S HE DOING HERE?!
I... I DIDN'T HAVE A CHOICE! I SWEAR. LOOK, I JUST FOLLOW ORDERS!
ALL THIS... IT... IT'S ALL HIS FAULT! IT'S PEOPLE LIKE HIM THAT MAKE US HAVE TO ACT IN SECRET!
I THINK I'M BEGINNING TO UNDERSTAND WHAT'S GOING ON...
STEP ASIDE.
PLEASE...

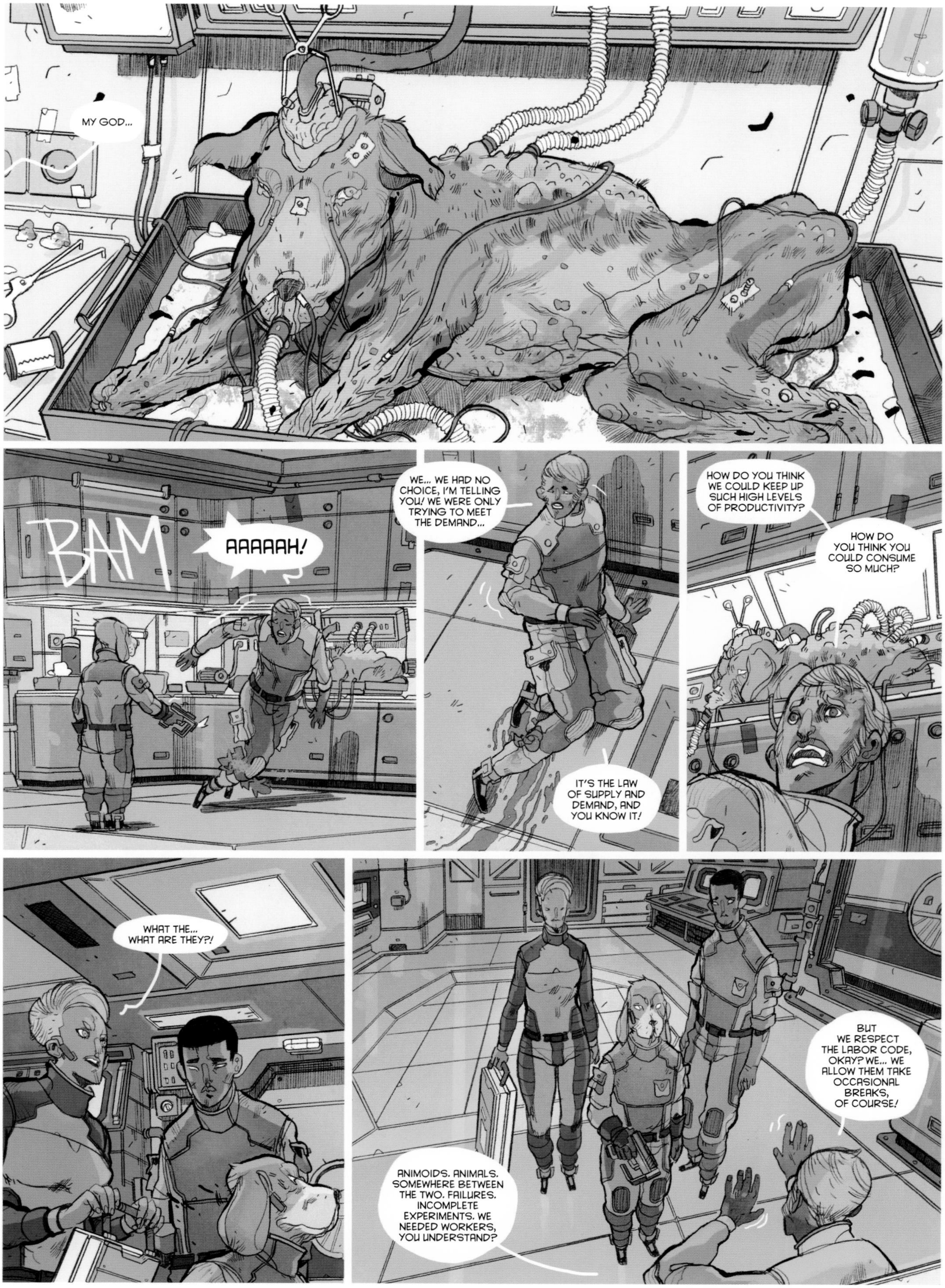
MY GOD...
BAM
AAAAAH!
WE... WE HAD NO CHOICE, I'M TELLING YOU! WE WERE ONLY TRYING TO MEET THE DEMAND...
IT'S THE LAW OF SUPPLY AND DEMAND, AND YOU KNOW IT!
HOW DO YOU THINK WE COULD KEEP UP SUCH HIGH LEVELS OF PRODUCTIVITY?
HOW DO YOU THINK YOU COULD CONSUME SO MUCH?
WHAT THE... WHAT ARE THEY?!
ANIMOIDS. ANIMALS. SOMEWHERE BETWEEN THE TWO. FAILURES. INCOMPLETE EXPERIMENTS. WE NEEDED WORKERS, YOU UNDERSTAND?
BUT WE RESPECT THE LABOR CODE, OKAY? WE... WE ALLOW THEM TAKE OCCASIONAL BREAKS, OF COURSE!

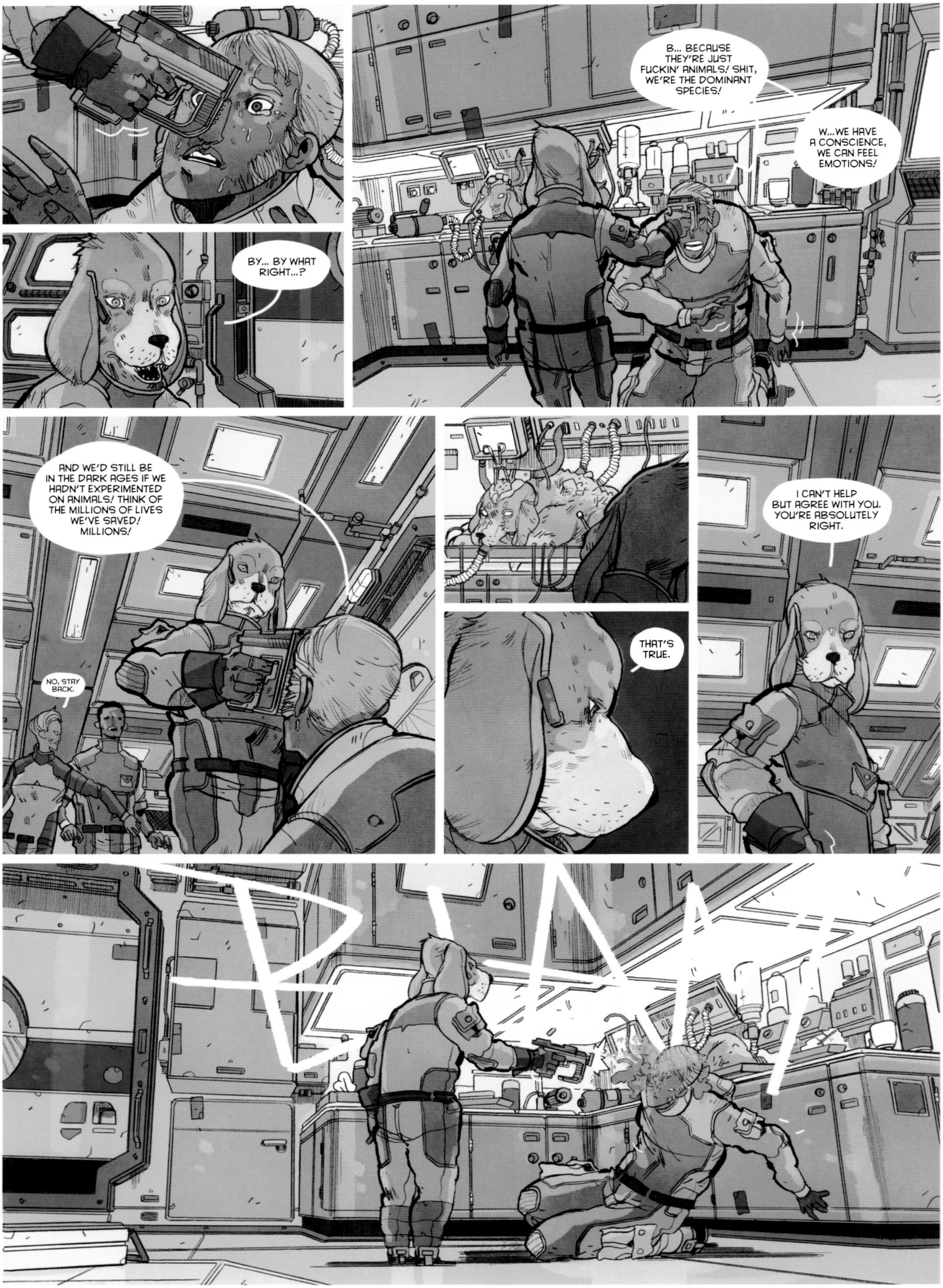
B... BECAUSE THEY'RE JUST FUCKIN' ANIMALS! SHIT, WE'RE THE DOMINANT SPECIES!
W...WE HAVE A CONSCIENCE, WE CAN FEEL EMOTIONS!
BY... BY WHAT RIGHT...?
AND WE'D STILL BE IN THE DARK AGES IF WE HADN'T EXPERIMENTED ON ANIMALS! THINK OF THE MILLIONS OF LIVES WE'VE SAVED! MILLIONS!
NO, STAY BACK.
THAT'S TRUE.
I CAN'T HELP BUT AGREE WITH YOU. YOU'RE ABSOLUTELY RIGHT.

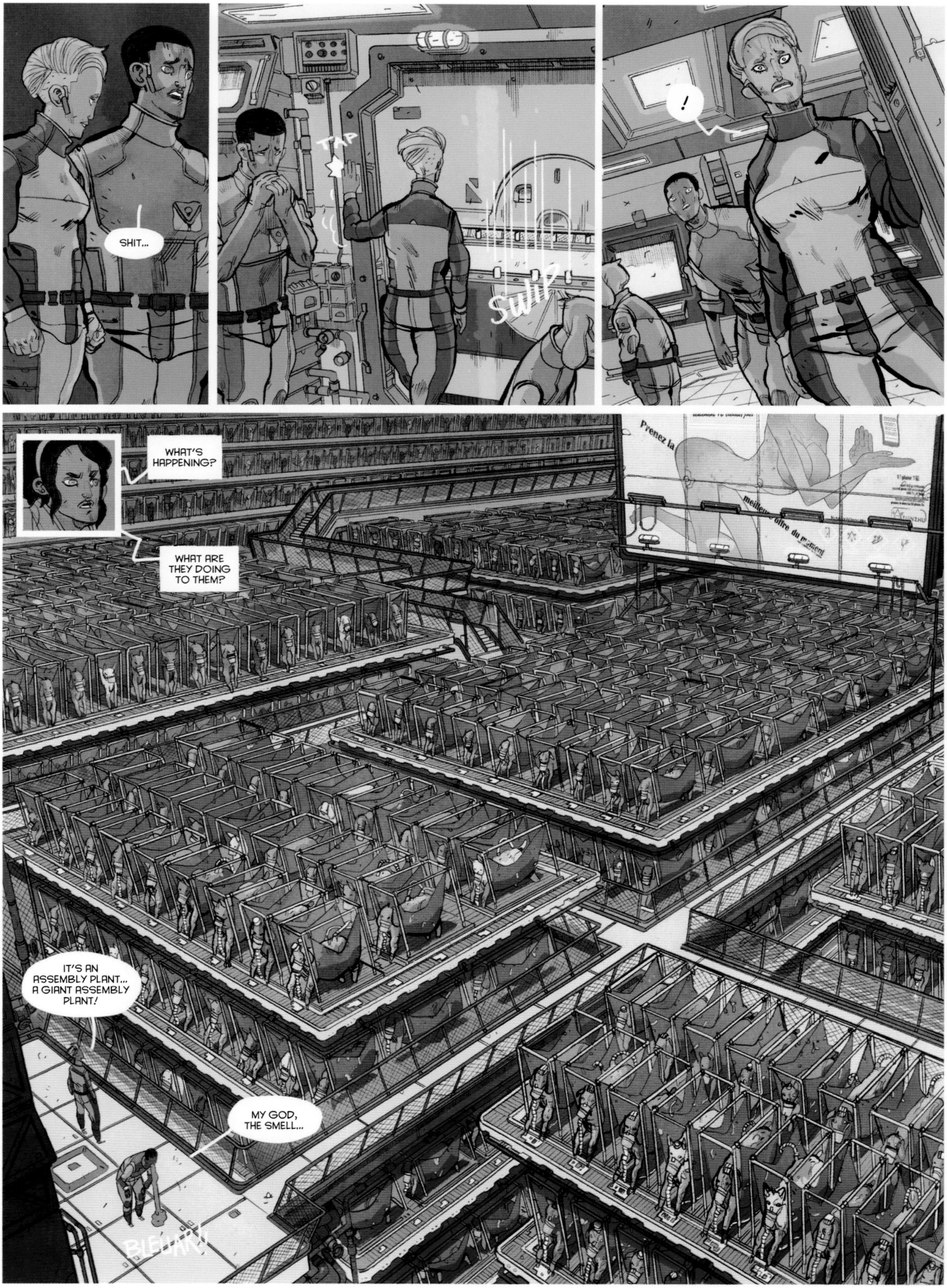
SHIT...
TAP
SWIP
!
WHAT'S HAPPENING?
WHAT ARE THEY DOING TO THEM?
Prenez la
IT'S AN ASSEMBLY PLANT... A GIANT ASSEMBLY PLANT!
MY GOD, THE SMELL...
BLEUAR!

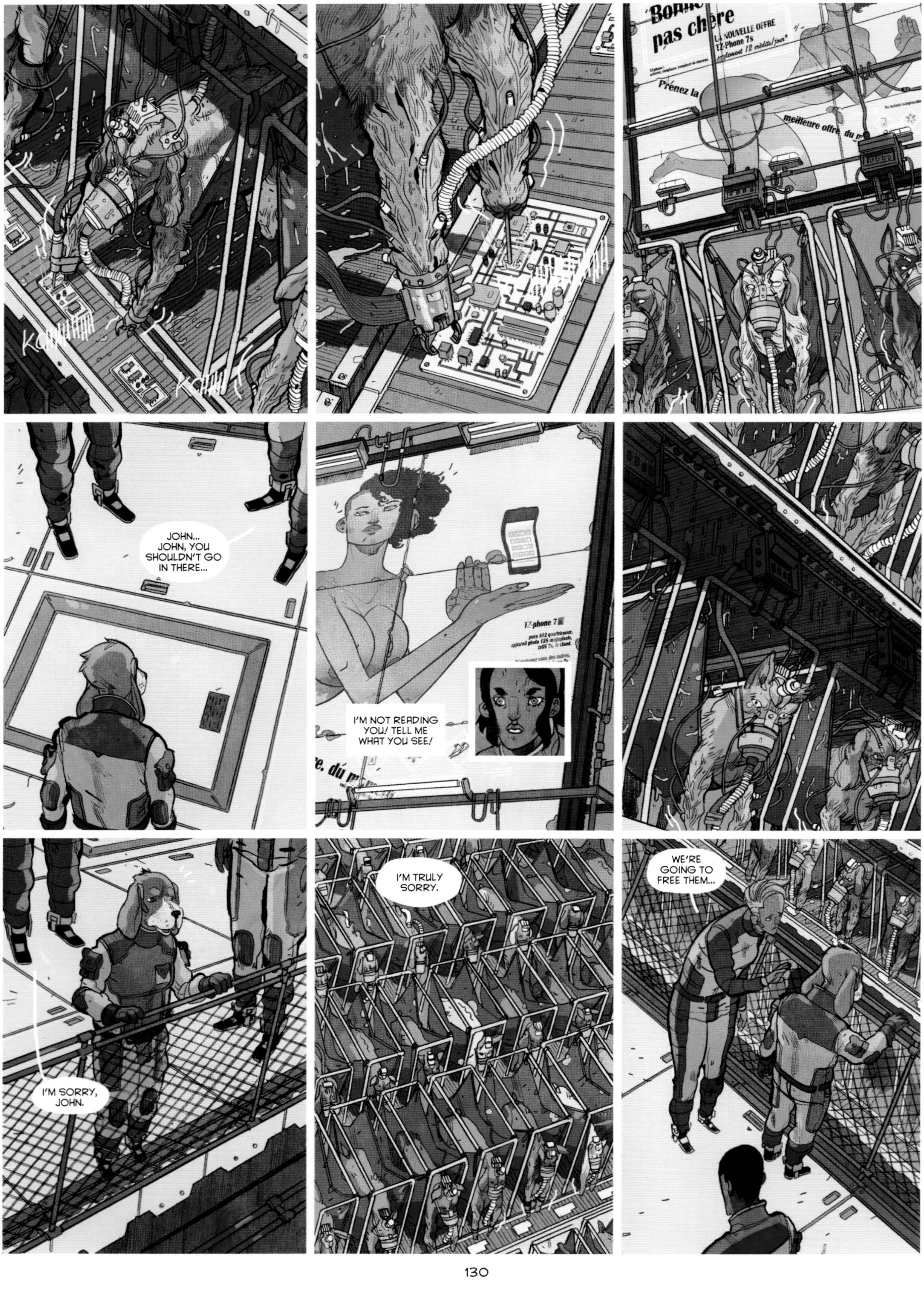
pas chère
LA NOUVELLE OFFRE
TZ-Phone 7s
Prénez la
meilleure offre du
JOHN... JOHN, YOU SHOULDN'T GO IN THERE...
TZ-phone 7
I'M NOT READING YOU! TELL ME WHAT YOU SEE!
I'M SORRY, JOHN.
I'M TRULY SORRY.
WE'RE GOING TO FREE THEM...

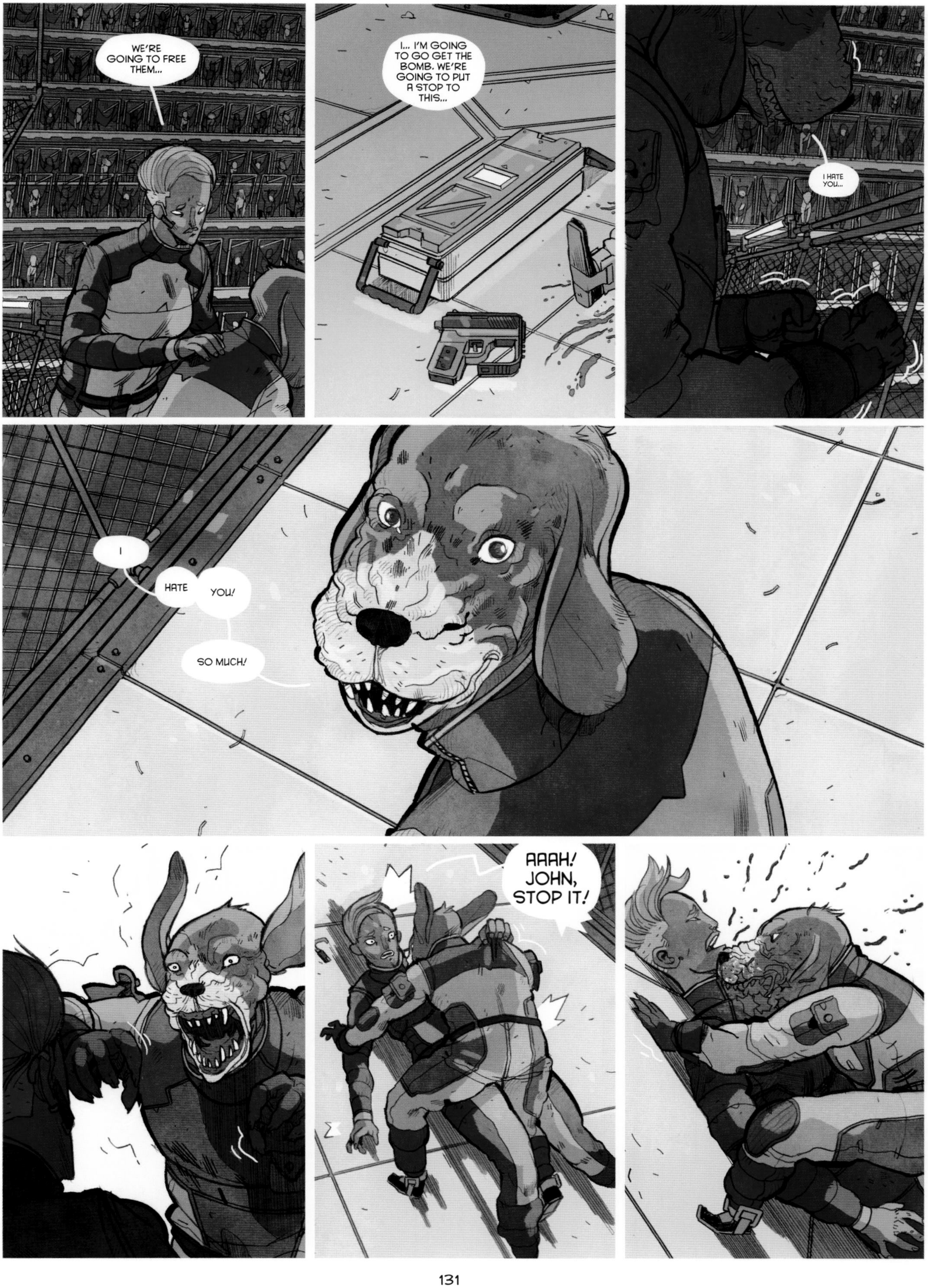
WE'RE GOING TO FREE THEM...
I... I'M GOING TO GO GET THE BOMB. WE'RE GOING TO PUT A STOP TO THIS...
I HATE YOU...
I
HATE
YOU!
SO MUCH!
AAAH! JOHN, STOP IT!

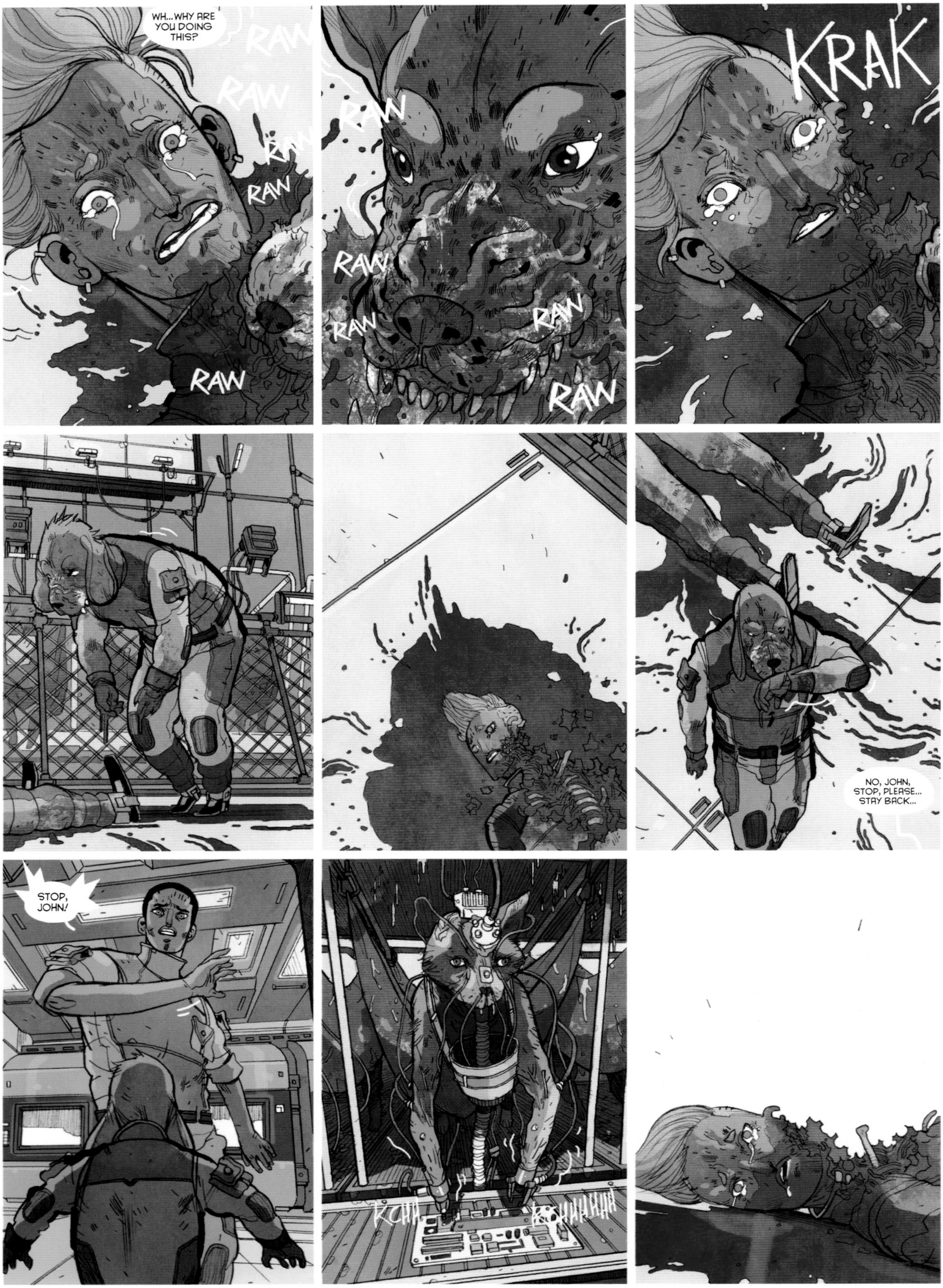
WH... WHY ARE YOU DOING THIS?
RAW
RAW
RAW
RAW
RAW
RAW
RAW
RAW
RAW
RAW
KRAK
NO, JOHN, STOP, PLEASE... STAY BACK...
STOP, JOHN!

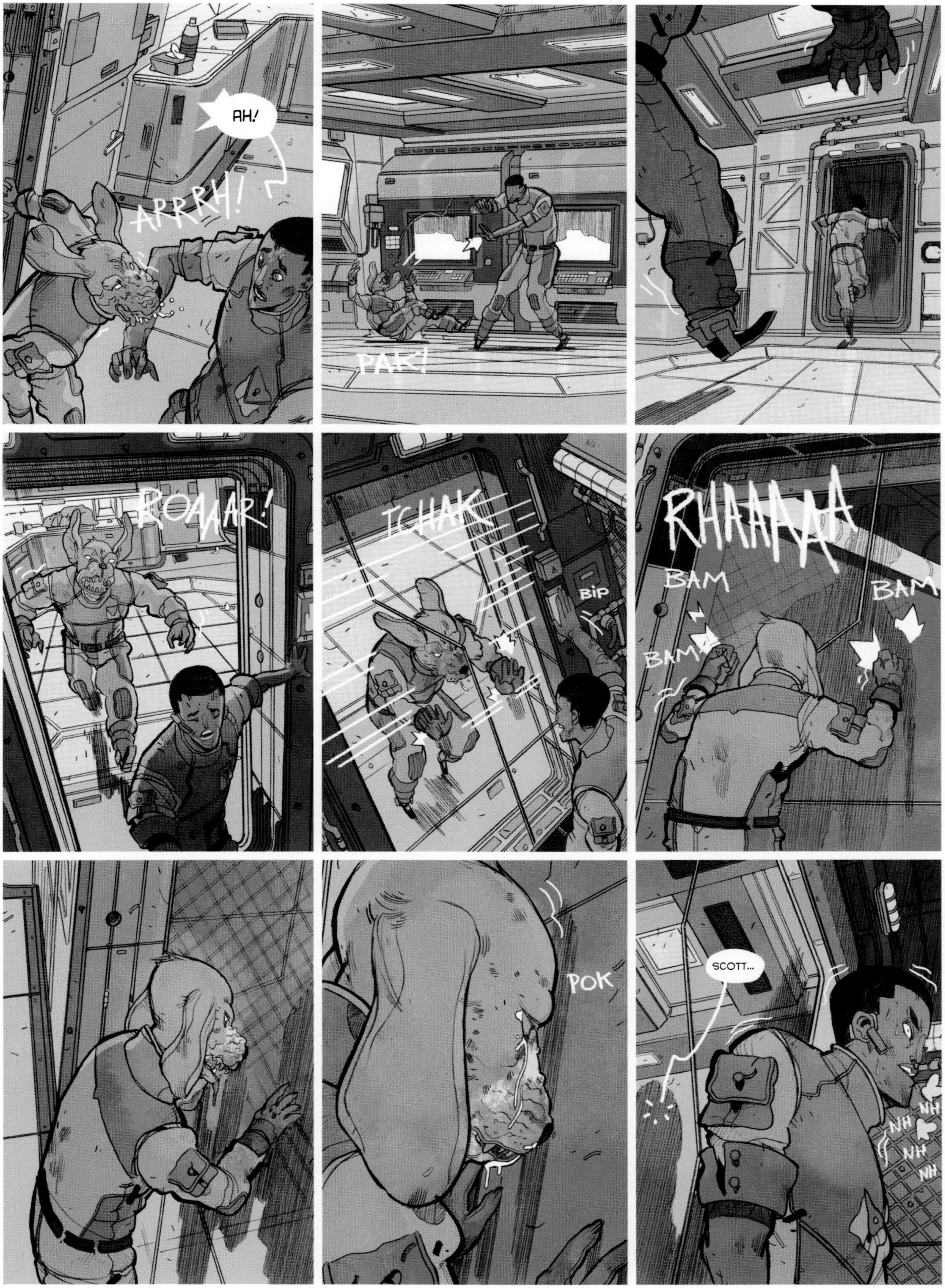
AH!
ARRRH!
PAK!
ROAAAR!
TCHAK
BIP
RHAAAAA
BAM
BAM
BAM
POK
SCOTT...
NH
NH
NH
NH

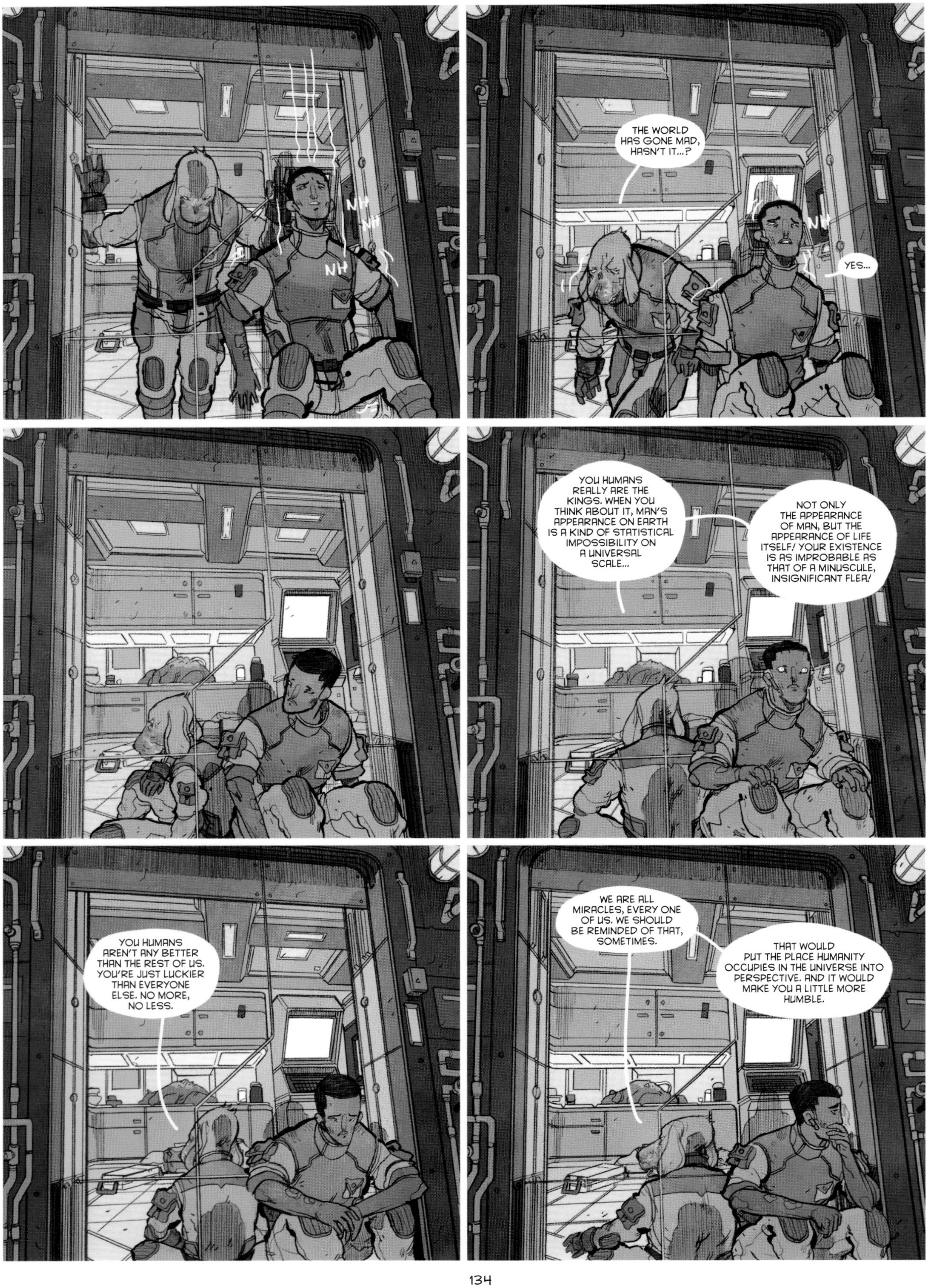
NH
NH
NH
THE WORLD HAS GONE MAD, HASN'T IT...?
NH
YES...
YOU HUMANS REALLY ARE THE KINGS. WHEN YOU THINK ABOUT IT, MAN'S APPEARANCE ON EARTH IS A KIND OF STATISTICAL IMPOSSIBILITY ON A UNIVERSAL SCALE...
NOT ONLY THE APPEARANCE OF MAN, BUT THE APPEARANCE OF LIFE ITSELF! YOUR EXISTENCE IS AS IMPROBABLE AS THAT OF A MINUSCULE, INSIGNIFICANT FLEA!
YOU HUMANS AREN'T ANY BETTER THAN THE REST OF US. YOU'RE JUST LUCKIER THAN EVERYONE ELSE. NO MORE, NO LESS.
WE ARE ALL MIRACLES, EVERY ONE OF US. WE SHOULD BE REMINDED OF THAT, SOMETIMES.
THAT WOULD PUT THE PLACE HUMANITY OCCUPIES IN THE UNIVERSE INTO PERSPECTIVE. AND IT WOULD MAKE YOU A LITTLE MORE HUMBLE.

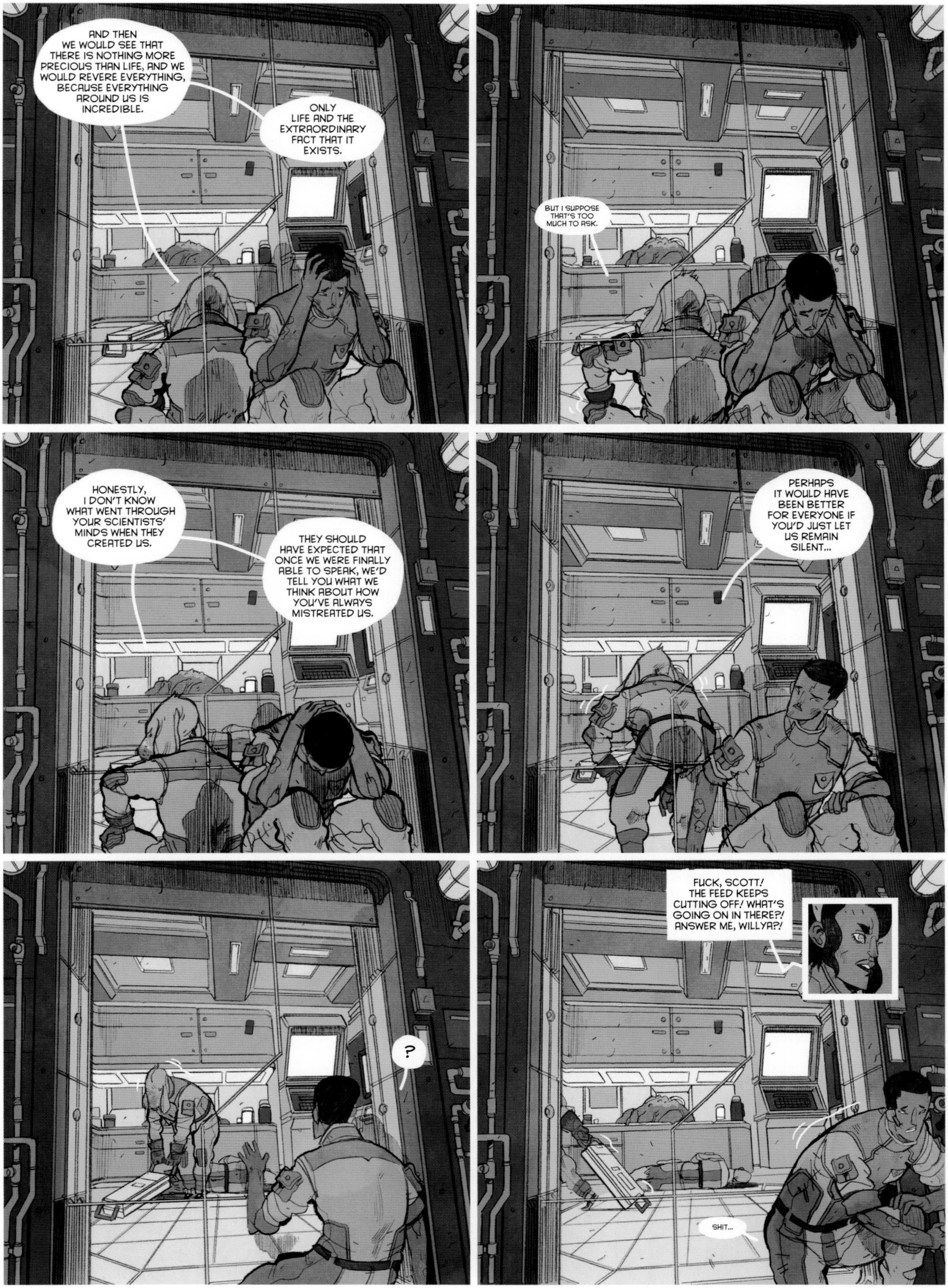
AND THEN WE WOULD SEE THAT THERE IS NOTHING MORE PRECIOUS THAN LIFE, AND WE WOULD REVERE EVERYTHING, BECAUSE EVERYTHING AROUND US IS INCREDIBLE.
ONLY LIFE AND THE EXTRAORDINARY FACT THAT IT EXISTS.
BUT I SUPPOSE THAT'S TOO MUCH TO ASK.
HONESTLY, I DON'T KNOW WHAT WENT THROUGH YOUR SCIENTISTS' MINDS WHEN THEY CREATED US.
THEY SHOULD HAVE EXPECTED THAT ONCE WE WERE FINALLY ABLE TO SPEAK, WE'D TELL YOU WHAT WE THINK ABOUT HOW YOU'VE ALWAYS MISTREATED US.
PERHAPS IT WOULD HAVE BEEN BETTER FOR EVERYONE IF YOU'D JUST LET US REMAIN SILENT...
?
FUCK, SCOTT! THE FEED KEEPS CUTTING OFF! WHAT'S GOING ON IN THERE?! ANSWER ME, WILLYA?!
SHIT...

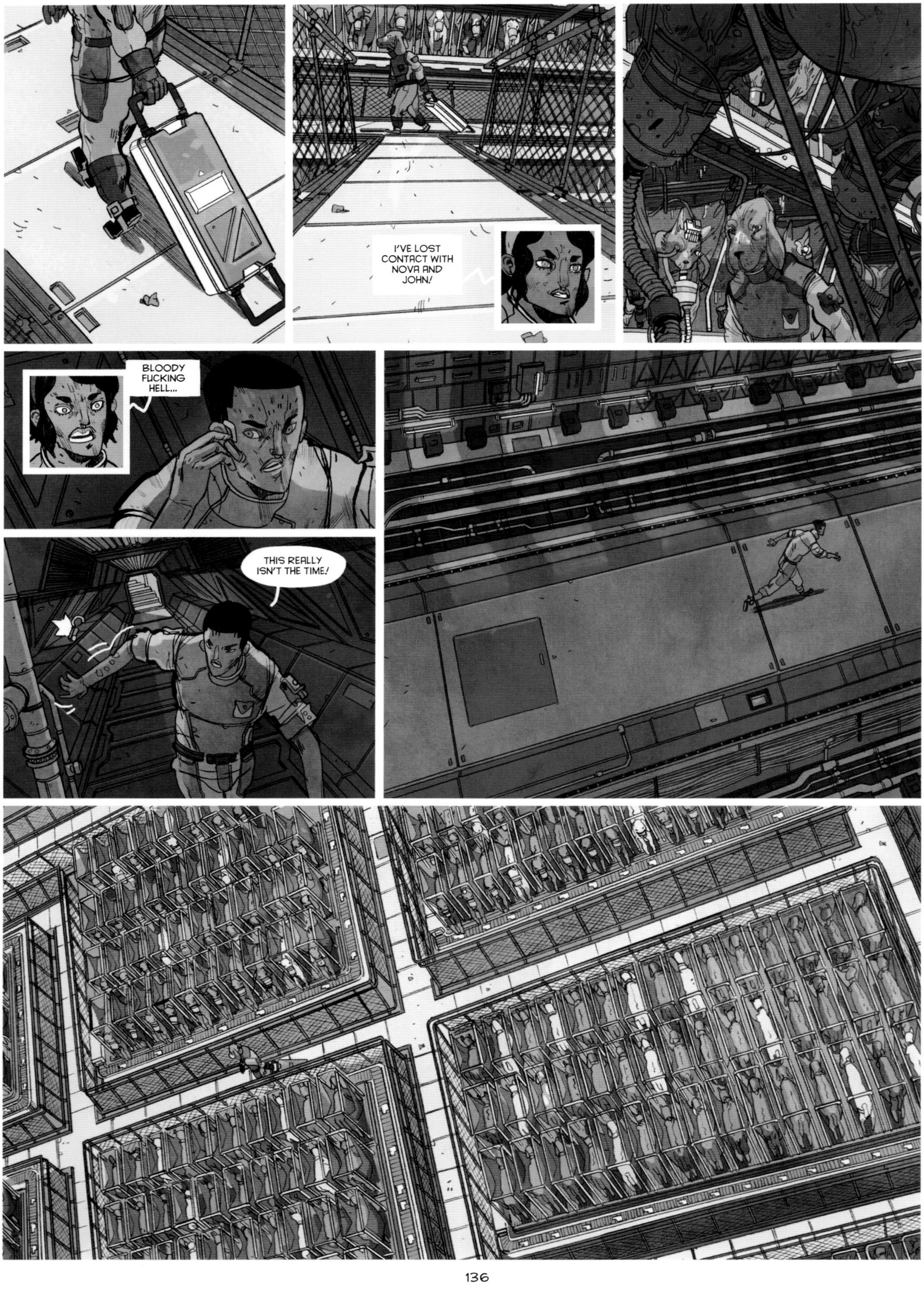
I'VE LOST CONTACT WITH NOVA AND JOHN!
BLOODY FUCKING HELL...
THIS REALLY ISN'T THE TIME!

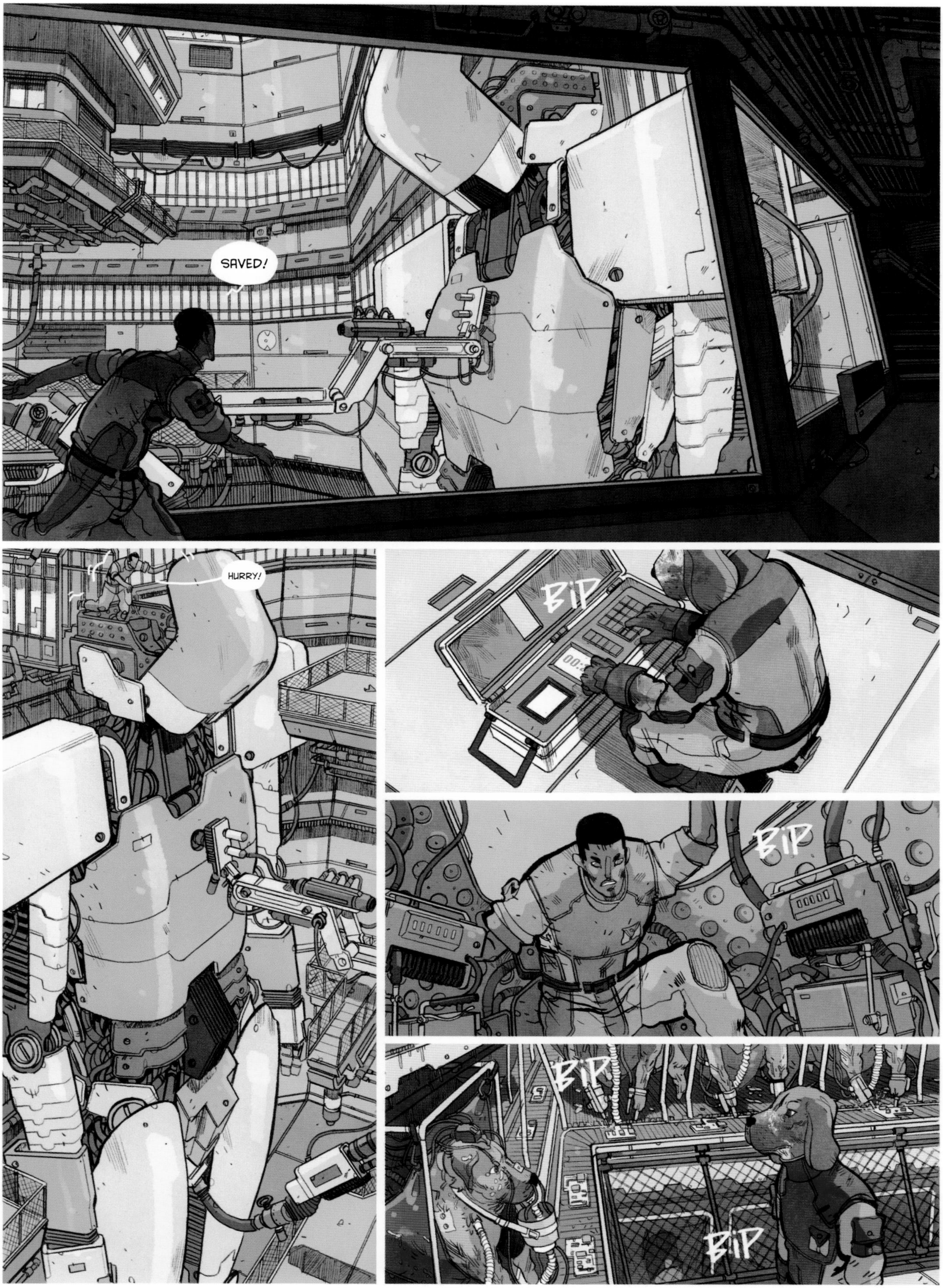
SAVED!
HURRY!
BIP
BIP
BIP
BIP

BIP

BIP

00:01

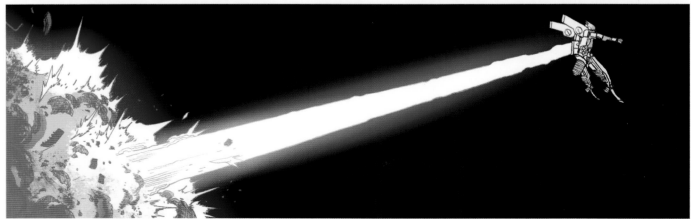

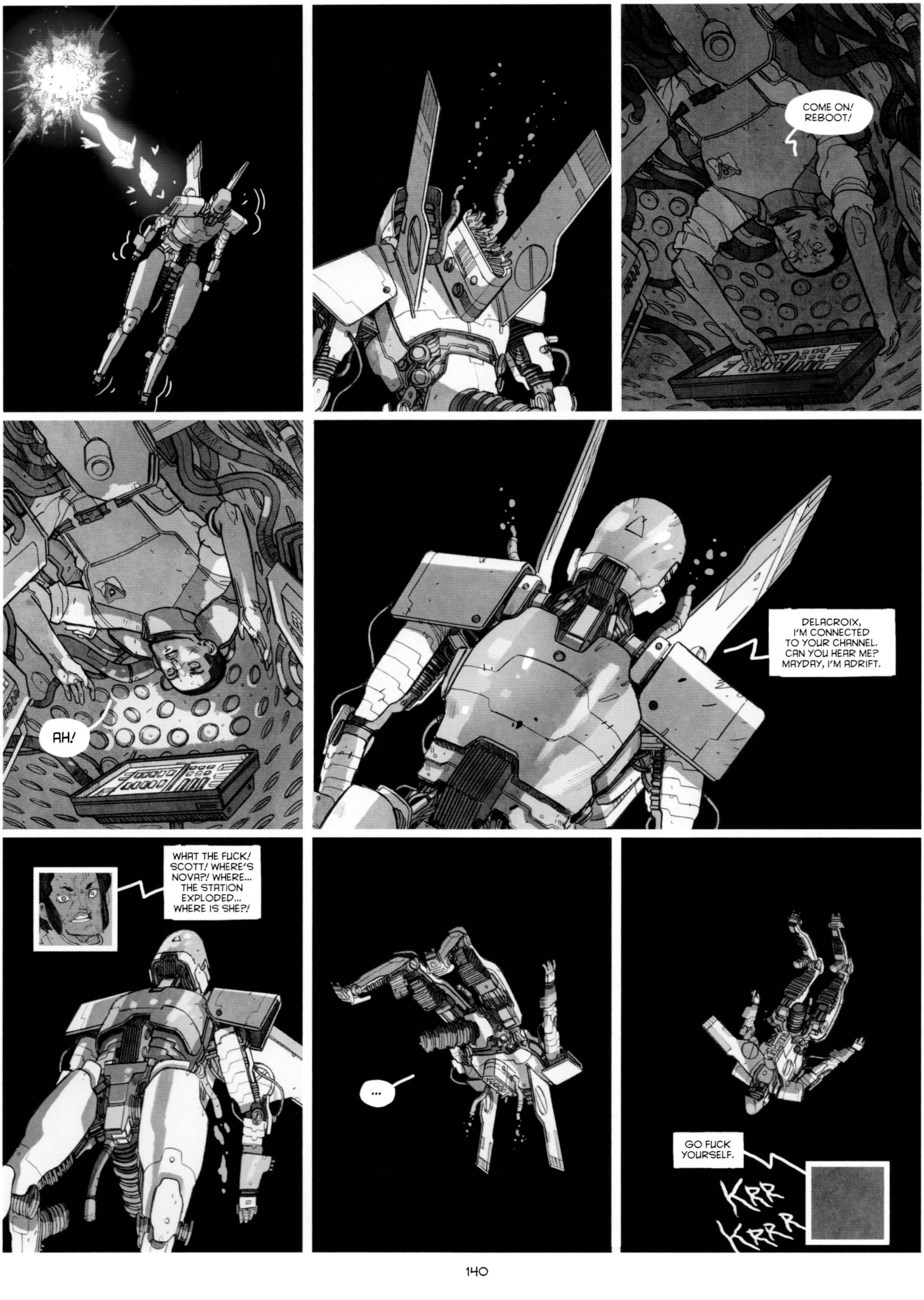
COME ON! REBOOT!
AH!
DELACROIX, I'M CONNECTED TO YOUR CHANNEL. CAN YOU HEAR ME? MAYDAY, I'M ADRIFT.
WHAT THE FUCK! SCOTT! WHERE'S NOVA?! WHERE... THE STATION EXPLODED... WHERE IS SHE?!
...
GO FUCK YOURSELF.
KRR
KRRR

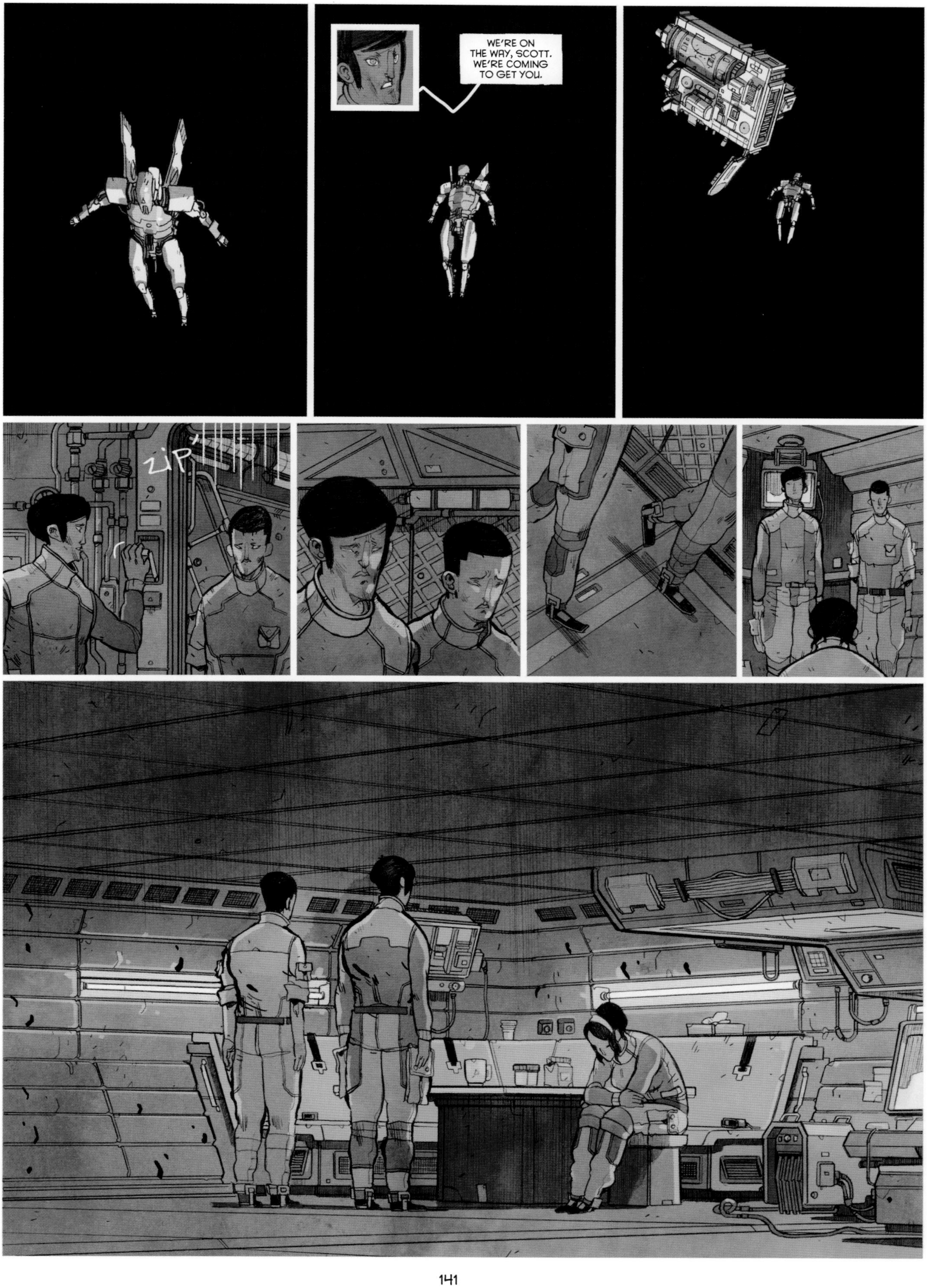
WE'RE ON THE WAY, SCOTT. WE'RE COMING TO GET YOU.
ZIP

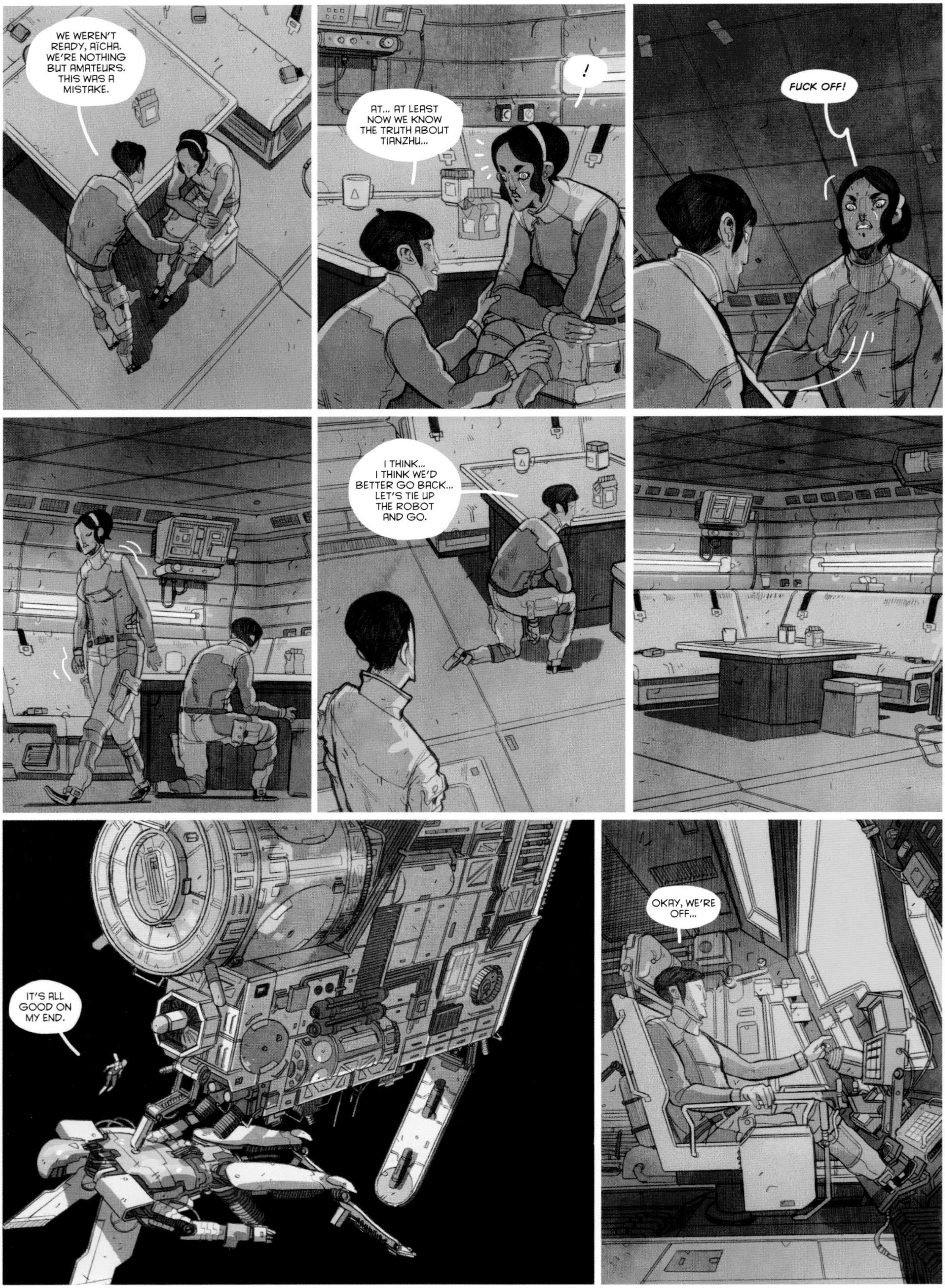
WE WEREN'T READY, AÏCHA. WE'RE NOTHING BUT AMATEURS. THIS WAS A MISTAKE.
AT... AT LEAST NOW WE KNOW THE TRUTH ABOUT TIANZHU...
!
FUCK OFF!
I THINK... I THINK WE'D BETTER GO BACK... LET'S TIE UP THE ROBOT AND GO.
IT'S ALL GOOD ON MY END.
OKAY, WE'RE OFF...

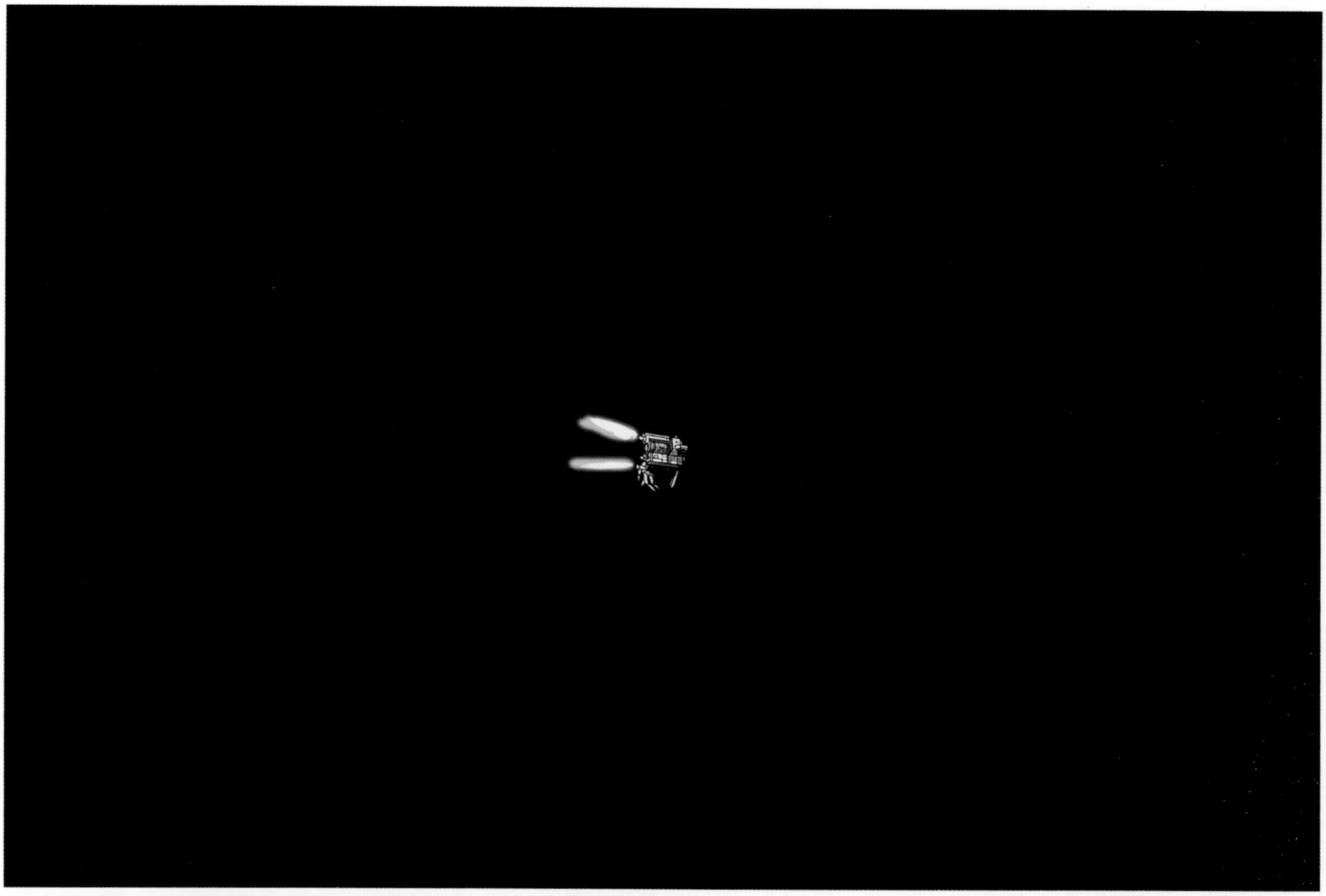

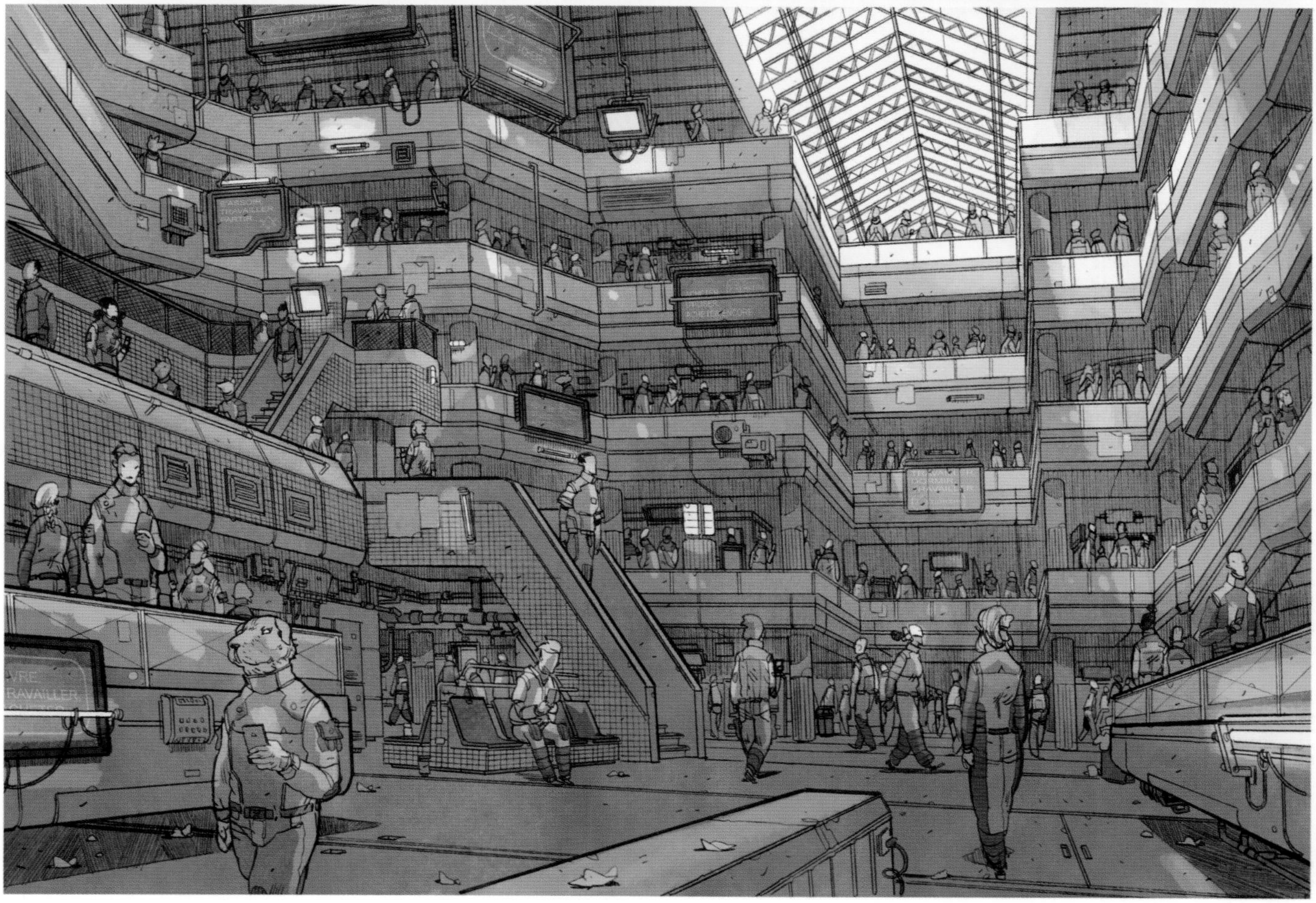

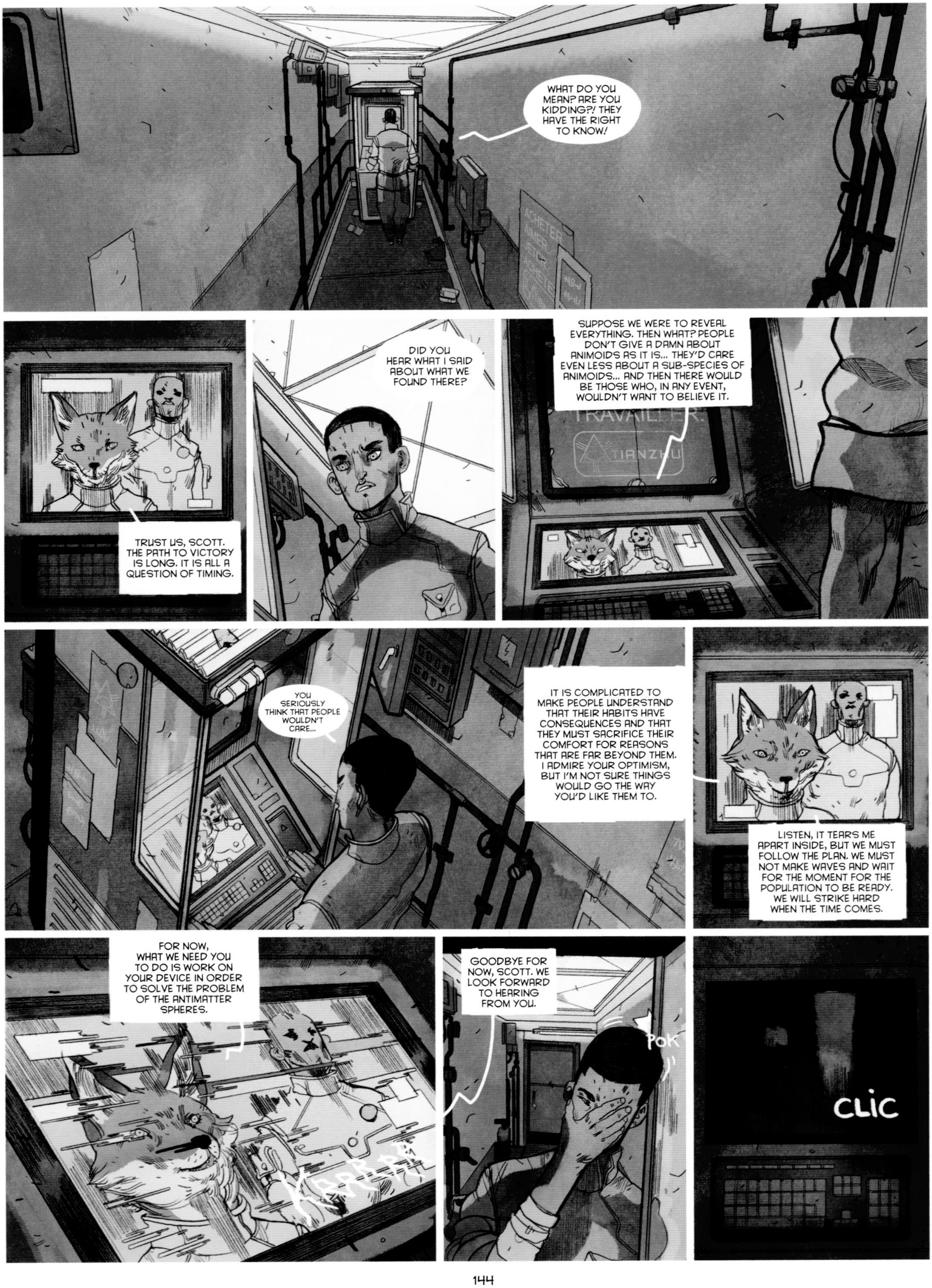

WHAT DO YOU MEAN? ARE YOU KIDDING?! THEY HAVE THE RIGHT TO KNOW!
TRUST US, SCOTT. THE PATH TO VICTORY IS LONG. IT IS ALL A QUESTION OF TIMING.
DID YOU HEAR WHAT I SAID ABOUT WHAT WE FOUND THERE?
SUPPOSE WE WERE TO REVEAL EVERYTHING. THEN WHAT? PEOPLE DON'T GIVE A DAMN ABOUT ANIMOIDS AS IT IS... THEY'D CARE EVEN LESS ABOUT A SUB-SPECIES OF ANIMOIDS... AND THEN THERE WOULD BE THOSE WHO, IN ANY EVENT, WOULDN'T WANT TO BELIEVE IT.
TIANZHU
YOU SERIOUSLY THINK THAT PEOPLE WOULDN'T CARE...
IT IS COMPLICATED TO MAKE PEOPLE UNDERSTAND THAT THEIR HABITS HAVE CONSEQUENCES AND THAT THEY MUST SACRIFICE THEIR COMFORT FOR REASONS THAT ARE FAR BEYOND THEM. I ADMIRE YOUR OPTIMISM, BUT I'M NOT SURE THINGS WOULD GO THE WAY YOU'D LIKE THEM TO.
LISTEN, IT TEARS ME APART INSIDE, BUT WE MUST FOLLOW THE PLAN. WE MUST NOT MAKE WAVES AND WAIT FOR THE MOMENT FOR THE POPULATION TO BE READY. WE WILL STRIKE HARD WHEN THE TIME COMES.
FOR NOW, WHAT WE NEED YOU TO DO IS WORK ON YOUR DEVICE IN ORDER TO SOLVE THE PROBLEM OF THE ANTIMATTER SPHERES.
GOODBYE FOR NOW, SCOTT. WE LOOK FORWARD TO HEARING FROM YOU.
POK
CLIC

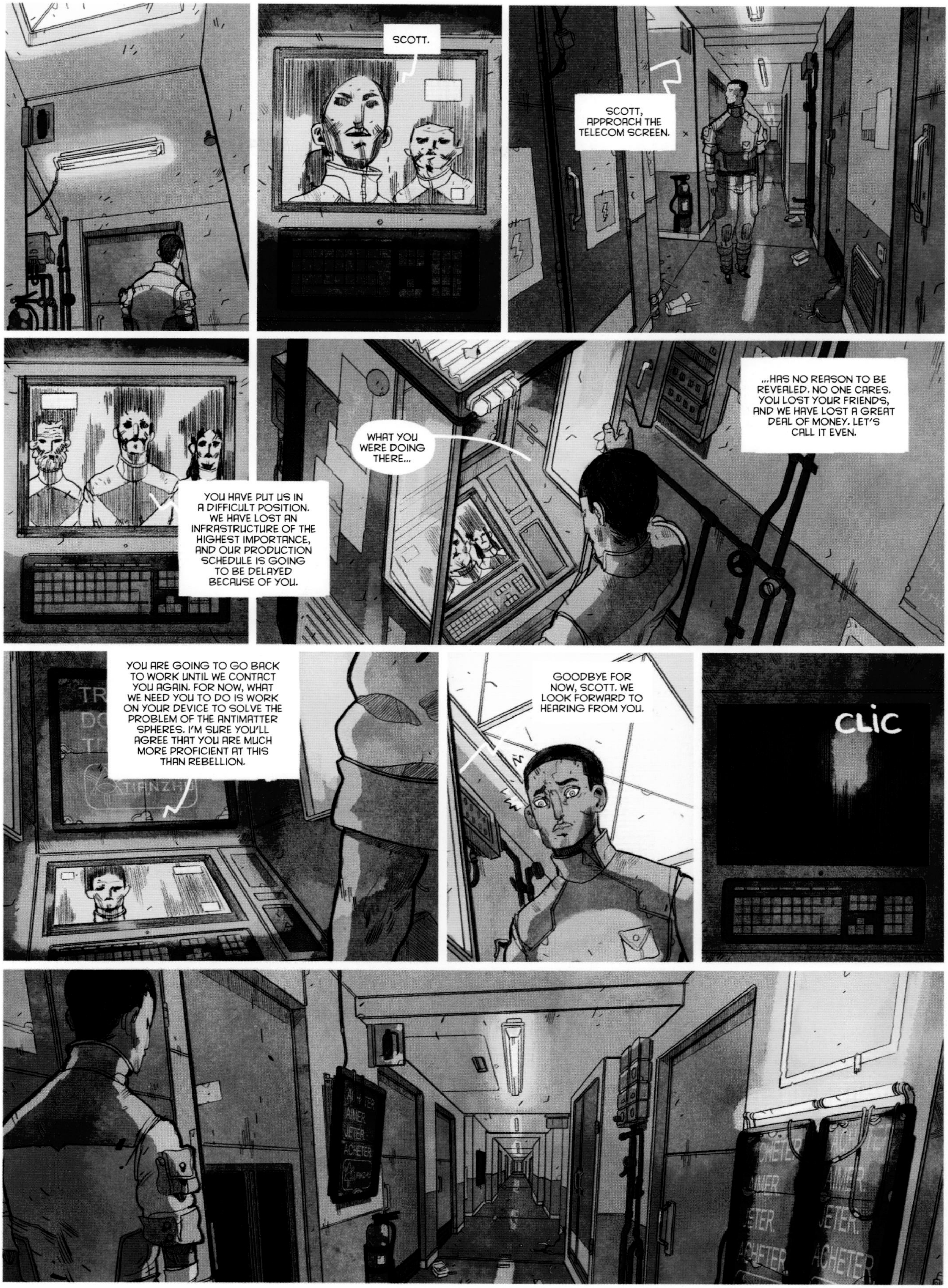
SCOTT.
SCOTT, APPROACH THE TELECOM SCREEN.
YOU HAVE PUT US IN A DIFFICULT POSITION. WE HAVE LOST AN INFRASTRUCTURE OF THE HIGHEST IMPORTANCE, AND OUR PRODUCTION SCHEDULE IS GOING TO BE DELAYED BECAUSE OF YOU.
WHAT YOU WERE DOING THERE...
...HAS NO REASON TO BE REVEALED. NO ONE CARES. YOU LOST YOUR FRIENDS, AND WE HAVE LOST A GREAT DEAL OF MONEY. LET'S CALL IT EVEN.
YOU ARE GOING TO GO BACK TO WORK UNTIL WE CONTACT YOU AGAIN. FOR NOW, WHAT WE NEED YOU TO DO IS WORK ON YOUR DEVICE TO SOLVE THE PROBLEM OF THE ANTIMATTER SPHERES. I'M SURE YOU'LL AGREE THAT YOU ARE MUCH MORE PROFICIENT AT THIS THAN REBELLION.
GOODBYE FOR NOW, SCOTT. WE LOOK FORWARD TO HEARING FROM YOU.
CLIC

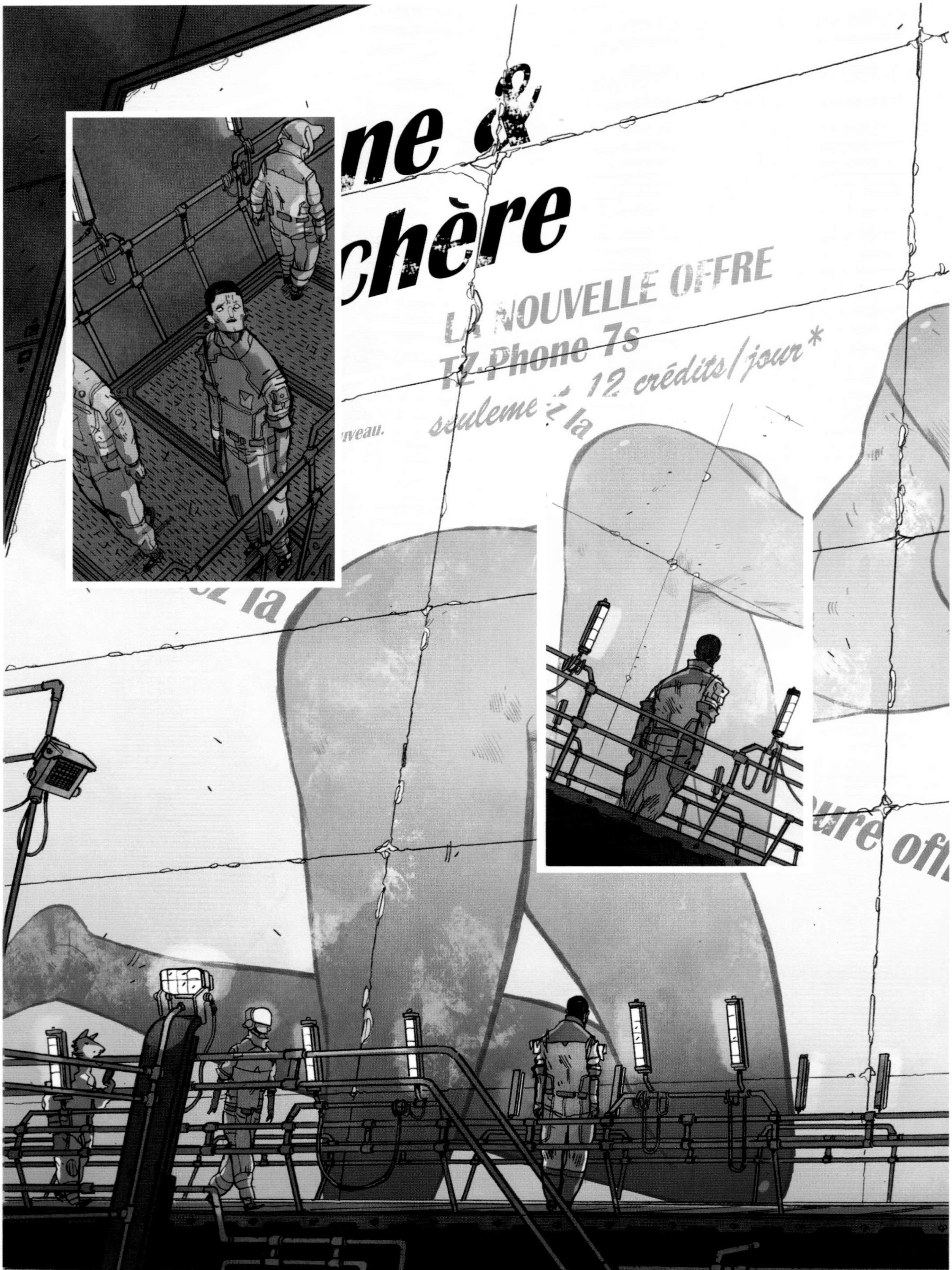
ne &
chère
LA NOUVELLE OFFRE
TZ-Phone 7s
12 crédits/jour*
uveau.
z la
ure off

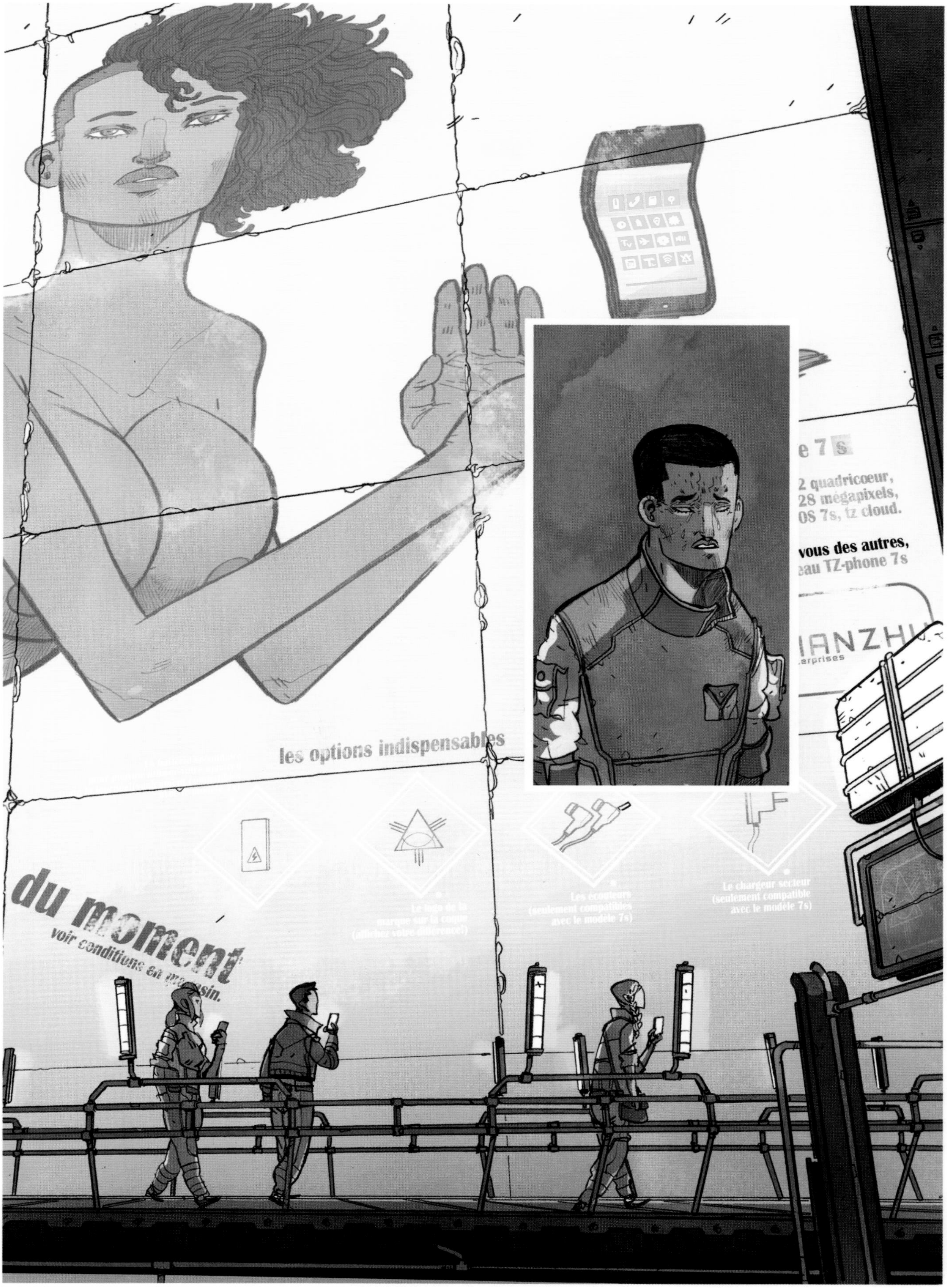
e 7 s
2 quadricoeur,
28 mégapixels,
OS 7s, tz cloud.
vous des autres,
eau TZ-phone 7s
IANZHU
erprises
les options indispensables
du moment
voir conditions en
Le logo de la marque sur la coque (affichez votre différence!)
Les écouteurs (seulement compatibles avec le modèle 7s)
Le chargeur secteur (seulement compatible avec le modèle 7s)

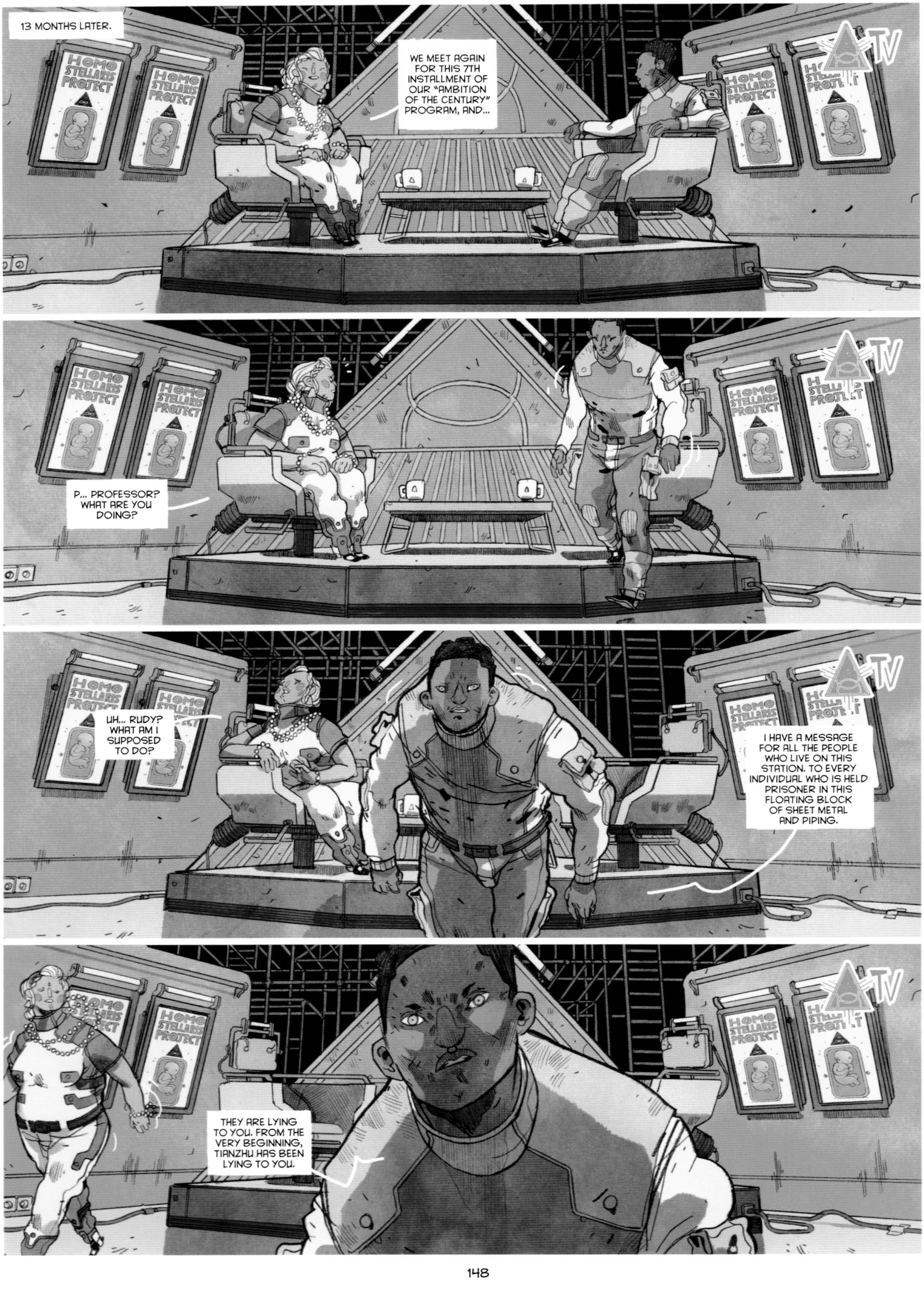
13 MONTHS LATER.
WE MEET AGAIN FOR THIS 7TH INSTALLMENT OF OUR "AMBITION OF THE CENTURY" PROGRAM, AND...
P... PROFESSOR? WHAT ARE YOU DOING?
UH... RUDY? WHAT AM I SUPPOSED TO DO?
I HAVE A MESSAGE FOR ALL THE PEOPLE WHO LIVE ON THIS STATION. TO EVERY INDIVIDUAL WHO IS HELD PRISONER IN THIS FLOATING BLOCK OF SHEET METAL AND PIPING.
THEY ARE LYING TO YOU. FROM THE VERY BEGINNING, TIANZHU HAS BEEN LYING TO YOU.

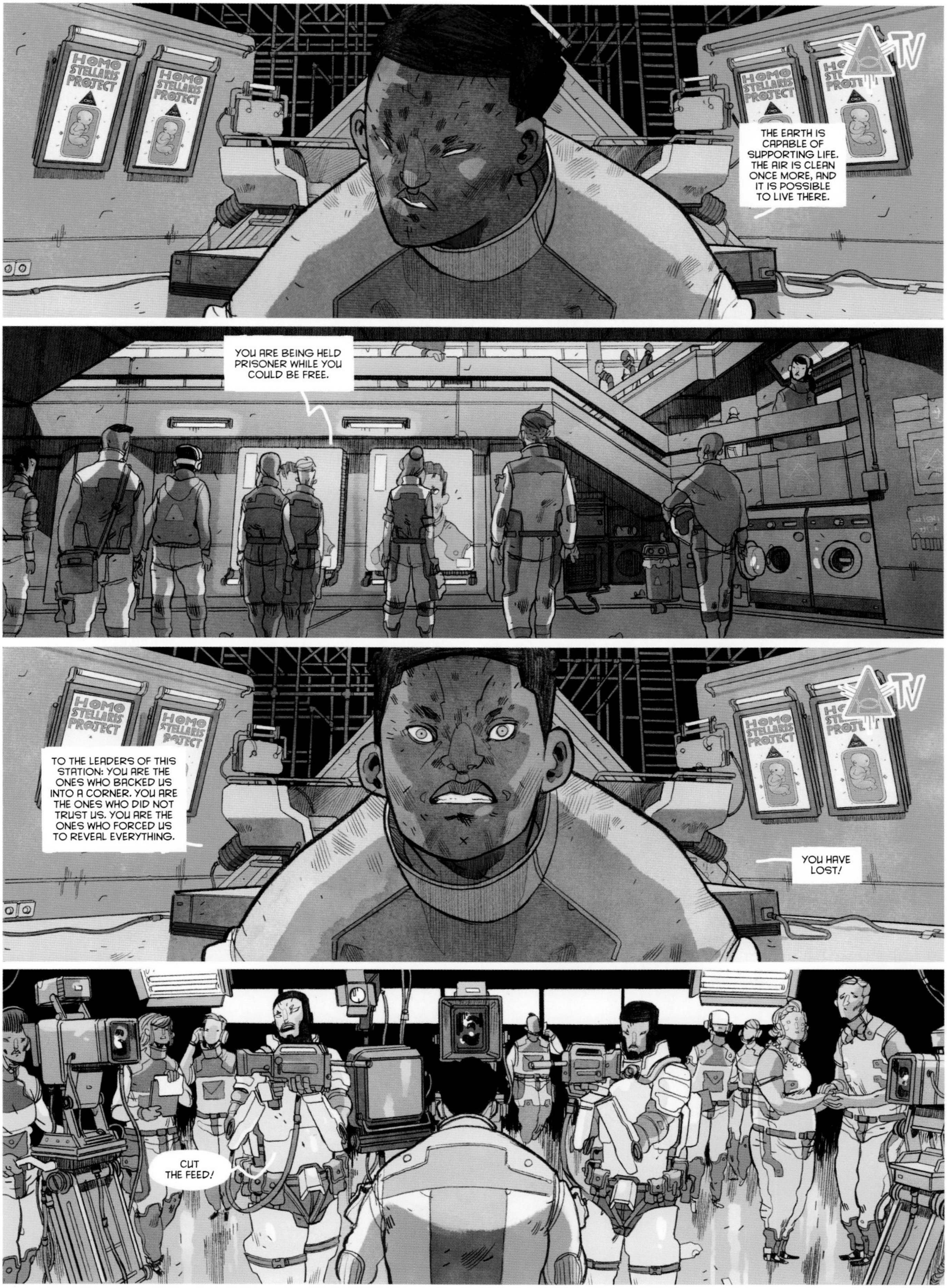
HOMO STELLARIS PROJECT
ATV
THE EARTH IS CAPABLE OF SUPPORTING LIFE. THE AIR IS CLEAN ONCE MORE, AND IT IS POSSIBLE TO LIVE THERE.
YOU ARE BEING HELD PRISONER WHILE YOU COULD BE FREE.
HOMO STELLARIS PROJECT
TO THE LEADERS OF THIS STATION: YOU ARE THE ONES WHO BACKED US INTO A CORNER. YOU ARE THE ONES WHO DID NOT TRUST US. YOU ARE THE ONES WHO FORCED US TO REVEAL EVERYTHING.
YOU HAVE LOST!
CUT THE FEED!

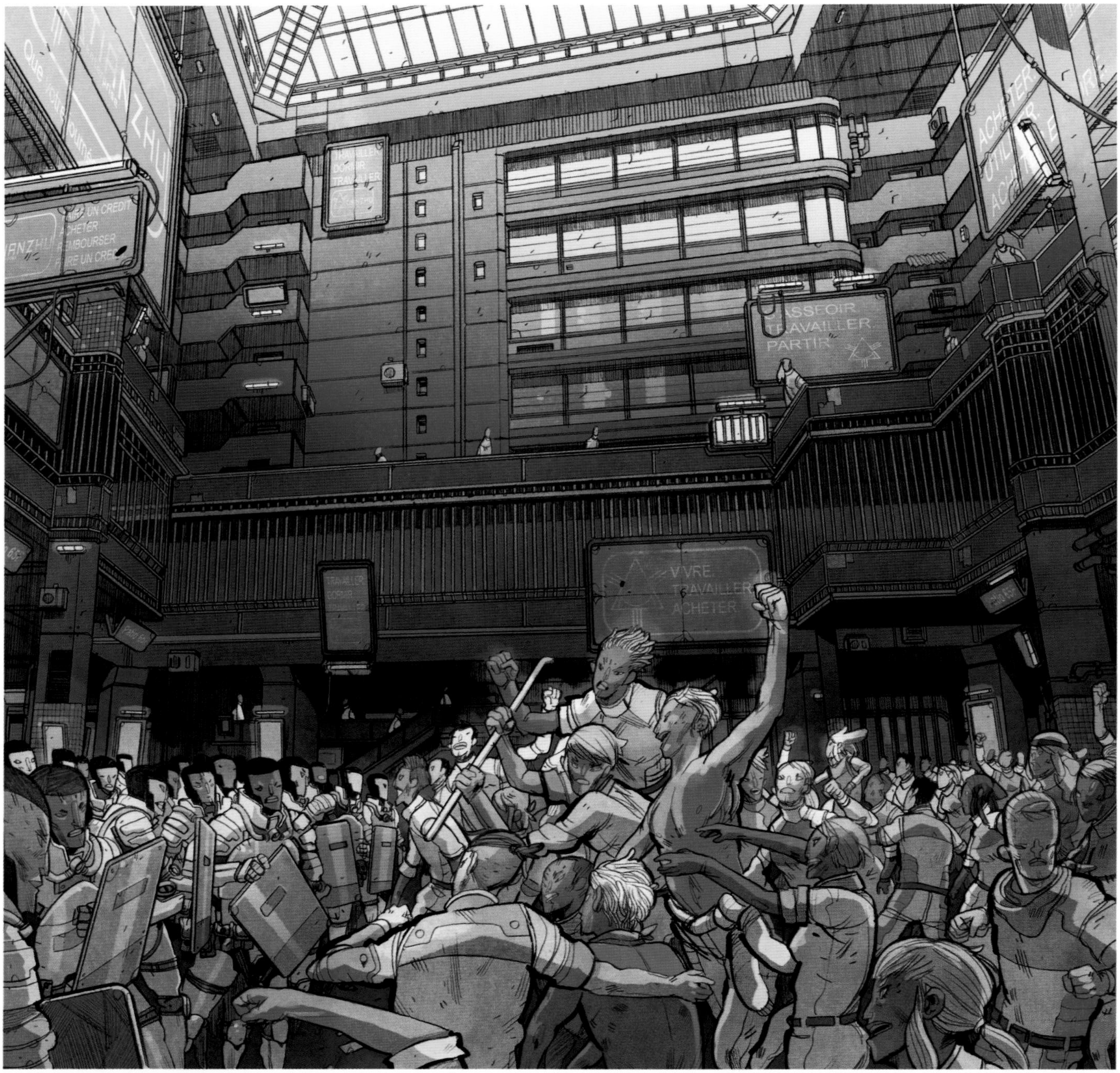
FAIRE UN CREDIT
ACHETER
REMBOURSER
TRAVAILLER
DORMIR
TRAVAILLER
ASSEOIR
TRAVAILLER
PARTIR
VIVRE,
TRAVAILLER,
ACHETER

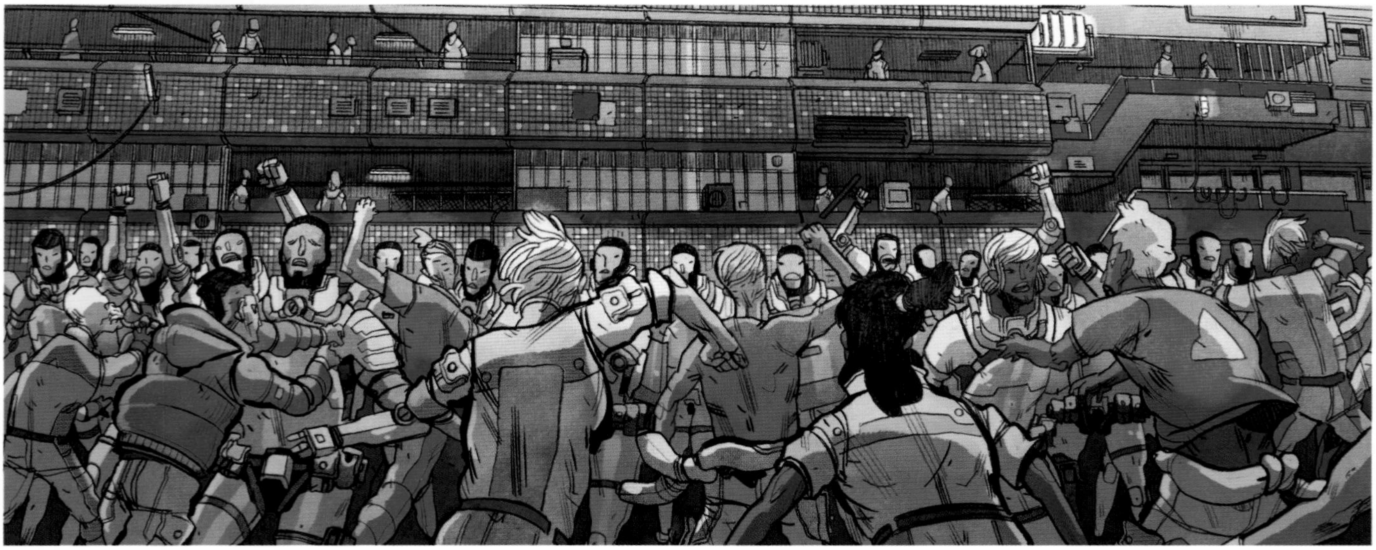

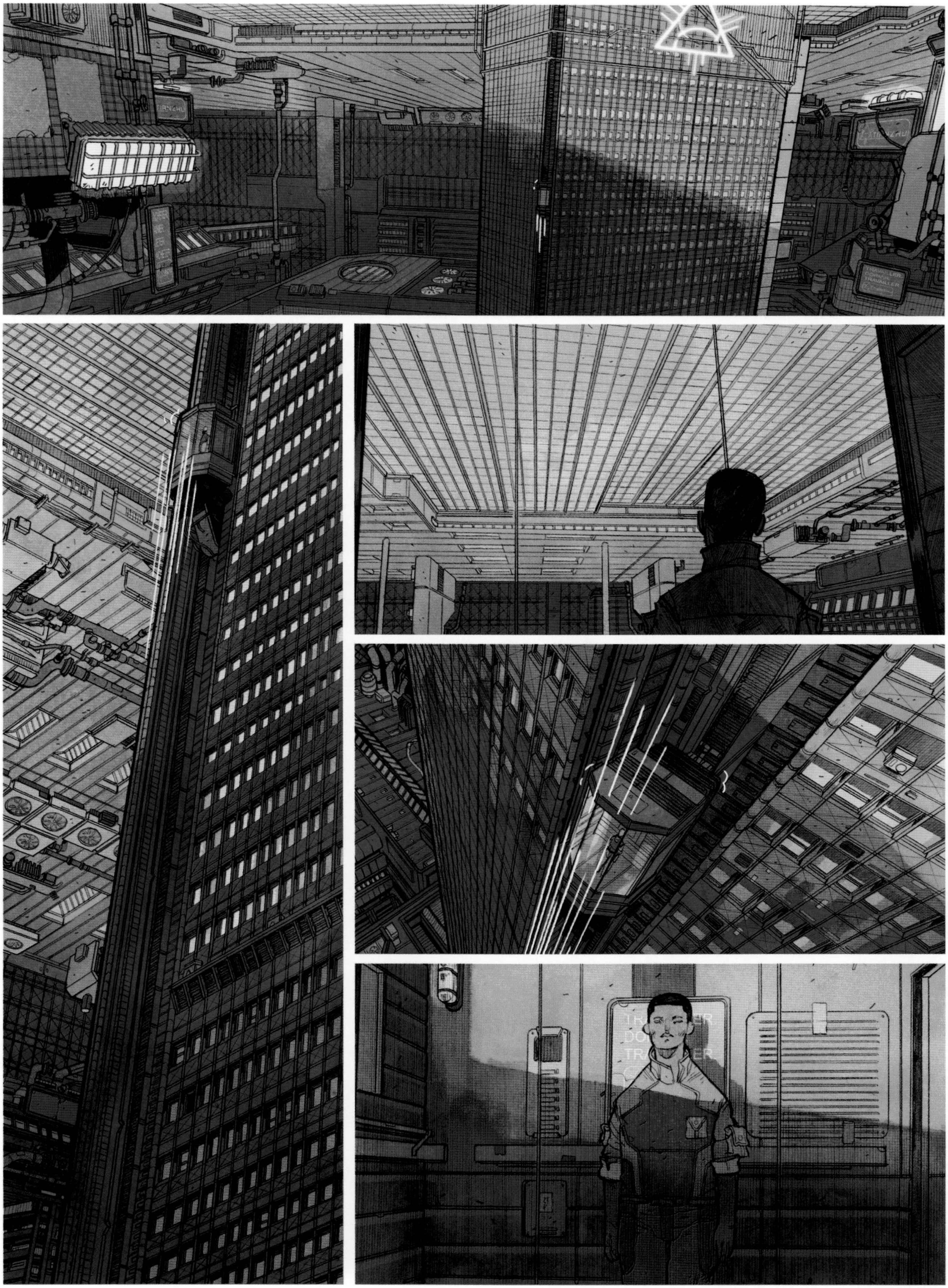

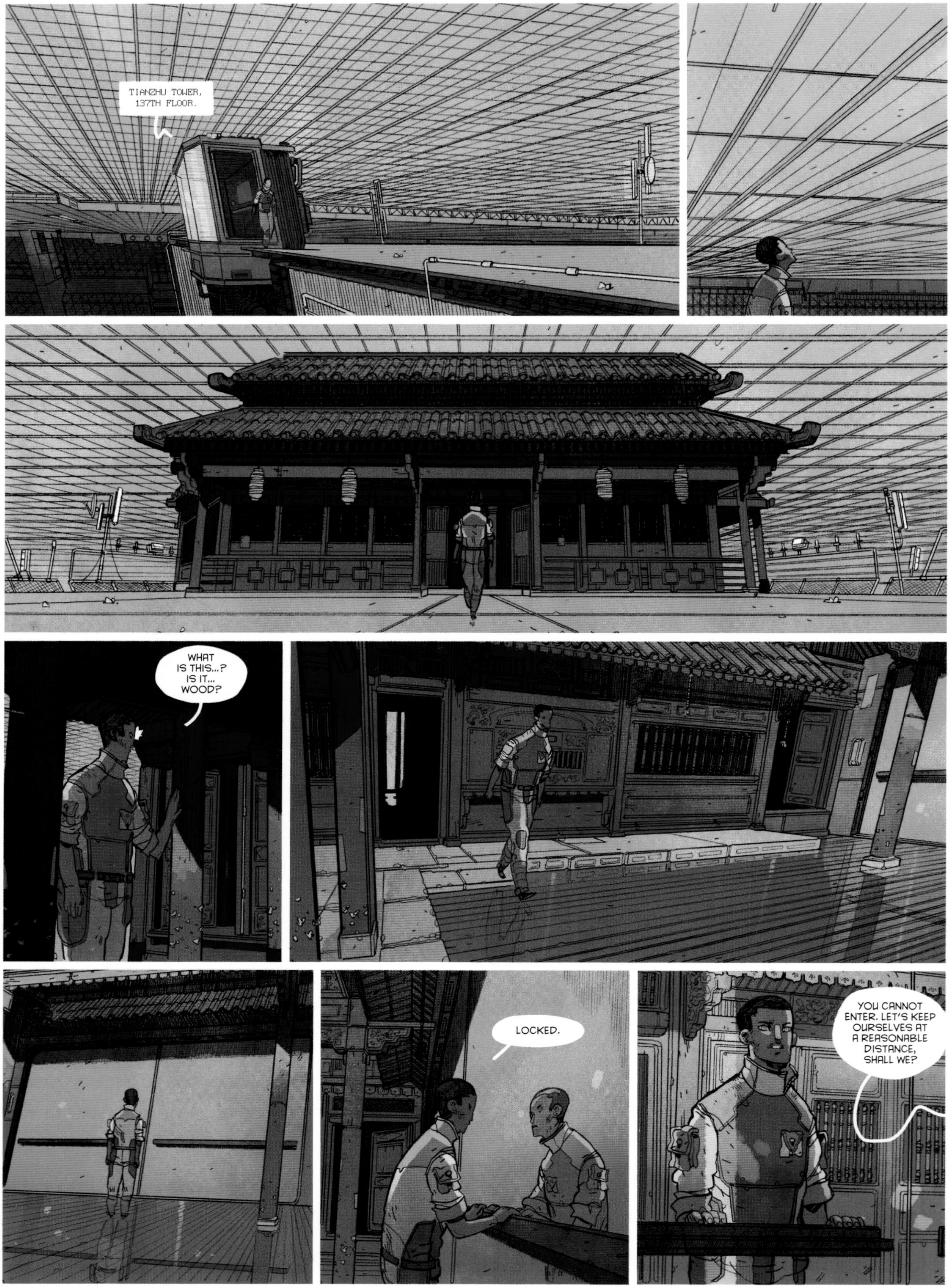
TIANZHU TOWER, 137TH FLOOR.
WHAT IS THIS...? IS IT... WOOD?
LOCKED.
YOU CANNOT ENTER. LET'S KEEP OURSELVES AT A REASONABLE DISTANCE, SHALL WE?

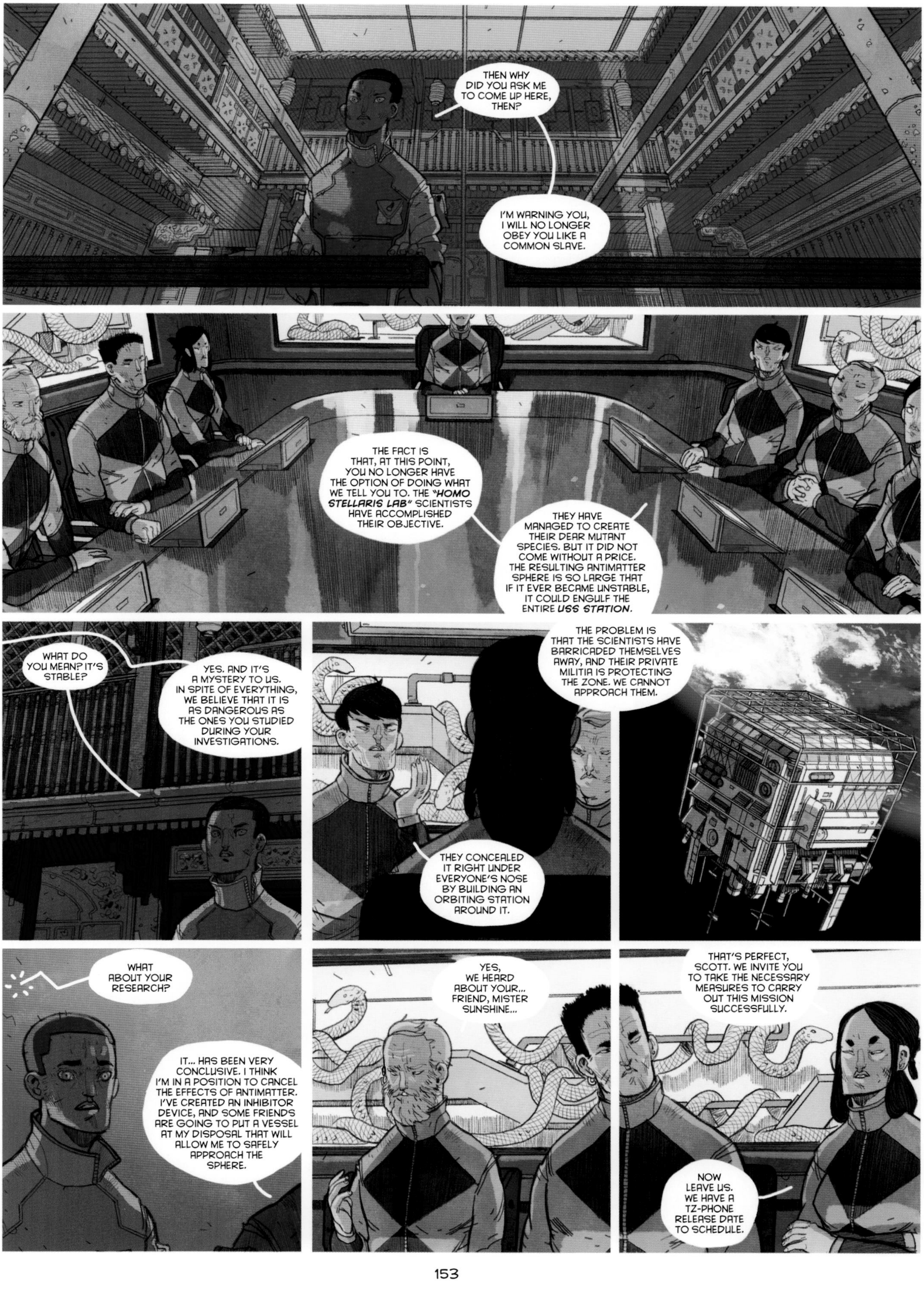
THEN WHY DID YOU ASK ME TO COME UP HERE, THEN?
I'M WARNING YOU, I WILL NO LONGER OBEY YOU LIKE A COMMON SLAVE.
THE FACT IS THAT, AT THIS POINT, YOU NO LONGER HAVE THE OPTION OF DOING WHAT WE TELL YOU TO. THE "HOMO STELLARIS LAB" SCIENTISTS HAVE ACCOMPLISHED THEIR OBJECTIVE.
THEY HAVE MANAGED TO CREATE THEIR DEAR MUTANT SPECIES. BUT IT DID NOT COME WITHOUT A PRICE. THE RESULTING ANTIMATTER SPHERE IS SO LARGE THAT IF IT EVER BECAME UNSTABLE, IT COULD ENGULF THE ENTIRE USS STATION.
WHAT DO YOU MEAN? IT'S STABLE?
YES. AND IT'S A MYSTERY TO US. IN SPITE OF EVERYTHING, WE BELIEVE THAT IT IS AS DANGEROUS AS THE ONES YOU STUDIED DURING YOUR INVESTIGATIONS.
THE PROBLEM IS THAT THE SCIENTISTS HAVE BARRICADED THEMSELVES AWAY, AND THEIR PRIVATE MILITIA IS PROTECTING THE ZONE. WE CANNOT APPROACH THEM.
THEY CONCEALED IT RIGHT UNDER EVERYONE'S NOSE BY BUILDING AN ORBITING STATION AROUND IT.
WHAT ABOUT YOUR RESEARCH?
IT... HAS BEEN VERY CONCLUSIVE. I THINK I'M IN A POSITION TO CANCEL THE EFFECTS OF ANTIMATTER. I'VE CREATED AN INHIBITOR DEVICE, AND SOME FRIENDS ARE GOING TO PUT A VESSEL AT MY DISPOSAL THAT WILL ALLOW ME TO SAFELY APPROACH THE SPHERE.
YES, WE HEARD ABOUT YOUR... FRIEND, MISTER SUNSHINE...
THAT'S PERFECT, SCOTT. WE INVITE YOU TO TAKE THE NECESSARY MEASURES TO CARRY OUT THIS MISSION SUCCESSFULLY.
NOW LEAVE US. WE HAVE A TZ-PHONE RELEASE DATE TO SCHEDULE.

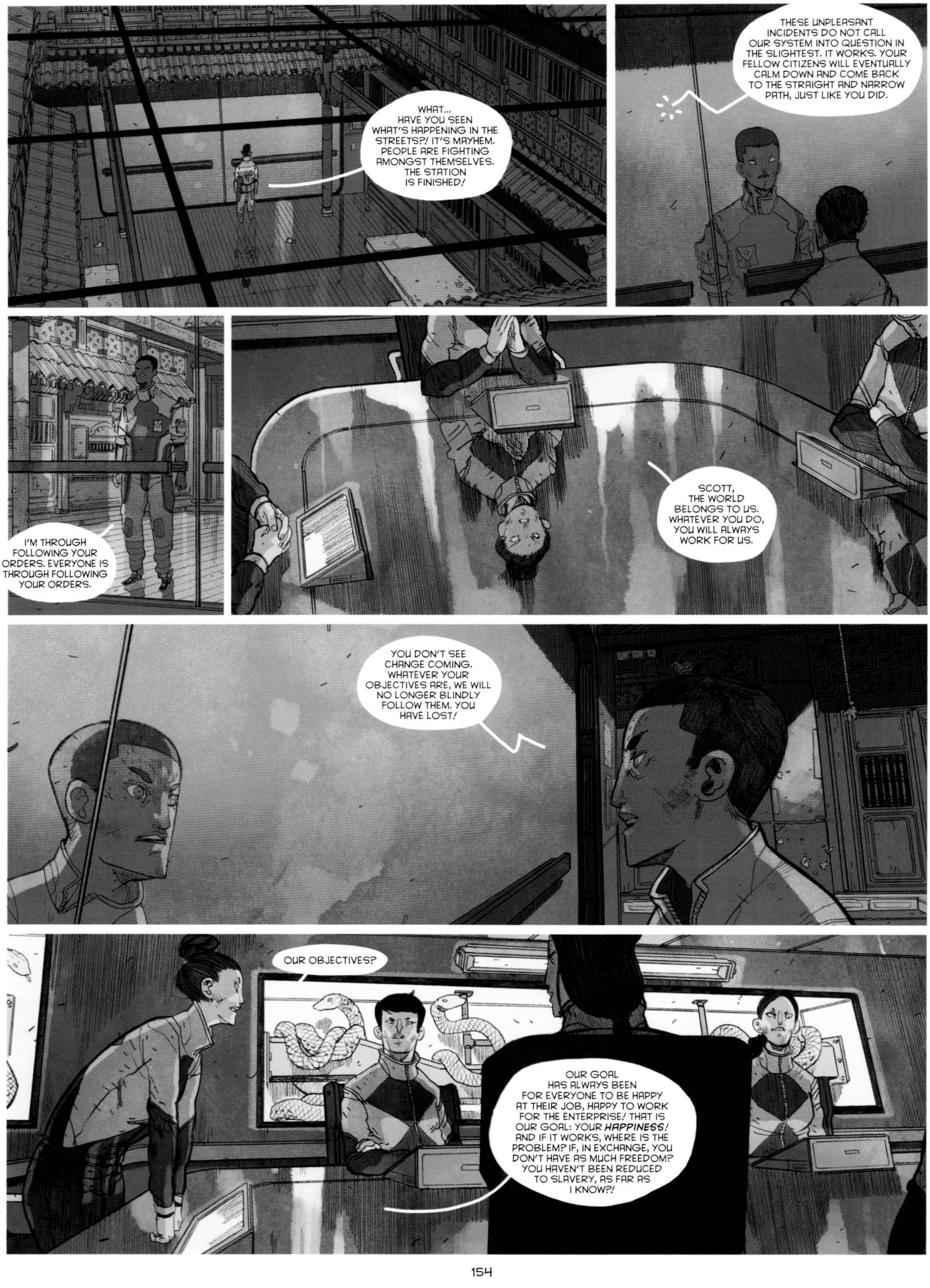
WHAT... HAVE YOU SEEN WHAT'S HAPPENING IN THE STREETS?! IT'S MAYHEM. PEOPLE ARE FIGHTING AMONGST THEMSELVES. THE STATION IS FINISHED!
THESE UNPLEASANT INCIDENTS DO NOT CALL OUR SYSTEM INTO QUESTION IN THE SLIGHTEST. IT WORKS. YOUR FELLOW CITIZENS WILL EVENTUALLY CALM DOWN AND COME BACK TO THE STRAIGHT AND NARROW PATH, JUST LIKE YOU DID.
I'M THROUGH FOLLOWING YOUR ORDERS. EVERYONE IS THROUGH FOLLOWING YOUR ORDERS.
SCOTT, THE WORLD BELONGS TO US. WHATEVER YOU DO, YOU WILL ALWAYS WORK FOR US.
YOU DON'T SEE CHANGE COMING. WHATEVER YOUR OBJECTIVES ARE, WE WILL NO LONGER BLINDLY FOLLOW THEM. YOU HAVE LOST!
OUR OBJECTIVES?
OUR GOAL HAS ALWAYS BEEN FOR EVERYONE TO BE HAPPY AT THEIR JOB, HAPPY TO WORK FOR THE ENTERPRISE! THAT IS OUR GOAL: YOUR **HAPPINESS**! AND IF IT WORKS, WHERE IS THE PROBLEM? IF, IN EXCHANGE, YOU DON'T HAVE AS MUCH FREEDOM? YOU HAVEN'T BEEN REDUCED TO SLAVERY, AS FAR AS I KNOW?!

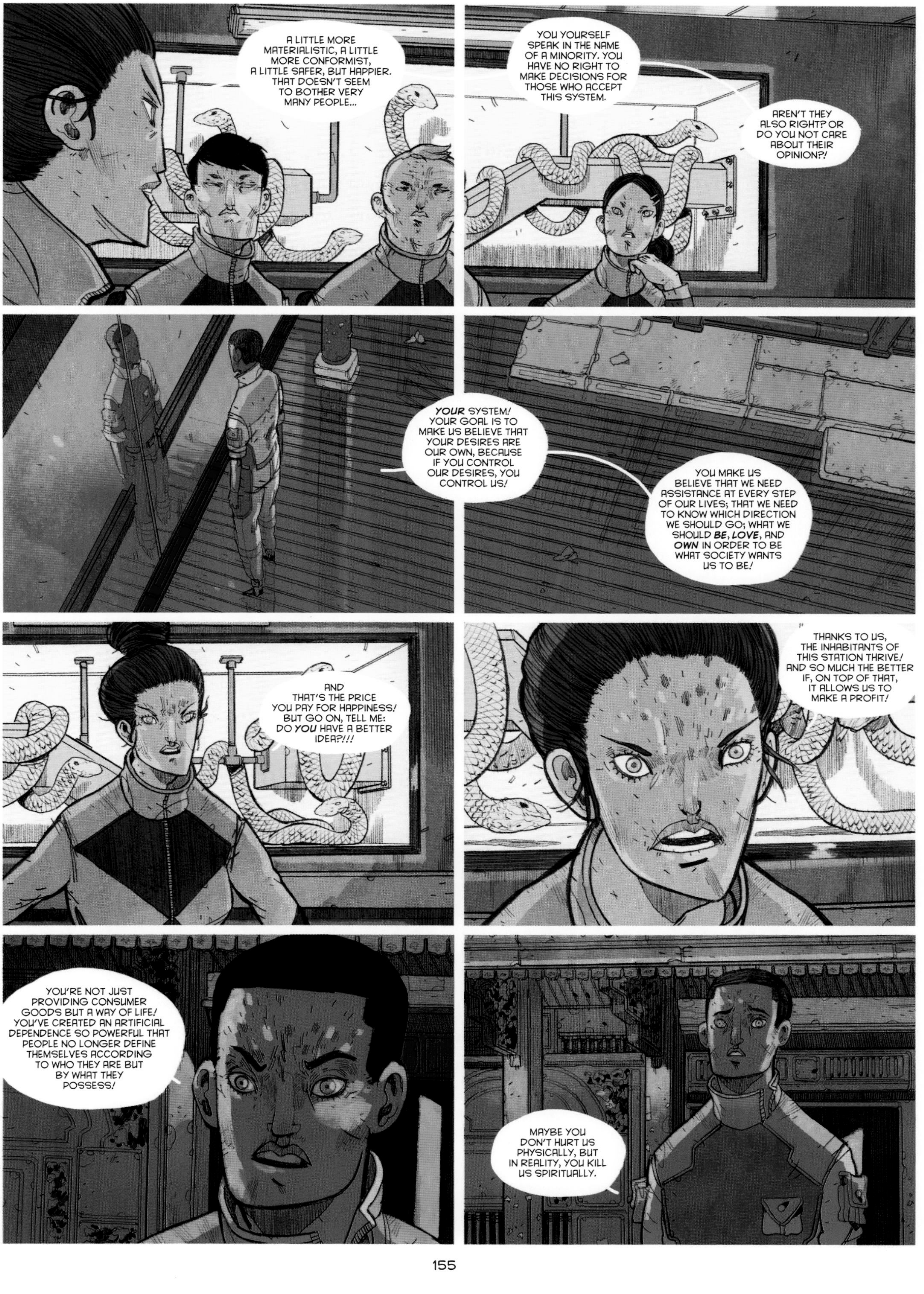
A LITTLE MORE MATERIALISTIC, A LITTLE MORE CONFORMIST, A LITTLE SAFER, BUT HAPPIER. THAT DOESN'T SEEM TO BOTHER VERY MANY PEOPLE...
YOU YOURSELF SPEAK IN THE NAME OF A MINORITY. YOU HAVE NO RIGHT TO MAKE DECISIONS FOR THOSE WHO ACCEPT THIS SYSTEM.
AREN'T THEY ALSO RIGHT? OR DO YOU NOT CARE ABOUT THEIR OPINION?!
YOUR SYSTEM! YOUR GOAL IS TO MAKE US BELIEVE THAT YOUR DESIRES ARE OUR OWN, BECAUSE IF YOU CONTROL OUR DESIRES, YOU CONTROL US!
YOU MAKE US BELIEVE THAT WE NEED ASSISTANCE AT EVERY STEP OF OUR LIVES; THAT WE NEED TO KNOW WHICH DIRECTION WE SHOULD GO; WHAT WE SHOULD BE, LOVE, AND OWN IN ORDER TO BE WHAT SOCIETY WANTS US TO BE!
AND THAT'S THE PRICE YOU PAY FOR HAPPINESS! BUT GO ON, TELL ME: DO YOU HAVE A BETTER IDEA?!!!
THANKS TO US, THE INHABITANTS OF THIS STATION THRIVE! AND SO MUCH THE BETTER IF, ON TOP OF THAT, IT ALLOWS US TO MAKE A PROFIT!
YOU'RE NOT JUST PROVIDING CONSUMER GOODS BUT A WAY OF LIFE! YOU'VE CREATED AN ARTIFICIAL DEPENDENCE SO POWERFUL THAT PEOPLE NO LONGER DEFINE THEMSELVES ACCORDING TO WHO THEY ARE BUT BY WHAT THEY POSSESS!
MAYBE YOU DON'T HURT US PHYSICALLY, BUT IN REALITY, YOU KILL US SPIRITUALLY.

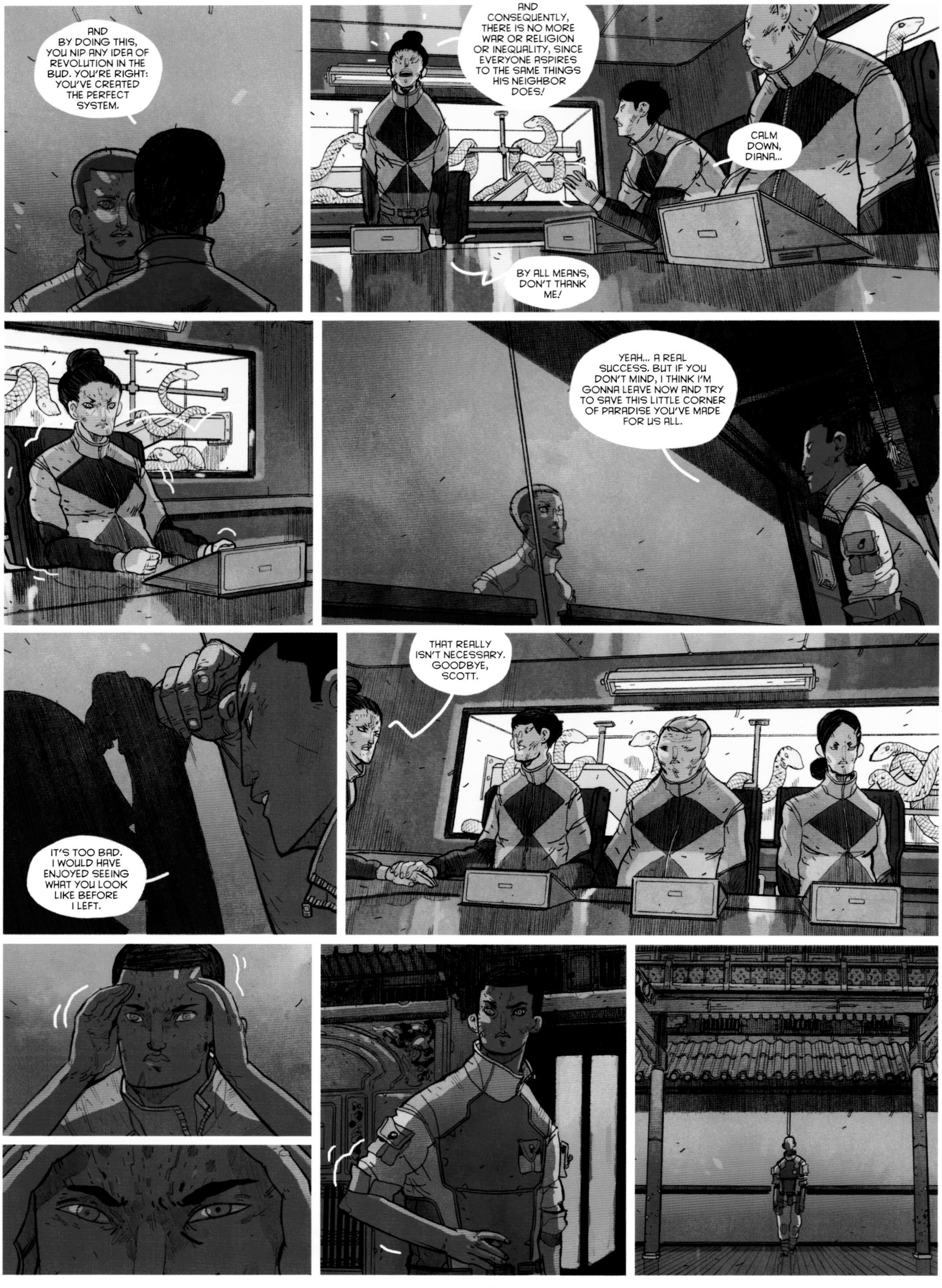
AND BY DOING THIS, YOU NIP ANY IDEA OF REVOLUTION IN THE BUD. YOU'RE RIGHT: YOU'VE CREATED THE PERFECT SYSTEM.
AND CONSEQUENTLY, THERE IS NO MORE WAR OR RELIGION OR INEQUALITY, SINCE EVERYONE ASPIRES TO THE SAME THINGS HIS NEIGHBOR DOES!
CALM DOWN, DIANA...
BY ALL MEANS, DON'T THANK ME!
YEAH... A REAL SUCCESS. BUT IF YOU DON'T MIND, I THINK I'M GONNA LEAVE NOW AND TRY TO SAVE THIS LITTLE CORNER OF PARADISE YOU'VE MADE FOR US ALL.
IT'S TOO BAD. I WOULD HAVE ENJOYED SEEING WHAT YOU LOOK LIKE BEFORE I LEFT.
THAT REALLY ISN'T NECESSARY. GOODBYE, SCOTT.

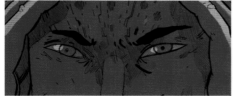

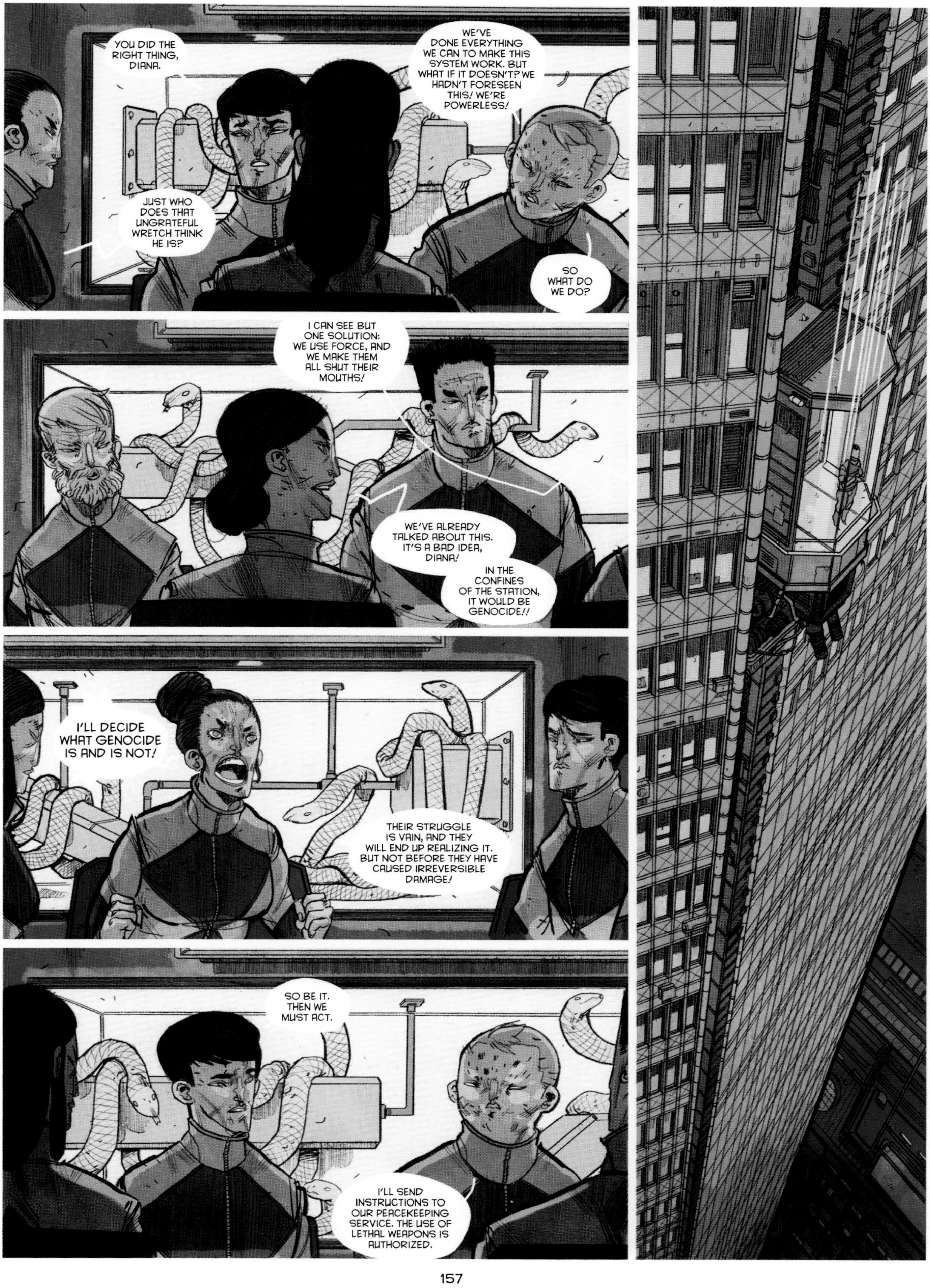
YOU DID THE RIGHT THING, DIANA.
WE'VE DONE EVERYTHING WE CAN TO MAKE THIS SYSTEM WORK. BUT WHAT IF IT DOESN'T? WE HADN'T FORESEEN THIS! WE'RE POWERLESS!
JUST WHO DOES THAT UNGRATEFUL WRETCH THINK HE IS?
SO WHAT DO WE DO?
I CAN SEE BUT ONE SOLUTION: WE USE FORCE, AND WE MAKE THEM ALL SHUT THEIR MOUTHS!
WE'VE ALREADY TALKED ABOUT THIS. IT'S A BAD IDEA, DIANA!
IN THE CONFINES OF THE STATION, IT WOULD BE GENOCIDE!!
I'LL DECIDE WHAT GENOCIDE IS AND IS NOT!
THEIR STRUGGLE IS VAIN, AND THEY WILL END UP REALIZING IT. BUT NOT BEFORE THEY HAVE CAUSED IRREVERSIBLE DAMAGE!
SO BE IT. THEN WE MUST ACT.
I'LL SEND INSTRUCTIONS TO OUR PEACEKEEPING SERVICE. THE USE OF LETHAL WEAPONS IS AUTHORIZED.

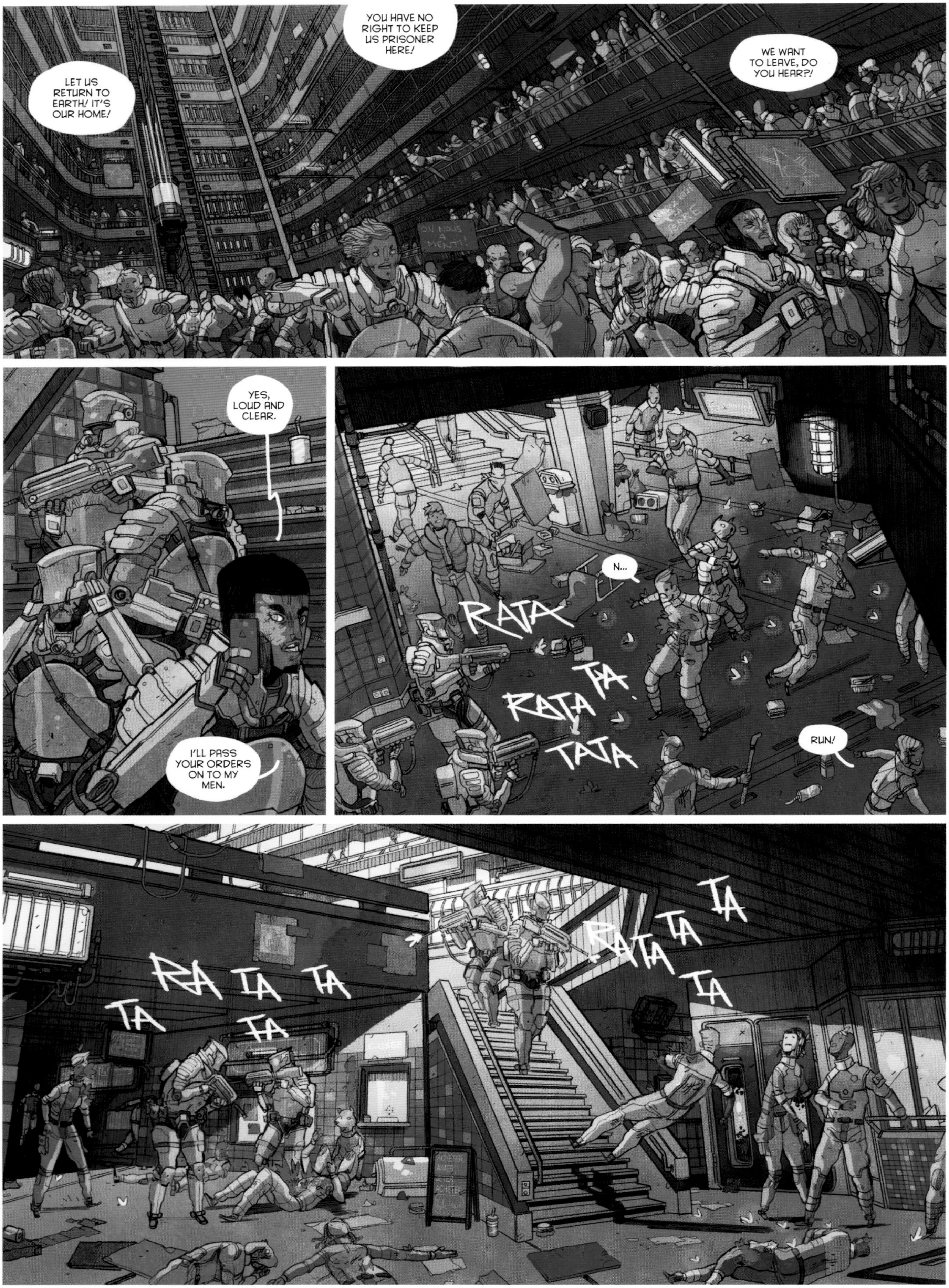
LET US RETURN TO EARTH! IT'S OUR HOME!
YOU HAVE NO RIGHT TO KEEP US PRISONER HERE!
WE WANT TO LEAVE, DO YOU HEAR?!
ON NOUS A MENTI!
YES, LOUD AND CLEAR.
I'LL PASS YOUR ORDERS ON TO MY MEN.
N...
RATA TA RATA TAJA
RUN!
TA RA TA TA TA
RATA TA TA TA TA
CAISSE

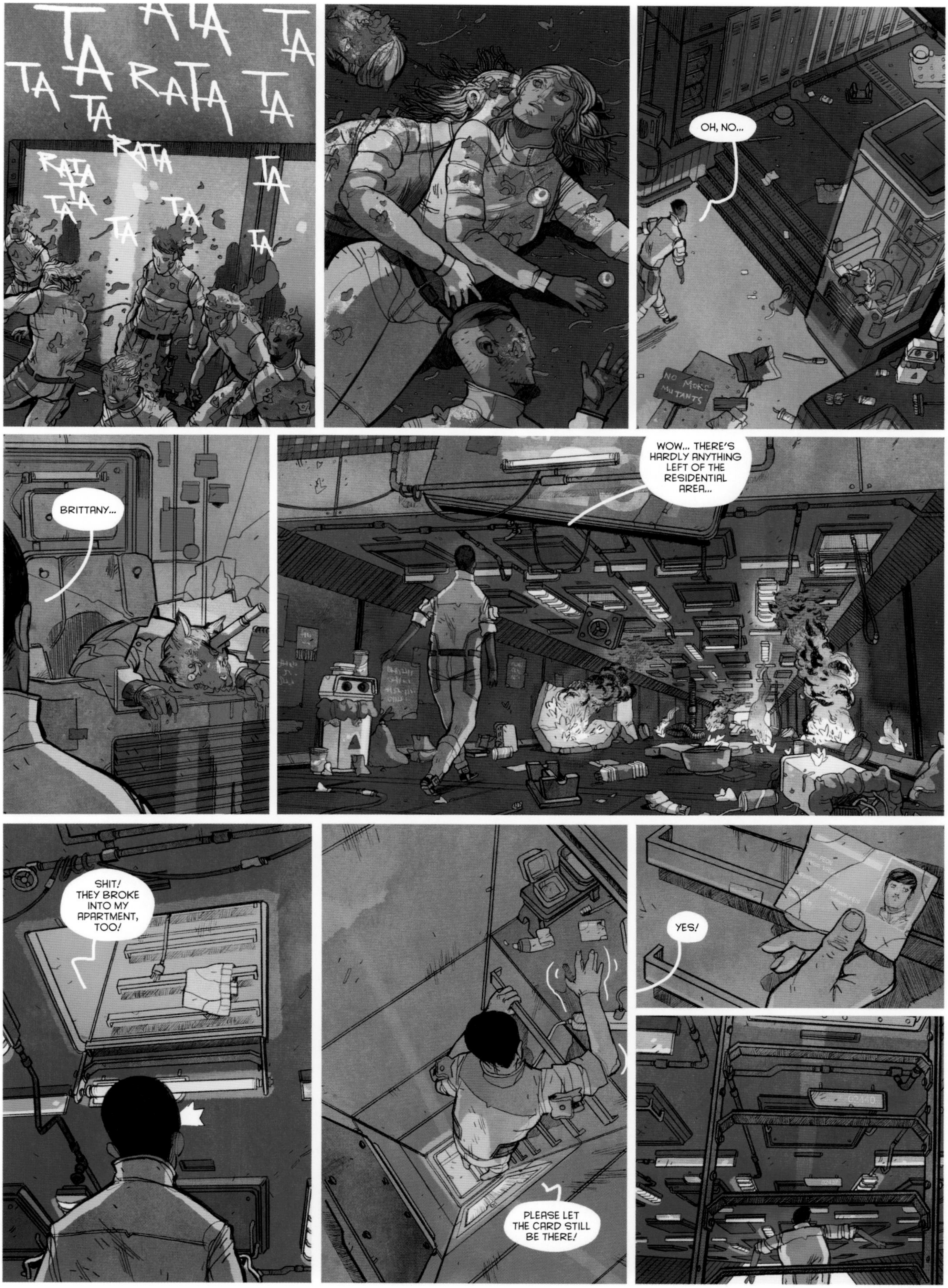
TA ALA TA
TA TA RATA TA
TA TA
RATA
RATA TA
TA TA TA TA
TA TA
OH, NO...
NO MORE MUTANTS
BRITTANY...
WOW... THERE'S HARDLY ANYTHING LEFT OF THE RESIDENTIAL AREA...
SHIT! THEY BROKE INTO MY APARTMENT, TOO!
PLEASE LET THE CARD STILL BE THERE!
YES!

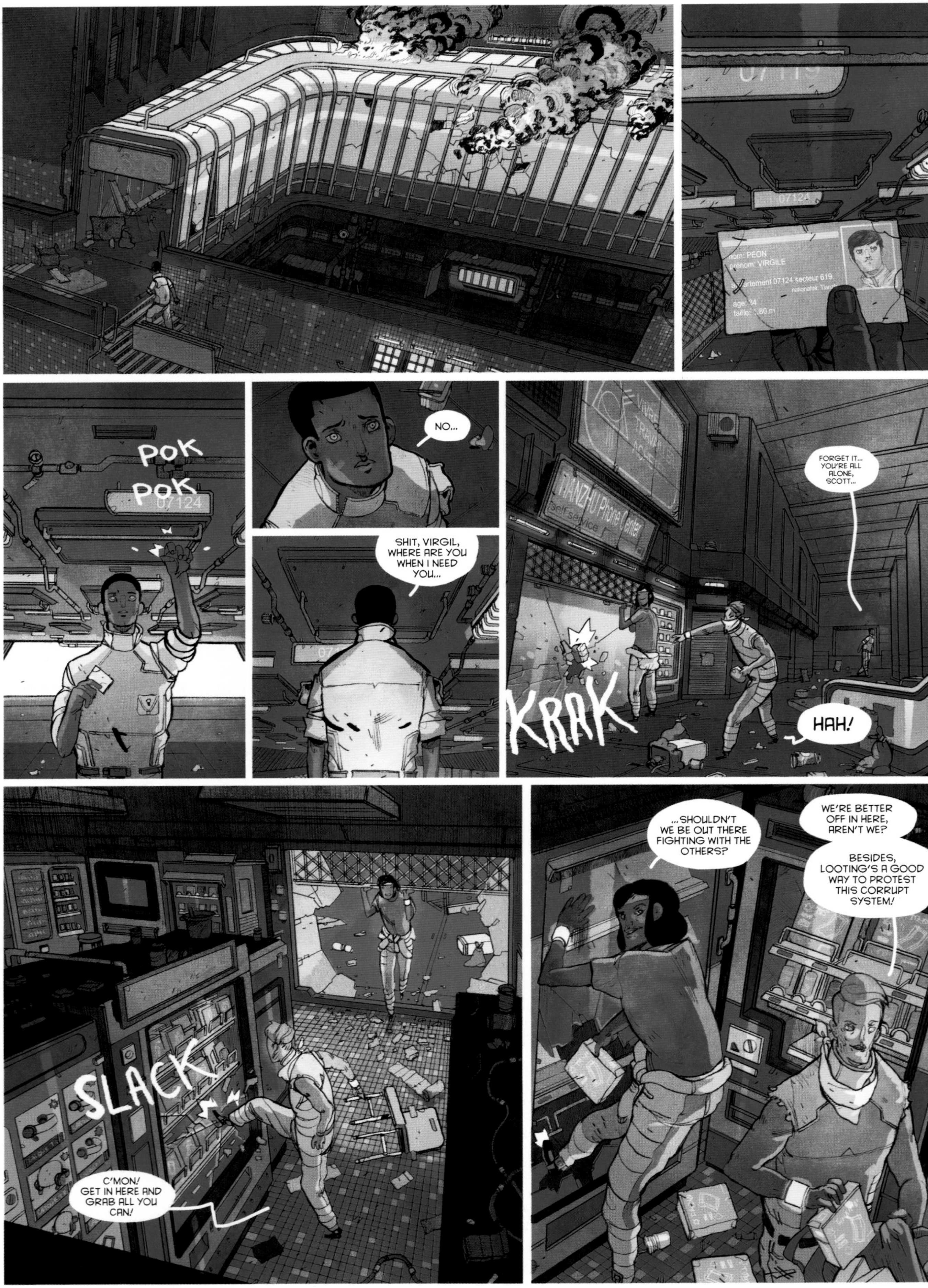
07124
nom: PEON
prénom: VIRGILE
secteur 619
POK
POK
07124
NO...
SHIT, VIRGIL, WHERE ARE YOU WHEN I NEED YOU...
Phone Center
Self service
FORGET IT... YOU'RE ALL ALONE, SCOTT...
KRAK
HAH!
SLACK
C'MON! GET IN HERE AND GRAB ALL YOU CAN!
...SHOULDN'T WE BE OUT THERE FIGHTING WITH THE OTHERS?
WE'RE BETTER OFF IN HERE, AREN'T WE?
BESIDES, LOOTING'S A GOOD WAY TO PROTEST THIS CORRUPT SYSTEM!

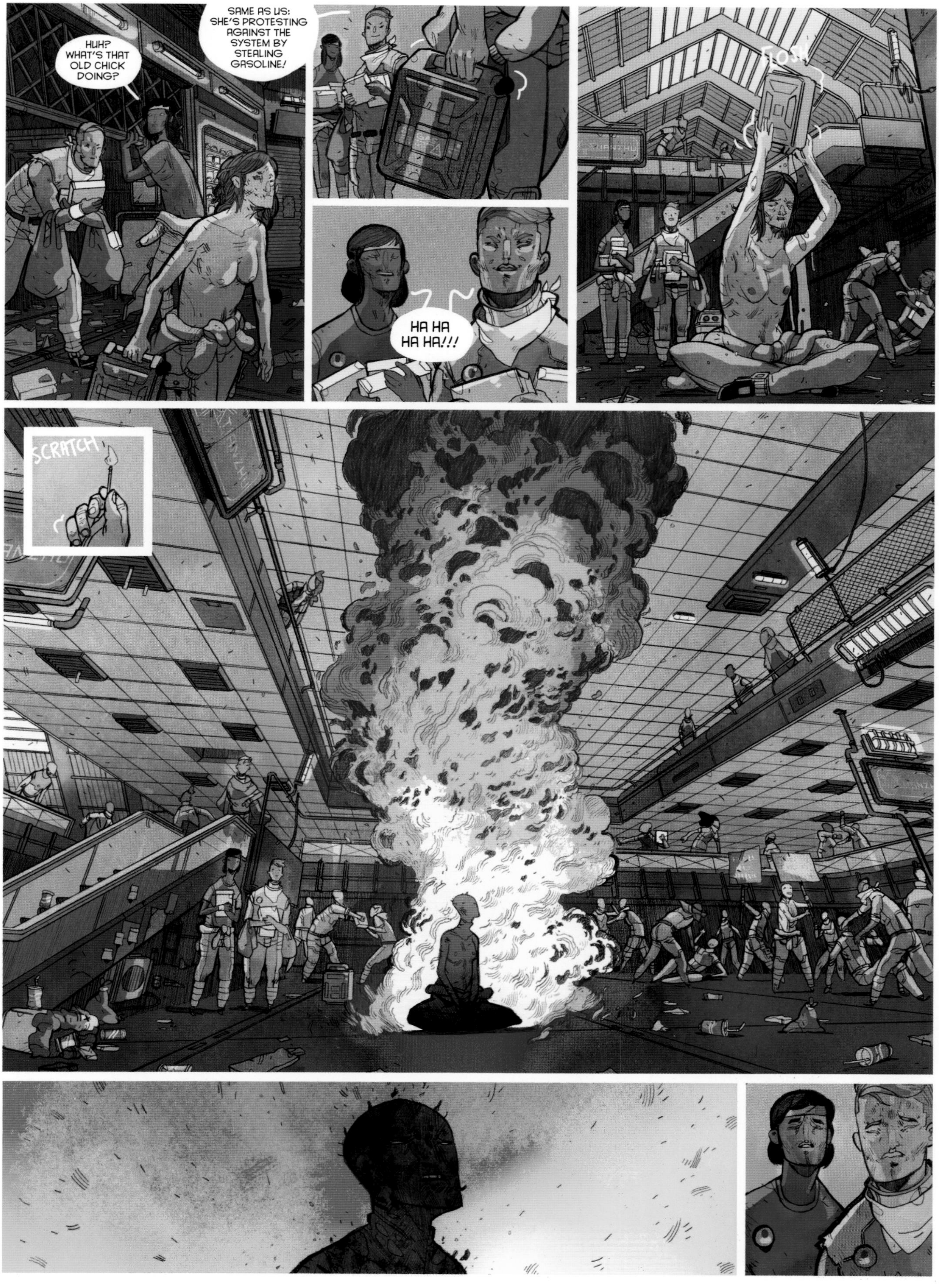
HUH? WHAT'S THAT OLD CHICK DOING?
SAME AS US: SHE'S PROTESTING AGAINST THE SYSTEM BY STEALING GASOLINE!
HA HA HA HA!!!
FLOSH
SCRATCH

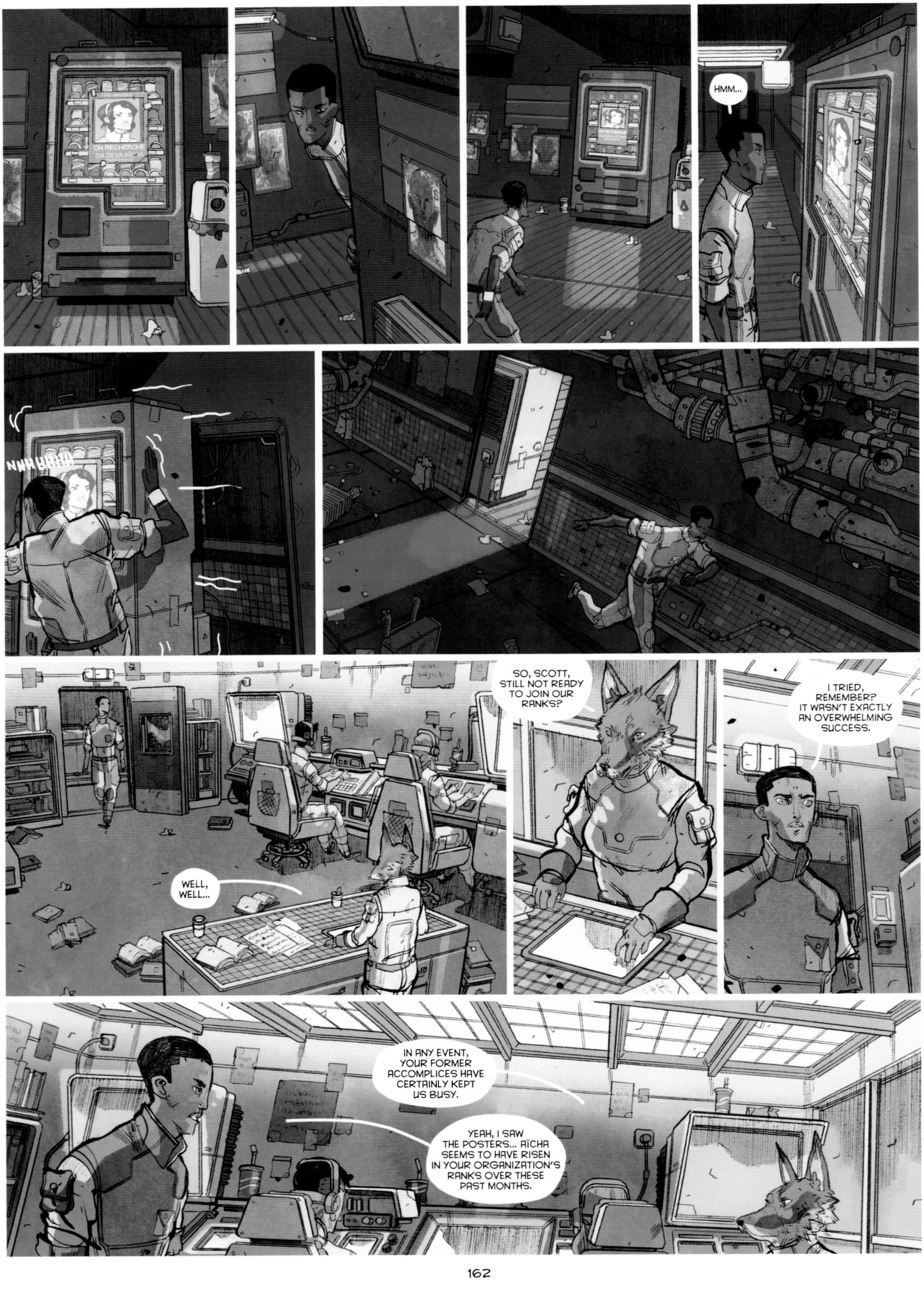
ON RECHERCHE
DA SILVA AÏCHA
HMM...
NNHHHH!!!
WELL, WELL...
SO, SCOTT, STILL NOT READY TO JOIN OUR RANKS?
I TRIED, REMEMBER? IT WASN'T EXACTLY AN OVERWHELMING SUCCESS.
IN ANY EVENT, YOUR FORMER ACCOMPLICES HAVE CERTAINLY KEPT US BUSY.
YEAH, I SAW THE POSTERS... AÏCHA SEEMS TO HAVE RISEN IN YOUR ORGANIZATION'S RANKS OVER THESE PAST MONTHS.

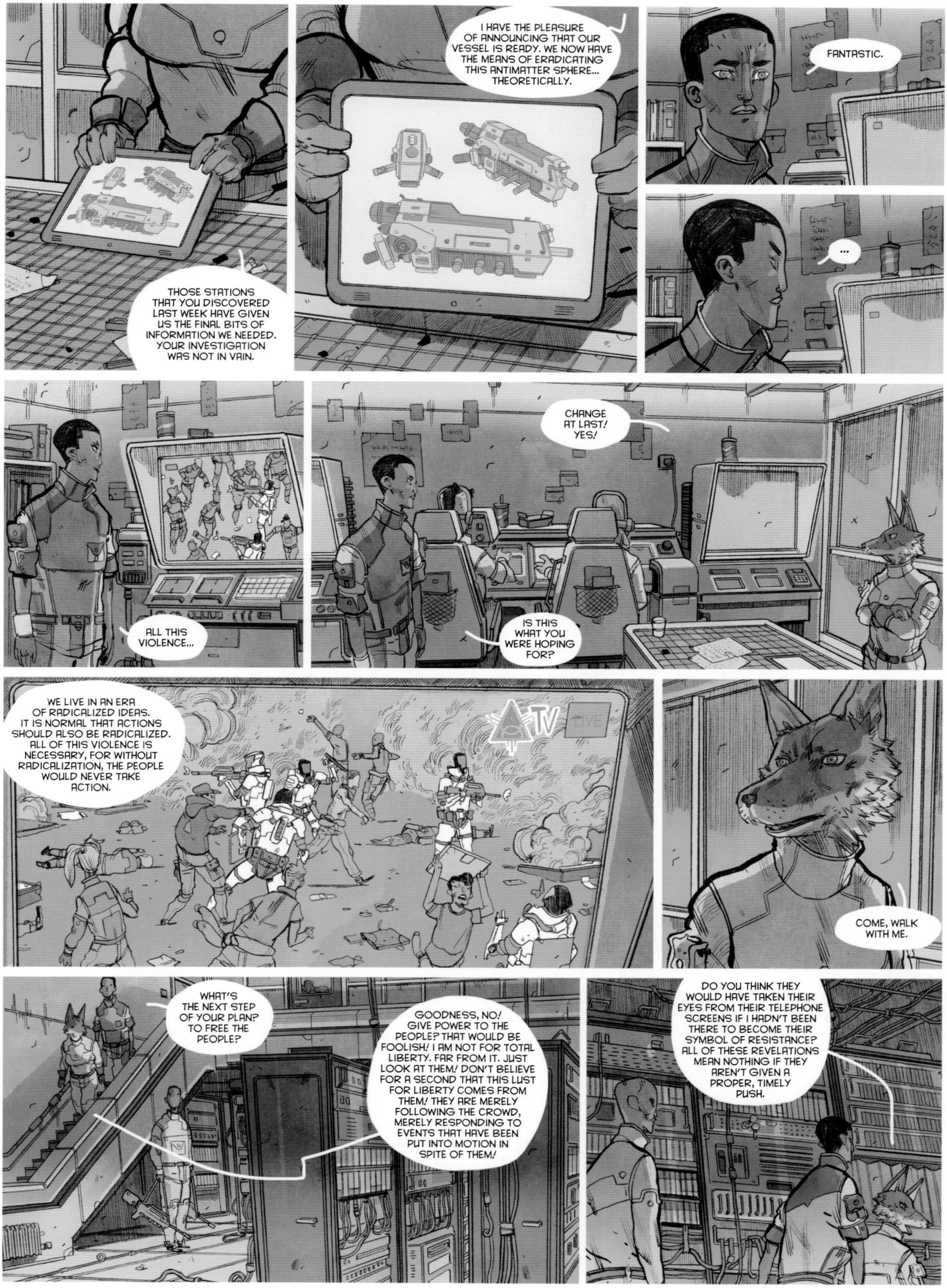
I HAVE THE PLEASURE OF ANNOUNCING THAT OUR VESSEL IS READY. WE NOW HAVE THE MEANS OF ERADICATING THIS ANTIMATTER SPHERE... THEORETICALLY.
THOSE STATIONS THAT YOU DISCOVERED LAST WEEK HAVE GIVEN US THE FINAL BITS OF INFORMATION WE NEEDED. YOUR INVESTIGATION WAS NOT IN VAIN.
FANTASTIC.
...
ALL THIS VIOLENCE...
CHANGE AT LAST! YES!
IS THIS WHAT YOU WERE HOPING FOR?
WE LIVE IN AN ERA OF RADICALIZED IDEAS. IT IS NORMAL THAT ACTIONS SHOULD ALSO BE RADICALIZED. ALL OF THIS VIOLENCE IS NECESSARY, FOR WITHOUT RADICALIZATION, THE PEOPLE WOULD NEVER TAKE ACTION.
TV
LIVE
COME, WALK WITH ME.
WHAT'S THE NEXT STEP OF YOUR PLAN? TO FREE THE PEOPLE?
GOODNESS, NO! GIVE POWER TO THE PEOPLE? THAT WOULD BE FOOLISH! I AM NOT FOR TOTAL LIBERTY. FAR FROM IT. JUST LOOK AT THEM! DON'T BELIEVE FOR A SECOND THAT THIS LUST FOR LIBERTY COMES FROM THEM! THEY ARE MERELY FOLLOWING THE CROWD, MERELY RESPONDING TO EVENTS THAT HAVE BEEN PUT INTO MOTION IN SPITE OF THEM!
DO YOU THINK THEY WOULD HAVE TAKEN THEIR EYES FROM THEIR TELEPHONE SCREENS IF I HADN'T BEEN THERE TO BECOME THEIR SYMBOL OF RESISTANCE? ALL OF THESE REVELATIONS MEAN NOTHING IF THEY AREN'T GIVEN A PROPER, TIMELY PUSH.

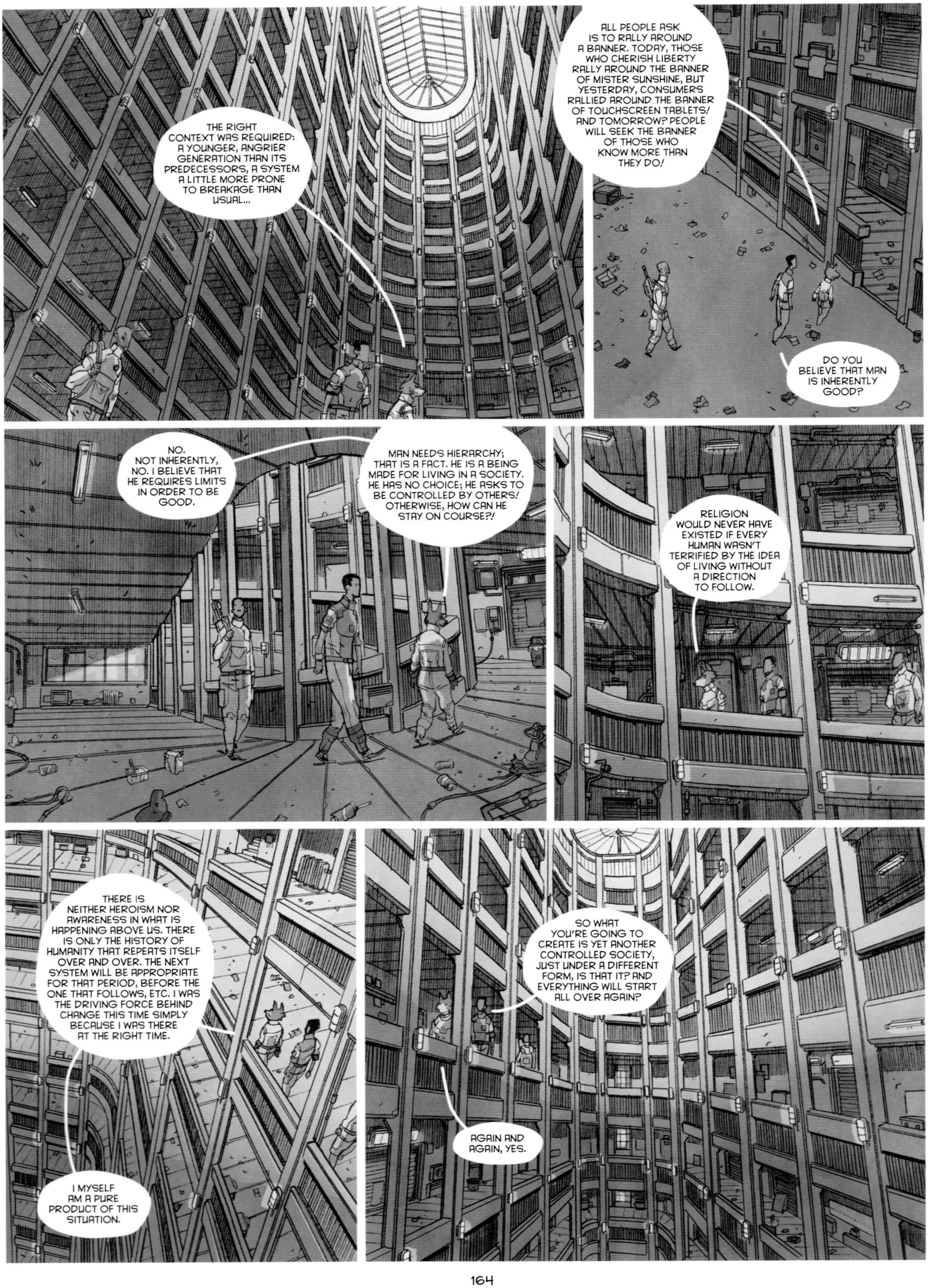
THE RIGHT CONTEXT WAS REQUIRED: A YOUNGER, ANGRIER GENERATION THAN ITS PREDECESSORS, A SYSTEM A LITTLE MORE PRONE TO BREAKAGE THAN USUAL...
ALL PEOPLE ASK IS TO RALLY AROUND A BANNER. TODAY, THOSE WHO CHERISH LIBERTY RALLY AROUND THE BANNER OF MISTER SUNSHINE, BUT YESTERDAY, CONSUMERS RALLIED AROUND THE BANNER OF TOUCHSCREEN TABLETS! AND TOMORROW? PEOPLE WILL SEEK THE BANNER OF THOSE WHO KNOW MORE THAN THEY DO!
DO YOU BELIEVE THAT MAN IS INHERENTLY GOOD?
NO. NOT INHERENTLY, NO. I BELIEVE THAT HE REQUIRES LIMITS IN ORDER TO BE GOOD.
MAN NEEDS HIERARCHY; THAT IS A FACT. HE IS A BEING MADE FOR LIVING IN A SOCIETY. HE HAS NO CHOICE; HE ASKS TO BE CONTROLLED BY OTHERS! OTHERWISE, HOW CAN HE STAY ON COURSE?!
RELIGION WOULD NEVER HAVE EXISTED IF EVERY HUMAN WASN'T TERRIFIED BY THE IDEA OF LIVING WITHOUT A DIRECTION TO FOLLOW.
THERE IS NEITHER HEROISM NOR AWARENESS IN WHAT IS HAPPENING ABOVE US. THERE IS ONLY THE HISTORY OF HUMANITY THAT REPEATS ITSELF OVER AND OVER. THE NEXT SYSTEM WILL BE APPROPRIATE FOR THAT PERIOD, BEFORE THE ONE THAT FOLLOWS, ETC. I WAS THE DRIVING FORCE BEHIND CHANGE THIS TIME SIMPLY BECAUSE I WAS THERE AT THE RIGHT TIME.
I MYSELF AM A PURE PRODUCT OF THIS SITUATION.
SO WHAT YOU'RE GOING TO CREATE IS YET ANOTHER CONTROLLED SOCIETY, JUST UNDER A DIFFERENT FORM, IS THAT IT? AND EVERYTHING WILL START ALL OVER AGAIN?
AGAIN AND AGAIN, YES.

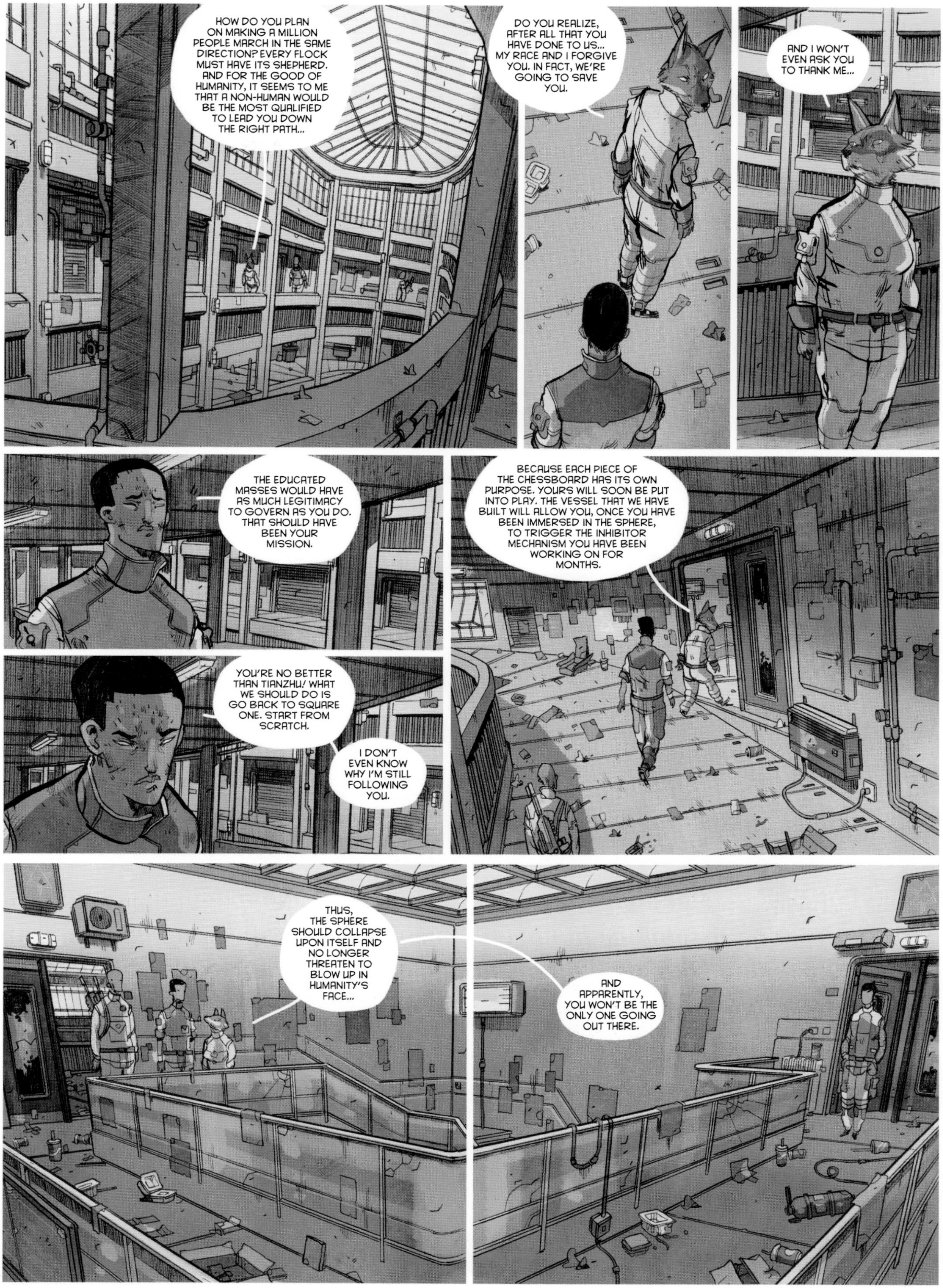
HOW DO YOU PLAN ON MAKING A MILLION PEOPLE MARCH IN THE SAME DIRECTION? EVERY FLOCK MUST HAVE ITS SHEPHERD. AND FOR THE GOOD OF HUMANITY, IT SEEMS TO ME THAT A NON-HUMAN WOULD BE THE MOST QUALIFIED TO LEAD YOU DOWN THE RIGHT PATH...
DO YOU REALIZE, AFTER ALL THAT YOU HAVE DONE TO US... MY RACE AND I FORGIVE YOU. IN FACT, WE'RE GOING TO SAVE YOU.
AND I WON'T EVEN ASK YOU TO THANK ME...
THE EDUCATED MASSES WOULD HAVE AS MUCH LEGITIMACY TO GOVERN AS YOU DO. THAT SHOULD HAVE BEEN YOUR MISSION.
YOU'RE NO BETTER THAN TIANZHU! WHAT WE SHOULD DO IS GO BACK TO SQUARE ONE. START FROM SCRATCH.
I DON'T EVEN KNOW WHY I'M STILL FOLLOWING YOU.
BECAUSE EACH PIECE OF THE CHESSBOARD HAS ITS OWN PURPOSE. YOURS WILL SOON BE PUT INTO PLAY. THE VESSEL THAT WE HAVE BUILT WILL ALLOW YOU, ONCE YOU HAVE BEEN IMMERSED IN THE SPHERE, TO TRIGGER THE INHIBITOR MECHANISM YOU HAVE BEEN WORKING ON FOR MONTHS.
THUS, THE SPHERE SHOULD COLLAPSE UPON ITSELF AND NO LONGER THREATEN TO BLOW UP IN HUMANITY'S FACE...
AND APPARENTLY, YOU WON'T BE THE ONLY ONE GOING OUT THERE.

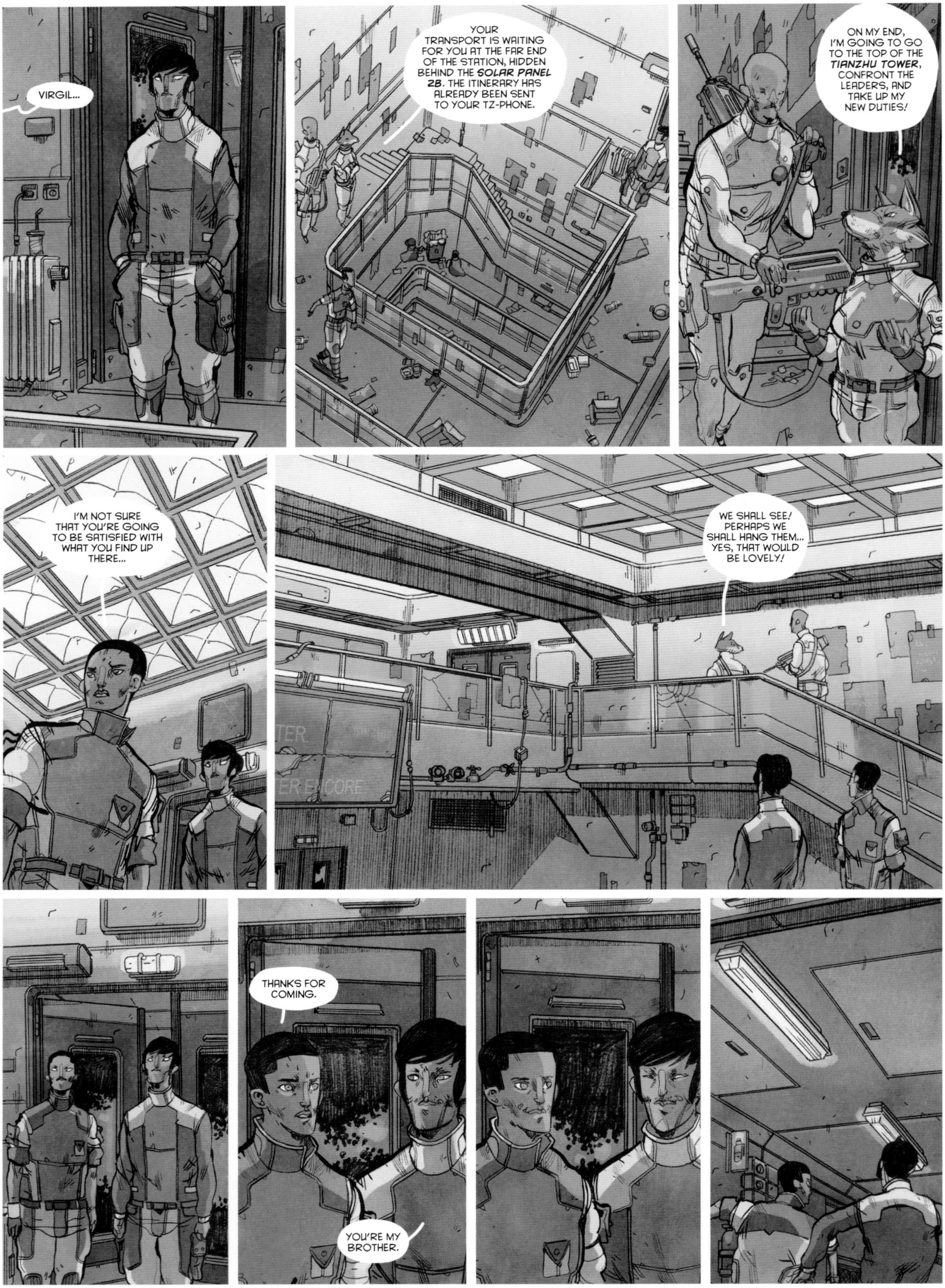
VIRGIL...
YOUR TRANSPORT IS WAITING FOR YOU AT THE FAR END OF THE STATION, HIDDEN BEHIND THE SOLAR PANEL 2B. THE ITINERARY HAS ALREADY BEEN SENT TO YOUR TZ-PHONE.
ON MY END, I'M GOING TO GO TO THE TOP OF THE TIANZHU TOWER, CONFRONT THE LEADERS, AND TAKE UP MY NEW DUTIES!
I'M NOT SURE THAT YOU'RE GOING TO BE SATISFIED WITH WHAT YOU FIND UP THERE...
WE SHALL SEE! PERHAPS WE SHALL HANG THEM... YES, THAT WOULD BE LOVELY!
THANKS FOR COMING.
YOU'RE MY BROTHER.

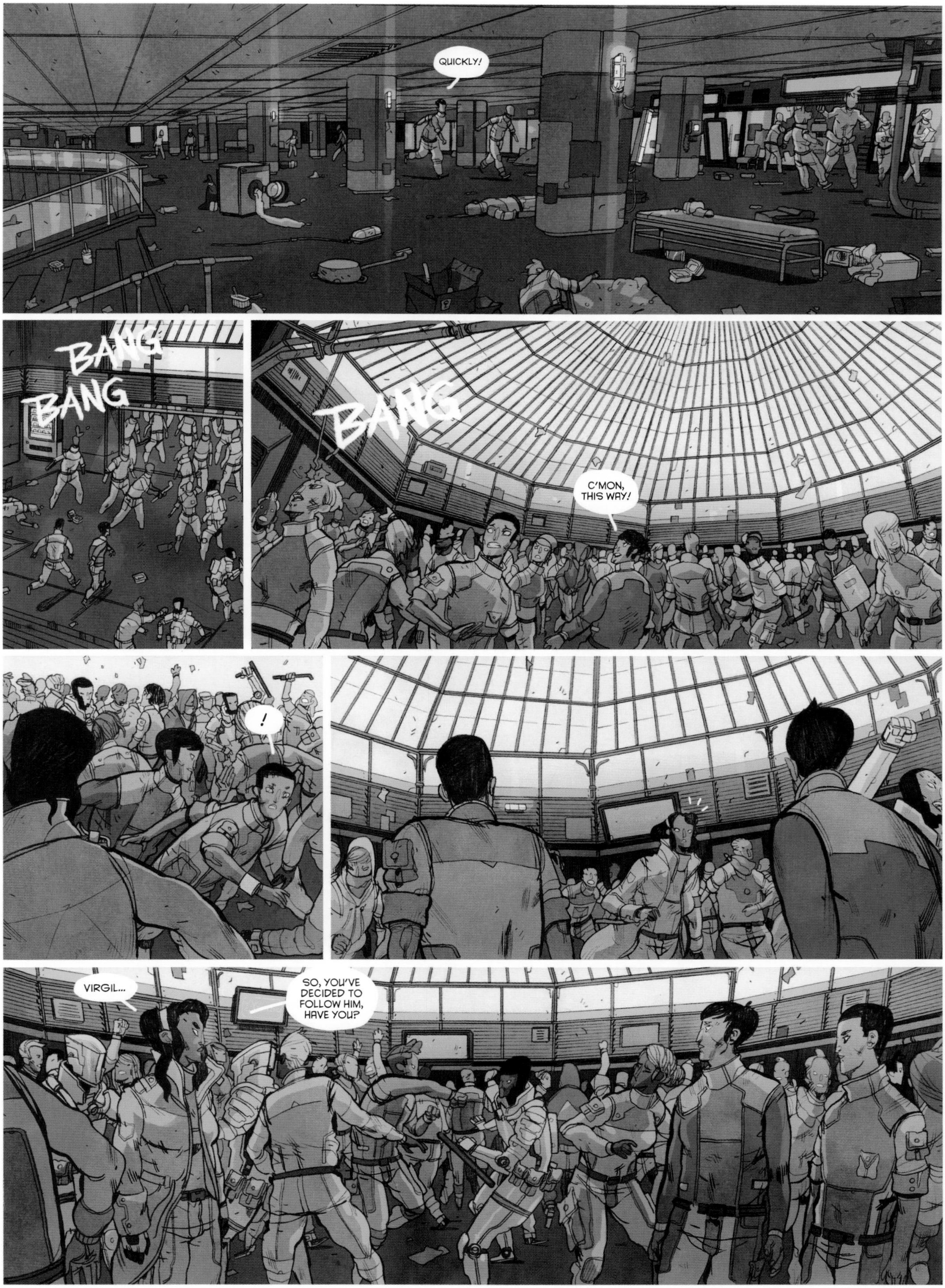
QUICKLY!
BANG
BANG
BANG
C'MON, THIS WAY!
!
VIRGIL...
SO, YOU'VE DECIDED TO FOLLOW HIM, HAVE YOU?

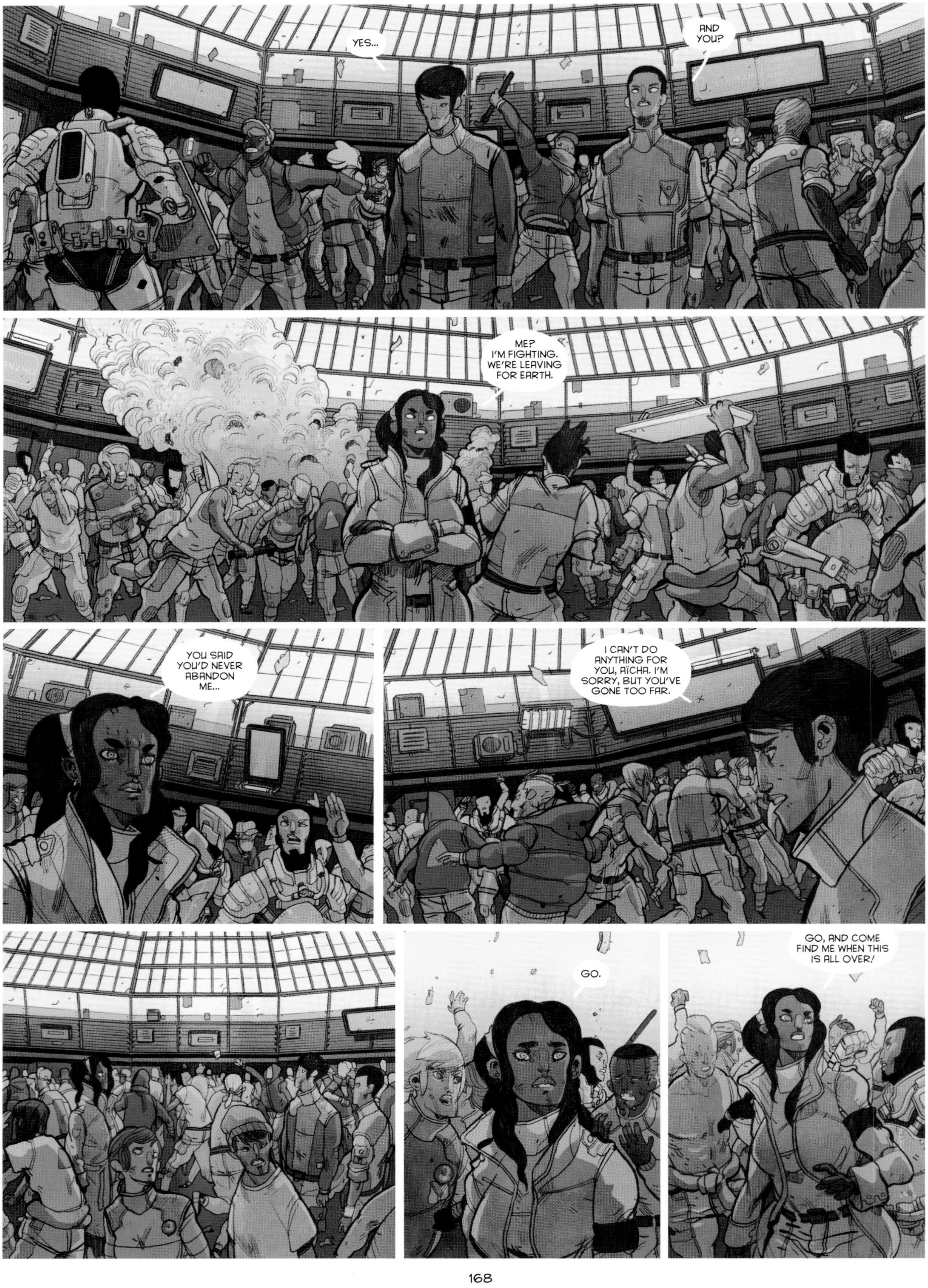
YES...
AND YOU?
ME? I'M FIGHTING. WE'RE LEAVING FOR EARTH.
YOU SAID YOU'D NEVER ABANDON ME...
I CAN'T DO ANYTHING FOR YOU, AÏCHA. I'M SORRY, BUT YOU'VE GONE TOO FAR.
GO.
GO, AND COME FIND ME WHEN THIS IS ALL OVER!

THIS WAY.
KLAK
THIS PART OF THE STATION HAS BEEN ABANDONED FOR AGES! WHAT ARE ALL THESE THINGS...?
NOTRE HISTOIRE...
THERE! HELP ME REMOVE THIS PANEL. IT'S THE ACCESS TO THE MAINTENANCE SYSTEM.
DANGER

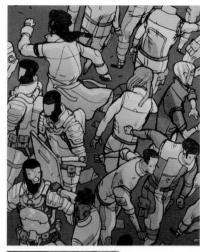

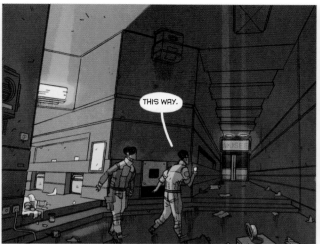

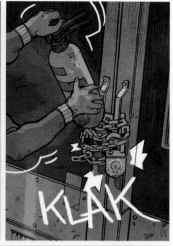

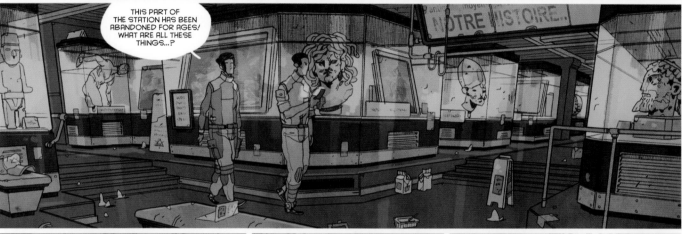

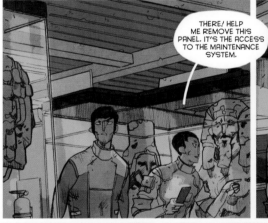

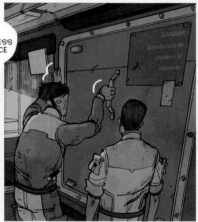

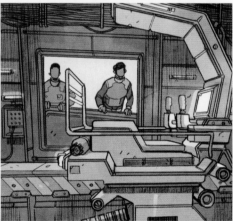

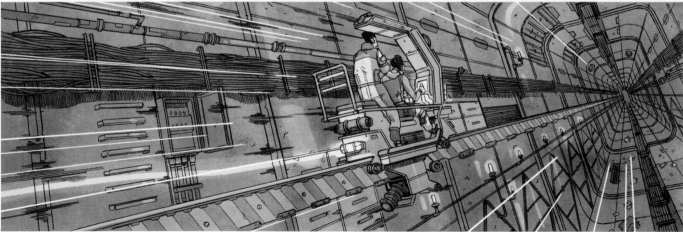

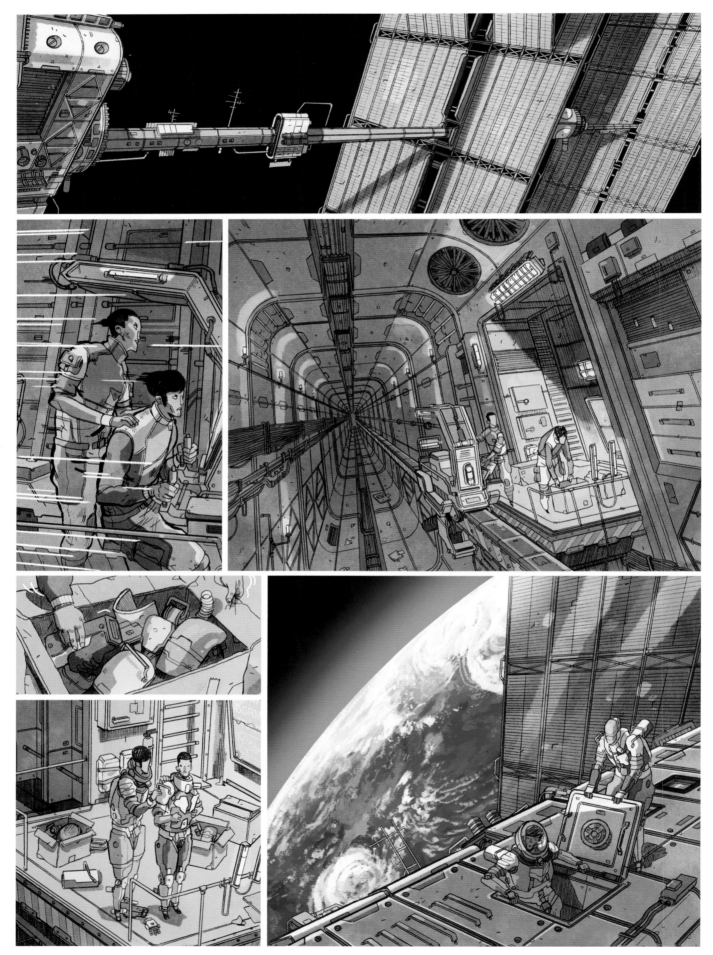

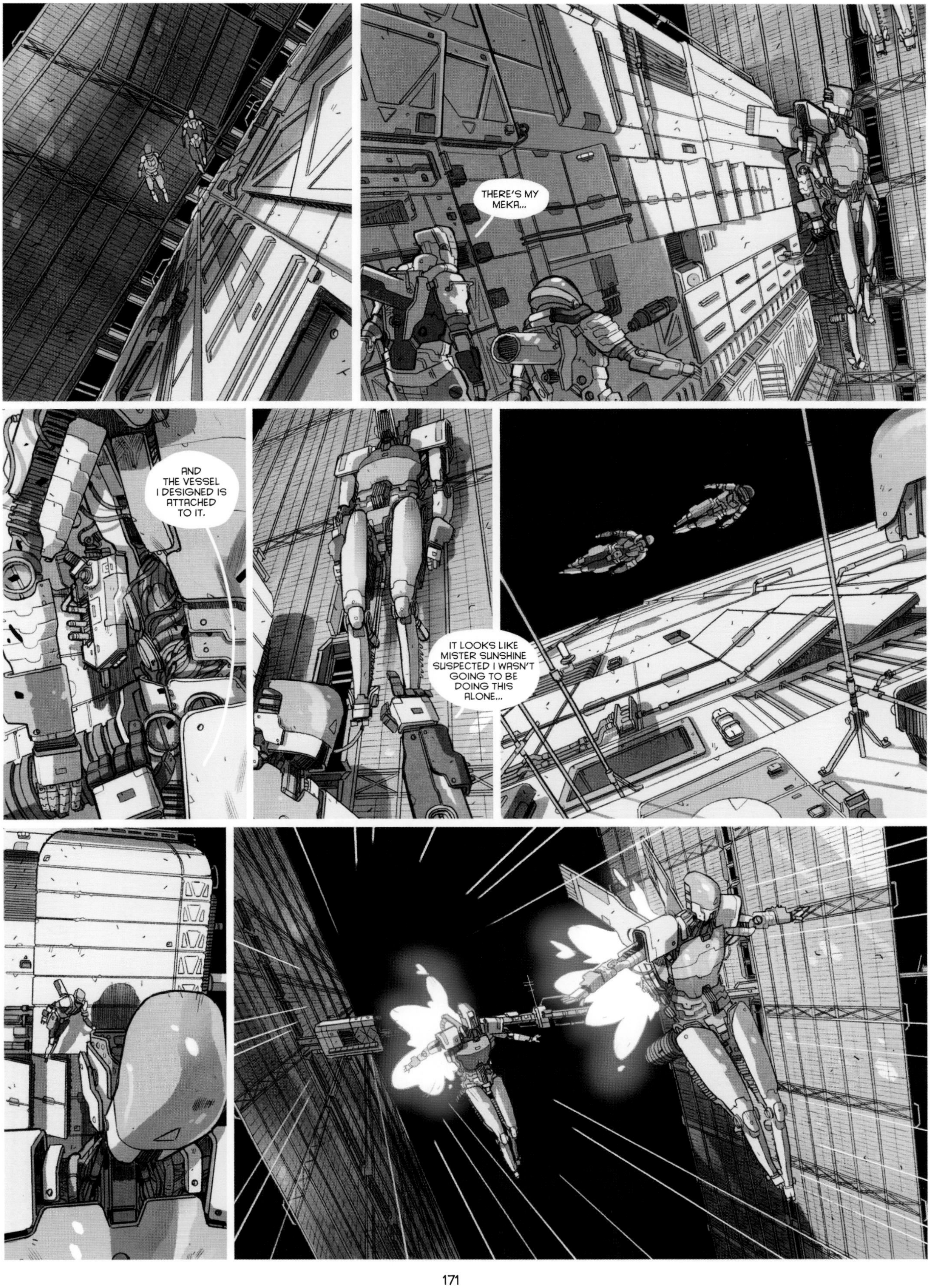
THERE'S MY MEKA...
AND THE VESSEL I DESIGNED IS ATTACHED TO IT.
IT LOOKS LIKE MISTER SUNSHINE SUSPECTED I WASN'T GOING TO BE DOING THIS ALONE...

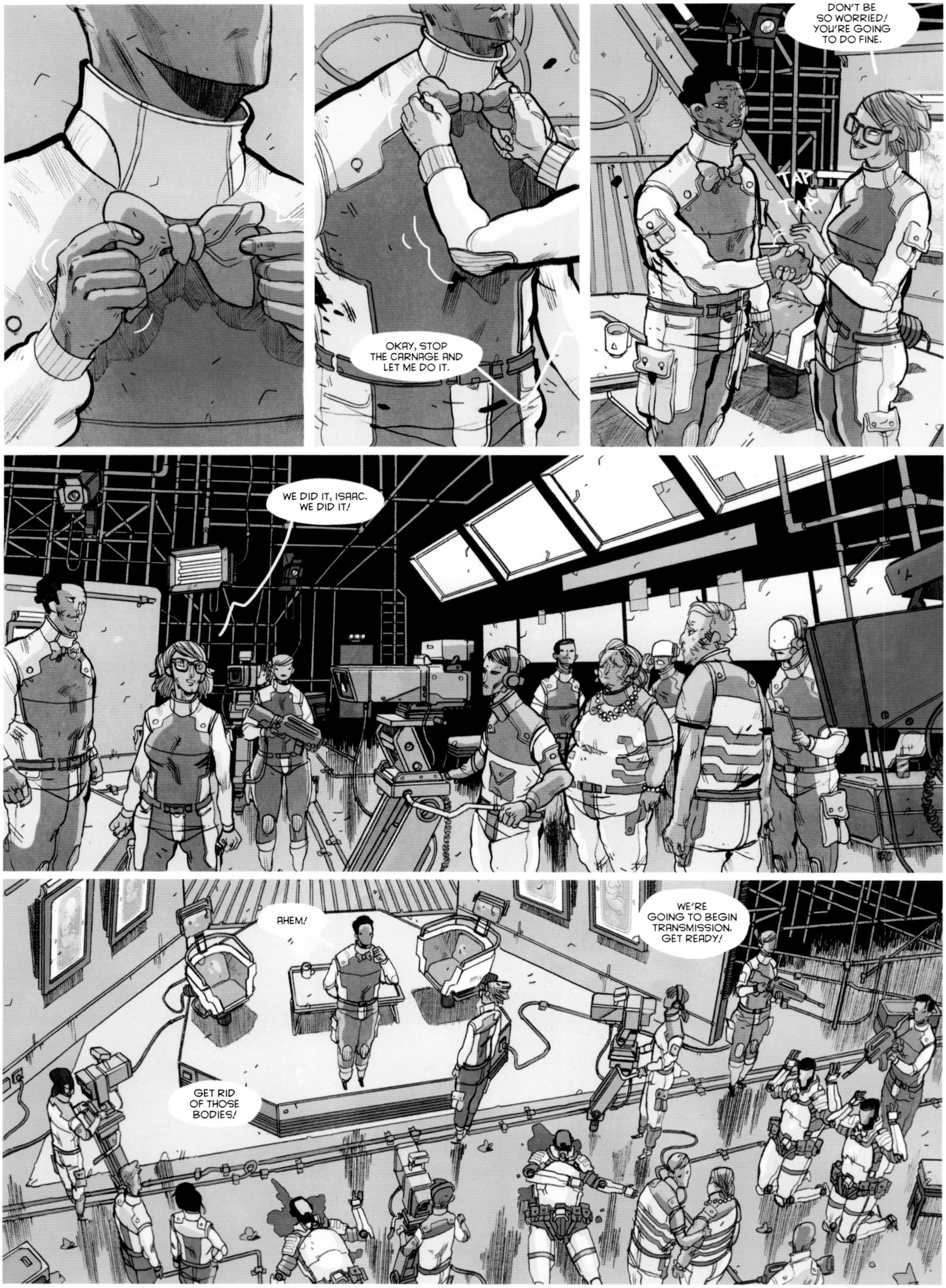
OKAY, STOP THE CARNAGE AND LET ME DO IT.
DON'T BE SO WORRIED! YOU'RE GOING TO DO FINE.
TAP TAP
WE DID IT, ISAAC. WE DID IT!
AHEM!
WE'RE GOING TO BEGIN TRANSMISSION. GET READY!
GET RID OF THOSE BODIES!

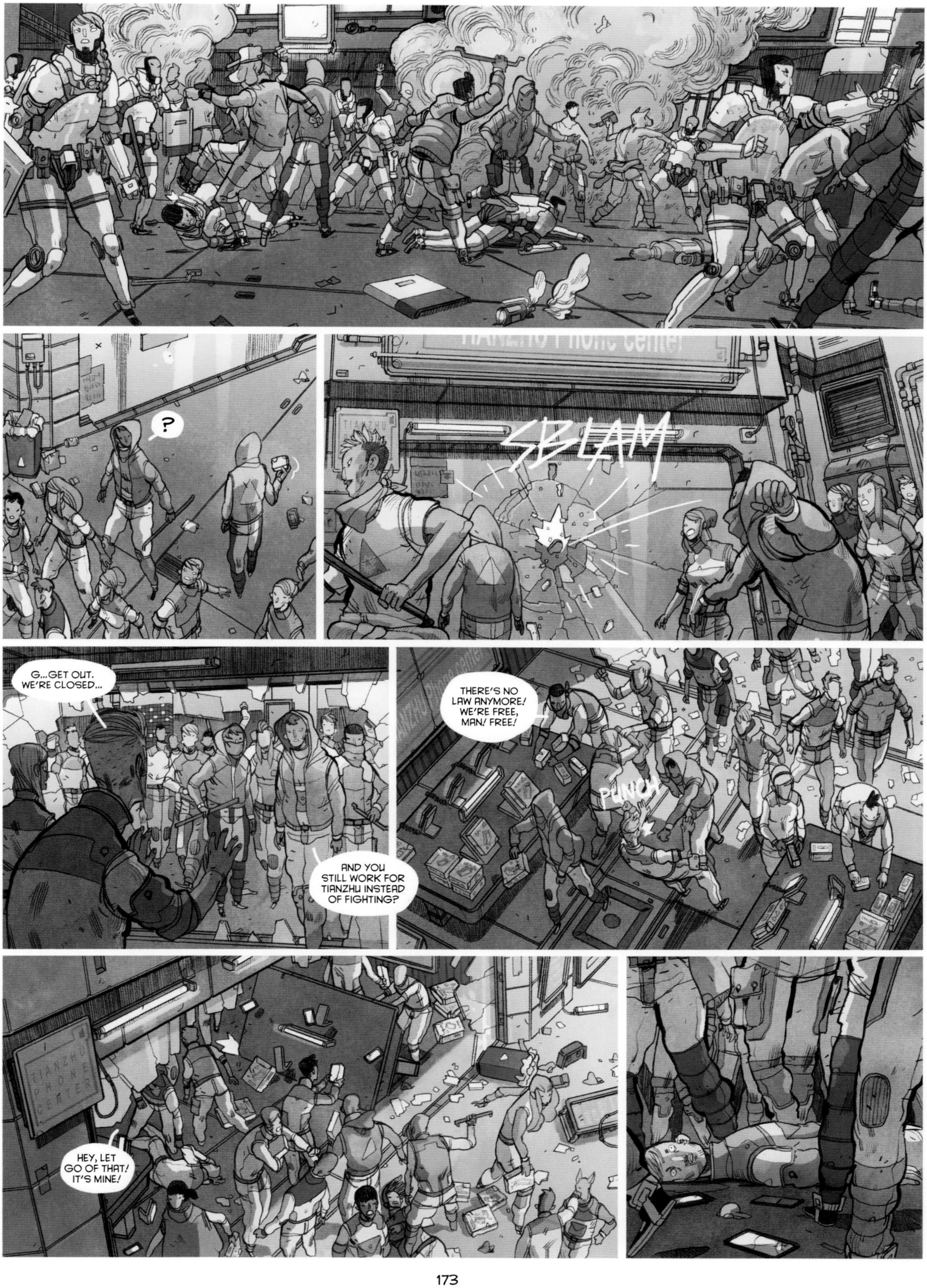
?
TIANZHU
SBLAM
G...GET OUT. WE'RE CLOSED...
AND YOU STILL WORK FOR TIANZHU INSTEAD OF FIGHTING?
THERE'S NO LAW ANYMORE! WE'RE FREE, MAN! FREE!
PUNCH
TIANZHU PHONE CENTER
HEY, LET GO OF THAT! IT'S MINE!

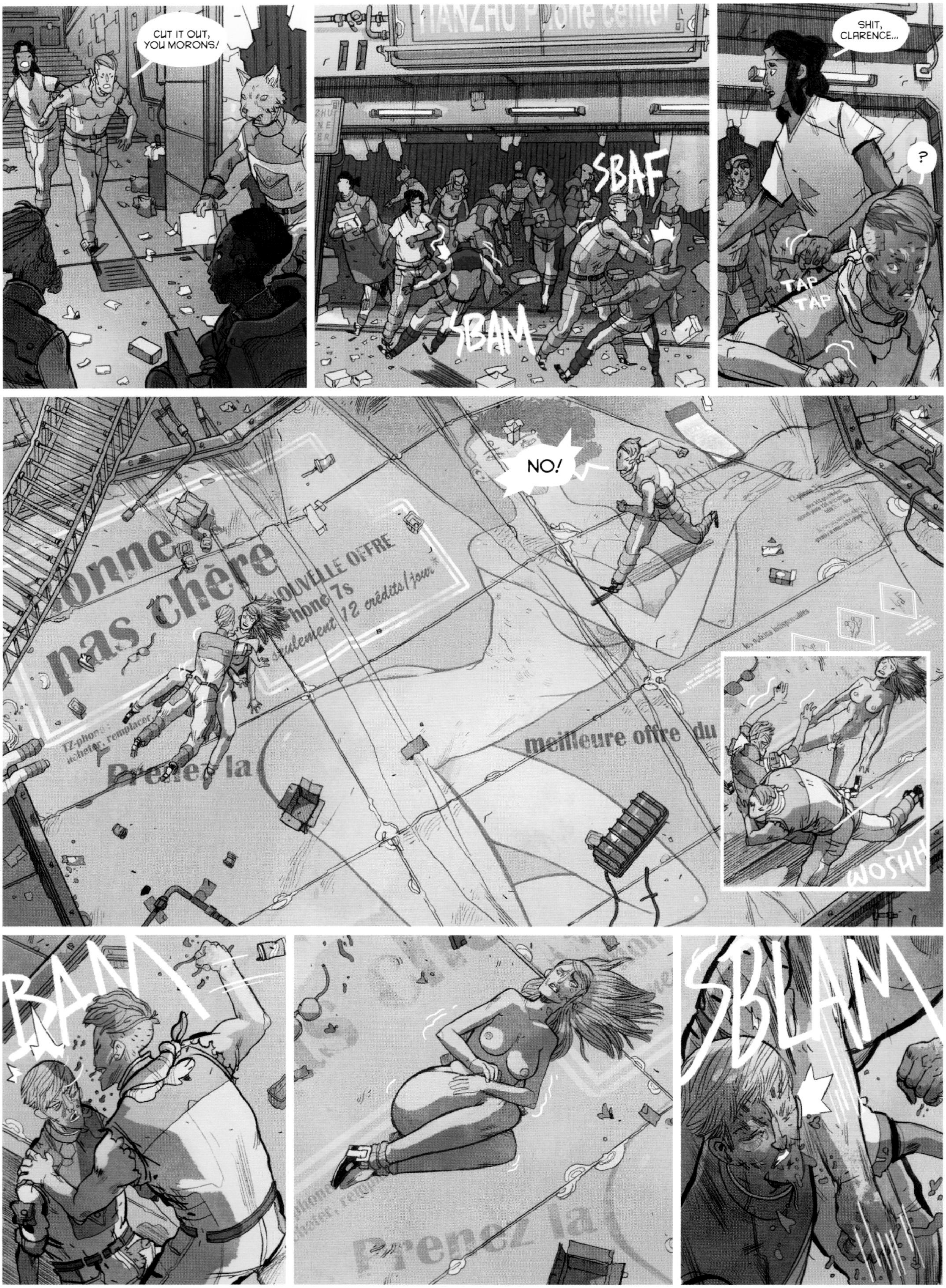
CUT IT OUT, YOU MORONS!
SBAF
SBAM
SHIT, CLARENCE...
?
TAP TAP
NO!
pas chère
NOUVELLE OFFRE
phone 7s
seulement 12 crédits/jour*
meilleure offre du
Prenez la
WOSHH
BAM
SBLAM

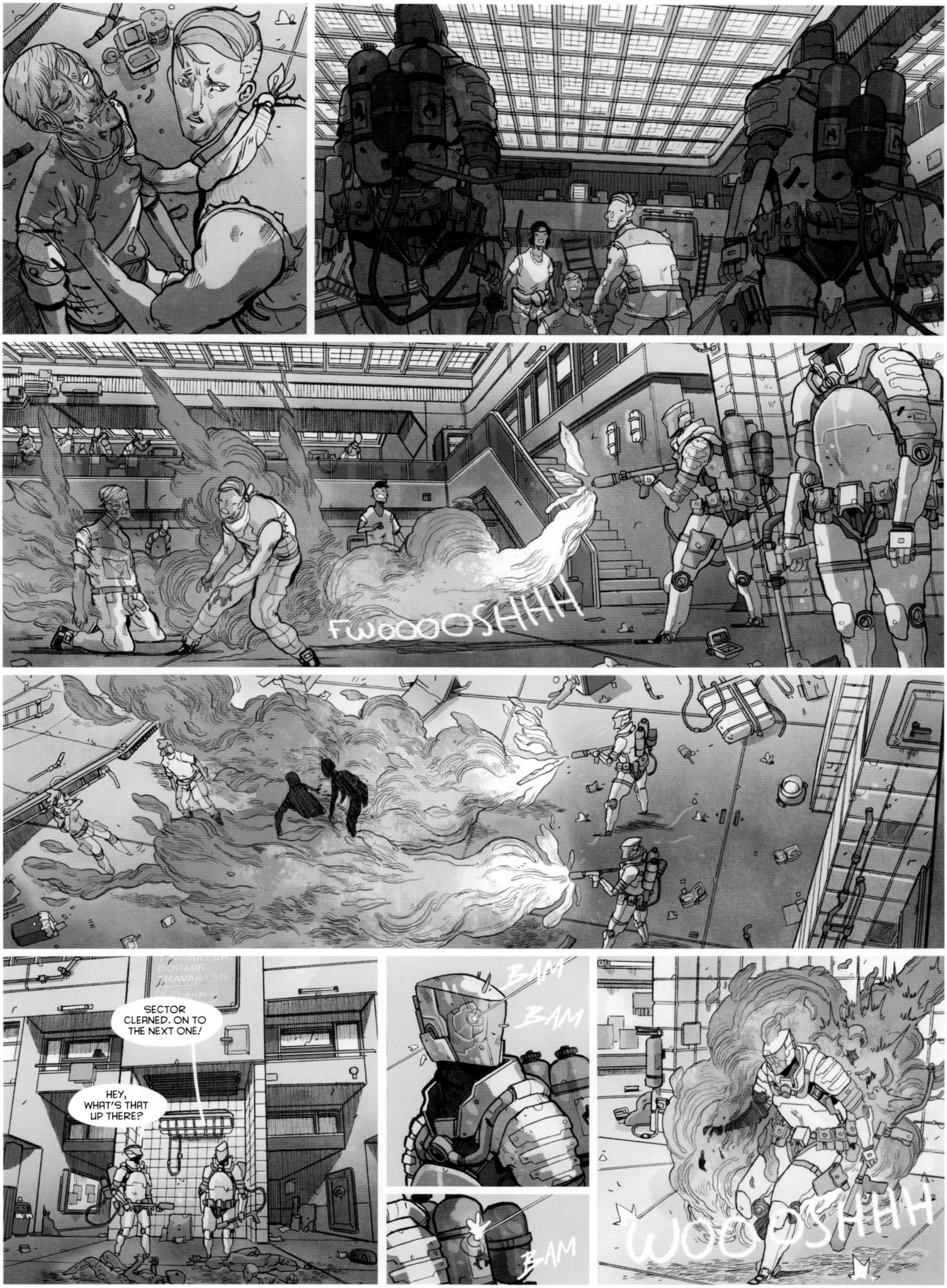
FWOOOOSHHH
SECTOR CLEANED. ON TO THE NEXT ONE!
HEY, WHAT'S THAT UP THERE?
BAM
BAM
BAM
WOOOOSHHH

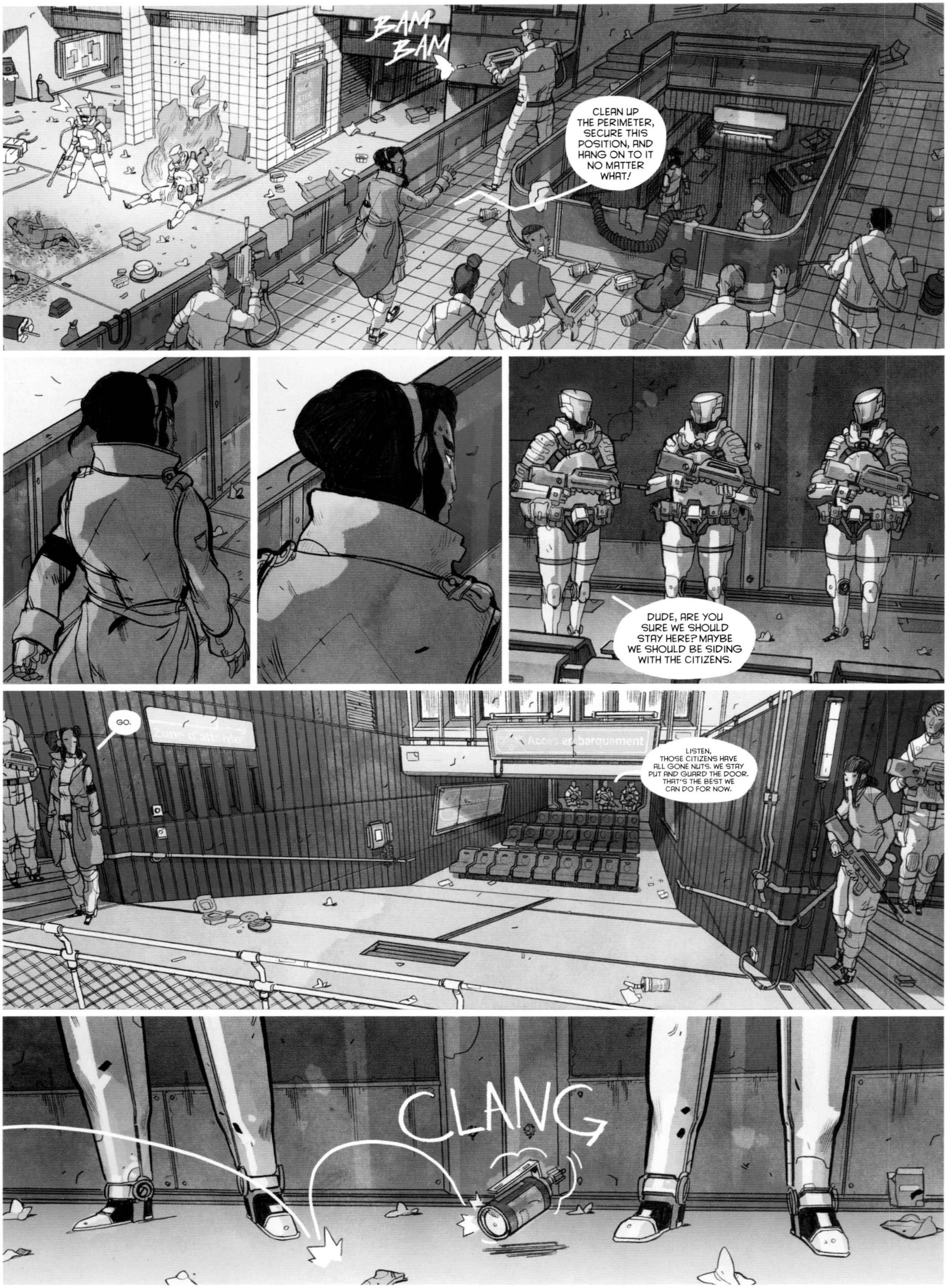
BAM BAM
CLEAN UP THE PERIMETER, SECURE THIS POSITION, AND HANG ON TO IT NO MATTER WHAT!
DUDE, ARE YOU SURE WE SHOULD STAY HERE? MAYBE WE SHOULD BE SIDING WITH THE CITIZENS.
GO.
Zone d'attente
Acces embarquement
LISTEN, THOSE CITIZENS HAVE ALL GONE NUTS. WE STAY PUT AND GUARD THE DOOR. THAT'S THE BEST WE CAN DO FOR NOW.
CLANG

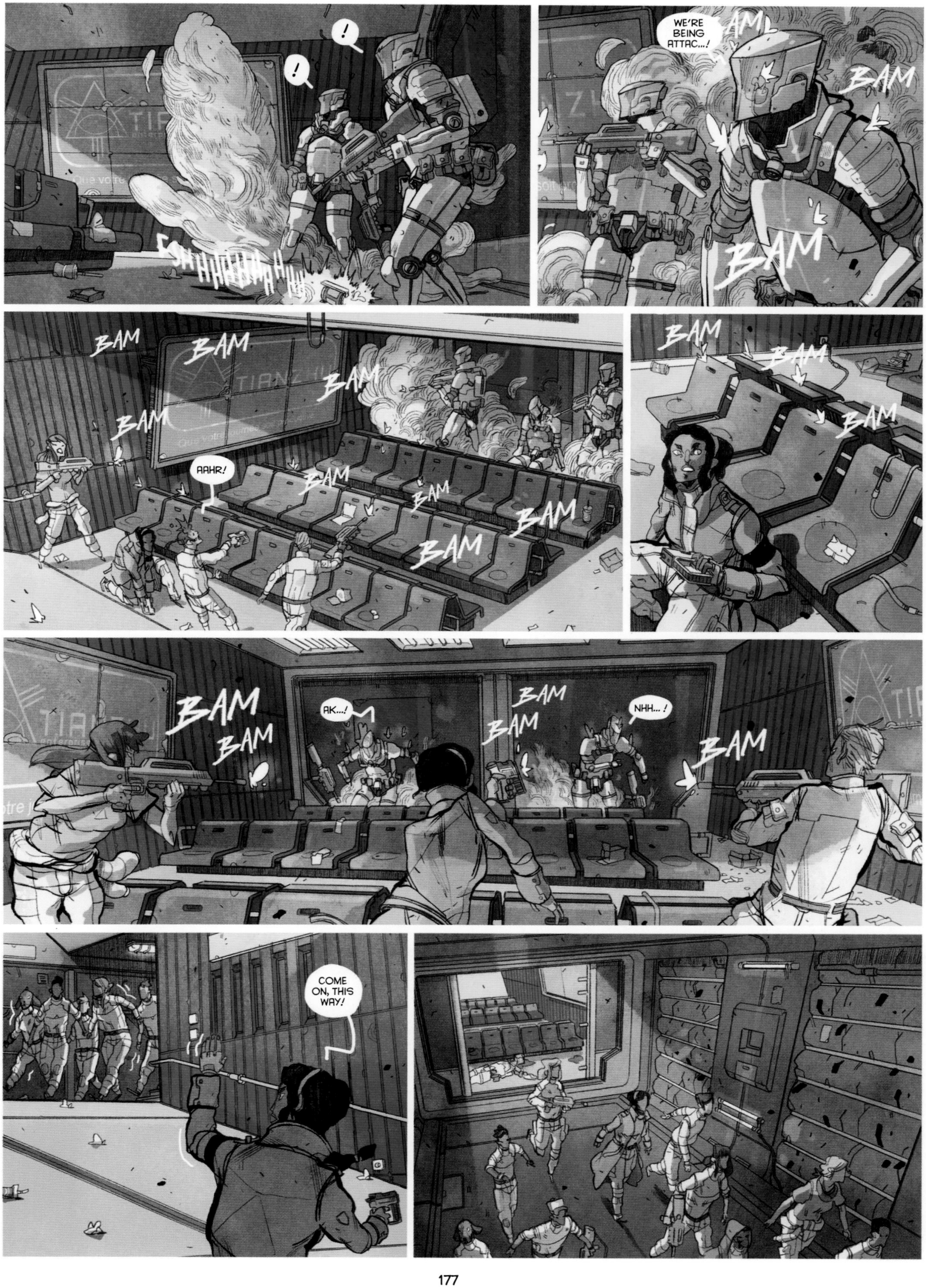
!
!
SHHHHHHHHHHH
WE'RE BEING ATTAC...!
BAM
BAM
BAM
BAM
BAM
BAM
BAM
AAHR!
BAM
BAM
BAM
BAM
BAM
BAM
BAM
BAM
BAM
AK...!
BAM
BAM
NHH...!
BAM
COME ON, THIS WAY!

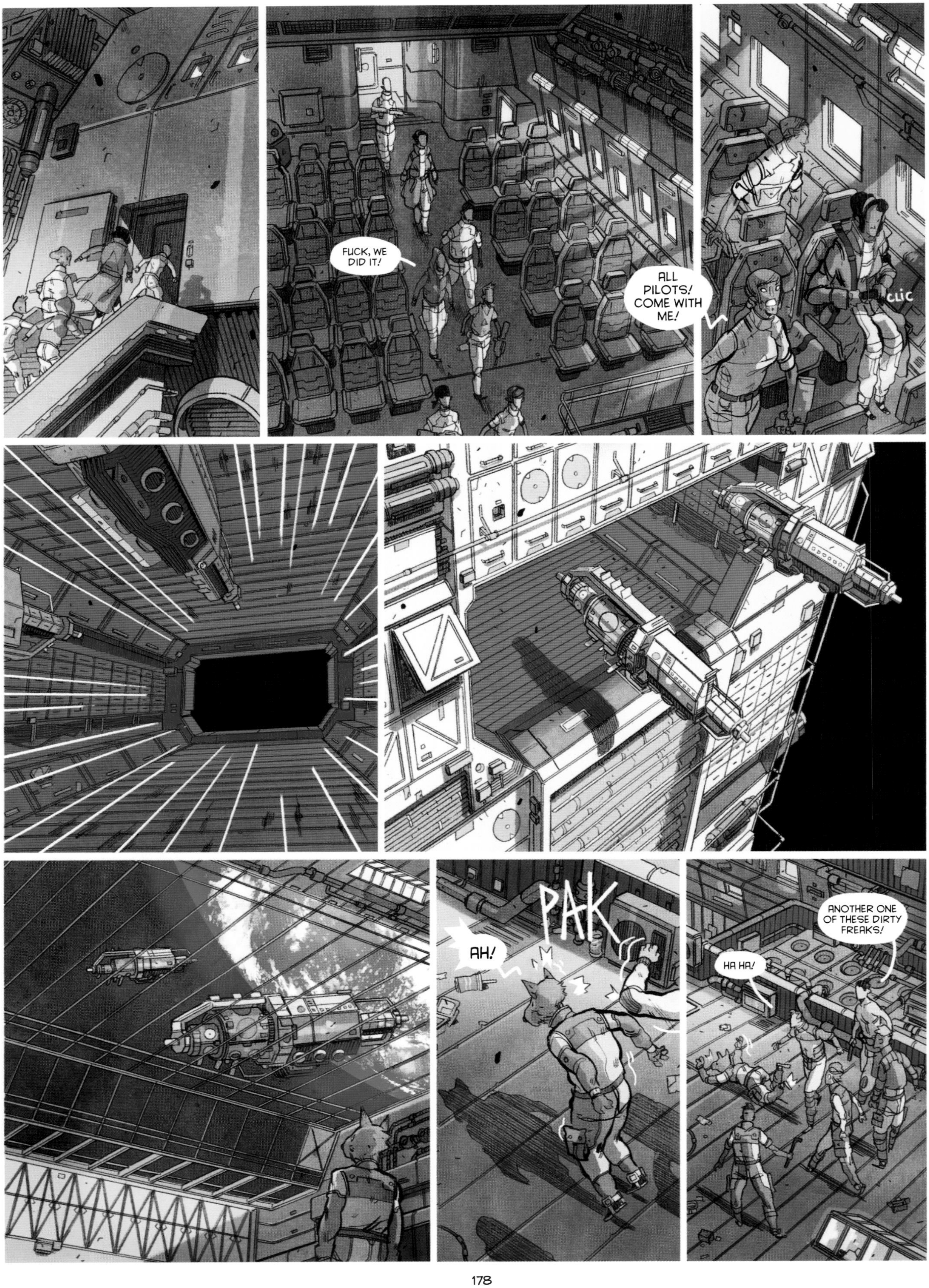
FUCK, WE DID IT!
ALL PILOTS! COME WITH ME!
CLIC
PAK
AH!
ANOTHER ONE OF THESE DIRTY FREAKS!
HA HA!

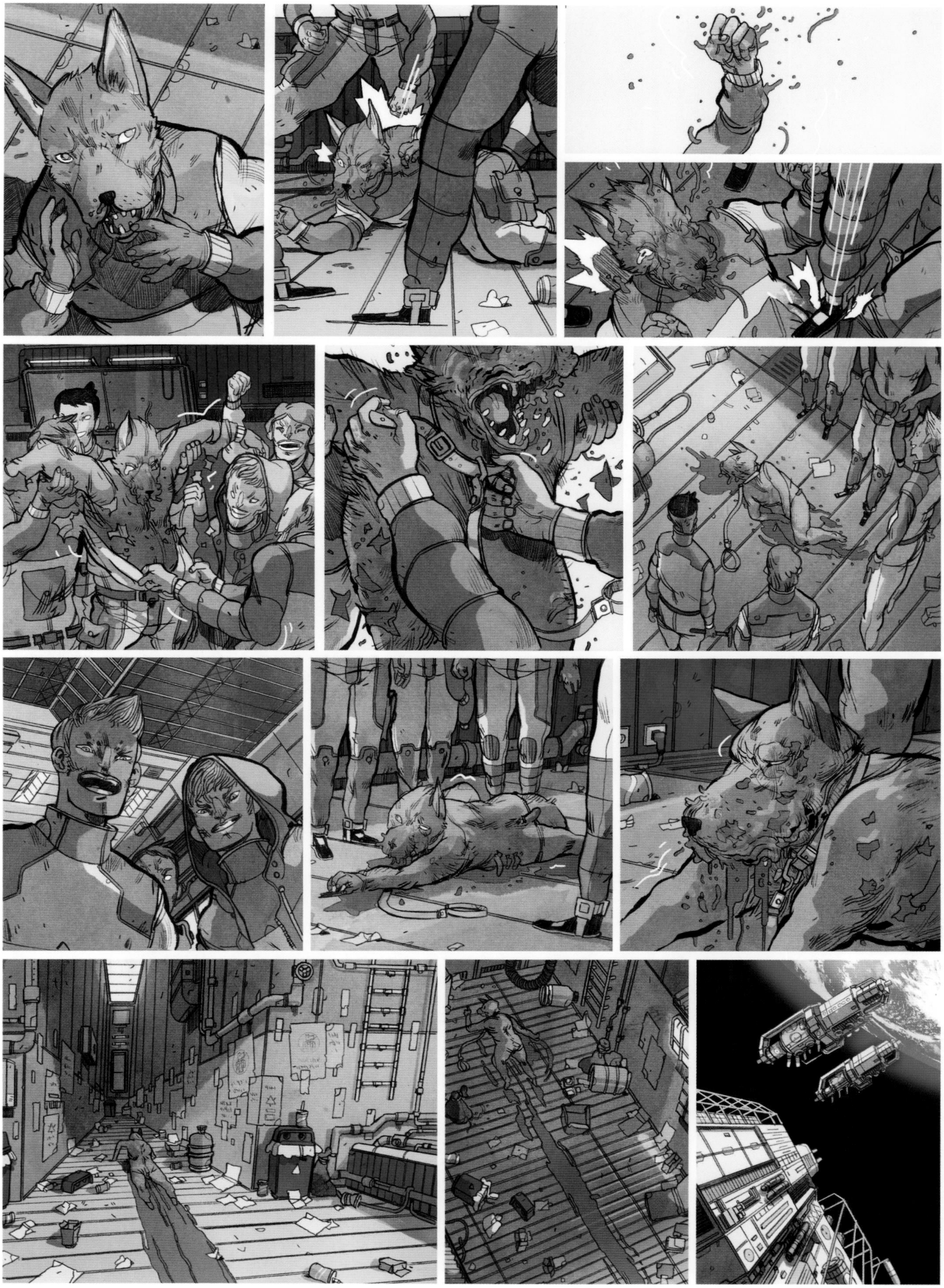

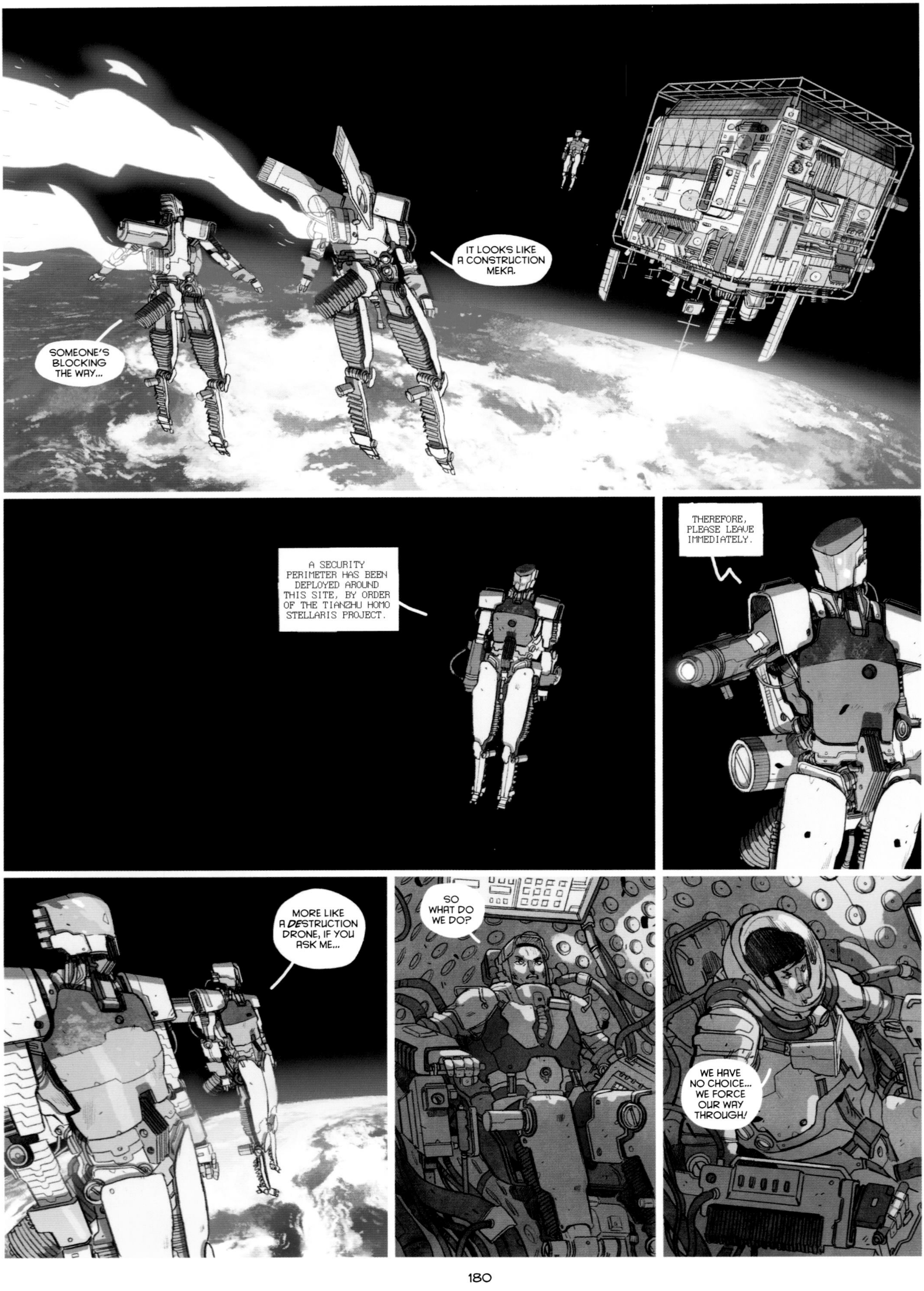

IT LOOKS LIKE A CONSTRUCTION MEKA.
SOMEONE'S BLOCKING THE WAY...
A SECURITY PERIMETER HAS BEEN DEPLOYED AROUND THIS SITE, BY ORDER OF THE TIANZHU HOMO STELLARIS PROJECT.
THEREFORE, PLEASE LEAVE IMMEDIATELY.
MORE LIKE A *DE*STRUCTION DRONE, IF YOU ASK ME...
SO WHAT DO WE DO?
WE HAVE NO CHOICE... WE FORCE OUR WAY THROUGH!

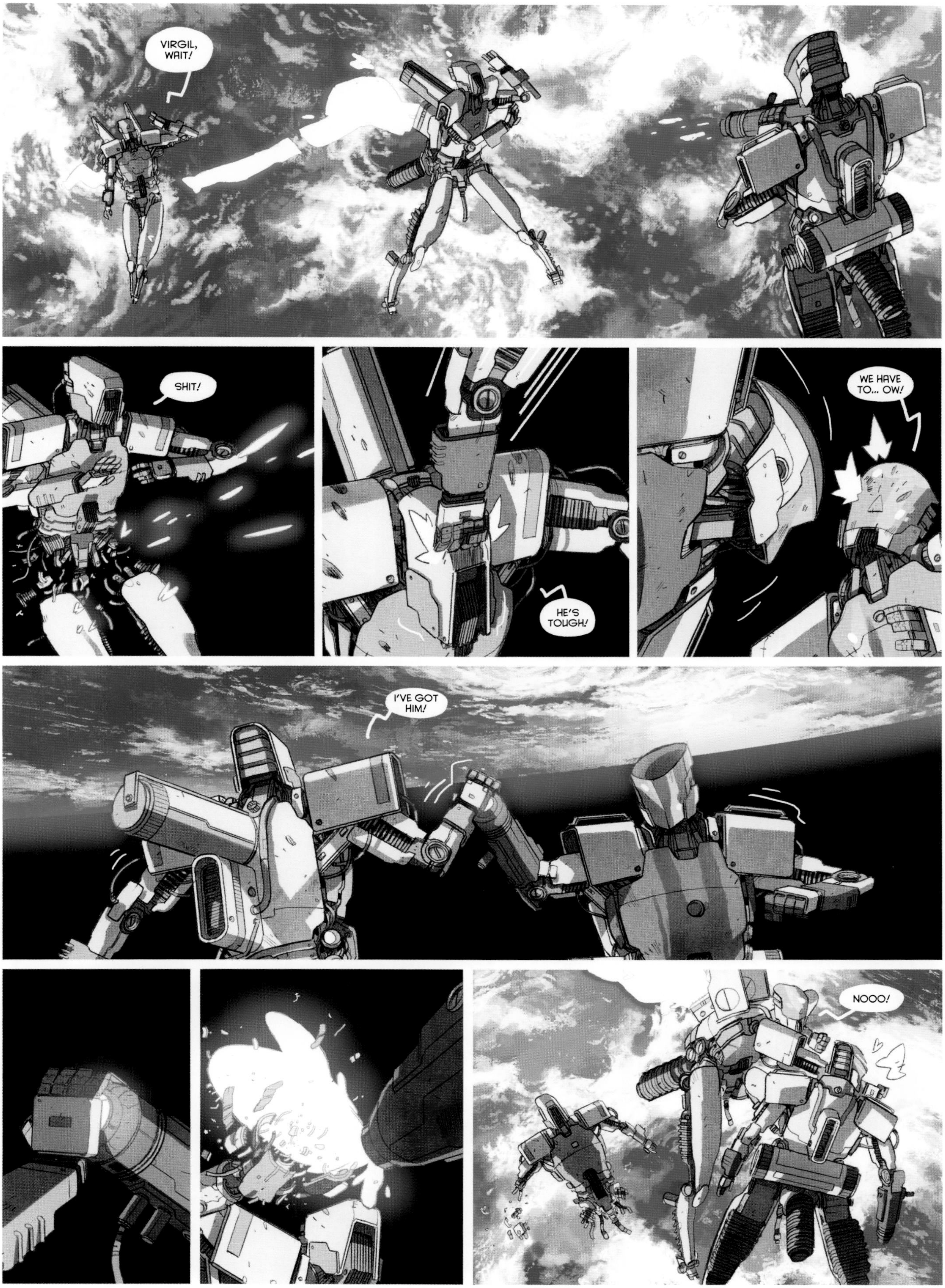

VIRGIL, WAIT!
SHIT!
HE'S TOUGH!
WE HAVE TO... OW!
I'VE GOT HIM!
NOOO!

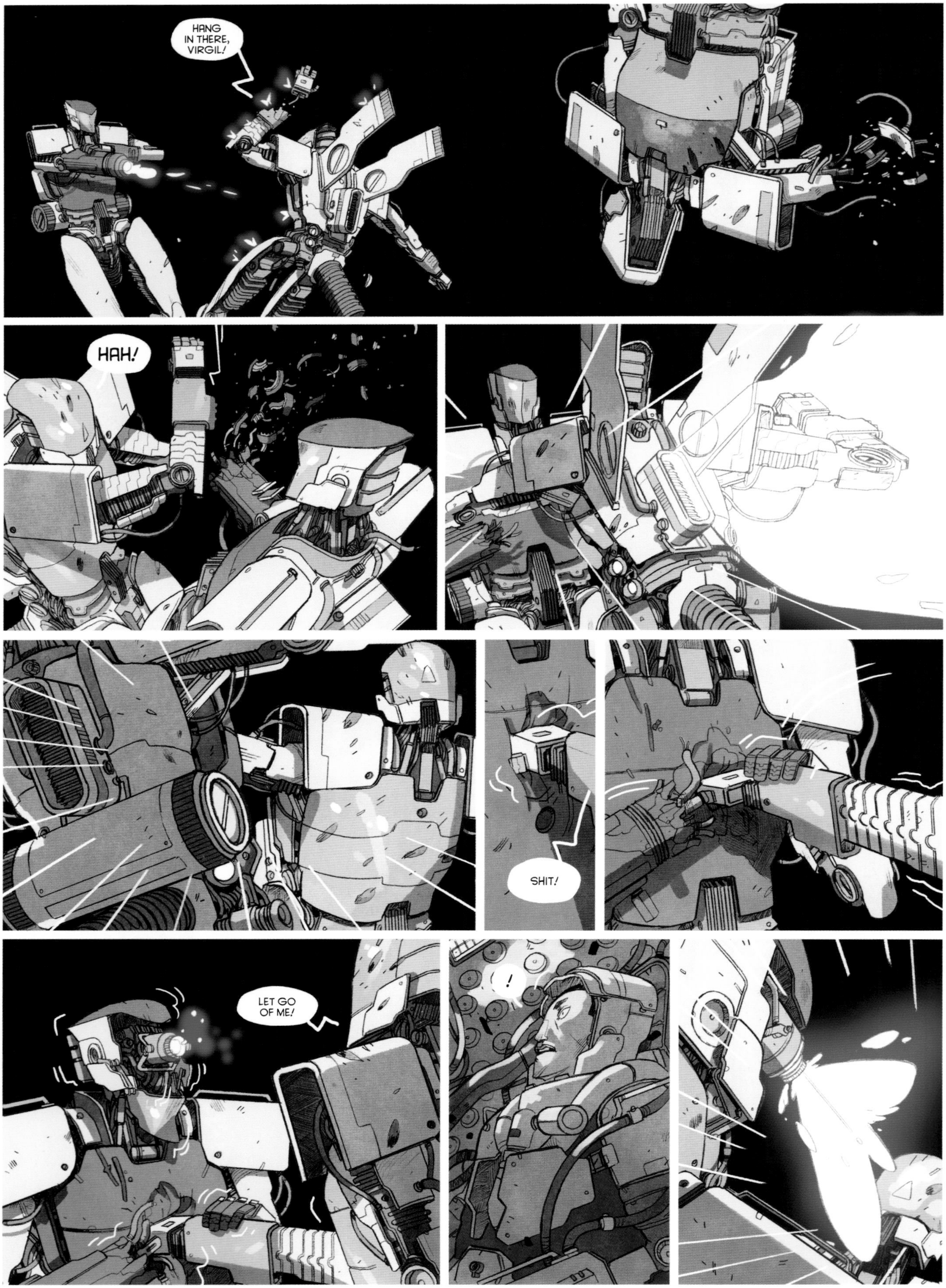
HANG IN THERE, VIRGIL!
HAH!
SHIT!
LET GO OF ME!
!

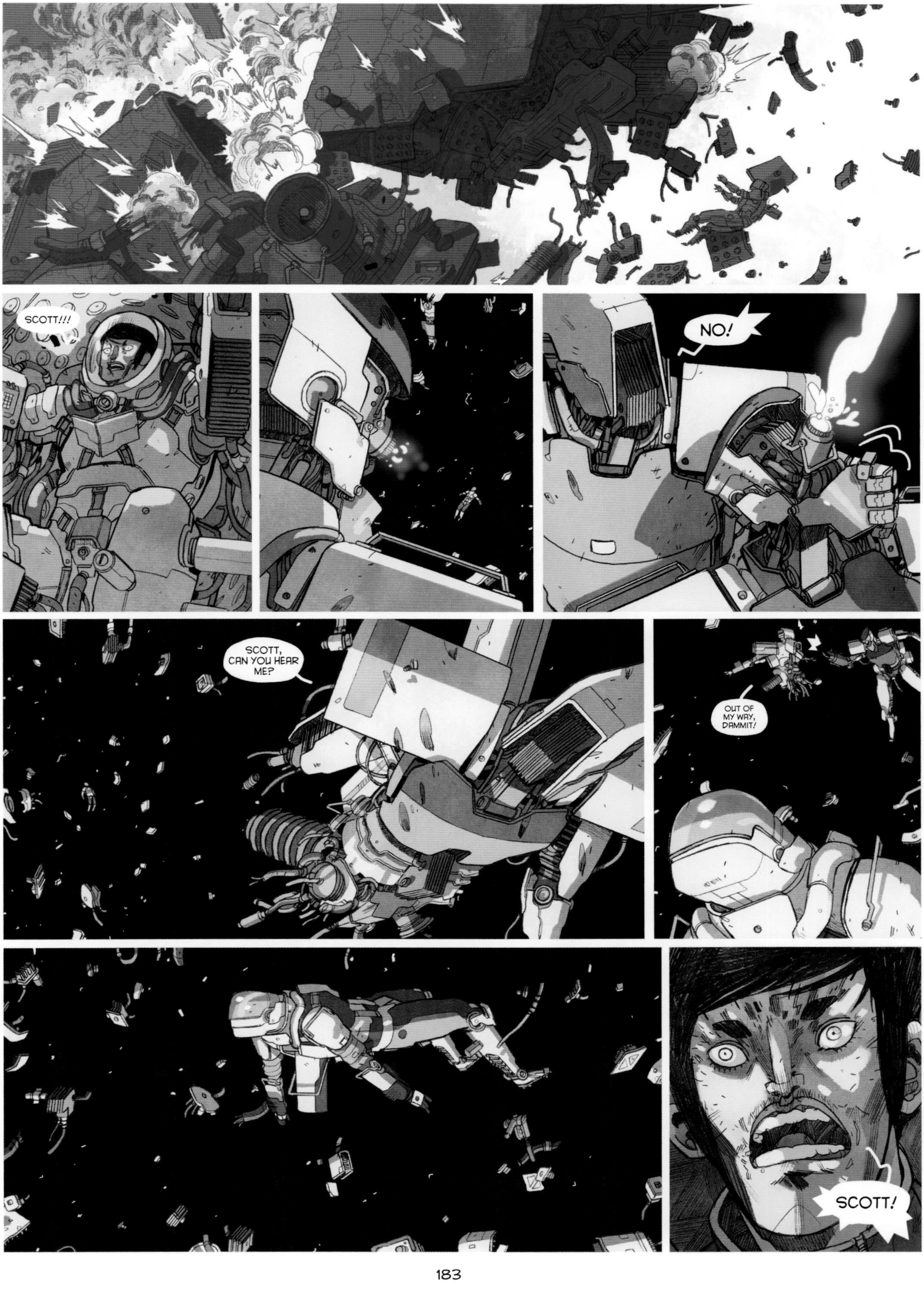
SCOTT!!!
NO!
SCOTT, CAN YOU HEAR ME?
OUT OF MY WAY, DAMMIT!
SCOTT!

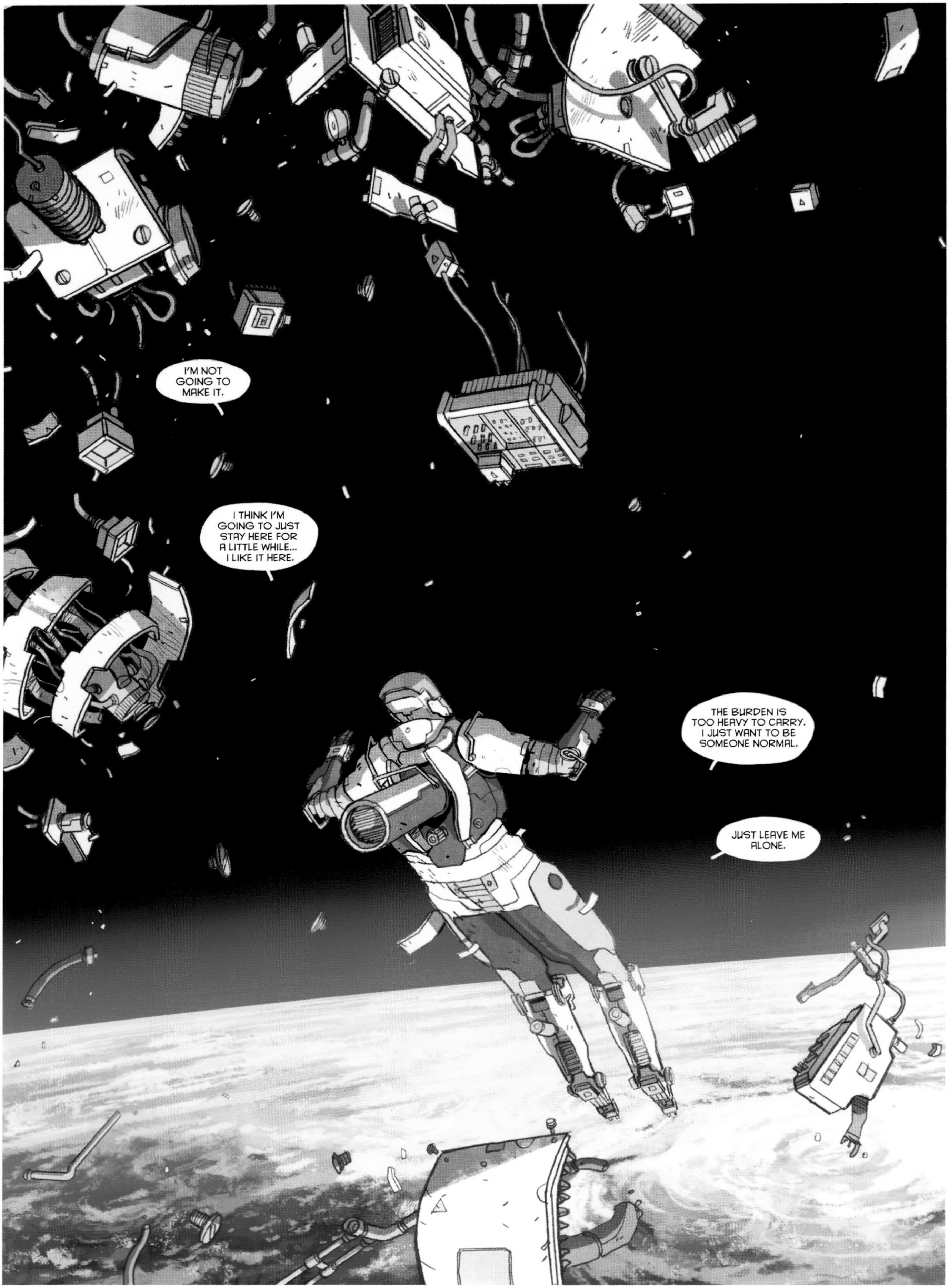
I'M NOT GOING TO MAKE IT.
I THINK I'M GOING TO JUST STAY HERE FOR A LITTLE WHILE... I LIKE IT HERE.
THE BURDEN IS TOO HEAVY TO CARRY. I JUST WANT TO BE SOMEONE NORMAL.
JUST LEAVE ME ALONE.

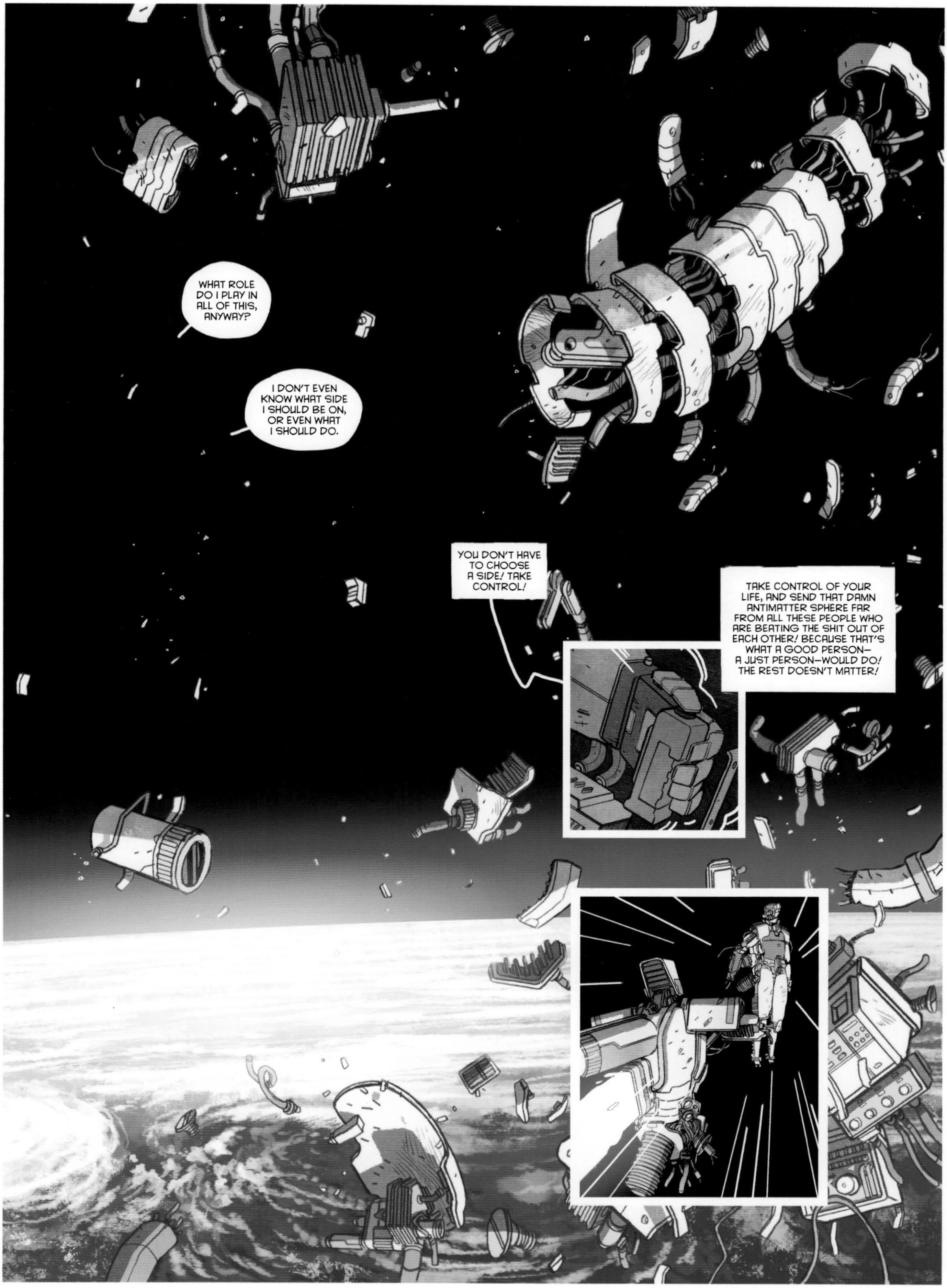
WHAT ROLE DO I PLAY IN ALL OF THIS, ANYWAY?
I DON'T EVEN KNOW WHAT SIDE I SHOULD BE ON, OR EVEN WHAT I SHOULD DO.
YOU DON'T HAVE TO CHOOSE A SIDE! TAKE CONTROL!
TAKE CONTROL OF YOUR LIFE, AND SEND THAT DAMN ANTIMATTER SPHERE FAR FROM ALL THESE PEOPLE WHO ARE BEATING THE SHIT OUT OF EACH OTHER! BECAUSE THAT'S WHAT A GOOD PERSON— A JUST PERSON—WOULD DO! THE REST DOESN'T MATTER!

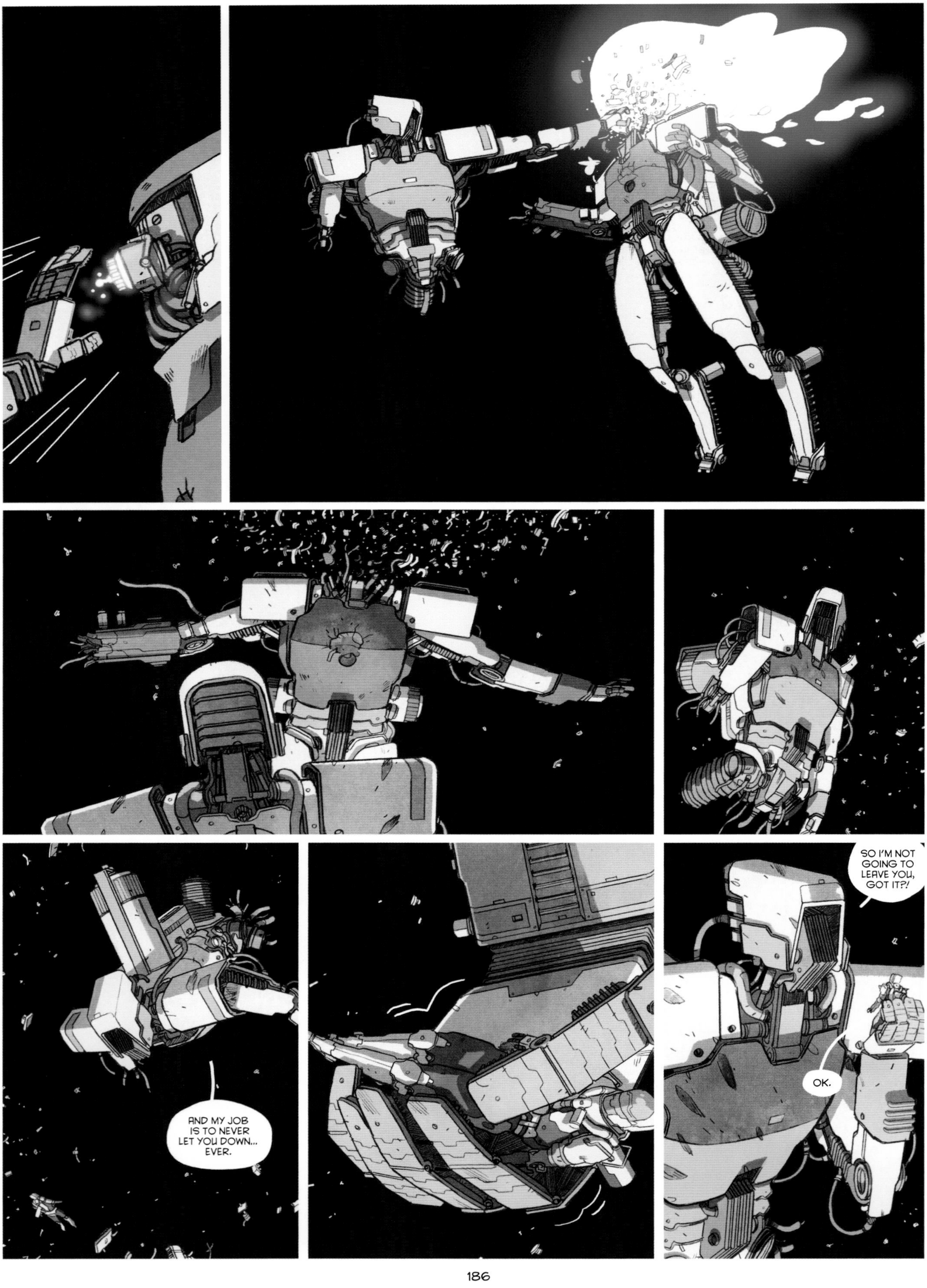
AND MY JOB IS TO NEVER LET YOU DOWN... EVER.
SO I'M NOT GOING TO LEAVE YOU, GOT IT?!
OK.

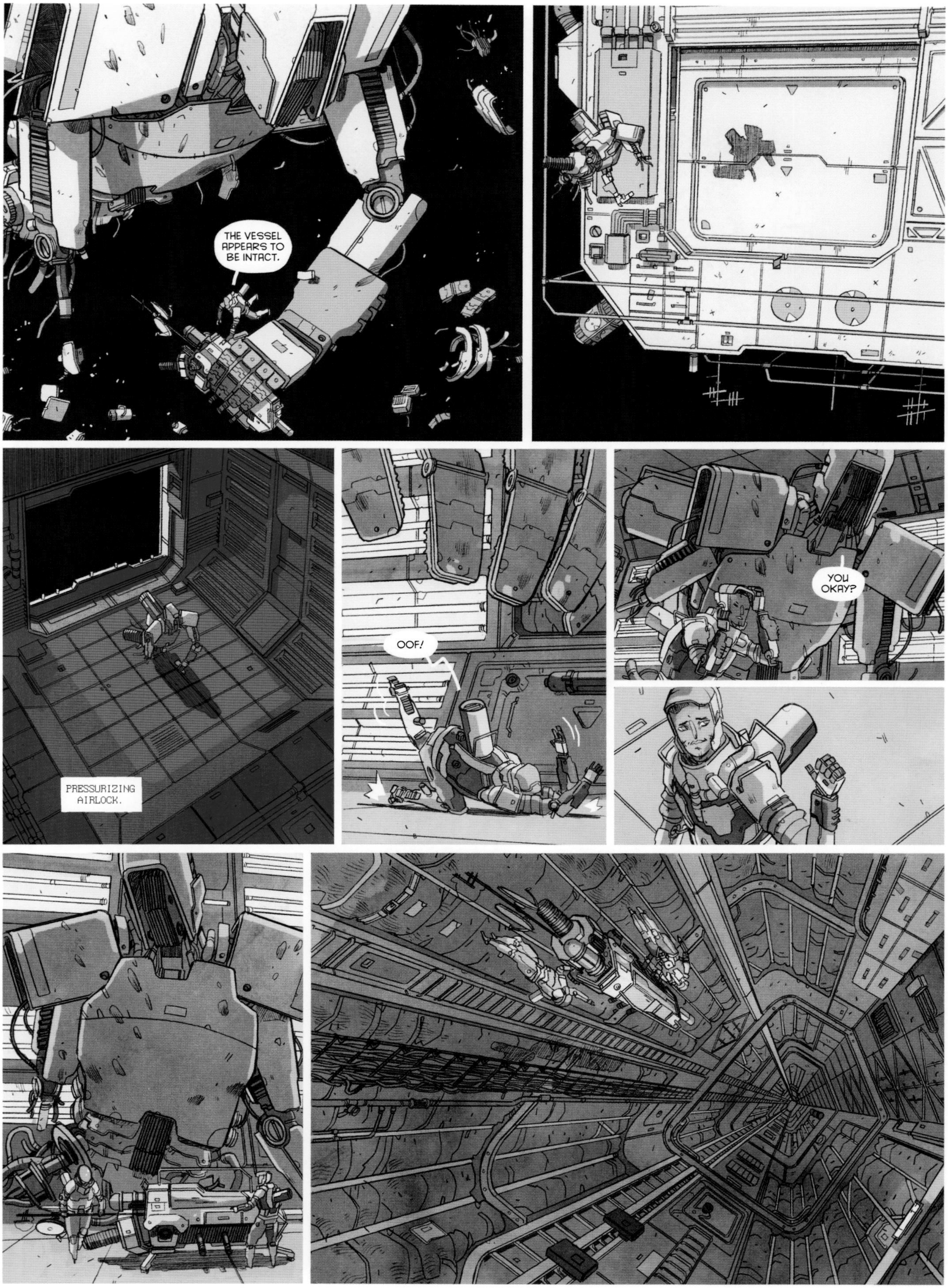
THE VESSEL APPEARS TO BE INTACT.
PRESSURIZING AIRLOCK.
OOF!
YOU OKAY?

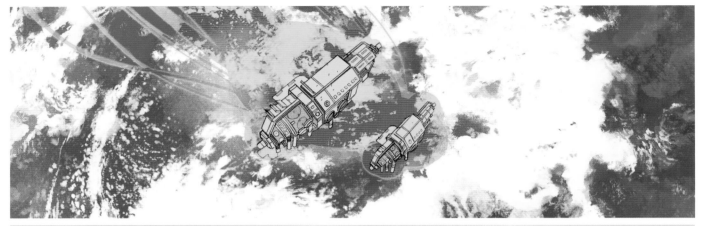

ACCORDING TO YOUR NOTES, THIS SUIT WILL CONTINUE TO STIMULATE YOUR MUSCLES, EVEN IF YOU REMAIN CONFINED AND IMMOBILE.

YOU COULD EVEN HOLD OUT A LONG TIME IN THIS THING, WITH ENOUGH OXYGEN, WATER, AND LIQUIDS THAT ARE PROBABLY SIMILAR TO FOOD.

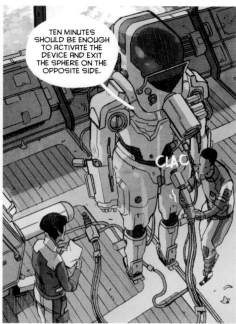

TEN MINUTES SHOULD BE ENOUGH TO ACTIVATE THE DEVICE AND EXIT THE SPHERE ON THE OPPOSITE SIDE.

CLAC

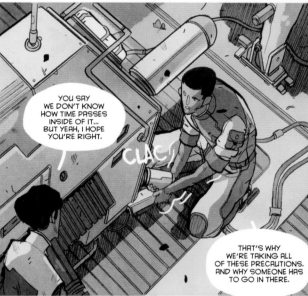

YOU SAY WE DON'T KNOW HOW TIME PASSES INSIDE OF IT... BUT YEAH, I HOPE YOU'RE RIGHT.

CLAC

THAT'S WHY WE'RE TAKING ALL OF THESE PRECAUTIONS. AND WHY SOMEONE HAS TO GO IN THERE.

I HOPE THAT MISTER SUNSHINE'S TEAMS FOLLOWED YOUR NOTES... AND THAT YOU DIDN'T MAKE ANY MISTAKES...

IT'S MY JOB AND MY RESEARCH THAT ALLOWED THIS DEVICE TO BE BUILT. MANNING IT FROM INSIDE IS PART OF MY JOB.

I'M NO GOOD AT A LOT OF THINGS, BUT THAT I KNOW HOW TO DO.

BESIDES, WE CAN'T ACTIVATE IT FROM A DISTANCE. NO SIGNAL CAN PENETRATE THE HULL.

SO WE WON'T BE ABLE TO MAINTAIN CONTACT WHILE YOU'RE INSIDE?

NOPE, RADIO SIGNALS WON'T GO THROUGH.

FROT

FROT FROT

SCOTT...

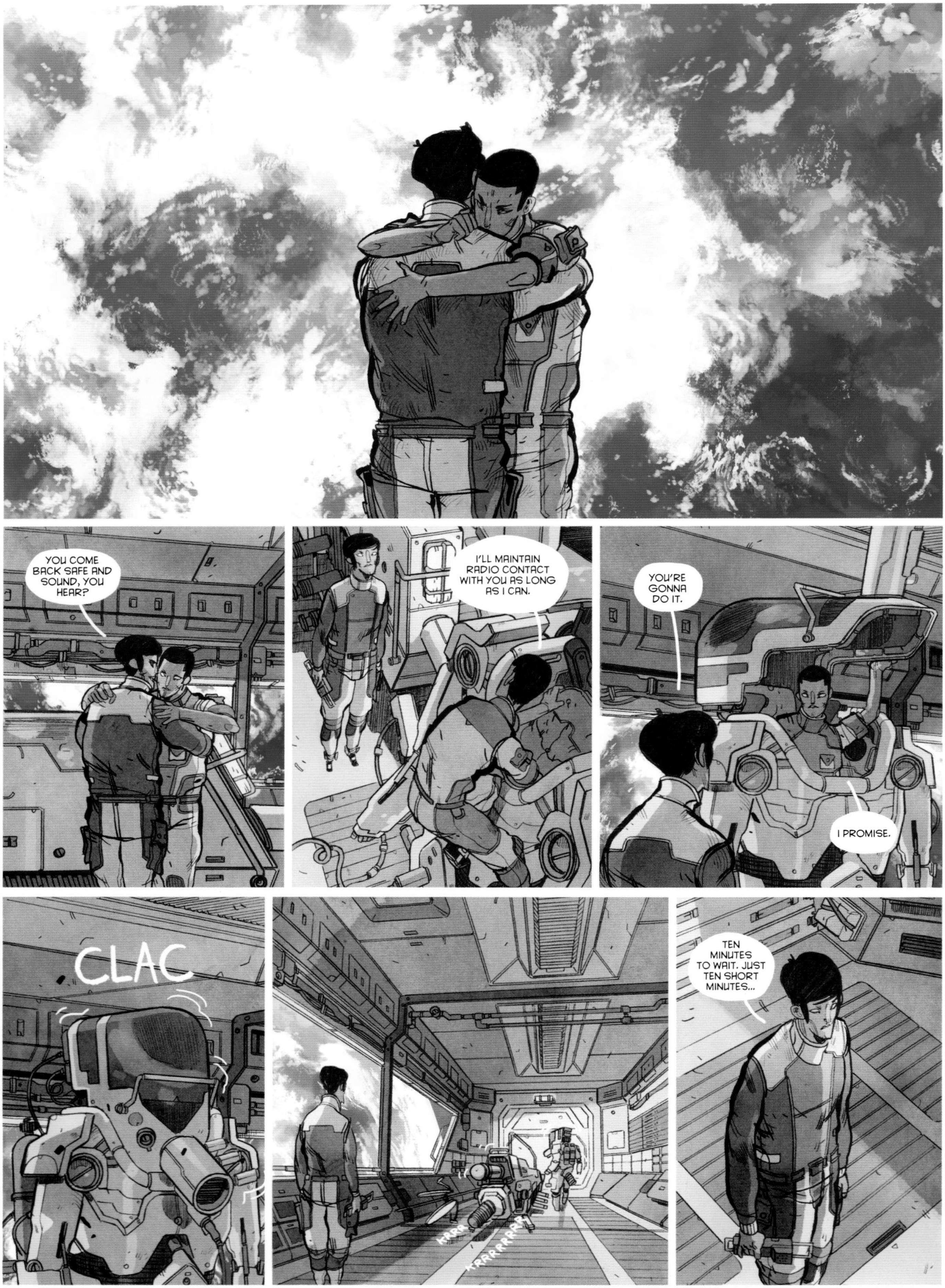
YOU COME BACK SAFE AND SOUND, YOU HEAR?
I'LL MAINTAIN RADIO CONTACT WITH YOU AS LONG AS I CAN.
YOU'RE GONNA DO IT.
I PROMISE.
CLAC
KRRR
KRRRRRRRRR
TEN MINUTES TO WAIT. JUST TEN SHORT MINUTES...

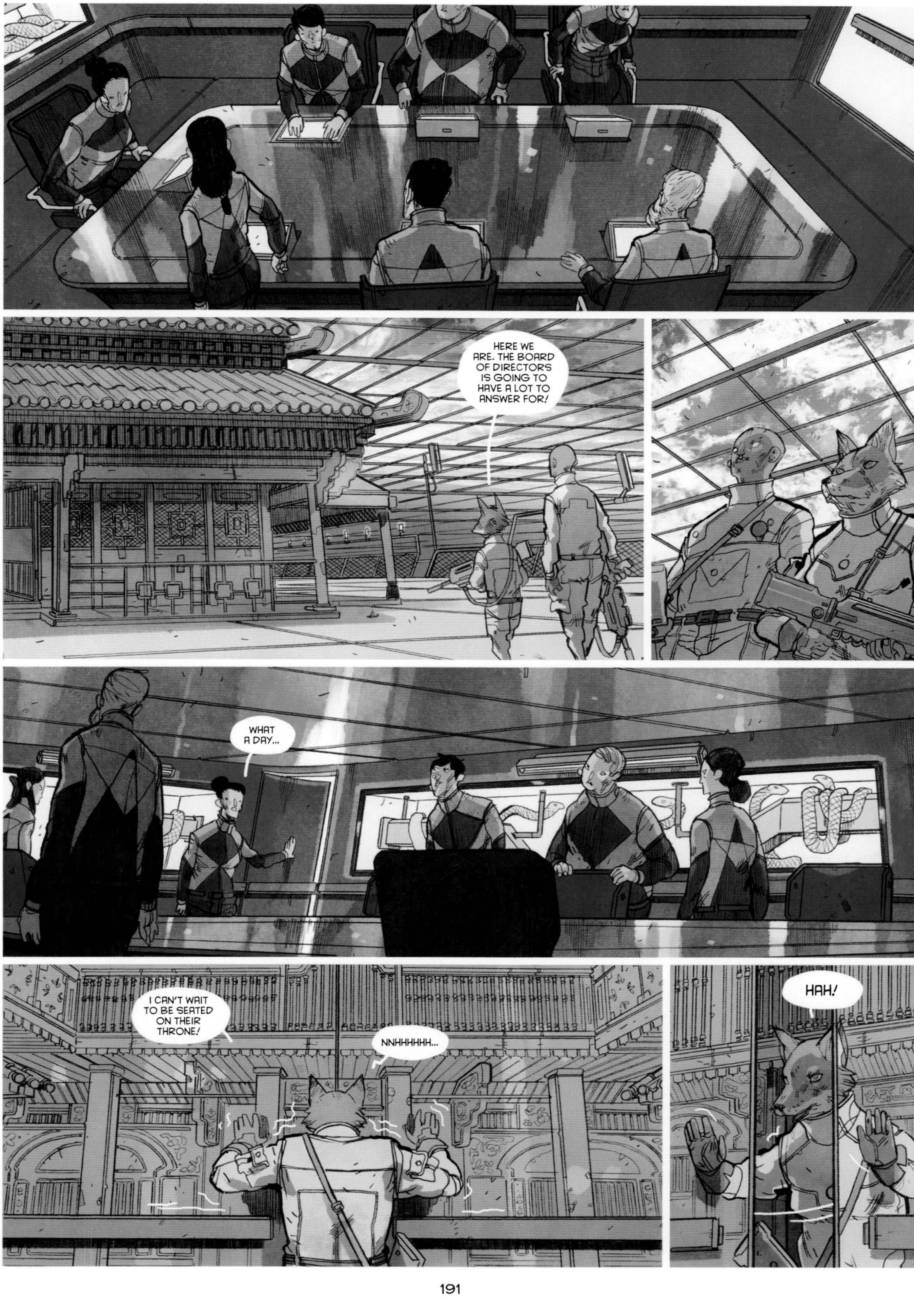
HERE WE ARE. THE BOARD OF DIRECTORS IS GOING TO HAVE A LOT TO ANSWER FOR!
WHAT A DAY...
I CAN'T WAIT TO BE SEATED ON THEIR THRONE!
NNHHHHHH...
HAH!

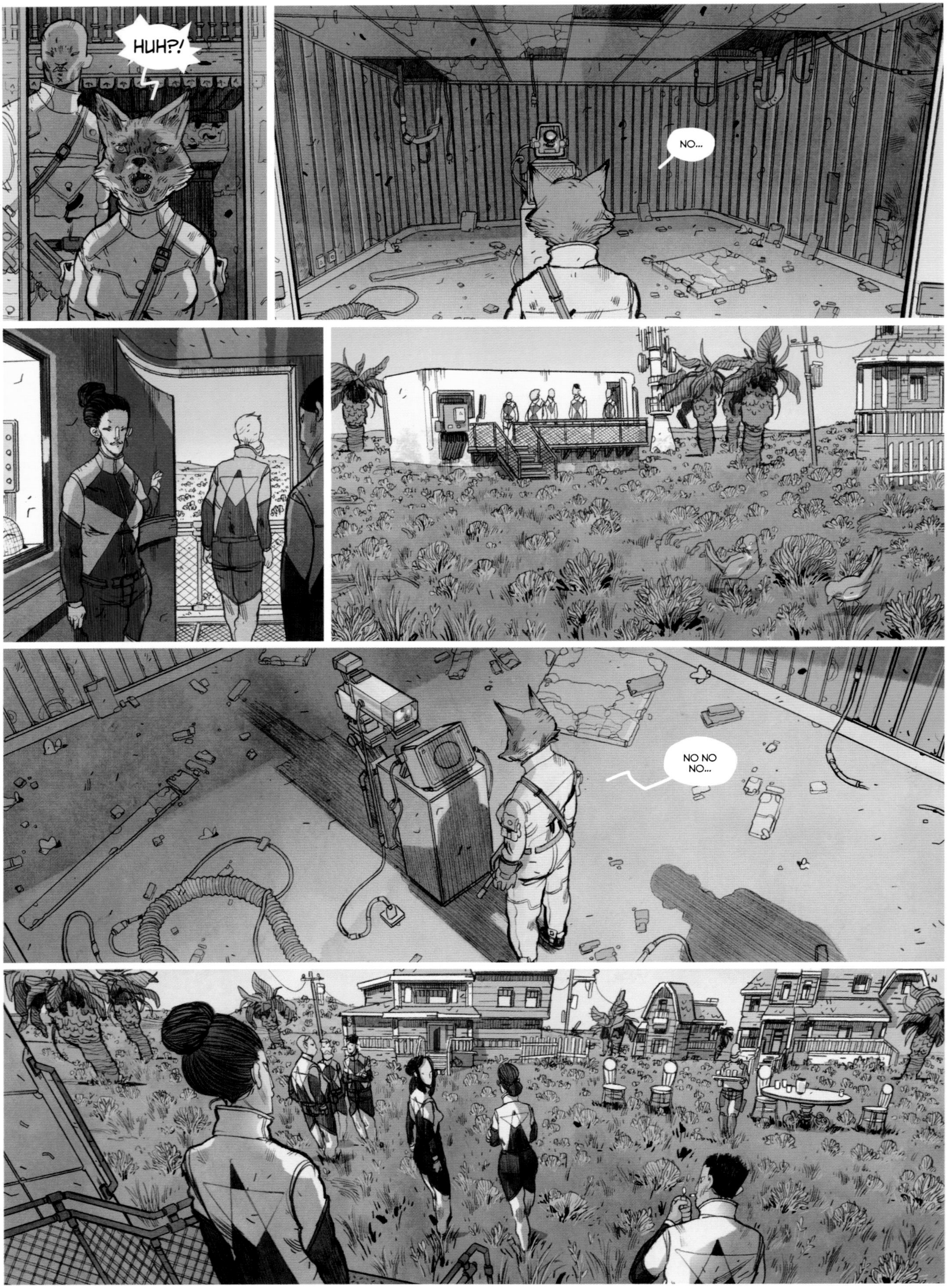
HUH?!
NO...
NO NO NO...

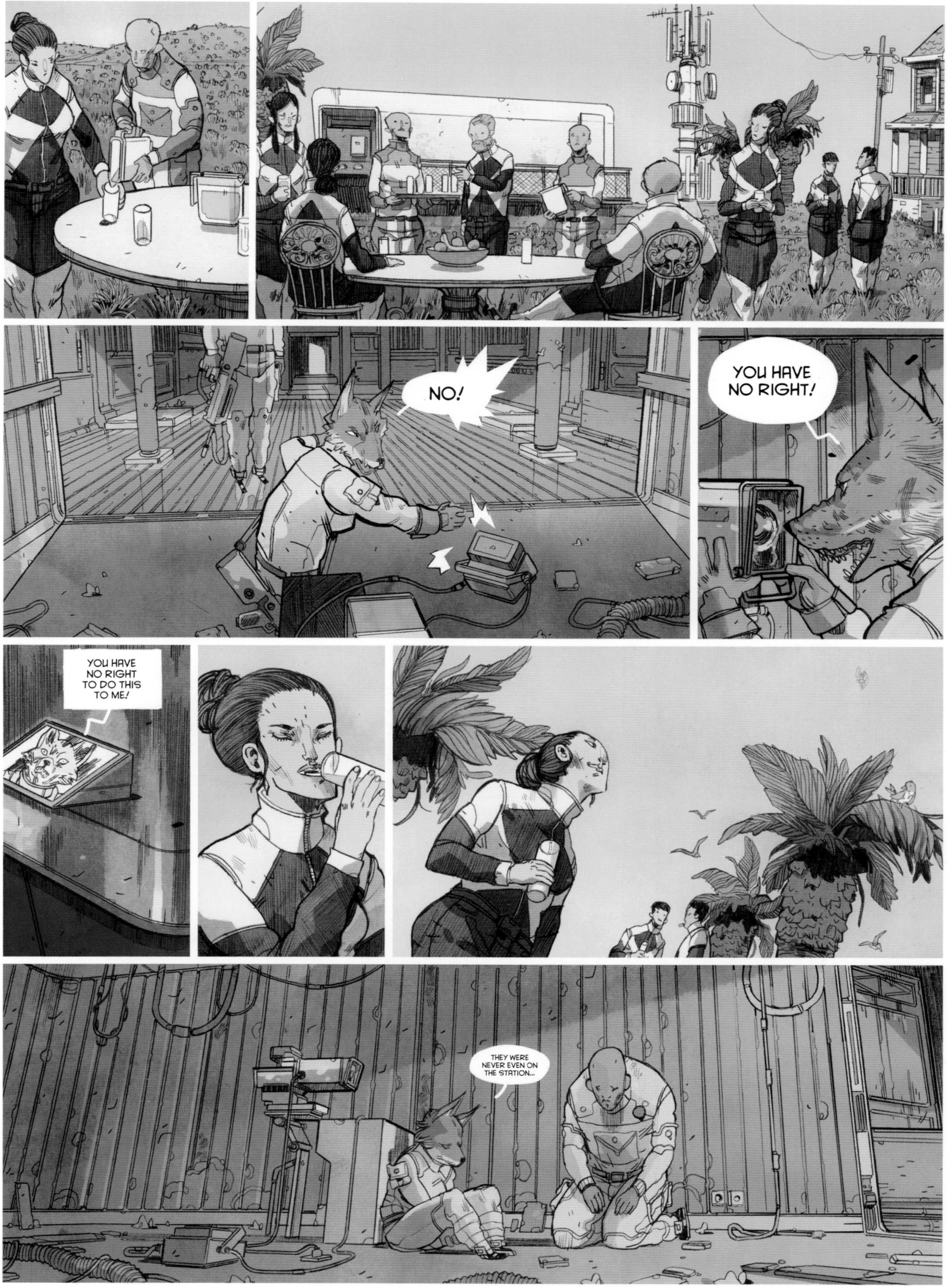
NO!
YOU HAVE NO RIGHT!
YOU HAVE NO RIGHT TO DO THIS TO ME!
THEY WERE NEVER EVEN ON THE STATION...

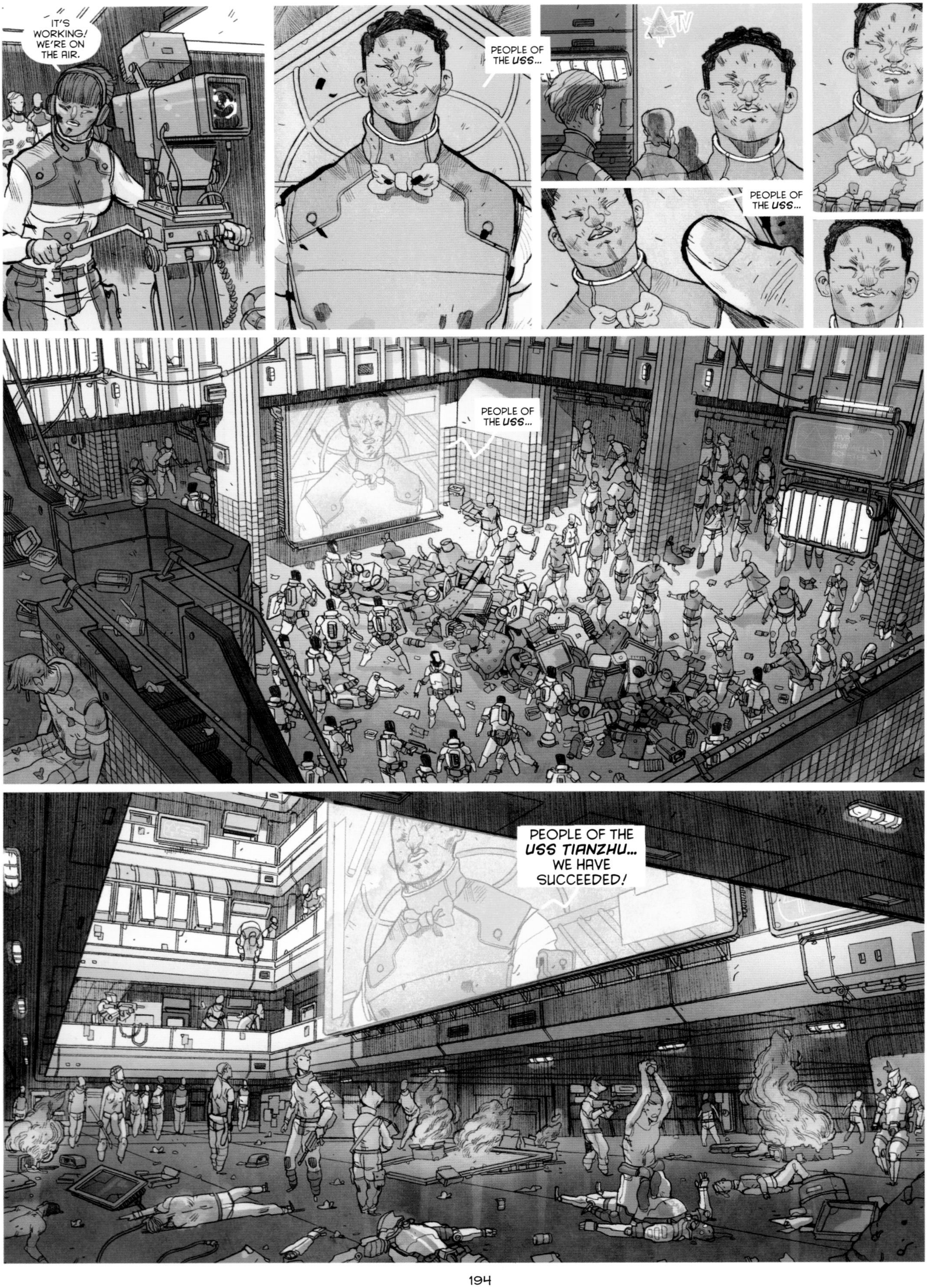
IT'S WORKING! WE'RE ON THE AIR.
PEOPLE OF THE USS...
PEOPLE OF THE USS...
PEOPLE OF THE USS...
PEOPLE OF THE USS TIANZHU... WE HAVE SUCCEEDED!

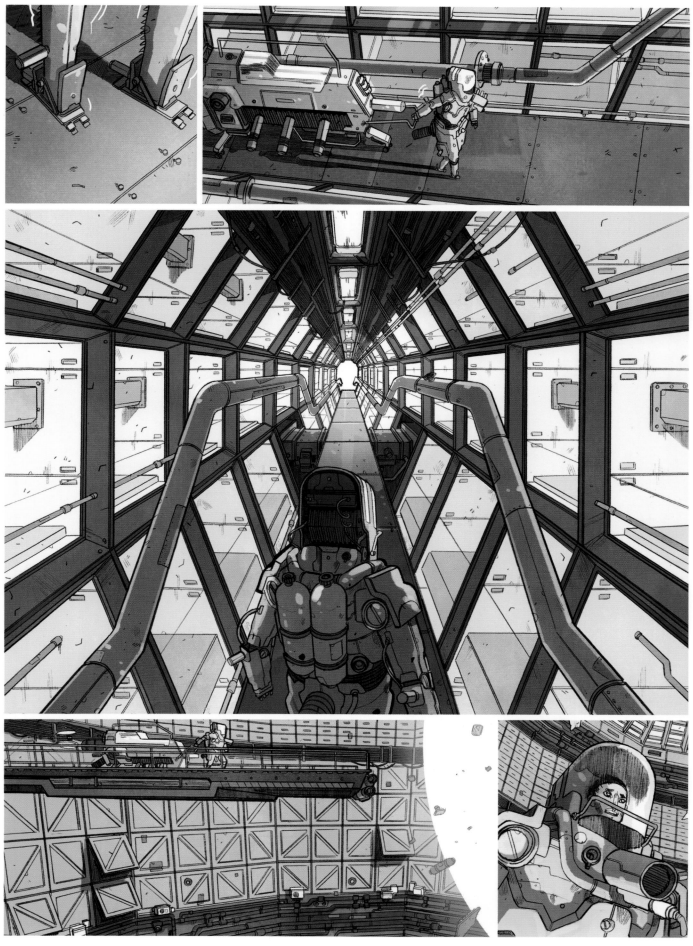

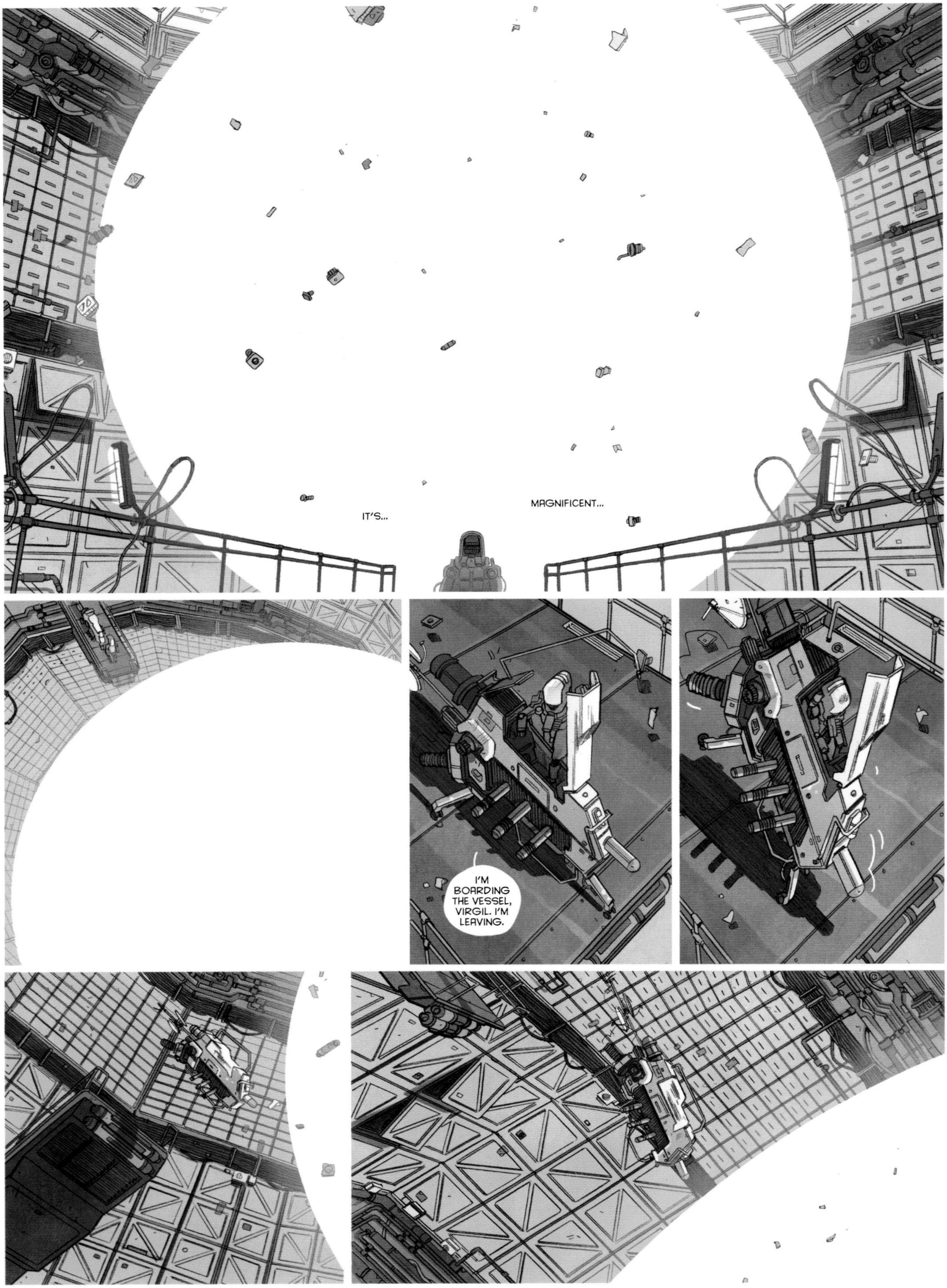

IT'S...
MAGNIFICENT...
I'M BOARDING THE VESSEL, VIRGIL. I'M LEAVING.

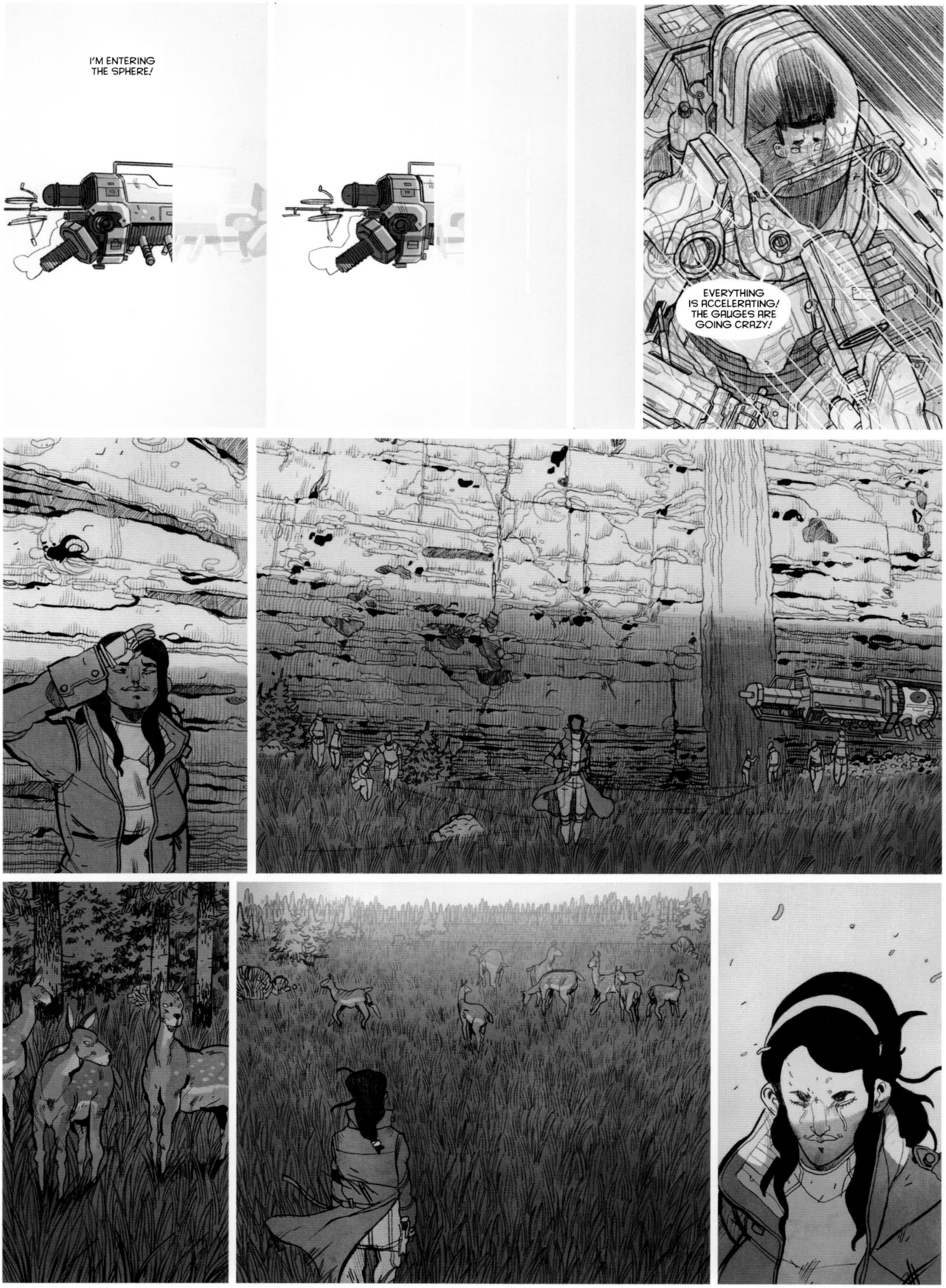
I'M ENTERING THE SPHERE!
EVERYTHING IS ACCELERATING! THE GAUGES ARE GOING CRAZY!

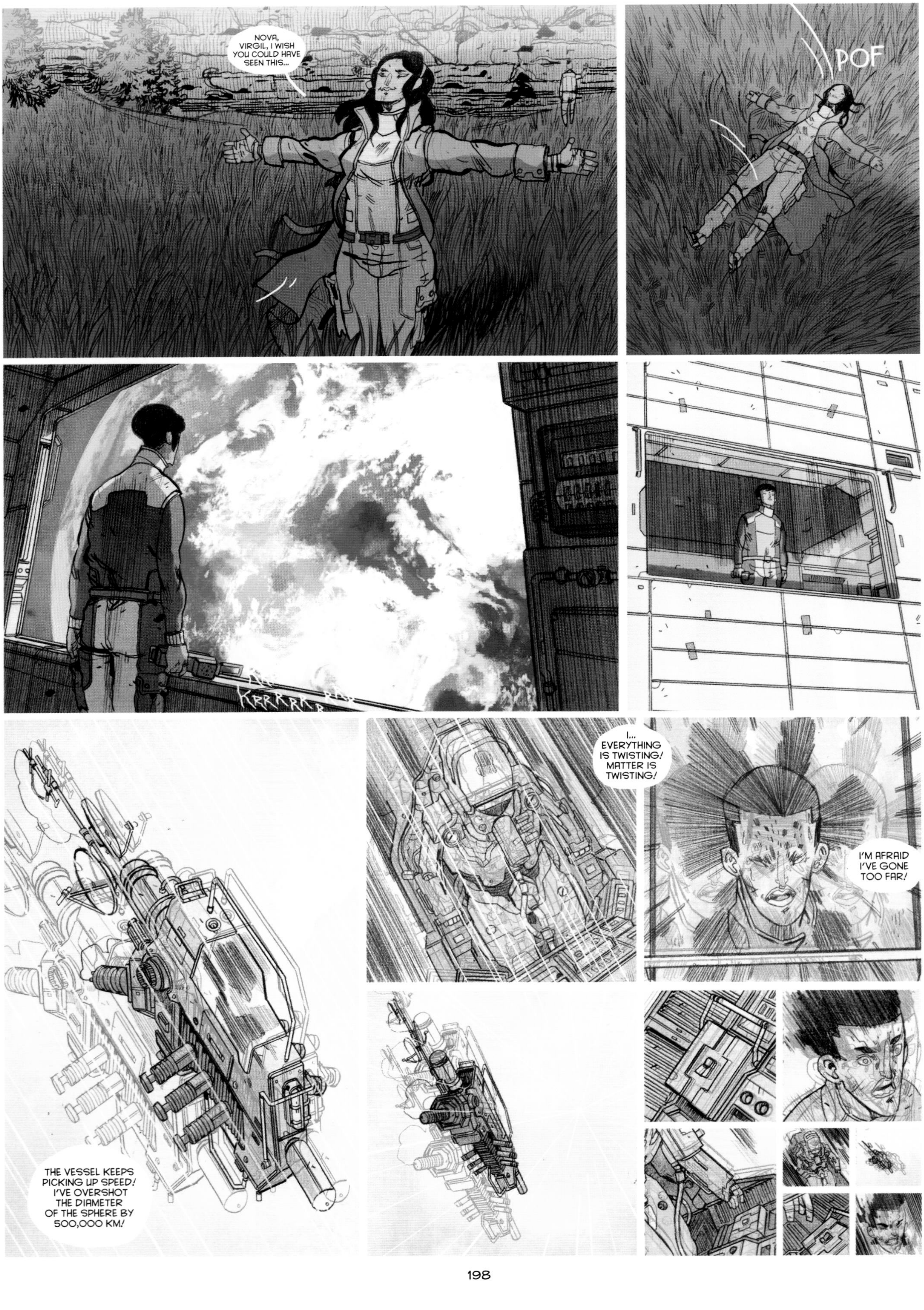
NOVA, VIRGIL, I WISH YOU COULD HAVE SEEN THIS...
POF
KRRRRRR
I... EVERYTHING IS TWISTING! MATTER IS TWISTING!
I'M AFRAID I'VE GONE TOO FAR!
THE VESSEL KEEPS PICKING UP SPEED! I'VE OVERSHOT THE DIAMETER OF THE SPHERE BY 500,000 KM!

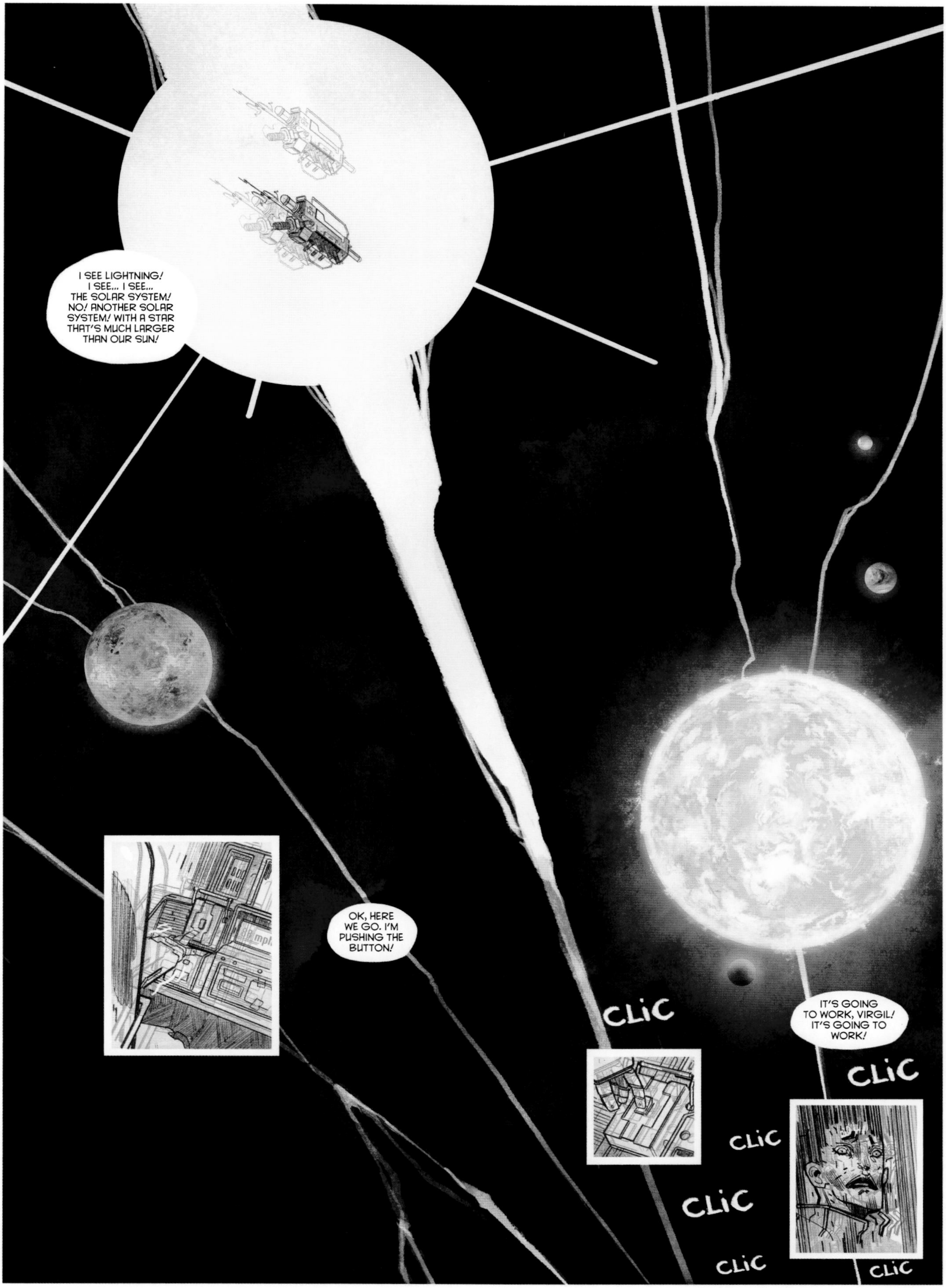
I SEE LIGHTNING! I SEE... I SEE... THE SOLAR SYSTEM! NO! ANOTHER SOLAR SYSTEM! WITH A STAR THAT'S MUCH LARGER THAN OUR SUN!
OK, HERE WE GO. I'M PUSHING THE BUTTON!
CLIC
IT'S GOING TO WORK, VIRGIL! IT'S GOING TO WORK!
CLIC
CLIC
CLIC
CLIC
CLIC

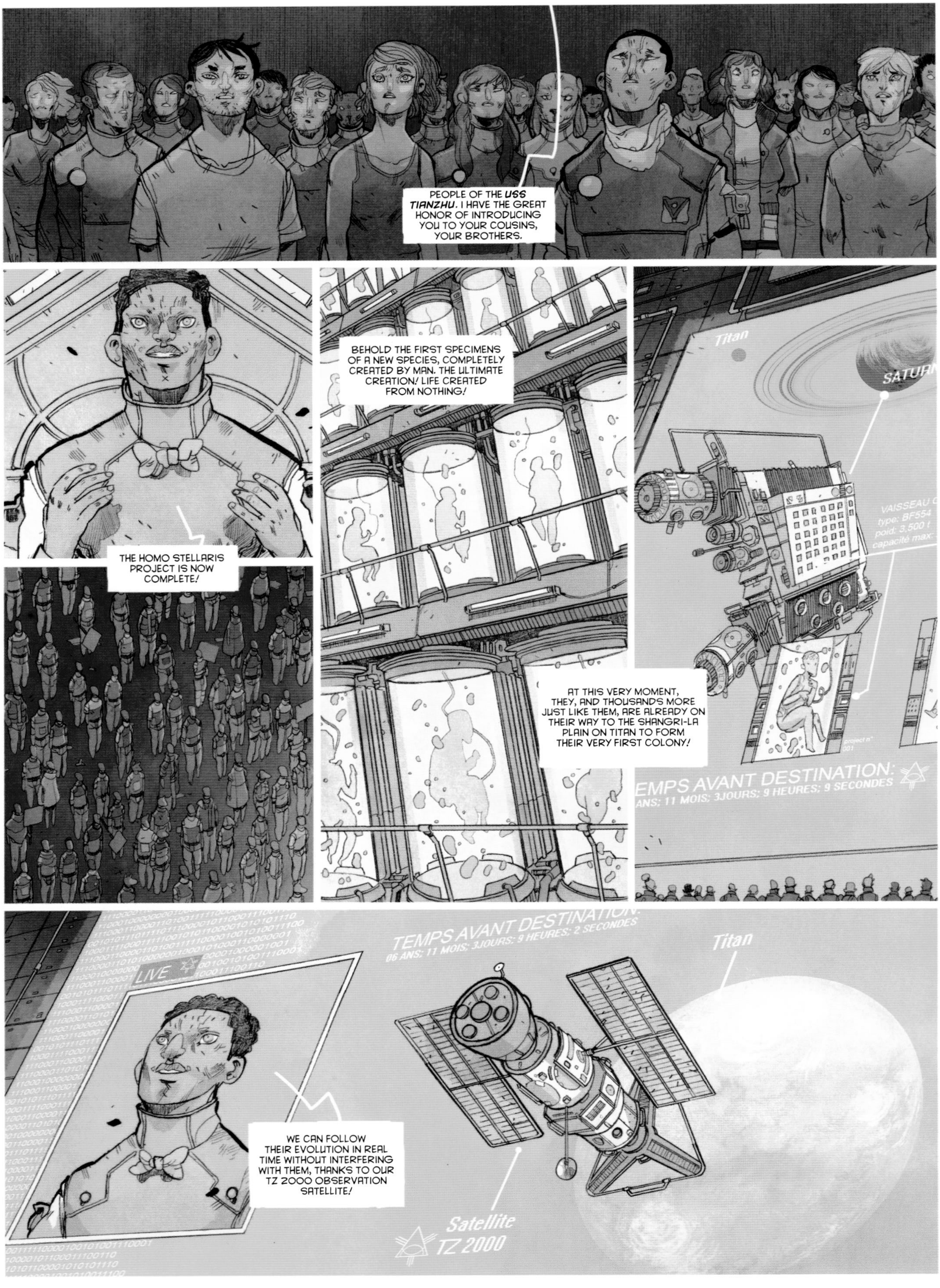
PEOPLE OF THE *USS TIANZHU*. I HAVE THE GREAT HONOR OF INTRODUCING YOU TO YOUR COUSINS, YOUR BROTHERS.
THE HOMO STELLARIS PROJECT IS NOW COMPLETE!
BEHOLD THE FIRST SPECIMENS OF A NEW SPECIES, COMPLETELY CREATED BY MAN. THE ULTIMATE CREATION! LIFE CREATED FROM NOTHING!
Titan
SATURN
VAISSEAU
type: BF554
poid: 3,500 t
capacité max:
project n° 001
AT THIS VERY MOMENT, THEY, AND THOUSANDS MORE JUST LIKE THEM, ARE ALREADY ON THEIR WAY TO THE SHANGRI-LA PLAIN ON TITAN TO FORM THEIR VERY FIRST COLONY!
EMPS AVANT DESTINATION:
ANS; 11 MOIS; 3JOURS; 9 HEURES; 9 SECONDES
TEMPS AVANT DESTINATION:
06 ANS; 11 MOIS; 3JOURS; 9 HEURES; 2 SECONDES
Titan
LIVE
WE CAN FOLLOW THEIR EVOLUTION IN REAL TIME WITHOUT INTERFERING WITH THEM, THANKS TO OUR TZ 2000 OBSERVATION SATELLITE!
Satellite TZ 2000

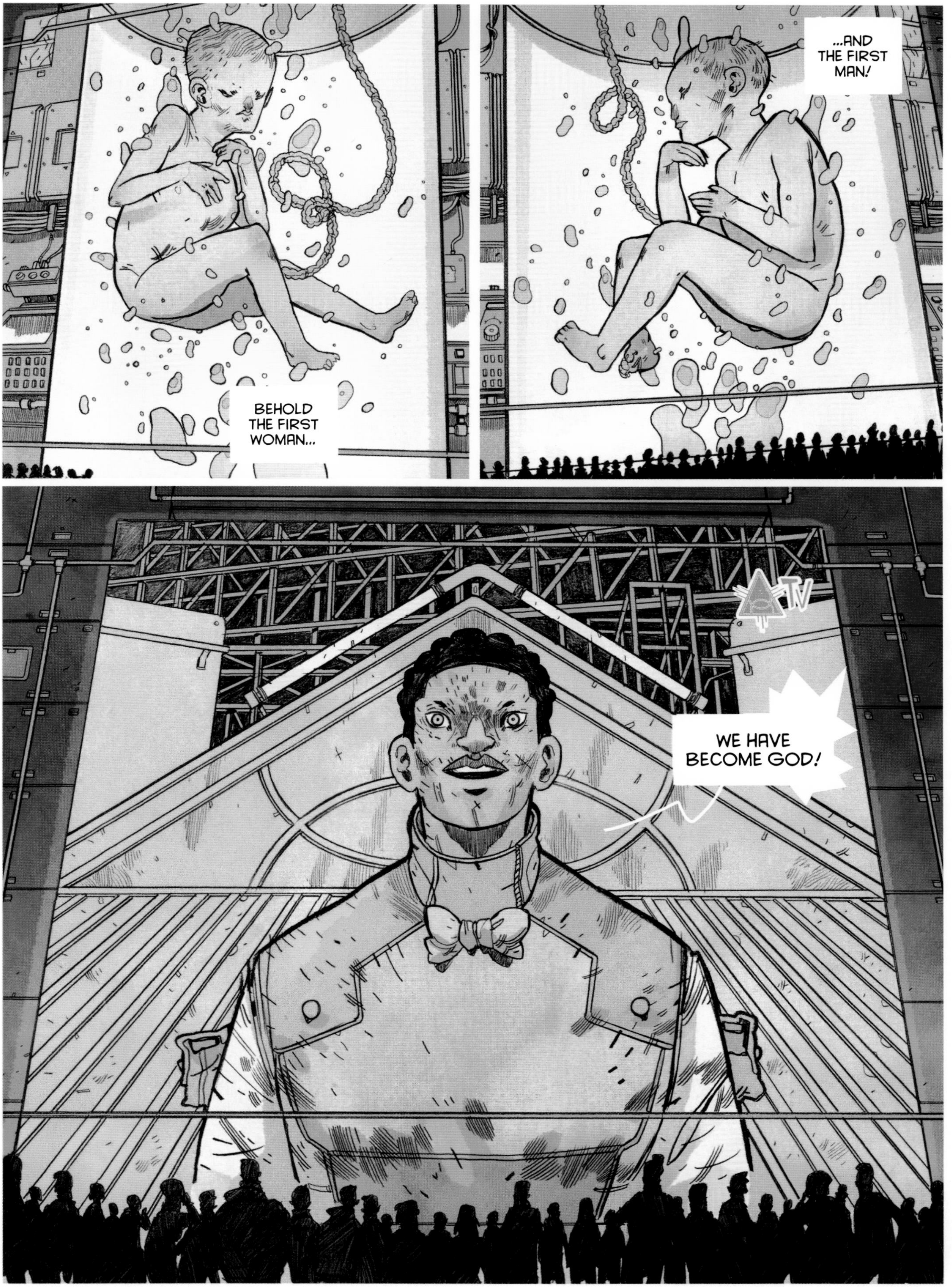
BEHOLD THE FIRST WOMAN...
...AND THE FIRST MAN!
TV
WE HAVE BECOME GOD!

CLIC

CLIC

CLIC

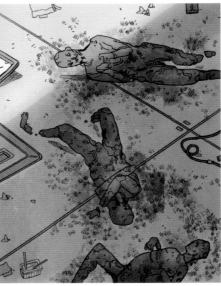

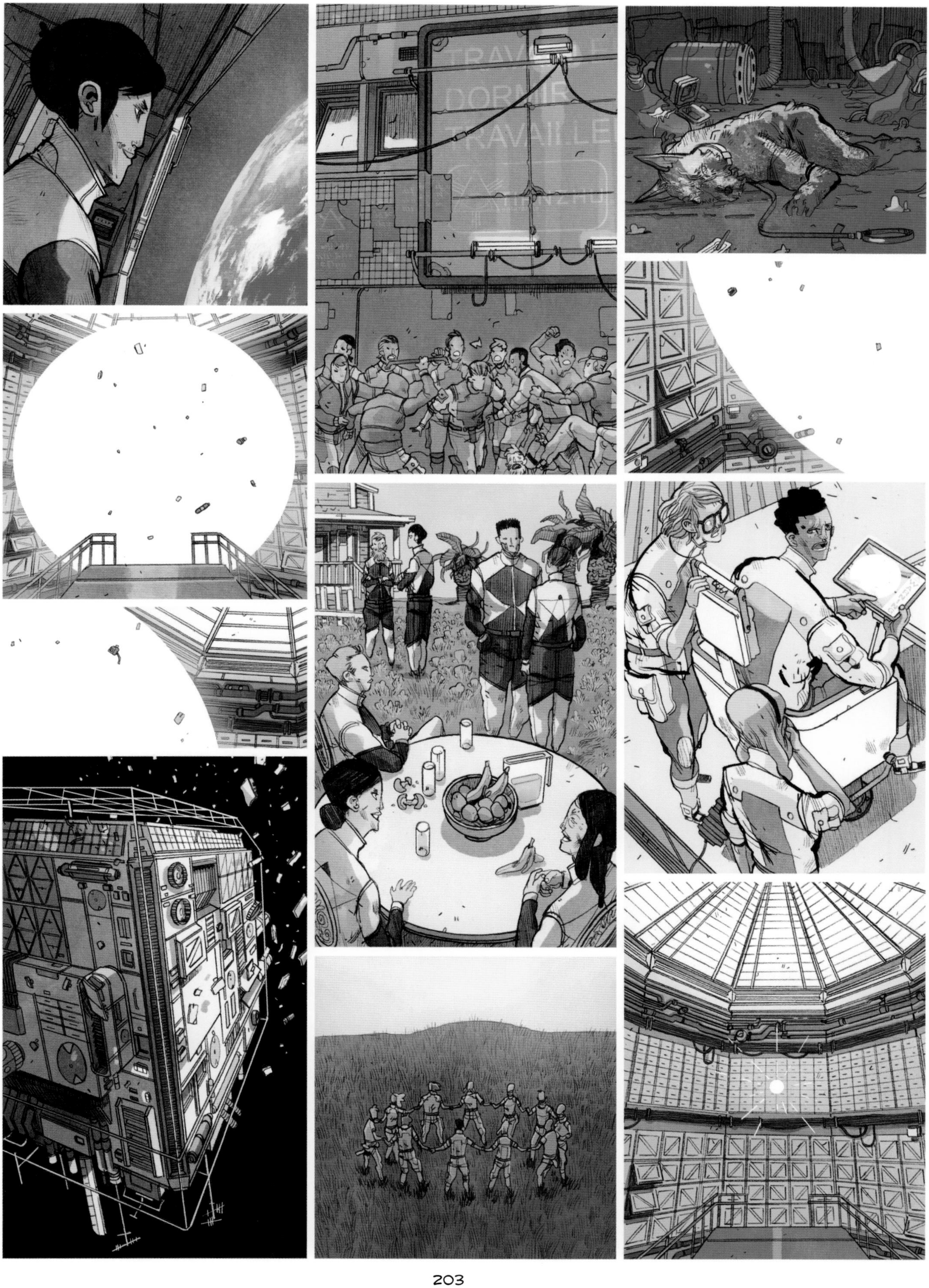
DORMIR

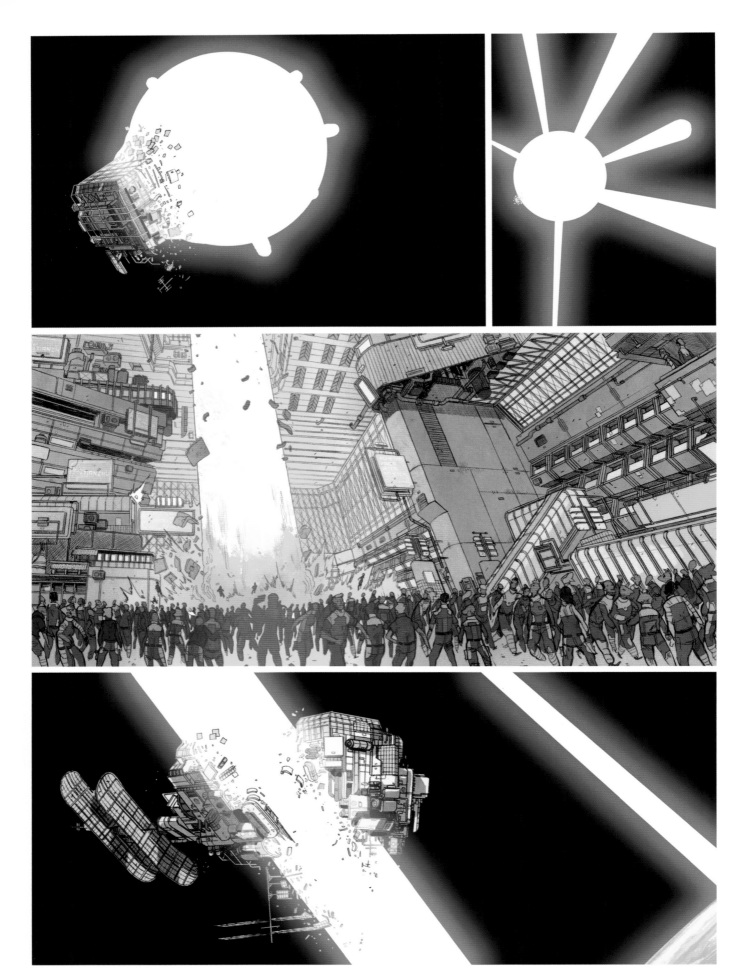

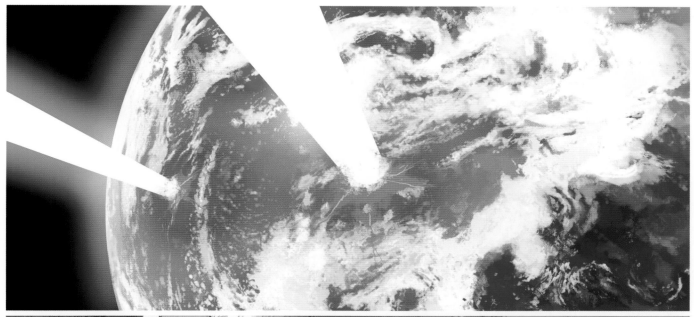

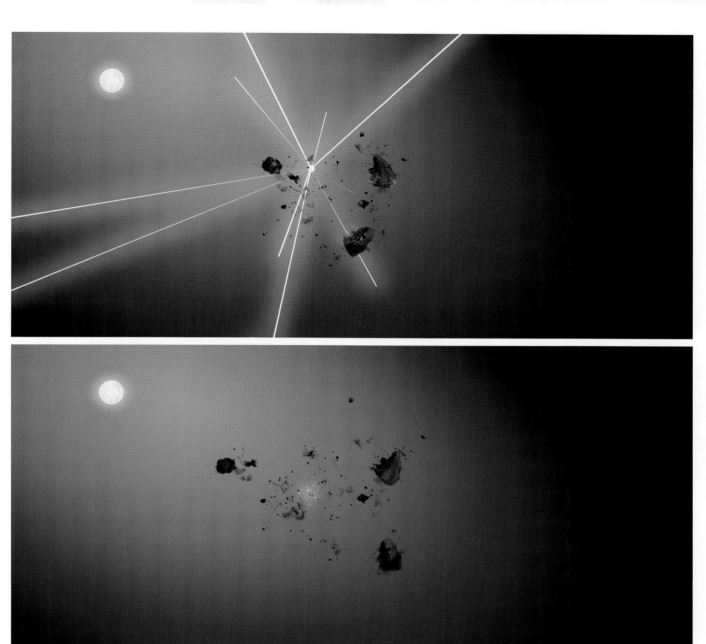

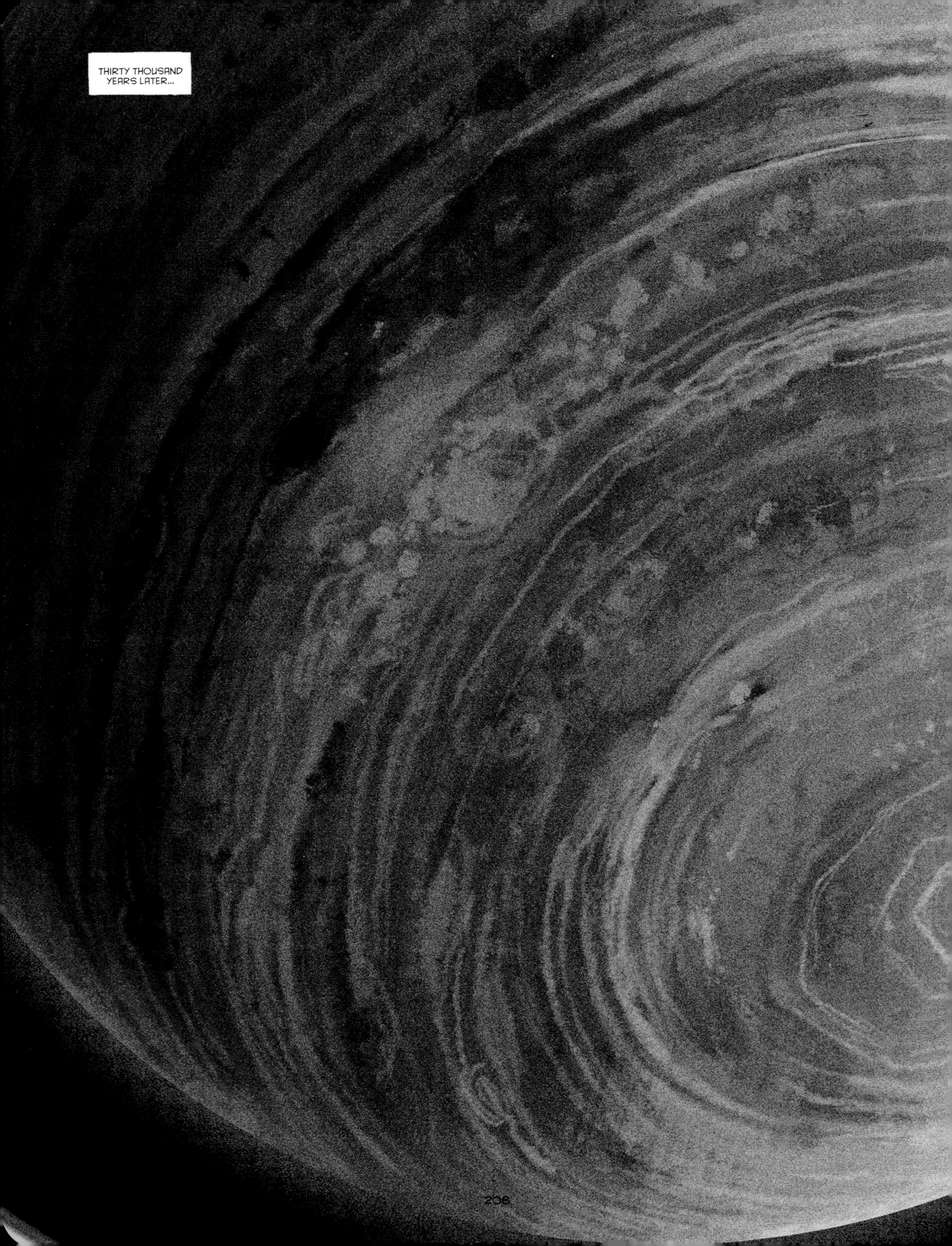
THIRTY THOUSAND YEARS LATER...

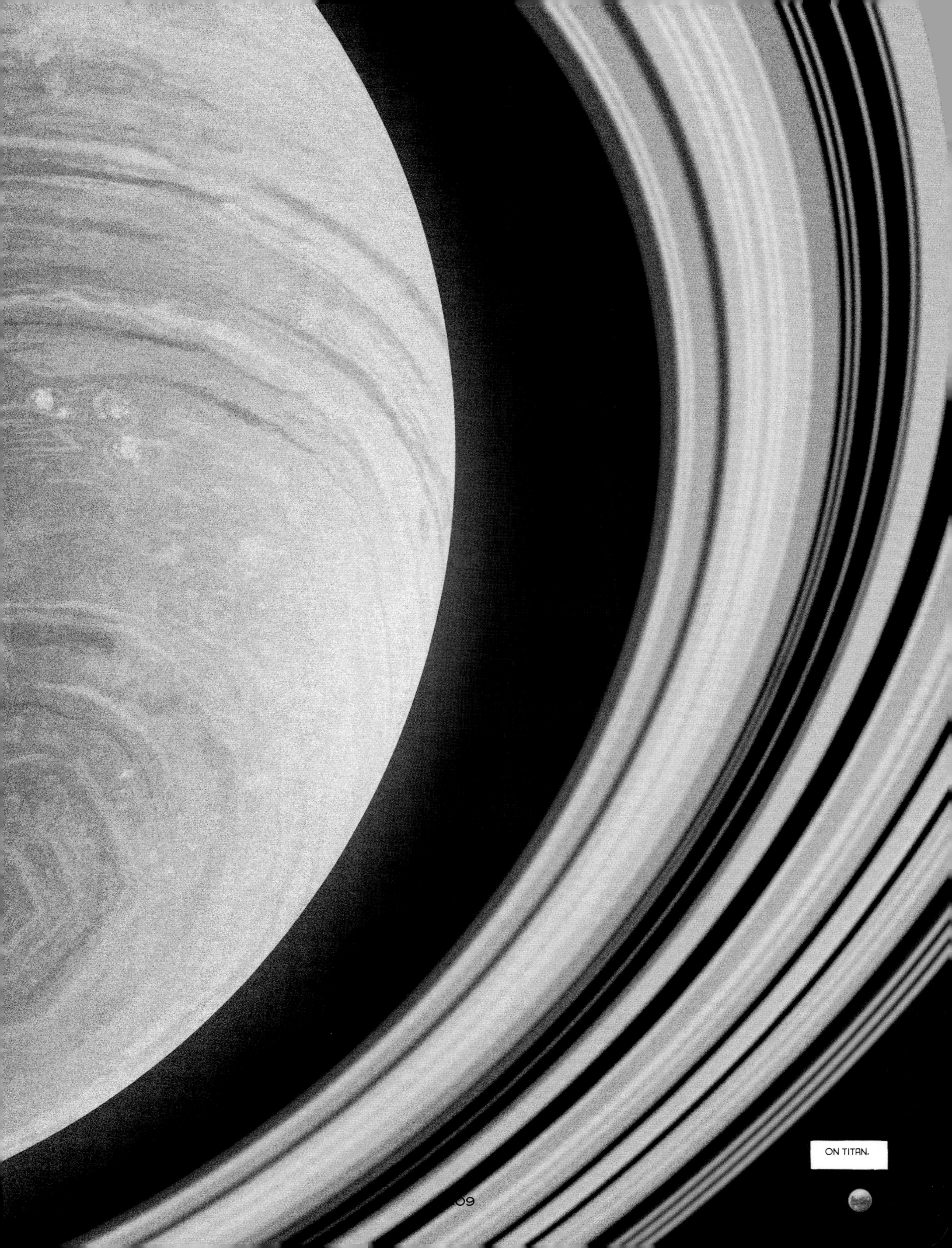
ON TITAN.

TZ2000

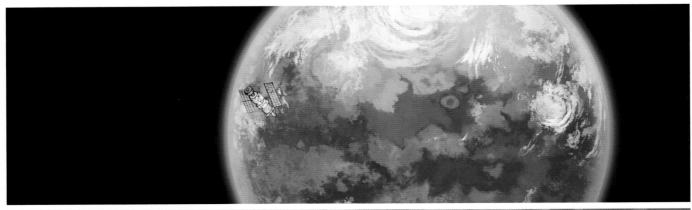

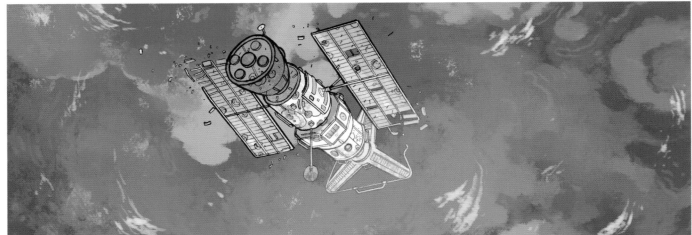

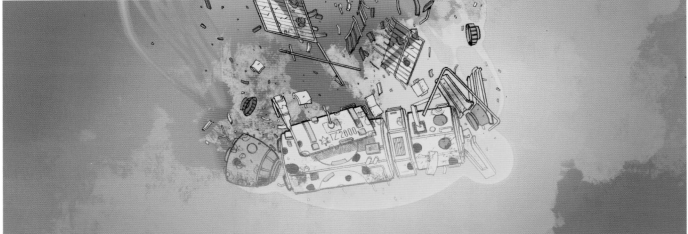

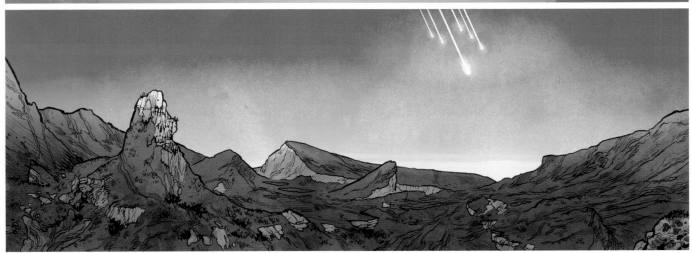

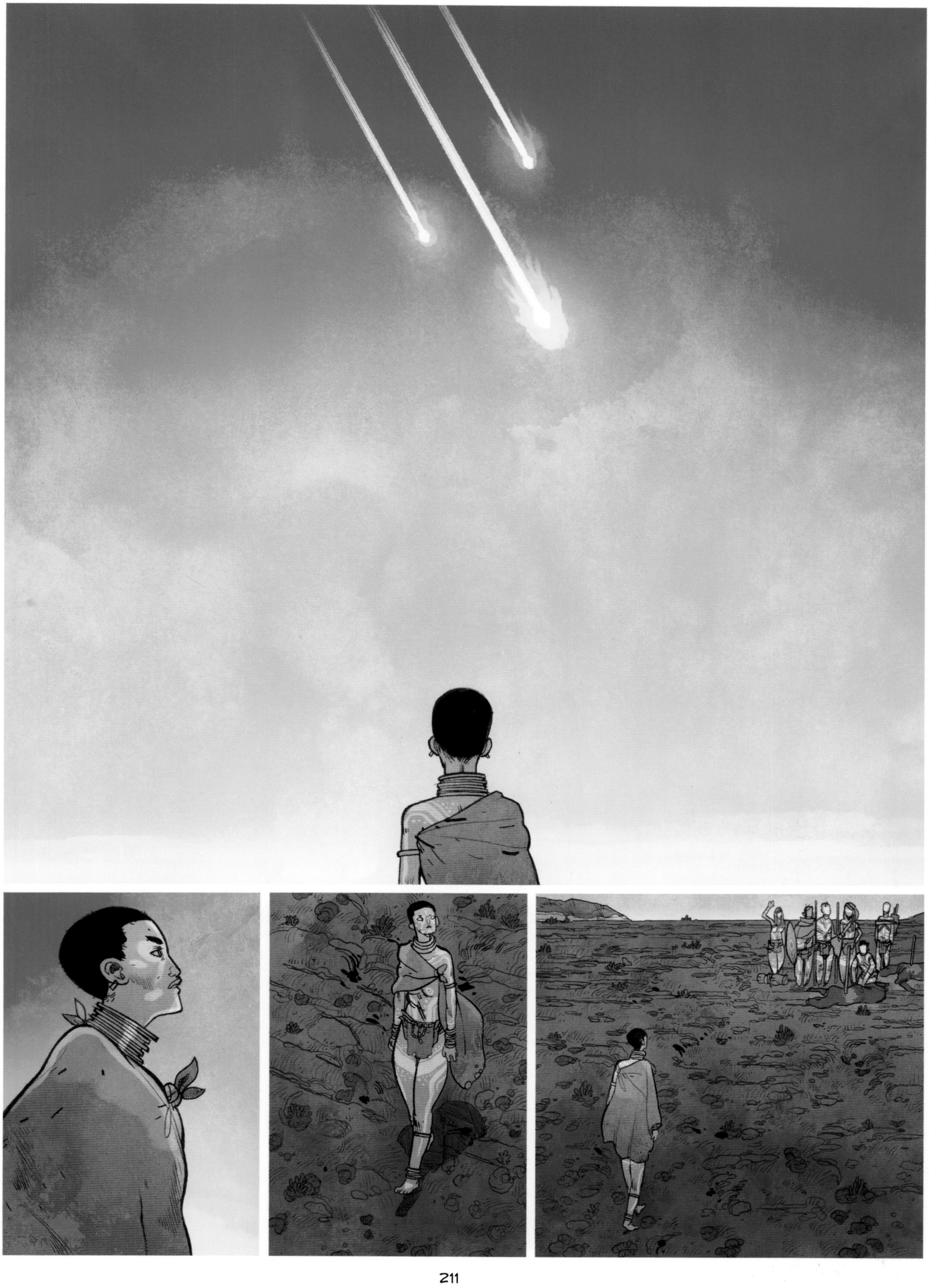

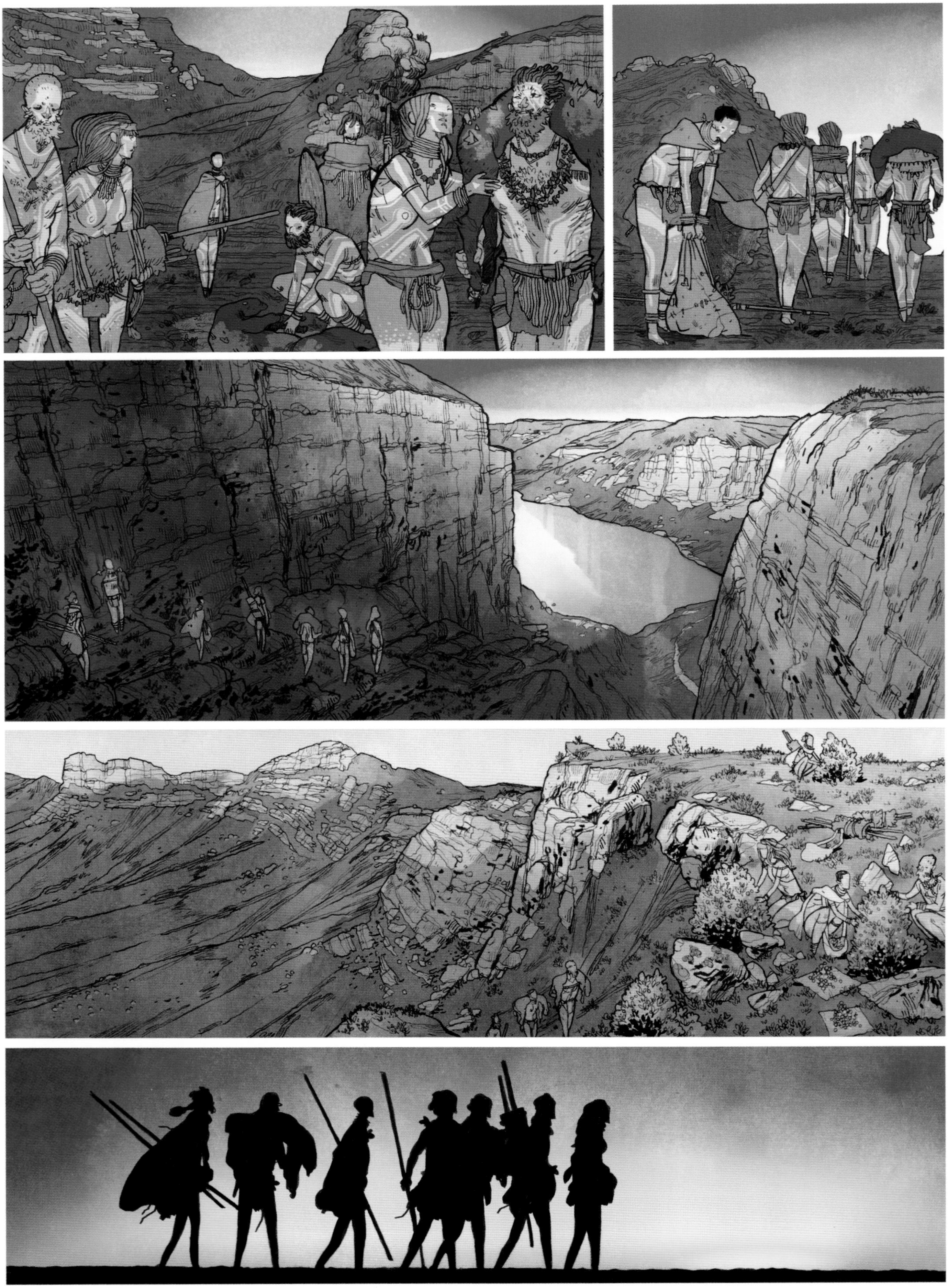

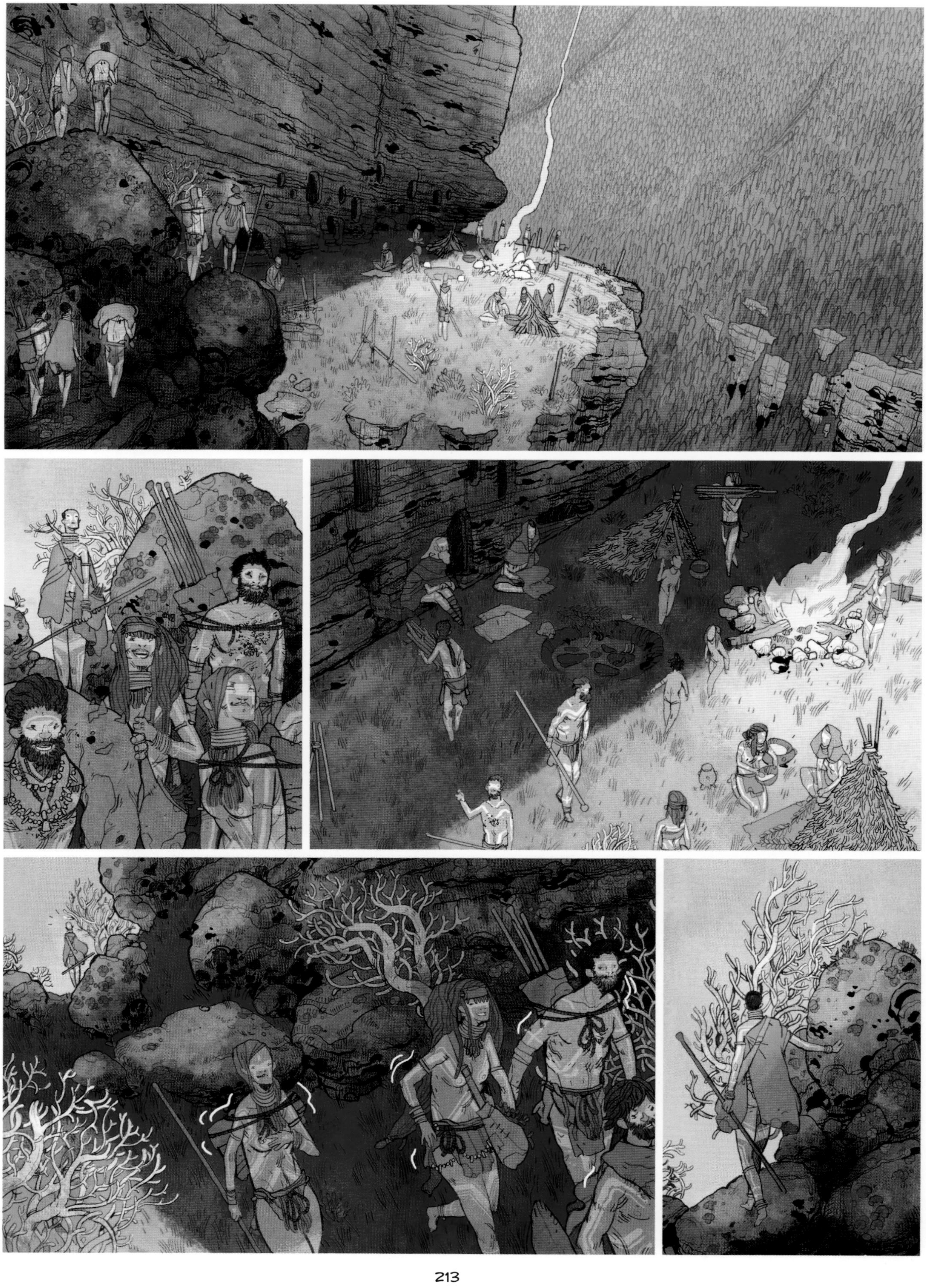

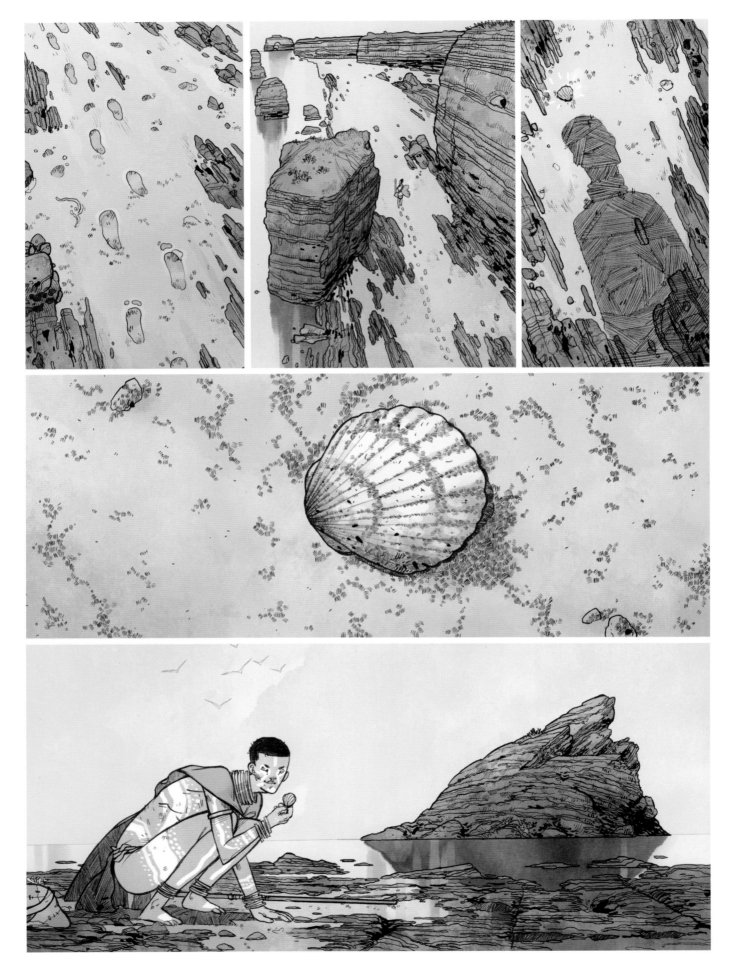

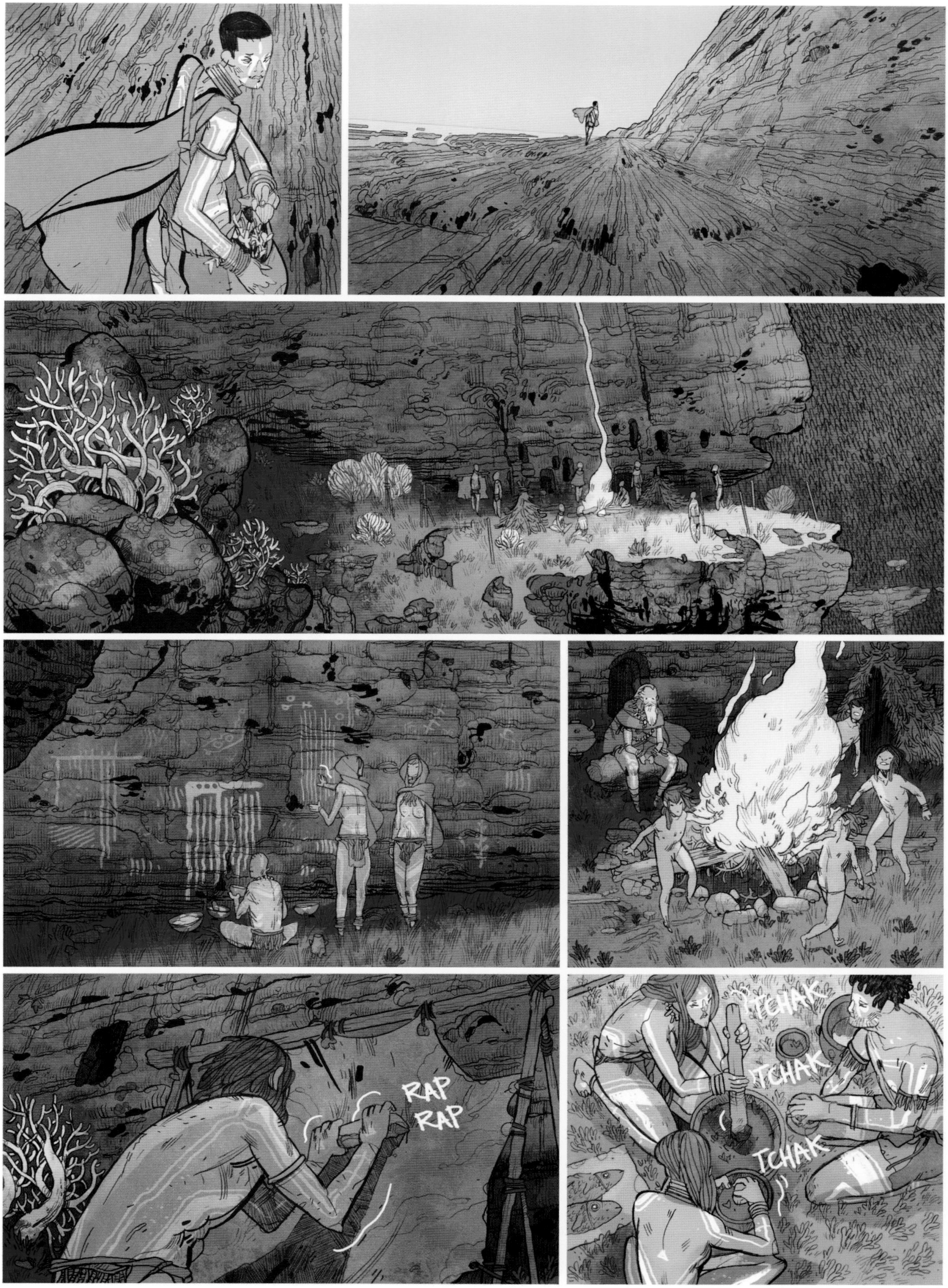
RAP
RAP
TCHAK
TCHAK
TCHAK

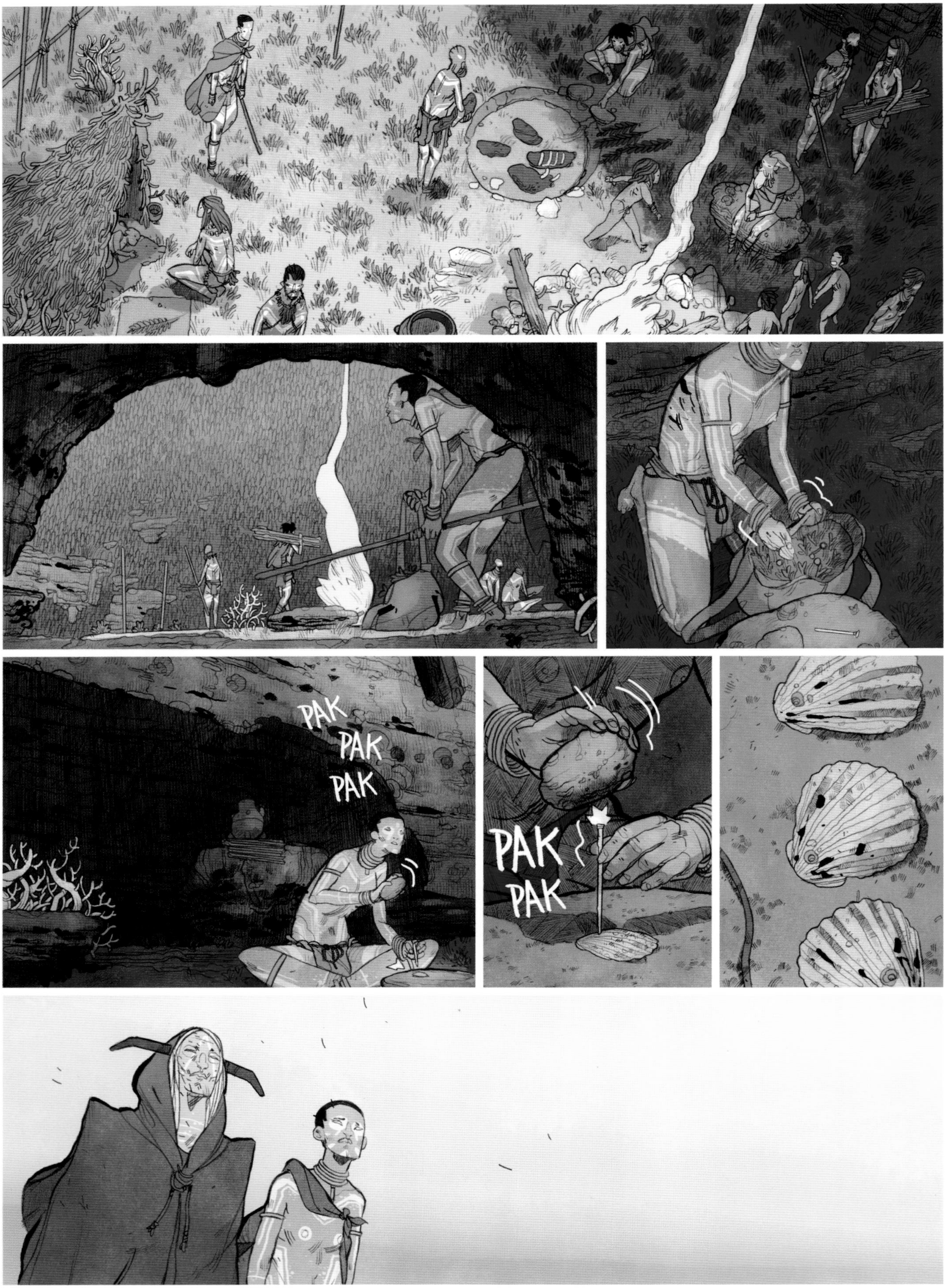
PAK
PAK
PAK
PAK
PAK

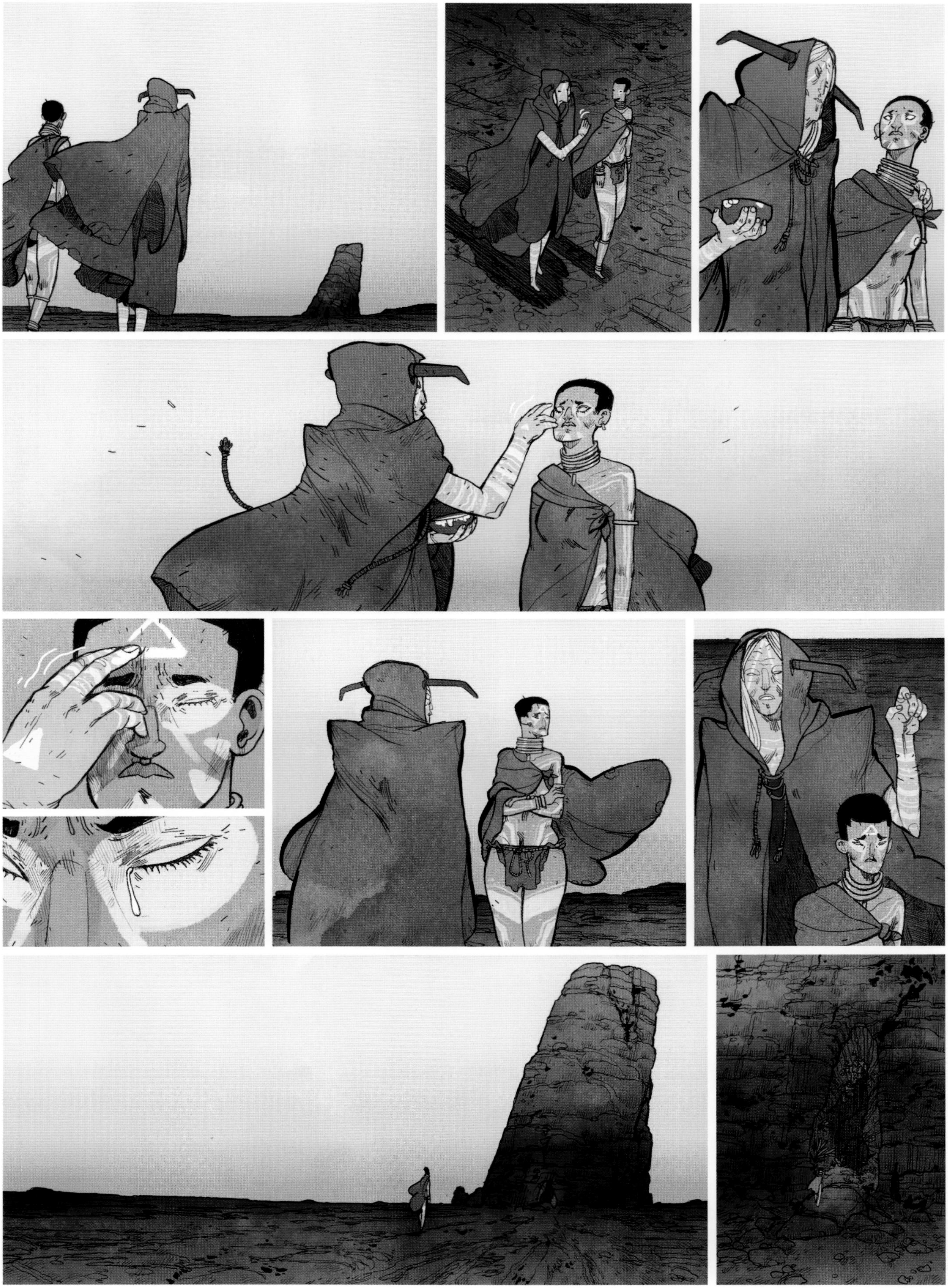

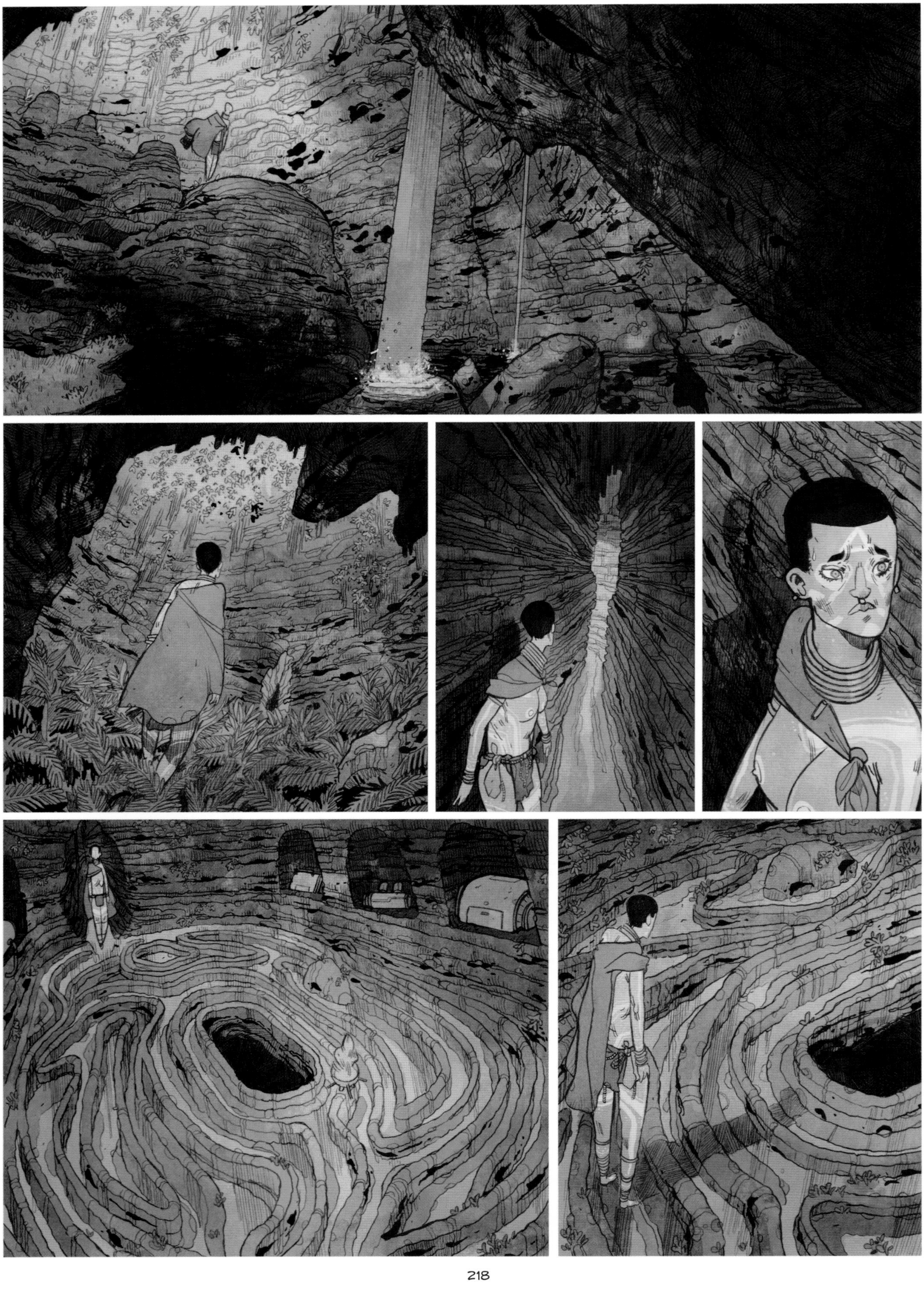

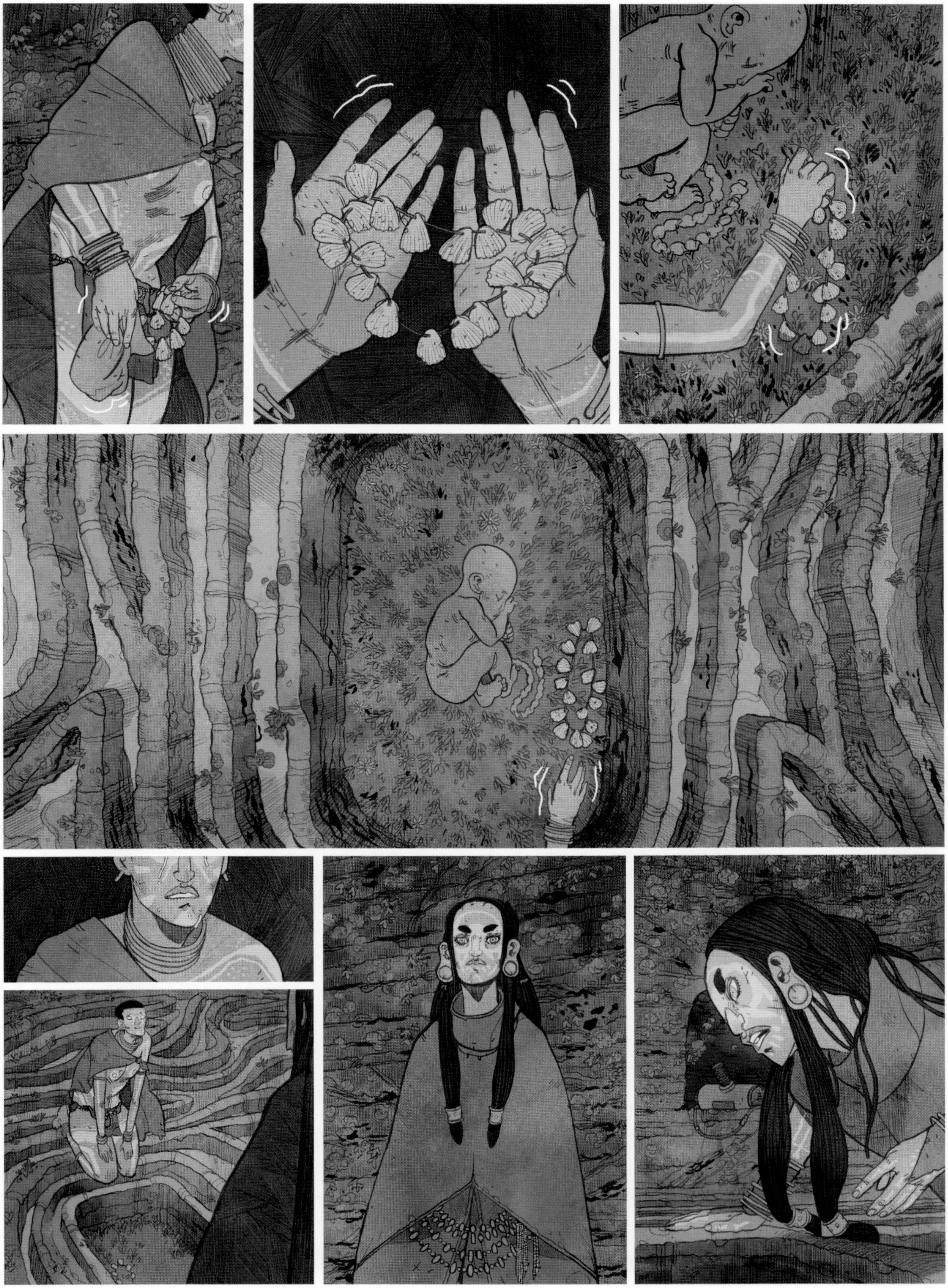

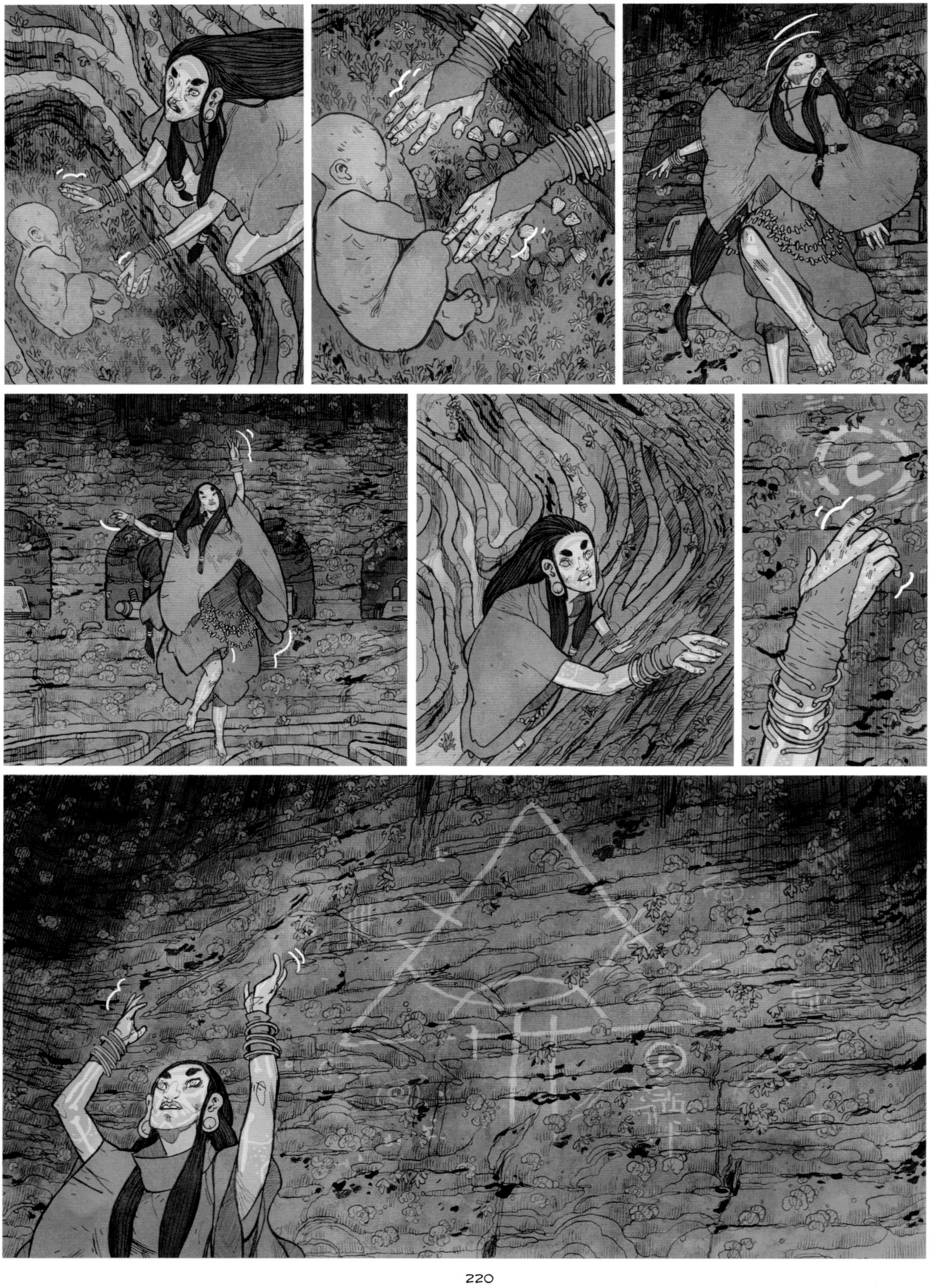

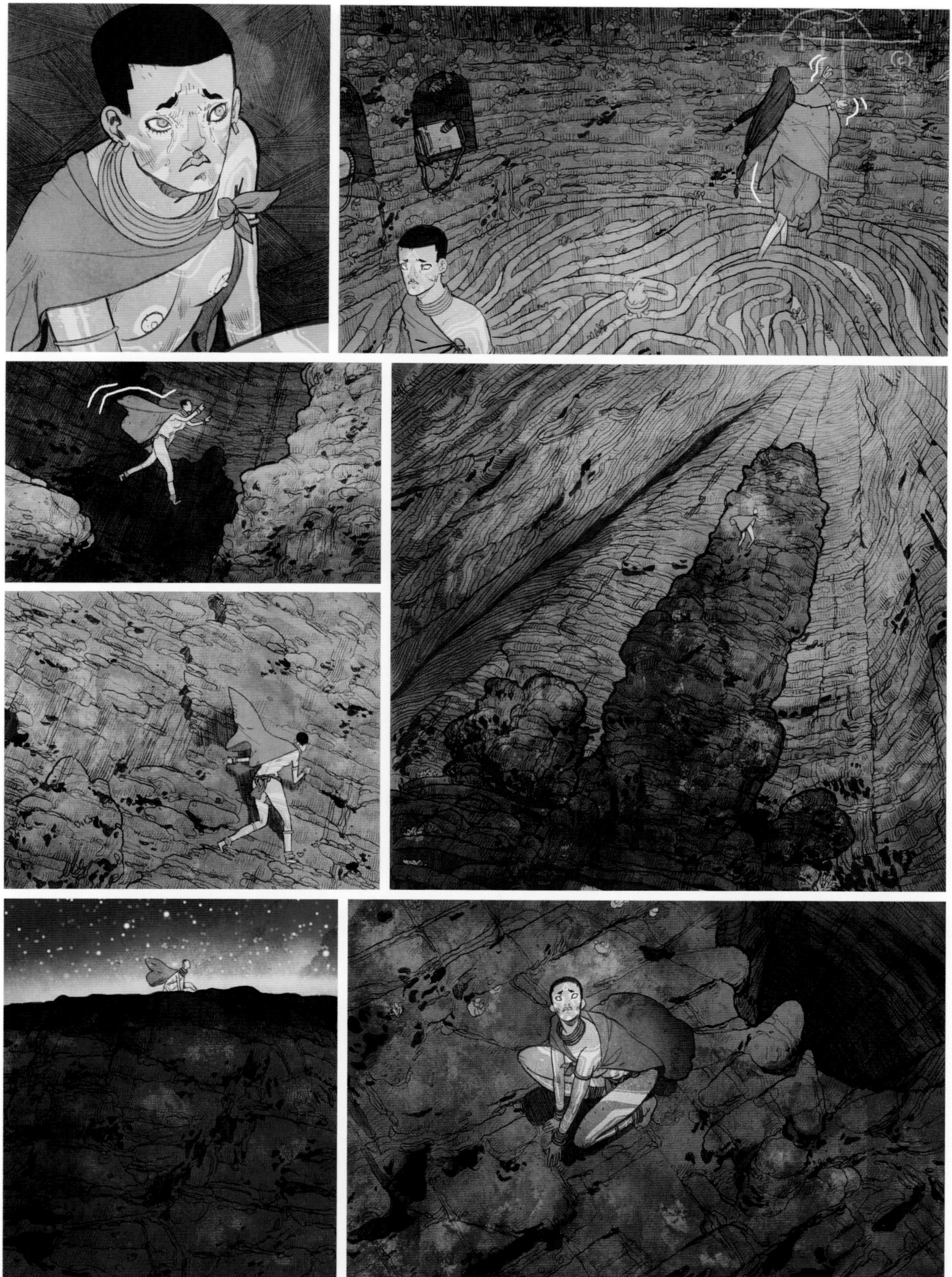

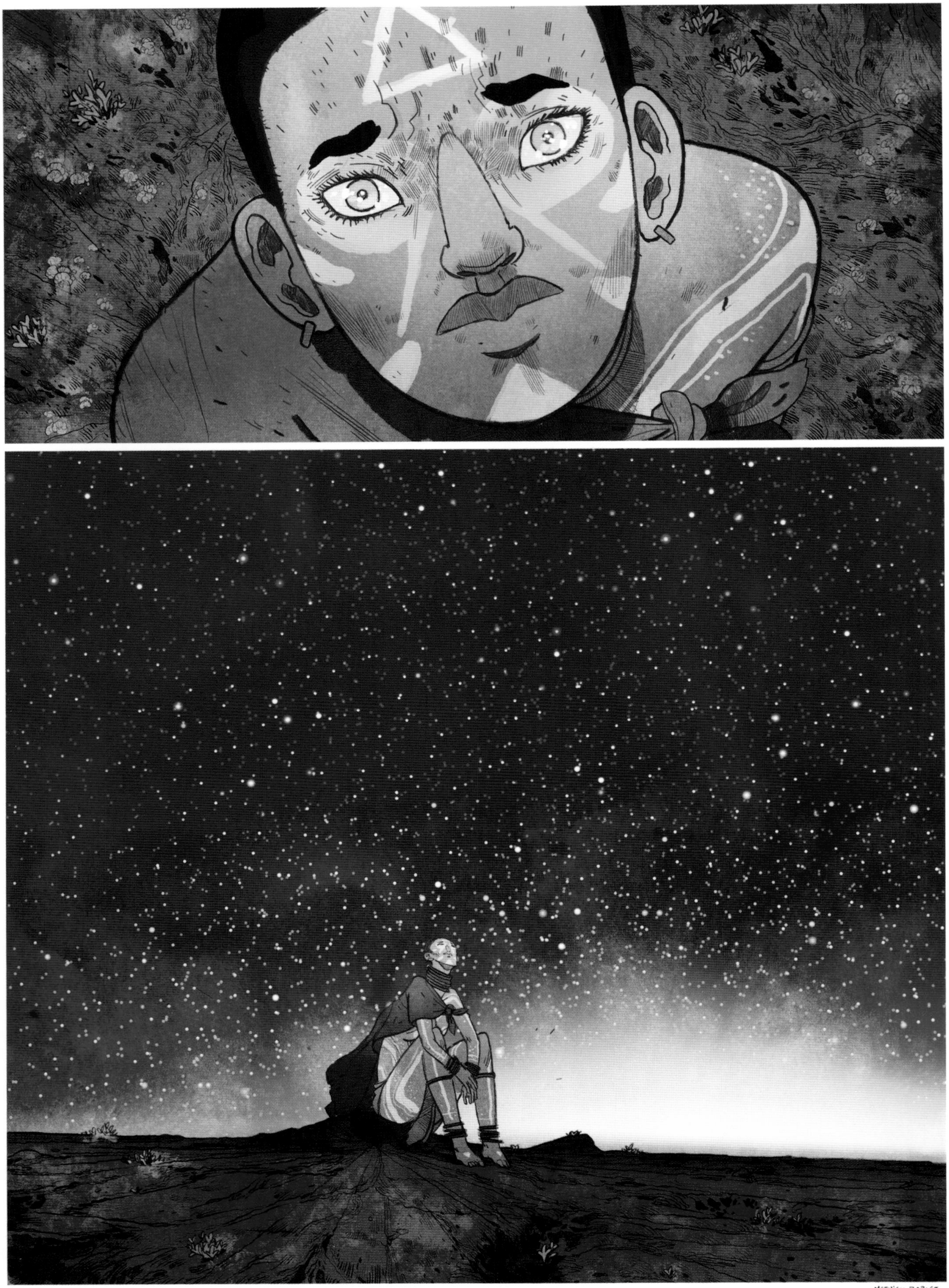

MATHIEU BABLET
15.05.16.

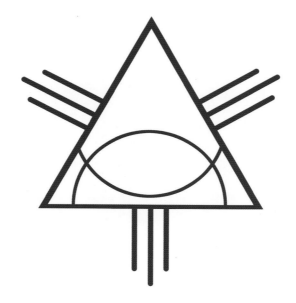

SHANGRI-LA

M.BABLET

SKETCHES AND CHARACTER DESIGN

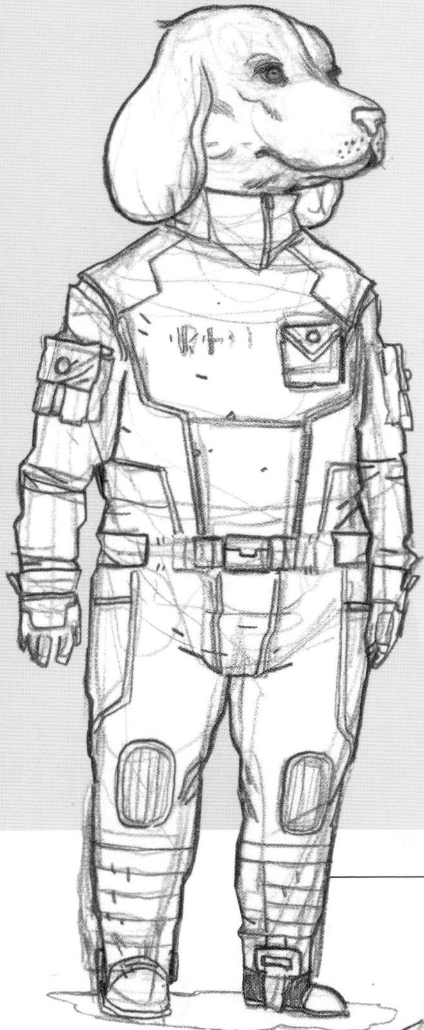

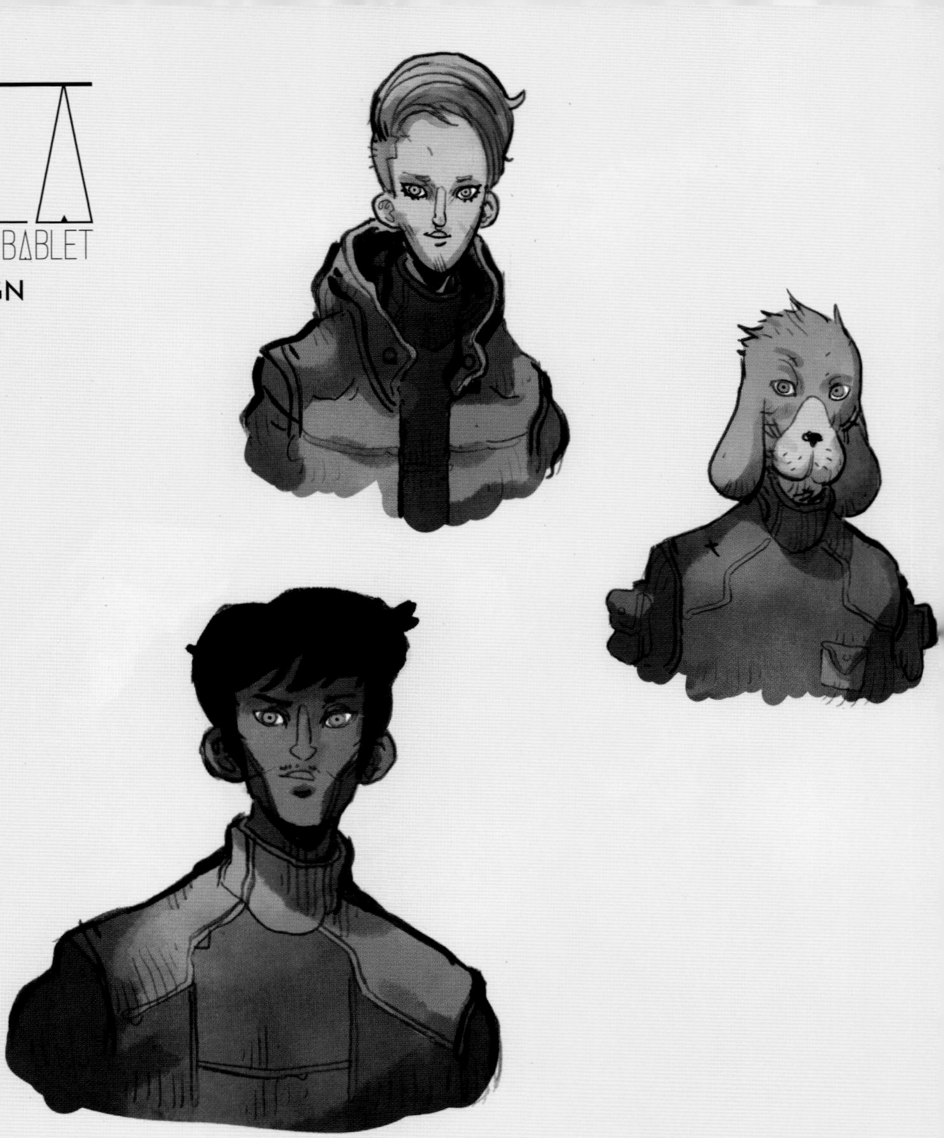

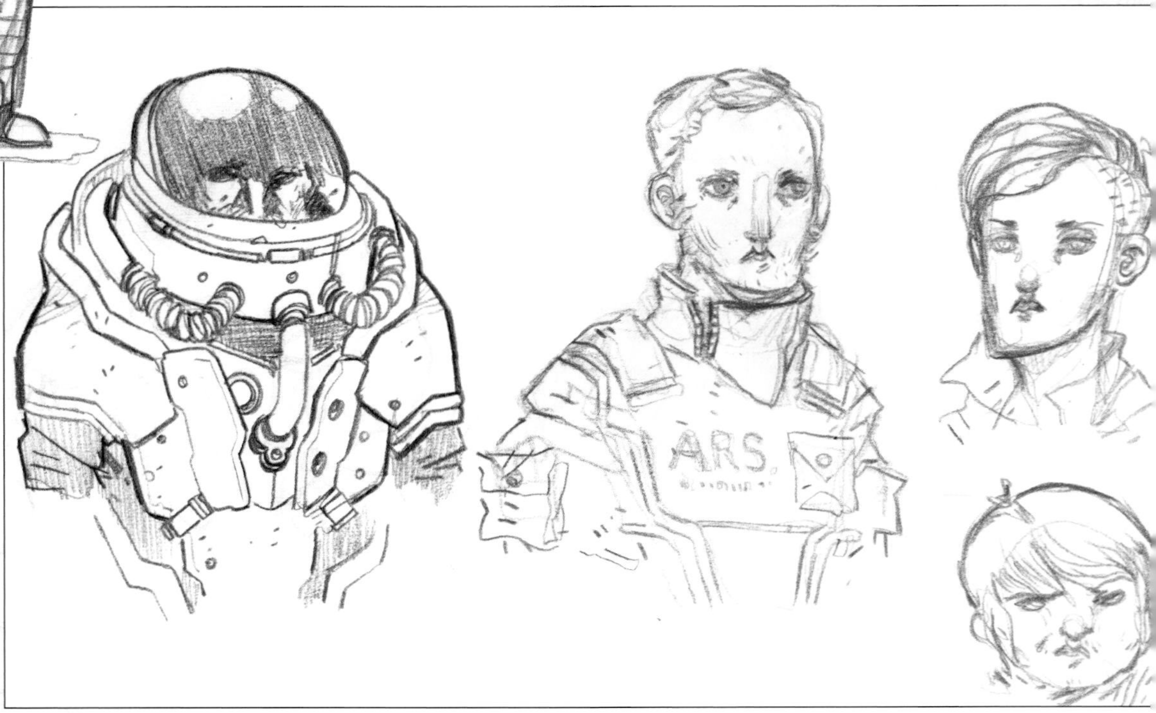
ARS.

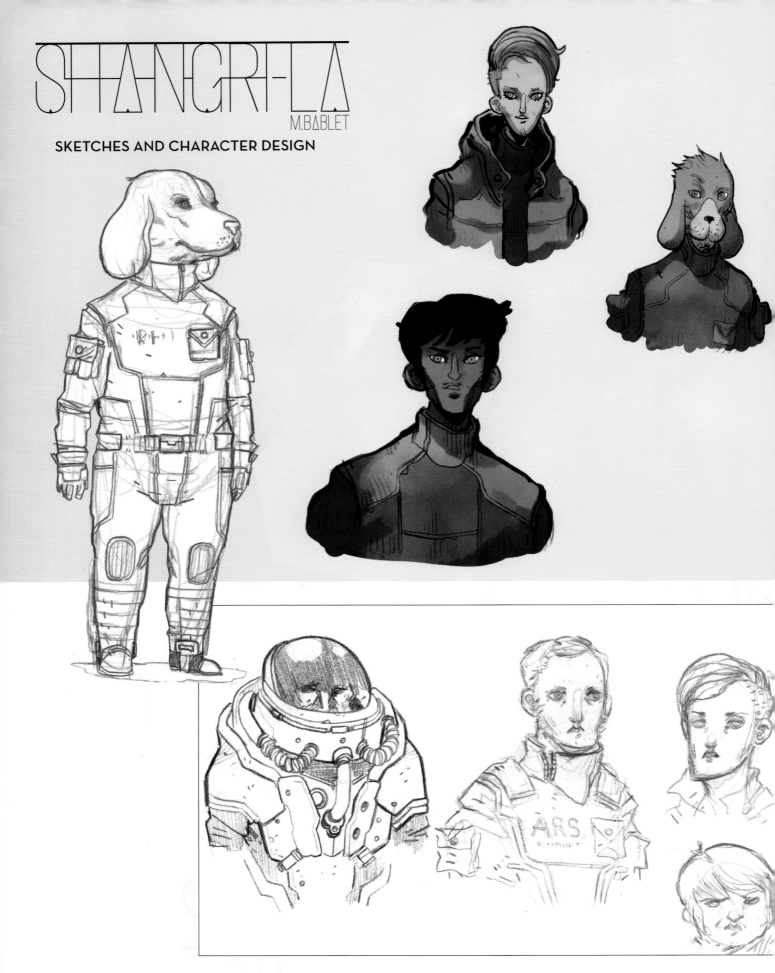

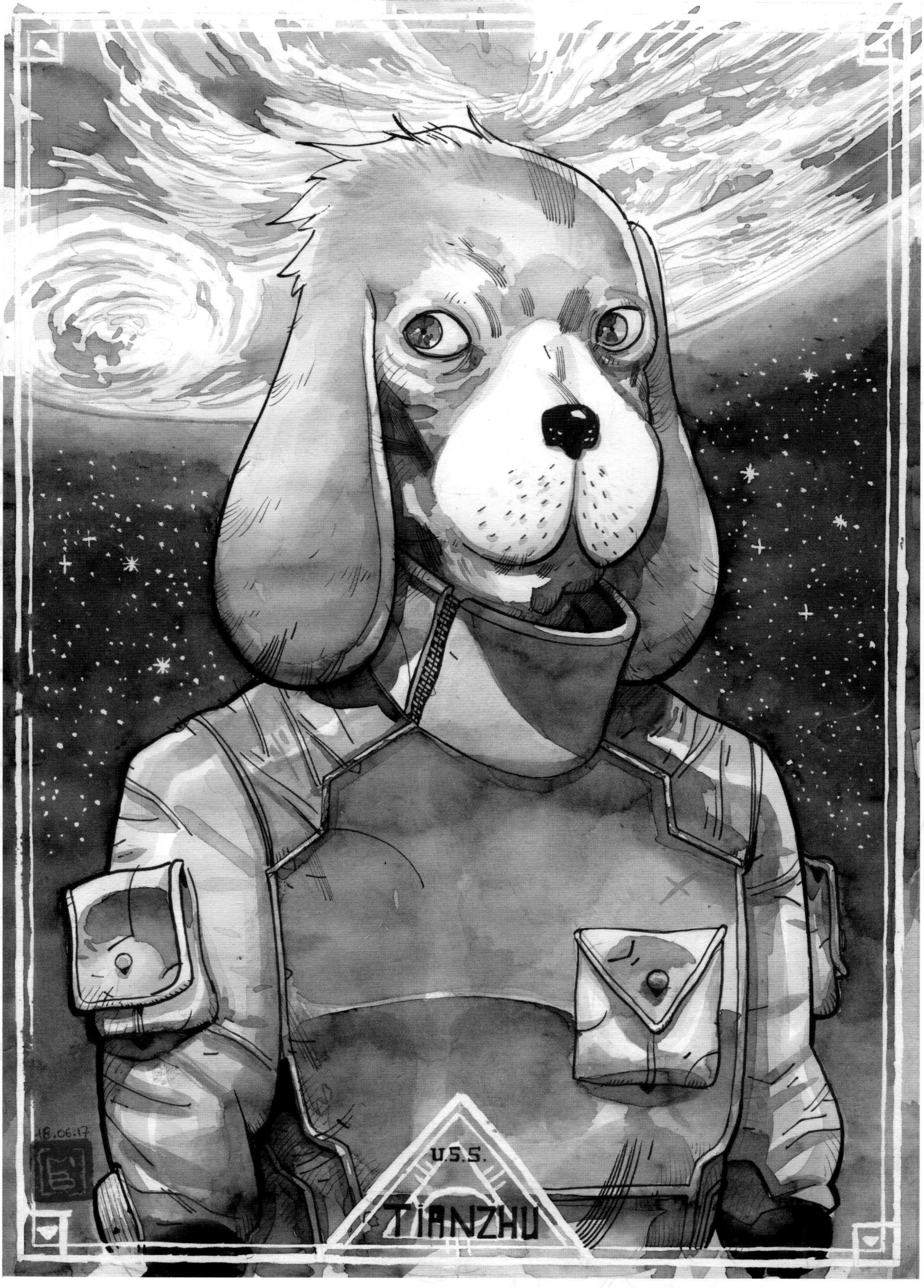
18.06.17
U.S.S.
TIANZHU

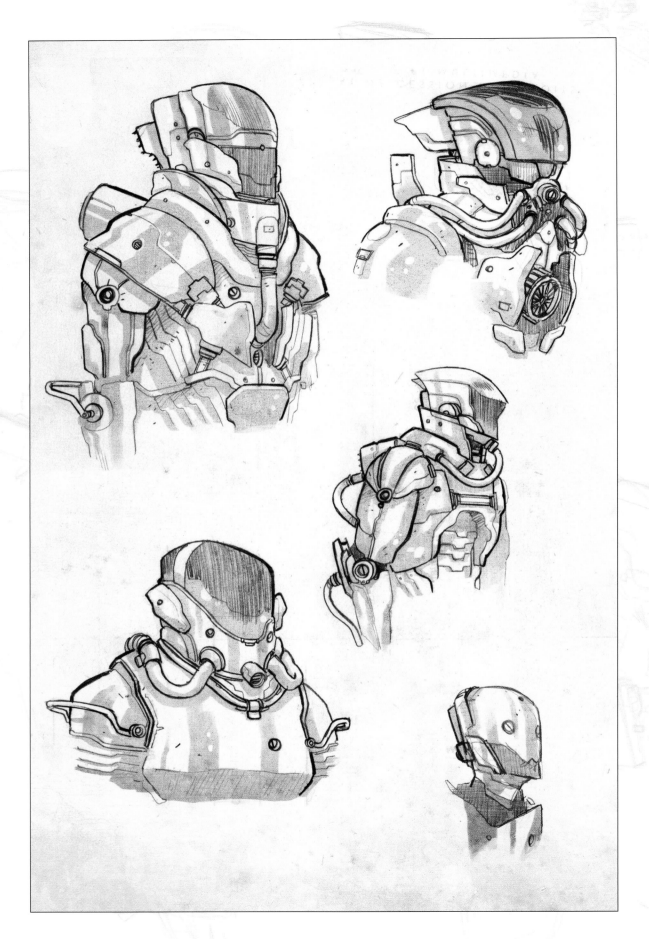

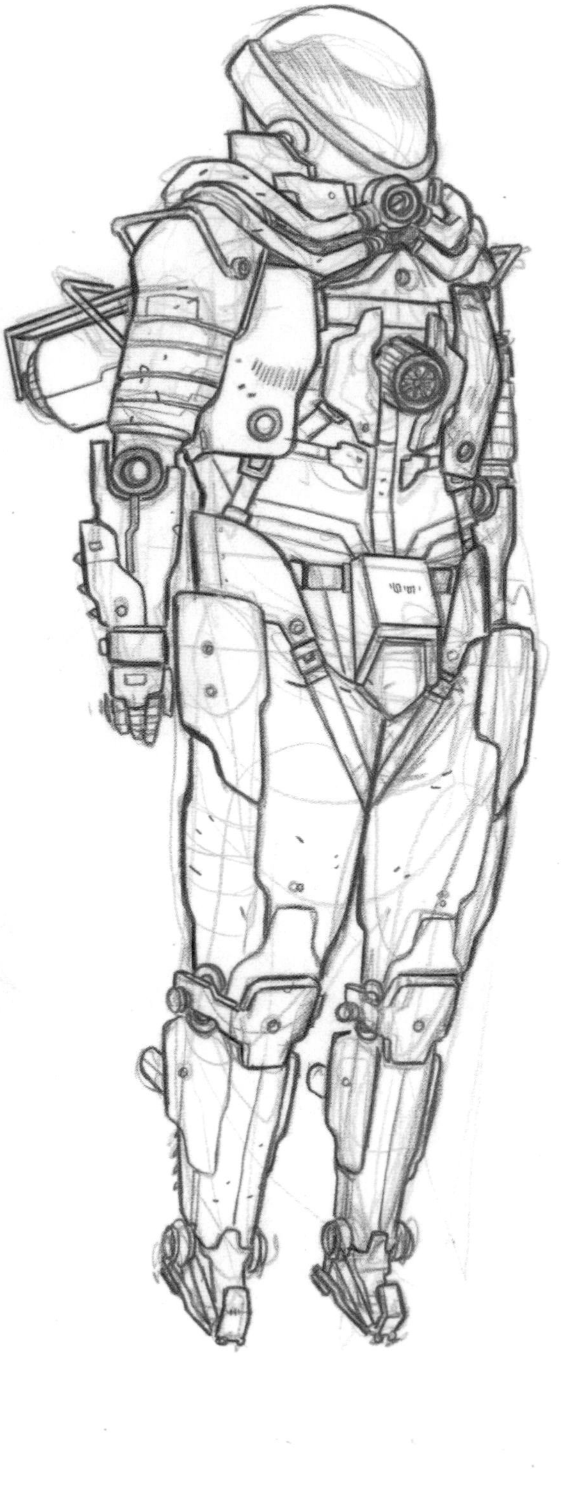

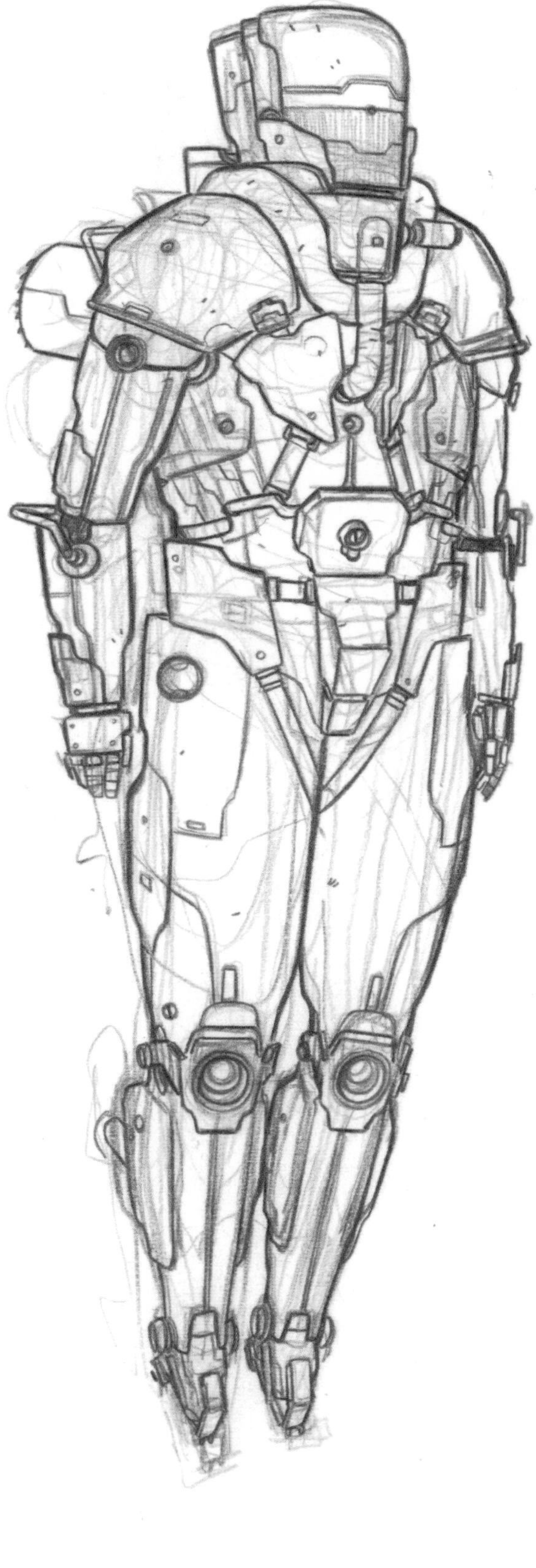

"First of all, I would like to thank Claire, who in addition to supporting me on a daily basis, always gives good counsel and advice. I can't count the number of times we re-read the story in order to refine the script and dialogue. There's some of her in this book, too.

I would like to thank my family, because they have always encouraged me to confidently pursue my dreams.

Thanks to Run, who continues to believe in me, and who rushes headlong into projects that I often don't explain very well. But he believes in them, which motivates me to do the best I can.

To all the people of Crew 619, who in addition to all being adorable, are responsible for the quality of the beautiful object that you hold in your hands."

Mathieu